FE 19

BEYOND THESE WALLS

BEYOND
THESE
WALLS

RETHINKING
CRIME and PUNISHMENT
in the UNITED STATES

TONY PLATT

St. Martin's Press   New York

www.stmartins.com

"It is early evening; the sun sets in a red-gold glow, / From my prison window I drink in its beauty." (appearing on page 179)
Elizabeth Gurley Flynn, "Venus Over Alderson—New Year's Eve 1956," in *The Alderson Story: My Life as a Political Prisoner* (New York: International Publishers, 1963), p. 204. **Reprinted by permission of International Publishers.**

"I live in a country / without love, / where the roses are red." (appearing on page 180)
Itaru Ina, "Haiku," translated by Hisako Ifshini and Leza Lowitz, *Modern Haiku* 34, no. 2 (Summer 2003), http://modernhaiku.org/essays/itaruinahaiku.html. **Reprinted by permission of Satsuki Ina.**

"Sun-stricken gun-towers." (appearing on page 191)
Fragment of poem by William Wantling, "From Sestina to San Quentin" (1979). **Reprinted by permission of Ruth Wantling.**

"The young eyes scared and the old eyes / tarnished like peeling boat hulls." (appearing on page 191)
Fragment of poem by Jimmy Santiago Baca, "The County Jail." **Reprinted by permission of Jimmy Santiago Baca.**

Designed by Kelly Too

Library of Congress Cataloging-in-Publication Data
Names: Platt, Tony, 1942– author.
Title: Beyond these walls : rethinking crime and punishment in the United States / Tony Platt.
Description: First edition. | New York : St. Martin's Press, [2019] | Includes bibliographical
    references and index.
Identifiers: LCCN 2018029156 | ISBN 9781250085115 (hardcover) | ISBN 9781250085122 (ebook)
Subjects: LCSH: Criminal justice, Administration of—United States—History. | Punishment—United
    States—History. | Crime—United States—History.
Classification: LCC HV9950 .P53 2019 | DDC 364.973—dc23
LC record available at https://lccn.loc.gov/2018029156

First Edition: January 2019

10 9 8 7 6 5 4 3 2 1

In memory of Stuart Hall (1932–2014),
who demanded intellectual rigor
and a fierce commitment to social justice

Beyond these walls
Sweet freedom calls.
  —Eugene V. Debs, 1918

It was a long time ago now. And it was yesterday.
  —Kate Atkinson, 2013

What we now call the present, this fleeting *nownownow*, is constantly overshadowed by a past now.
  —Günter Grass, 2007

The suppressed past will rankle and return.
  —Eva Hoffman, 2004

CONTENTS

I

1. State of Injustice   3
2. Double System   25

II

3. Except For   57
4. On Guard   84
5. The Insecurity Syndrome   117

III

6. The Perils of Reform   149
7. Radical Visions   175

IV

8. The Distant Present   205
9. Limbo   227

Author's Note   257
Resources   265
Appendix   277
Acknowledgments   285
Photo Credits   289
Notes   291
References   335
Index   365

I

STATE OF INJUSTICE

Why we need a broad vision and deep history
in order to understand the current state of
criminal injustices in the United States.

Stand too close to horror, and you get fixation, paralysis, engulfment;
stand too far, and you get voyeurism or forgetting. Distance matters.
—Eva Hoffman, *After Such Knowledge*

ANYTHING BUT

In December 2006 the South Salt Lake Police Department received an anonymous tip that a local residence was being used for drug dealing. After a week of surveillance, tracking suspected buyers as they came and went, the narcotics detective Douglas Fackrell stopped and interrogated Edward Strieff on suspicion that he had purchased illegal drugs. When Fackrell learned from a dispatcher that Strieff had an outstanding arrest warrant for a traffic violation, the detective searched him and found methamphetamine and drug paraphernalia.

This kind of police activity happens thousands of times every day in the United States: cops stopping and searching poor people on the flimsiest of excuses, behaving in ways that would get the officers in trouble if they treated the rich and middle class in the same way. These arbitrary street stops are the bread and butter of police work. They typically occur anonymously, hidden from justice, their outcomes predictable: the police chalk up another successful arrest. With the help of a publicly paid lawyer the defendant pleads guilty in order to receive a reduced sentence. And the poorhouse jails effortlessly stay jam-packed.

What was unusual about this case was that, a decade later, the arrest of Edward Strieff generated a remarkable dissent from a U.S. Supreme Court justice.

Occasionally the smooth process of punishment without trial is interrupted when the police carelessly treat a big shot as though he is a powerless nonentity or when a public defender, despite being hard-pressed for time and resources, takes a case to trial or, even more rarely, appeals a legal decision to a higher court.

What happened to the retired tennis star James Blake is an example of the police roughing up the wrong African American. In 2015 a New York officer, James Frascatore, mistook Blake for another black man suspected of credit card fraud and slammed Blake to the ground outside a hotel. Unlike the overwhelming majority of black men who have been similarly accosted, Blake made his experience a public matter and eventually settled with the city for damages. He also had the resources and patience to file a grievance of police misconduct with the city's Civilian Complaint Review Board, a process that took more than two years to complete, and concluded with the prosecutor asking only for Frascatore to be docked ten days of vacation pay. Even this kind of token victory is a rarity.[1]

Edward Strieff is the one-in-a-million defendant who had the good luck to be represented by a public defender who saw an opportunity to raise a constitutional challenge to the misuse of police power. Typically, defendants like Strieff end up in jail unable to make bail, and sooner or later they plead guilty rather than do "dead time" while waiting for their case to be decided. Contrary to the widely held impression—derived from police procedurals and courtroom dramas on television—a trial by jury is rare, and a debate about constitutional issues provoked by an illegal arrest is even more rare.

Strieff was not a typical defendant. At the time of his arrest, as the brief by his lawyer, Joan Watt of the nonprofit Salt Lake Legal Defenders Association, stated, the police "had no idea whether Strieff was a short-term visitor, or a permanent resident, or the pizza delivery man." She moved to suppress evidence gathered during the stop on the ground that the police had exceeded their authority. Utah's Supreme Court agreed, finding that

Strieff's Fourth Amendment right to security against unreasonable search and seizure had been violated. But on appeal the U.S. Supreme Court, in a 5–3 decision written by Justice Clarence Thomas, upheld the power of the police to stop and search people on the street on the basis of nothing more than a hunch and an outstanding traffic ticket. Strieff's guilt was affirmed.[2]

The decision of the Supreme Court was expected, given its long-standing tendency to make it difficult for civilians to prevail in complaints against the police. What stands out in the Strieff case, however, was Justice Sonia Sotomayor's brutally frank and caustic dissent. Although Strieff is white, Sotomayor used the occasion to express her views about police and race as well as class. "Writing only for myself," she noted, the police treat too many people as though they are "second-class citizens," and "it is no secret that people of color are disproportionate victims of this kind of scrutiny."

Drawing on a long tradition of African American critics of racial injustice—from W.E.B. Du Bois and James Baldwin to Michelle Alexander and Ta-Nehisi Coates—and expressing herself with a passion not usually heard from the highest court in the land, Sotomayor declared:

> This case tells everyone, white and black, guilty and innocent, that an officer can verify your legal status at any time. It says that your body is subject to invasion while courts excuse the violation of your rights. It implies that you are not a citizen of a democracy but the subject of a carceral state, just waiting to be catalogued. We must not pretend that the countless people who are routinely targeted by the police are "isolated." They are the canaries in the coalmine whose deaths, civil and literal, warn us that no one can breathe in this atmosphere. They are the ones who recognize that unlawful police stops corrode all our civil liberties and threaten all our lives. Until their voices matter too, our justice system will continue to be anything but.[3]

Justice Sotomayor's "countless people" make up a sizable segment of American society. Police arrest about fourteen million people annually in the United States; sixty-five million people have a criminal record; and at least twenty million have been incarcerated at some point in their lives.

On a single day state and federal prisons and local jails hold 2.3 million people; another 3.7 million are on probation, and 840,000 are on parole, subject to restrictions and conditions that limit their civil rights.[4]

That means nearly seven million people are enmeshed in criminal justice institutions that employ, at a minimum, another 4.3 million people as police and guards and in other capacities at a cost of hundreds of billions of dollars.

Compared with other nations, the United States is an outlier in its reliance on prisons and jails. By 2015 thirty-one American states had the highest incarceration rates (per 100,000 population) in the world, higher even than Turkmenistan, a Central Asian country identified by Human Rights Watch as having one of the world's most repressive regimes. Thirty-eight states lock up a larger proportion of their residents than El Salvador, a country recovering from a civil war and dealing with one of the highest homicide rates in the world.[5]

When you look carefully, the inequities are blatant: macho policing that is routinely indifferent to human rights in impoverished communities and that reduces citizens and residents to objects of fear and loathing; astonishing cruelties that characterize day-to-day life in jails and prisons, including widespread use of solitary confinement and sensory deprivation in violation of international human rights standards; taken-for-granted and clearly evident institutionalized racism that confirms the widespread prejudice that people of color are the most criminal, most dangerous, and most deserving of social exclusion and persistent distrust.

African American, Latino, Native American, and poor white communities carry the heaviest burden of punishment. By 2014 African Americans, who comprise about 13 percent of the U.S. population, dominated prison statistics: they are incarcerated in state prisons nationwide at five times the rate of whites, and they account for 35 percent of people in prison and jail, 48 percent of those serving life sentences, 56 percent of those sentenced to life without the possibility of parole, and 42 percent of death row prisoners. Although men comprise the overwhelming majority of prisoners, 30 percent of the world's incarcerated women are in the United States, and African American women's rate of imprisonment is twice that of white women.[6]

Most people in the United States are so used to thinking of criminal justice institutions as reserved for the desperate and marginalized, and of criminality as the monopoly of poor folks that these attitudes appear to be predetermined and the way the world works rather than the product of specific historical developments and a double standard that routinely exempts corporate and government perpetrators from punishment.

In 2012 a U.S. Senate committee carried out an exhaustive investigation of illegal operations by the global bank HSBC. After reviewing 1.4 million documents and interviewing seventy-five witnesses, the committee concluded that the bank had reaped massive profits by laundering billions of dollars for drug cartels, pariah states, and organizations linked to terrorism. Mexico's Sinaloa cartel, which is implicated in tens of thousands of murders, even designed a special cash box that was compatible with HSBC's teller windows. The bank's malpractice was not simply a matter of negligence or poor oversight of low-level functionaries but rather stemmed from systematic criminal behavior approved by top executives. "This is something that people knew was going on at that bank," said then-senator Carl Levin, the Michigan Democrat who chaired the investigation.

Yet nobody went to prison. Nobody was even criminally prosecuted. HSBC's chief executive officer said he was "profoundly sorry," and the corporation paid a $1.9 billion fine that represents about four weeks' worth of profits from its forty million customers worldwide.[7]

In 2016 Wells Fargo was implicated in similar conduct when the Consumer Financial Protection Bureau revealed that the bank had created as many as 3.5 million deposit and credit-card accounts without the knowledge or permission of consumers. Employees described a toxic work atmosphere in which they were pressured to meet impossible sales goals. "If one of your tellers took a handful of $20 bills out of the cash drawer," Senator Elizabeth Warren (D-Mass.) told the bank's CEO during a congressional hearing, "they'd probably be looking at criminal charges for theft. They could end up in prison. But you squeezed your employees to the breaking point so they would cheat customers and you could drive up the value of your stock and put hundreds of millions of dollars in your own pocket." Wells Fargo responded by firing 5,300 mostly low-level employees, paying a fine of $185 million, and forcing CEO John Stumpf to resign. In 2018 the Consumer Financial Protection Bureau added a $1 billion fine that was more than triply compensated by the windfall benefit from the

Trump administration's Tax Cuts and Jobs Act. No Wells Fargo executives have been criminally prosecuted.[8]

What Sotomayor calls a "carceral state," with its obsessive attention to cataloging the dangerousness of working-class communities and turning a blind eye to crimes in high places, was long in the making and involves a wide range of enthusiastic participants. The blame cannot be heaped only on the Trump administration, which came to power dedicated to unleashing the police "to do their job the way they know how to do it," for the *Strieff* decision was issued during the Obama presidency amid much talk about criminal justice reforms. Several government investigations already had exposed police lawlessness, and Black Lives Matter activists had forced the world to pay attention to what was happening on city streets.[9]

The state of injustice is attributable in part to right-wing politicians in both parties who clamor for tough measures, and to the self-interest of professional functionaries who personally benefit from the business of policing and guarding human misery. Among those functionaries are George Zoley, chief executive of a private prison company who personally made $9.6 million in 2017, and the psychologists James Mitchell and John Jessen, whose business received more than $75 million from the CIA to devise "enhanced interrogation techniques" for extracting information from suspected terrorists. They signed off on tormenting prisoners with sleep deprivation, cells filled with mice, naked humiliation, and physical pain. We learned the details of this abuse when some of Mitchell and Jessen's victims, who had been held in a secret American prison in Aghanistan, sued for compensation and won a settlement.[10]

But the problem is not limited to a few bad apples such as Mitchell and Jessen. It is endemic, not selective.

Do not forget the gun manufacturers, prison builders, and surveillance system engineers who service and profit from public agencies, and the knowledge professionals who articulate the logic of punishment.

A city of intellectuals, researchers, policy makers, experts, educators, bureaucrats, and pundits is necessary to figure out the details, make the plans, manage operations, and come up with a plausible rationale for why poor and working-class people are more despicable than those who commit war crimes, cover up government malfeasance, and defraud the public.

To insulate the know-how from its human impact demands a cold, calculating disengagement not unlike what is required to launch a drone or function like the technocrat in Franz Kafka's fictitious penal colony who created a sophisticated machine to forcibly tattoo the names of crimes on prisoners' bodies until they slowly bleed to death.[11]

A real-life architect in Arizona plans a prison in which windows are virtually eliminated and incarcerated bodies are moved "without creating situations in which inmates are together"; a technology company in San Diego invents a long-range acoustic device capable of blasting demonstrators with earsplitting noise, the sonic equivalent of a fire hose; and business consultants market "spit bud" masks that prevent prisoners from hawking at guards and stackable bunks so that more prisoners can be crammed into less space.

Medical and legal functionaries debate which drugs produce the best way to execute people, and the legal system orders the execution of seventy-five-year-old Tommy Arthur, who had been on Alabama's death row for thirty-four years.

The carceral state puts to work a public relations guru in Hawaii who advises the police to call the homeless "residentially challenged" as they issue them tickets for sitting on the sidewalks in tourist zones; a sheriff's SWAT team in rural Georgia that boasts an armored Humvee, machine guns, a door-breaching shotgun, and flash-bang grenades to carry out no-knock search warrants; and counterterrorism experts who are eager to construct ways of dividing "the civilian world into two, separating the trustworthy cooperators from the non-cooperators," and to teach government agencies how "to watch and track everything that moves."[12]

Despite so much purposeful rationality, "the 'system' itself may be mad," says the anthropologist Lorna Rhodes in her frank description of a maximum-security prison. Here the lockdown and isolation of prisoners for twenty-three hours a day, constant surveillance, and electronic control of movement generate "raging, depressed, or hallucinating men who 'knot up' within the tiny confines of their cells" and make themselves into sites of resistance by hurling body fluids at guards, thereby finding in their desperation a way to violate the prohibition on human contact.

Rhodes' insights about the immaculately maintained twenty-first-century, high-tech prison that does its best to drive convicts crazy reminds me of Charles Dickens' visit in 1842 to Pennsylvania's Eastern Penitentiary. The writer, like many European intellectuals of the mid-nineteenth century, visited the United States to investigate the American political experiment and report to his readers, who were curious for news about innovations in the New World. Several European governments and U.S. states, facing the need to modernize dilapidated prisons or build new ones, wanted to know in particular about the effectiveness of innovative American penitentiaries on the east coast in making prisoners economically productive and submissive workers, just as experts from around the world were dispatched to the west coast more than a century later to investigate California's efforts to rehabilitate and depoliticize activist prisoners. The United States has always been in the business of exporting its criminal justice policies and institutions.

Prison authorities in Philadelphia were proud to show off to Dickens what they considered to be the latest innovation in prison management. Unlike other prisons in the region, which used the Auburn, or "congregate," system that assembled prisoners in factory-like workshops during the day and isolated them in cells at night, the Pennsylvania system kept prisoners isolated day and night, working individually in their cells under a code of strictly enforced silence. The Quaker-influenced regime was based on the assumption that prisoners would return to society ready for "honest industry" as the result of deep reflection and penitence.[13]

Dickens came to a different conclusion. Eastern, he wrote, was indeed a "beautifully—exquisitely—kept and thoroughly well managed" institution but one that subjected prisoners to the "torturing anxieties and horrible despair of hopeless solitary confinement." Dickens was quickly convinced that the so-called silent system was "cruel and wrong. I never in my life was more affected by anything which was not strictly my own grief than I was by this sight." Witnessing a new prisoner being put through a degradation ritual that became a daily habit—the placing of a black hood with narrow eye slits over the head—was especially shocking to the visitor. Its purpose was to disorient a newcomer, make him more pliable, and limit interaction with other prisoners. To Dickens it symbolized "an emblem of the curtain dropped between him and the living world . . . He is a man buried alive; to be dug out in the slow round of years; and in the meantime dead to everything."[14]

A sense of humanity compels many people today to feel what Dickens felt more than 175 years ago and to express the conviction that our criminal justice institutions should be profoundly changed, even dismantled and transformed. But indignation and idealism are not enough. Demanding intellectual work also is required. Without conceding a sense of moral outrage at a web of injustices constructed with extraordinary ingenuity and extraordinary inhumanity, we also need to stand back to see the big picture—yet not so far back that we risk becoming voyeurs. Finding the right combination of anger, passion, and analytical complexity is the challenge.[15]

DISTANCE MATTERS

The expansion of the U.S. criminal justice system in recent decades is startling, and the investment of public resources in tracking, guarding, and punishing is extraordinary. In 1950 a staff of twenty-three thousand guarded all U.S. jails and prisons. Today more than seven hundred thousand are needed to do the job.

How we came to live in a society that still selectively processes millions of people as though they are "dead to everything" and what we can do about it are the subjects of this book. *Beyond These Walls* is a call to think in new and bolder ways about familiar issues, such as what prisons might have in common with barrios, ghettos, and reservations, and to consider the importance of unfamiliar issues, such as the central role played by private security in policing and how the public welfare system catalogs and dehumanizes poor women in ways that are similar to how the jails catalog and dehumanize poor men.

First we need to see the breadth of the problem and not be limited by a focus on *only* the most publicized issues, such as urban police violence, mass incarceration, and the sensational felony cases that come to mind when we think about crime control in the United States. No question, these issues are important, but much more happens under the auspices of criminal justice institutions. Moreover, criminalization is only one of many ways to exercise coercive power and social control.[16]

Beyond splashy government commissions calling for a restoration of trust in criminal justice in the United States and the daily spectacle on YouTube of police killing people, the wheels of injustice grind away invisibly, turning petty mischief and personal idiosyncrasies into crimes.

Local authorities have the power to invoke "civility codes" to banish the "disreputable" poor from city centers without judicial review.

Administrative bodies that do their work in relative obscurity return pa-
rolees to prison. Sex offenders and debtors can be sentenced to incarceration by means of civil proceedings. City councils, hard up for funds,
enable the police to make arrests for "manner of walking," saggy pants,
loitering in a park, even firing up a barbecue in the wrong place. The jails
are full of people sitting out tickets for minor infractions they cannot afford to pay.

Women and children are direct victims, not simply collateral damage:
imprisoning their family members deepens community poverty, aggravates
interpersonal violence, and sharpens divisions between women and men.
One in every twenty-eight children now has an incarcerated parent whose
family is bilked as much as $25 for a fifteen-minute in-state phone call.[17]

Criminal justice is generally framed as a local and state issue, with the
federal government occasionally mobilized to set standards and issue new
policy guidelines, such as during efforts to professionalize policing in the
1920s. Academics, journalists, and politicians typically make a distinction between the everyday stuff of policing and guarding and the federal
preoccupations with homeland security and border control. In contrast,
Beyond These Walls argues that crime control is as much a national as a
local issue and that an important and deeply rooted relationship exists between local law-and-order campaigns and national mobilizations against
perceived threats to the nation's moral-political health.

How can we understand, for example, the cultural construction of the
"black criminal" without tracing how for decades during the twentieth
century the nation's leading law enforcement agency, the FBI, employing
a panoply of dirty tricks, did its best to halt, slow down, and undermine
the struggle for civil rights? The criminalization of sexuality is similarly
influenced by national policies. When the federal government announced
during World War I that sexually predatory women were sapping the vitality of male conscripts, or during the Cold War that leftists and gays
were a threat to national security, local police forces obliged by carrying
out raids and roundups that ruined the lives of hundreds of thousands of
people.

The functions of intelligence and security agencies, such as the CIA,
FBI, and Department of Homeland Security, are intimately tied to what
happens every day in criminal justice agencies. Federal campaigns against
subversion, immorality, movements for social justice, undocumented

immigration, and terrorism have significantly shaped local policing and state legislation. There is a symbiotic relationship between efforts to criminalize and demonize groups in the United States and the deployment of criminal justice operations on behalf of U.S. foreign policy, as exemplified by the role played by the U.S. Office of Public Safety (OPS, part of the U.S. Agency for International Development from 1962 to 1974) in helping client states crack down on progressive movements in Latin America. In the case of Chile, OPS enabled the military to topple the democratically elected Salvador Allende government.

Domestic counterinsurgency operations are routinely entangled with everyday criminal justice operations, as in maintaining public order at political events and monitoring social movements; typically they focus on the same communities targeted by the local police. In July 2014 New York police arrested Eric Garner for selling loosies (single cigarettes) without a license. Officer Daniel Pantaleo used a chokehold, which is prohibited by departmental regulations, on the African American father of six. Witnesses reported that Garner gasped for breath and said, "I can't breathe" eleven times before passing out. Garner was dead by the time he reached the hospital. In December of that year, when a grand jury failed to indict Pantaleo, who had been the subject of previous civil rights lawsuits accusing him of abusing people he arrested, thousands took to the streets in anger. Instead of protecting the right to protest, undercover agents infiltrated organizations, such as Black Lives Matter, and accessed their internal communications and text messages to collect evidence for criminal prosecution. This practice of trying to discredit and criminalize groups critical of the police has a long history, going back at least to the early days of the FBI in the 1920s.[18]

Many urban police departments have large intelligence units, with agents even posted abroad. To criminalize activists the police regularly invoke laws relating to disorderly behavior, trespass, and illegal assembly. In 2017 several states passed legislation that restricts the right to protest; the laws included increased penalties for blocking traffic and for "disobeying a public safety order."[19]

The millions of people employed in criminal justice are not only public cops and prison guards, and their work does not stop at the U.S. borders. From the war in the Philippines at the beginning of the twentieth century through the Cold War to today's counterterrorism operations, the United

States has always exported advice, expertise, personnel, and equipment to client states in the name of fighting crime and subversion. By the early 1970s, for example, more than seven thousand police officials—more than half of whom were from Latin America—had received counterinsurgency training in the United States. When the George W. Bush administration told the Iraqi government in 2003 how to set up Abu Ghraib prison, where prisoners were routinely humiliated and tortured, the advice represented a long-standing and routine practice. Today global issues pervade every aspect of criminal justice policy, from border control to drug enforcement to urban security.[20]

The work of criminalizing, punishing, excluding, marginalizing, humiliating, subordinating, and discarding large groups of people does not only take place in criminal justice institutions. It involves millions of functionaries at an extraordinary and mostly unaccountable cost. A variety of public and private agencies have the authority to impose punishments and hardships, ostracize large numbers of people, and whittle away basic rights. This process is sometimes referred to as carceral, as in Justice Sotomayor's usage, to capture the myriad ways—public and private, formal and informal, legal and political—in which they exercise social control.

Although *carceral* is linguistically associated with a physical barrier, and thus prison (from the Latin *carcer*), it is also used symbolically and metaphorically to evoke the range of ways in which the human body can be contained beyond walls—from slavery, in which physical and psychological violence was seamlessly incorporated into the everyday round of life, to contemporary public housing projects that restrict the movement of tenants. "We are in jail outside," members of the Black Panther Party noted in 1971, "and jail inside."[21]

Physical punishments and exclusion include not only prisons and jails but also banishment, exile, transportation, deportation, reservations, and refugee camps. The increasing use of electronic monitoring makes it possible to expand institutional control into people's everyday lives. Already, enterprising criminologists are developing plans for "technological incarceration" that would monitor prisoners in their homes via ankle bracelets and remote sensors and immobilize violators with electroshock delivered by "Conducted Energy Devices."[22]

Punishments extend to placing limits on people's rights and status, such as denial of the right to vote and access to public services, which typically result in temporal and spatial restrictions that deprive individuals and groups of time to live full lives and the ability to move freely in society. An estimated six million people, for example, are barred from voting because they have a record of felony convictions.[23]

Now under the auspices of the cabinet-level U.S. Department of Homeland Security (DHS), which was created in 2002 in the wake of September 11 and expanded the following year, immigration control looks and acts much like a criminal justice operation but one that is better coordinated and funded and acknowledges even fewer rights than the criminal courts. Incarceration, surveillance, and deportation are now significant components of immigration enforcement. Detention of undocumented immigrants and documented immigrants accused of crimes has become commonplace, growing from about 20,000 detentions in 1961 to an average of 450,000 a year during the Obama presidency. The number of noncitizens, mostly Mexicans, formally removed from the United States increased sixteenfold from 1986 to 2012, and immigration-related prosecutions saw an unprecedented increase. Under the Trump administration Immigration and Customs Enforcement (ICE) agents became emboldened to round up folks who had committed minor criminal infractions or violated immigration laws. "Before, we used to be told, 'You can't arrest those people,'" said a ten-year ICE veteran. "Now those people are priorities again. And there are a lot of them here." In the first six months of 2017 arrests of undocumented immigrants increased by almost 38 percent over the previous year.[24]

Policing encompasses much more than publicly funded urban law enforcement, as revealed in cultural and political preoccupations with securing our streets, security measures, security services, national security, securing the border, secure communities, and homeland security. Builders of gated communities seamlessly incorporate security planning, including "armed response," in the architectural design of suburban communities that are expected to be defensible as well as comfortable.[25]

Private security operations are an integral component of policing. Private and public policing have long been intertwined, from the second half of the nineteenth century, when business-controlled security forces served as a model for urban police forces, to the long-standing hiring of former police administrators by security firms (whether as employees or consultants), and the innovative function provided by the corporate-security sector in creating and responding to what Étienne Balibar calls the "insecurity syndrome."[26]

Today private police perform exactly the same functions as public police, either as subcontracted by government agencies or as the direct employees of industries, businesses, malls, and middle-class communities. As of 2010, security workers outnumber public police by more than 25 percent, and companies that provide personnel and make security-related products are the recipients of government contracts that far exceed the amount of public money spent on criminal justice operations nationally.[27]

The work of social control stretches from the physical isolation and mind-shredding regimes of maximum-security prisons to techniques of co-optation and psychological manipulation used in schools and other social institutions; from regulating the disorderly behavior of truant children and downtown beggars to cooling out disruptive patients in hospital emergency rooms and patroling the stairwells and corridors of public housing projects.[28]

The line between agencies of social control and service institutions is often blurred. Public schools, for example, now incorporate security measures in their routine functioning, while prisons and jails increasingly incorporate medical and psychological techniques in the work of guarding. Public welfare in the United States puts millions of women and children in a limbo between desperate poverty and a criminalized status, and the system condemns millions of former prisoners to civil death.[29]

Criminal justice institutions, whether narrowly or expansively defined, do not monopolize the job of social control. The millions of people who come under their purview do not remain in police cells, criminal courts, reformatories, jails, and prisons. They also are subject to discipline in schools and punishment if they are on welfare; stopped and frisked, entered into data banks, corralled on the streets, and herded out of malls and city centers; deported across borders and locked away in military prisons, black sites, and refugee camps; and engaged in resistance, from hunger strikes in prison to street protests urgently demanding that black lives matter.

Punishment is not a single, decisive act with clear parameters and time limits. The arrestee, the incarcerated, the suspect, the welfare recipient, and the deportee are subject to an unfolding process in which they become a category of person to be followed, tracked, documented, and constantly made visible, as if they had a blazon attached to their clothes or a tattoo permanently imprinted on their body. "I know that on the day after my release," Oscar Wilde wrote to his literary executor from a jail near London in the late 1890s, "I will merely be moving from one prison into another, and there are times when the whole world seems to be no larger than my cell, and as full of terror for me."[30]

Former prisoners typically "carry their prison with them into the air, and hide it as a secret disgrace in their hearts," Wilde observed after doing two years at hard labor, picking oakum, and walking a treadmill. Having been convicted of "gross indecency," namely "the love that dare not speak its name," he left prison a broken man and died three years later, convinced that the state had abandoned him "at the very moment when its highest duty . . . begins. For me," he wrote, "the world is shriveled to a handsbreath, and everywhere I turn my name is written on the rocks in lead . . . I have come . . . from a sort of eternity of fame to a sort of eternity of infamy."[31]

Half a century later the 120,000 Japanese Americans and Japanese immigrants in the western United States who were incarcerated without trial during World War II on suspicion of potential subversion experienced deprivation and indignities before, during, and after their imprisonment. Officials from the War Relocation Authority, authorized by Franklin D. Roosevelt's Executive Order 9066, gave them only a few days to prepare for their banishment. They were told to pack only what they could carry and were not informed of their destinations. Aside from hardships in prison, the experience, Karen Inouye writes, had a "long afterlife" and left her family "in a constant state of distress and uncertainty about their safety and future." After his release her father would buy cars only from U.S.-owned companies so that his patriotism would not be questioned.[32]

Through rituals of "social death," to use the sociologist Orlando Patterson's evocative term, large groups of people are simultaneously excluded and included, made marginal and integrated, a part of society and "yet apart from it." It is a dynamic as well as destructive process that both discards people deemed expendable and makes them subordinate and potentially useful: deported workers who can be recalled when needed; formerly incarcerated people who are tracked into menial service work; welfare recipients "working off their debt to society" and thus depressing the wages of government workers; and marginalized urban youth competing with the most recent immigrants for part-time, minimum-wage work.[33]

Second, making sense of this extensive, complex, and multilayered labyrinth of social control requires a historical investigation of how the past bleeds into the present and how the present transforms the past.

"America is famously ahistorical," a sardonic Barack Obama observed in 2015. "That's one of our strengths—we forget things." This tendency is visible from both sides of the political divide. The Right conveniently ignores how the police and courts target crime only in poor and working-class communities and invokes the need for authoritarian measures as though this is a new idea. The Trump administration's views about crime and justice represented a sharp shift to the right and a break with the prevailing discourse of modest and selective change promoted by leading Republicans and Democrats in 2015–16, but they were not unprecedented. When Donald Trump injected racist rhetoric of unvarnished law and order into his presidential campaign, grossly exaggerating the problem of "illegal criminal immigrants" and calling for a ban on "other countries' undesirables," what he said was both shocking and familiar. Shocking because it was at odds with a growing political consensus about the need to reduce the incarcerated population, rein in the police, and give the states some economic relief from the cost of prisons. Familiar because it resurrected and polished up deeply embedded cultural imagery that has considerable staying power.[34]

The Left has a tendency to make extravagant claims about the exceptional horrors of the current U.S. prison system—that it is, for example, "historically unprecedented and internationally unique"—forgetting about, inter alia, regimes of terror in the American South after the defeat of Reconstruction and in fascist Europe in the 1930s and 1940s. Critiques of police hawkishness generally go no deeper than discussions of SWAT teams in the 1970s and acquisition of armaments during the Iraq War, ignoring how the modern police originally were organized along military lines in the late nineteenth century. The weapons and technology may have been upgraded, but the assumptions and attitudes about the need for a strong state to hold the line against the "dangerous classes" has an established pedigree.[35]

This is not to suggest that the present is merely history repeating itself or that nothing has changed significantly in the last 150 years. Continuities in the racial composition of who gets arrested and incarcerated run deep, and national initiatives against progressive organizations are nothing new. But today's racist police practices are not simply a holdover from the past. They have been given new life and new rationales in a society marked by segregated housing and education, and inequalities of the job market, that are quite different from conditions associated with slavery and Jim Crow. Similarly national security and counterterrorism operations in the wake of September 11 have been much more complex and extensive than the campaigns waged against communists, socialists, feminists, and civil rights activists in the early twentieth century.

Beyond These Walls is a dynamic genealogy that zigzags in time, searching for persistent patterns and ruptures in history. The targeting of African Americans, from chain gangs to solitary confinement, is central to this investigation, but a wider lens makes clear that historically this kind of victimization is neither exclusive nor unusual. The carceral imagination is quite prolific, as illustrated during the nineteenth century in the use of prison-like reservations to contain Native Americans, ethnic cleansing campaigns to rid rural communities of Chinese immigrants and herd them into Chinatowns on the west coast, and the demonization of Mexican immigrants that made lynching during the California Gold Rush a regular occurrence.

In critical discussions of policing and prisons, race is the most obvious and visible master narrative. But other important social dynamics are at play. Modern urban policing was originally organized to control working-class European immigrant communities, and to this day the people who end up in jails and prisons are almost exclusively drawn from the most impoverished communities. If you search the cells of the more than 2.3 million people incarcerated, you will be hard pressed to find more than a handful of upper-middle-class and wealthy felons in each institution, just enough to give the impression that, in Anatole France's memorable adage, "the law, in all its majesty, forbids the rich as well as the poor to sleep under bridges, to beg in the streets, and to steal bread." The incarceration of a leading political figure, such as former member of Congress Anthony Weiner, who received a twenty-one-month sentence for sending sexual texts to a fifteen-year-old girl, is so rare that it provokes a media frenzy.[36]

Also, criminal justice institutions have been centrally involved in attempting to keep women subordinate and in line, and in policing the boundaries of heterosexuality. In 2017 many Republican-controlled state legislatures rushed to enact laws, according to a former editor-in-chief of the *New England Journal of Medicine*, that "treat pregnant women like errant children."[37] Current efforts to limit access to abortion services, criminalize public welfare, and provoke moral panics about the dangers of sexual diversity have a long history, going back to the early-twentieth-century eugenics movement.

It is not possible to determine whether today's carceral state is unprecedented, as some critics have suggested, in part because relatively reliable, albeit incomplete, data on criminal justice institutions have been available only since the 1960s and in part because the experiences of different historical eras are not easily transferable.

How, for example, can we compare today's mass imprisonment with the extraordinarily high death rate of African American convict laborers in the South after the Civil War? Or with the disproportionate incarceration of Chinese immigrants in California following the Gold Rush? Or with the forced transfer of Native American children to boarding schools in the late nineteenth and early twentieth centuries? Or with the cramming of Mexican immigrants into Los Angeles jails in the 1930s? Or with the widespread institutionalization of the mentally ill in the 1950s?[38]

Rather than trying to quantify the relative harmfulness or magnitude of these injustices, I look at parallels, continuities, and breaks with the past and try to understand how these deeply rooted tectonic fissures trouble the here and now.

Third, it is important not to overstate the power and reach of the state. While the state is indeed extensive, multifaceted, and resourceful, it is not omnipotent or coherent but rather full of tensions and internal conflicts, more like Kafka's penal colony than Orwell's Big Brother.

Pick up any book on prisons, police, and crime, and you will find widespread use of the phrase "criminal justice system" to designate a group of interrelated institutions, framed by criminal laws and implemented by government: police, courts, jails and prisons and community corrections, probation and parole, and juvenile justice.

The use of *system* is problematic because it obscures the chaos, decentralization, and irrationality that typically characterize what passes for criminal justice in the United States. Recognizing what Primo Levi called the "grey zones" that permeate institutions of social control is important.[39]

Political consensus may have gelled, for example, around the rhetoric of the "war on crime" in the 1970s or "war on drugs" in the 1980s, but no national plan of action existed, nor did cities, regions, and states coordinate their efforts. Shifts in criminal justice policies usually occur haphazardly and chaotically, reflecting responses to crises, partisan political decisions, and global events. Capital punishment, although authorized by the U.S. Supreme Court, is carried out in only a few states. More than half of the thirty-nine executions carried out in 2013 took place in Texas and Florida. Even at the height of the prison boom, penal practices varied widely by region: rates of imprisonment per 100,000 adults ranged from 1,300 in Oklahoma and 1,130 in Texas to 350 in Maine and 450 in the District of Columbia. More recently, while New Jersey's prison population dropped by 35 percent, North Dakota's increased by 20 percent.[40]

The sense of unity of purpose is a delusion. Commentators from different ends of the political spectrum point out that the criminal justice apparatus "has gone astray, lost in a dark wood of its own making," and is dysfunctional and unraveling. Whatever goes on in the name of criminal justice, it is not an organized system. Instead I prefer to refer to "criminal justice institutions" and describe what they do as operations, thus conveying the idea of the exercise of organized power for specific purposes and of procedures performed on a living body.[41]

This distinction is not a mere linguistic quibble. Recognizing the irrational and fragmented nature of the carceral state means that space exists for a politics of critical resistance. Recent events suggest that social activism and organized opposition can have far-ranging impact on criminal justice institutions, which always bend to the arc of power but are vulnerable to movements from below. For example, collectively planned hunger strikes by isolated, degraded, and demonized prisoners, held in solitary confinement for decades in a remote hellhole of a prison in northern California, were what forced prison officials in 2015 to negotiate a reduction in cruel and usual punishments. Highly localized, often spontaneous street protests that quickly morphed into the Black Lives Matter movement were able to command a meeting with a president and issue a manifesto of political demands. And in the wake of the killing of seventeen people at Marjory Stoneman Douglas High School in Florida in February 2018, widespread protests by students, many of whom had never previously participated in political activism, jolted a former U.S. Supreme Court justice into calling for repeal of the Second Amendment.[42]

However, for reformers and activists, the years from 2010 to 2016 represented hope and possibility more than achievements, a trend that is symptomatic of previous efforts since the early twentieth century. Despite unusually bipartisan political efforts to reduce the prison population during the Obama administration the results were disappointingly modest and in some states ineffective. Though California, for example, has reduced the number of people in its state prisons, it still spends almost eight times more per prisoner than it spends on each K–12 student.[43]

Extraordinary attention may have been paid in recent years to the killing of citizens by police, but the number of deaths has not changed and was about the same for the first six months of 2017 as in 2016. According to nongovernmental accounts, police are still killing about three people every day, with young African American men aged fifteen to thirty-four nine times more likely to be killed than white young men. One in sixty-five deaths of young African Americans is attributable to police actions. And after all the task forces, investigations, and exposés in the 2010s, the structure, philosophy, and governance of policing remained essentially unchanged.

"Don't be too nice" to suspects, President Trump told a gathering of police officers in July 2017. Emboldened by the support of the president, when St. Louis police cleared the streets of demonstrators in September following the acquittal of a white cop for killing yet another black man, they appropriated the popular chant of the protest movement—"Whose street? Our street!"—and abandoned any pretense of professional neutrality.[44]

"I am aware of how much work is left unfinished," Obama said in a comprehensive criminal justice policy statement issued just before he left office.[45] Yet some significant sectors of the carceral state were not even up for reform before Trump became president. Deportations and incarceration of immigrants during the Obama administration reached a record high with almost no opposition from Congress. Nor was there any political outcry about millions of women denied welfare or about the treatment of those on welfare as though they are inherently criminal or about the billions of dollars contracted out with little accountability to the private sector for homeland security.

Fourth, we need to grapple with the legacy of stubborn resistance to meaningful structural change. A historical perspective enables us to face many frustrated efforts to significantly transform criminal justice agencies and to consider why so many reforms in the past soured or even made matters worse for the intended beneficiaries. Not all reforms are equal. Great harms are often committed in the name of benevolence.

Top-down criminal justice reformism has a long history. "Houses of correction," the forerunner of the modern prison that emerged in the Netherlands in the sixteenth century, replaced brutal public punishments with brutal punishments administered behind walls. Prisoners who resisted forced labor could be locked in a water cellar, where they had to pump out the water day and night to keep from drowning. Nothing was soft or sentimental about the first penal reformers.[46]

Perhaps the most famous example of idealism gone badly wrong is the Quakers' promotion of the silent system of solitary confinement in Pennsylvania in the late eighteenth century. "In its intention," Dickens wrote in a letter after his visit in 1842, "I am well convinced that it is kind, humane, and meant for reformation; but I am persuaded that those who devised this system of Prison Discipline, and those benevolent gentlemen who carry it into execution, do not know what it is that they are doing. I believe that very few men are capable of estimating the immense amount of torture and agony which this dreadful punishment, prolonged for years, inflicts upon the sufferers." About 130 years later the American Friends Service Committee, a Quaker organization, acknowledged "the blunders that an uncritical faith can produce."[47]

Many benevolent reforms advocated by middle-class philanthropists and professionals turned out to have a nasty, repressive underside and sometimes a topside that expanded rather than reduced the net of social control. The child-saving campaign during the Progressive Era rounded up working-class kids for petty infractions and sent them to highly regimented youth prisons for reformation. Between the world wars the eugenics movement justified the involuntary sterilization of tens of thousands of working-class women in the name of protecting racial purity. The policy of indeterminate sentencing in the 1960s added time to prisoners' sentences in the guise of rehabilitation.

A close inspection of past criminal justice campaigns undertaken in the name of reform reveals the heavy hand of managerial imperatives and a politics of pacification rather than a commitment to social justice. But the historical record is not all bad news. A bottom-up tradition, mostly submerged and forgotten, offers some insights about the possibility of structural reforms that alleviate suffering, improve people's everyday lives, and attempt to change the assumptions and governance of criminal justice.

Long before civil rights and black power organizations in the 1960s tried to make the police more accountable to communities they policed, before prisoners in the 1970s actively participated in building revolutionary organizations and made Malcolm X and George Jackson into popular heroes, there were writers, poets, artists, activists, and visionaries who took on the carceral state and imagined a world that does not require such a massive apparatus of social control. Revisiting this tradition is important, not out of nostalgia for what might have been or to search for a lost blueprint of radical change, but rather to help us understand the immense challenges we face.

2

DOUBLE SYSTEM

*Issues of class, race, and gender shape how crime
is defined, the police are deployed, the courts process
defendants, and the social welfare is neglected.*

___

The law locks up the man or woman
Who steals the goose from off the common,
But leaves the greater villain loose
Who steals the common from off the goose.

—Seventeenth-century English verse

NOT A QUESTION OF CRIME

In a memorable passage in *The Souls of Black Folk*, published in 1903,
W.E.B. Du Bois describes how the South, after defeating Reconstruction,
established a system of policing that "was arranged to deal with blacks
alone, and tacitly assumed that every white man was *ipso facto* a member
of that police. Thus grew up a double system of justice, which erred on
the white side by undue leniency and the practical immunity of red-handed
criminals, and erred on the black side by undue severity, injustice, and
lack of discrimination . . . It was not then a question of crime, but rather
one of color that settled a man's conviction on almost any charge."[1]

More than a century later "a large body of evidence," in Barack Obama's
words, documents that a double system of justice, from arrest to imprisonment, punishes African Americans, Latinos, and Native Americans
more harshly than their white counterparts. A mountain of compelling
studies details how race shapes police abuse of their broad discretion to

stop and frisk, ticket traffic violators, enforce drug-related crimes, and kill civilians. Racial considerations also permeate sentencing practices and capital punishment, as well as conditions of incarceration while awaiting or serving time.[2]

Nowhere is the disparity of the double system more evident than in the contrast between state and local prosecutors who take pride in getting convictions and sending poor folks to prison and federal prosecutors who do their best to keep corporate criminals out of prison, minimize their sentences, or divert them from criminal prosecutions.

In 2015 the U.S. Justice Department tried Don Blankenship, CEO of the Massey Energy Company, on a charge of criminal negligence in relation to the 2010 explosion at the Upper Big Branch coal mine in West Virginia that killed twenty-nine workers. The U.S. Department of Labor had cited the mine for more than five hundred safety violations a year earlier. The case was widely reported because charging a high-level corporate executive with a crime is so unusual. While awaiting trial for more than five years, the defendant was free on bail and cosseted by a team of defense lawyers, including William W. Taylor III, one of the country's top litigators. The jury found the executive guilty of only the misdemeanor charge of violating federal safety rules, and the judge sentenced him to one year in prison. Unlike most people with records, when Blankenship completed his sentence, he did not face a long afterlife of humiliation and exclusion. Instead he ran as a Republican for one of West Virginia's U.S. Senate seats and claimed the Environmental Protection Agency under Obama was trying to destroy the coal industry. Despite opposition from the political establishment and President Trump, he won the support of one in five Republican voters.[3]

About eighteen months after Blankenship avoided a felony conviction, New York State tried and convicted Lashawn Marten for a random act of street violence that caused the death of a passerby. The press reported that Marten was a "crazed convict," his crime a "senseless attack." After his arrest Marten was not convinced that he had killed Jeffrey Babbitt. "Where's the death certificate?" he asked.

At the time of his arrest Marten lived in a shelter for mentally ill homeless people. He was on medication for schizophrenia and had a history of assaultive behavior, for which he had done short stretches in jail. On the afternoon of September 4, 2013, after playing chess in Union Square, the forty-year-old African American man stood up and declared that he was going to knock out the next white person he met. His random victim was sixty-four-year-old Babbitt, a retired train conductor on his way from a subway station to a comic book store. Marten sucker-punched Babbitt, hitting him with such force that he died later from a head wound.

The defendant, who was held in jail for almost four years pending trial, was that rare impoverished defendant who received a jury trial. "Lashawn Marten targeted victims solely on the basis of their skin color," Cyrus Vance, Jr., the Manhattan district attorney, said in a statement after the verdict. Marten's court-appointed lawyer, Michael Croce, argued that his client was off his medication and delusional. The trial took eight days. The defense did not call any expert witnesses to testify about Marten's state of mind or about how his mental illness might have affected his behavior. After the jury quickly returned a guilty verdict for manslaughter aggravated by a hate crime, Justice Melissa Jackson handed down a maximum sentence of twenty-five years, claiming that the defendant had received "an abundance of resources" from government services, including housing and antipsychotic drugs. "You're a powder keg ready to ignite," the judge said, ignoring the plea of Marten's lawyer for mercy and compassion.[4]

Lashawn Marten received what is increasingly the treatment of last resort for the impoverished mentally ill, namely time in jails and prisons that function as de facto mental hospitals. These fill the vacuum created by the closing of mental institutions in the 1970s and the gutting of community-based social services beginning in the 1980s. As a result it is estimated that nearly 15 percent of men and 33 percent of women in local jails suffer from serious mental illnesses, and about 60 percent report cognitive and emotional problems.

The mentally ill poor are at much greater risk of incarceration than their middle-class counterparts who have access to private care subsidized by insurance policies. Up to 25 percent of Marten's fellow state prisoners are diagnosed with a psychotic illness. Jails and prisons aggravate the illnesses that prisoners have when they arrive and are incubators of disease, physical and mental, for those who arrive relatively healthy. Jeffrey Babbitt was a victim of not only Lashawn Marten's erratic violence but also of a society that criminalizes mental illness.[5]

The double system involves more than racial discrimination by individuals. It encompasses how criminal justice personnel carry out their mandate, where the police are dispatched, how legislators and prosecutors determine what constitutes social harm, and how criminality becomes politically and culturally identified as the exclusive preserve of the poor. The double system works internally through racial and ethnic profiling and economic biases that permeate criminal justice operations, and it works externally through the diversion of corporate criminals and other perpetrators of large-scale harm to civil and noncriminal resolutions.

The double system influences how Americans think about what constitutes social problems. The war on crime is highly selective, failing to address the most socially harmful issues. Black-on-black homicides (2,205 in 2014) receive much media and political attention, whereas we hear no comparable outrage about the 13,435 African Americans who died that year from diabetes or the 98,456 who died from cardiovascular illnesses.

The murder rate is a topic of constant attention, yet death and injury on the roads affect twice as many people as homicides. In 1967 Lyndon Johnson's prestigious Crime Commission, the President's Commission on Law Enforcement and the Administration of Justice, noted that economic losses resulting from automobile accidents were more than six times greater than losses resulting from everyday crimes. In 1975 the National Safety Council reported almost five million auto-related injuries during the year, with an economic loss of $35.9 billion. "In order to maintain our economic stability and lifestyle," a leading researcher noted in 1979, "we continue to tolerate this more costly source of danger." About thirty-five years later deaths on the roads were still double the annual number of homicides, whereas the economic losses associated with accidents had skyrocketed to $242 billion. Yet we had no war on automobiles.[6]

The double system means that when malpractice and abuse in criminal justice agencies are exposed, staffers at the lowest level tend to get the blame. The misanthropic practices of criminal justice functionaries aggravate but do not create the problem. Proposals to diversify the workforce, improve police-community relations, and educate individual police and guards to recognize their own unconscious biases are to be welcomed as sensible public policies, but they do not address structural inequities that permeate the carceral state.[7]

The focus on individual attitudes and the racial composition of personnel obscures a much deeper set of issues: the criminalization of public space through updated versions of banishment and antivagrancy policies, such as the regular removal of homeless tent encampments in San Francisco without the formality of arrests or prosecutions; the unglamorous judicial processing without due process of millions of petty offenders who end up in jails that are holding pens for the homeless, unemployed, and distraught; a bail system that explicitly favors middle- and upper-class defendants who can afford to stay out of jail while awaiting trial; administration of criminal courts that serves best those who can afford the best lawyers; immigration policies that keep hundreds of thousands of undocumented workers caught between exploitation and criminalization; and a welfare system that turns millions of women and children into hustling, stigmatized dependents, and denies desperately needed jobs, education, child care, and decent housing to the communities of the imprisoned.[8]

Four interrelated issues—the tracking of youth into juvenile justice institutions, selective definitions of criminality, gender bias and the criminalization of public welfare, and the myth of criminal courts as an adversary system—demonstrate how prejudice and discrimination are not only a by-product but are constitutive of the carceral state and how the double system operates through omissions as well as commissions.

WHO YOU ARE

Juvenile justice institutions are the gateway to an officially inscribed identity marked as delinquent and criminal. Studies show that teens who are arrested, held in detention, put on probation, or incarcerated are likely to enter the school-to-prison pipeline and do time later as adults. What triggers this initiation process is primarily who you are, not what you do. "The criminal justice system," Obama observed in January 2017, "takes young people who made mistakes no worse than my own and traps them in an endless cycle of marginalization and punishment."[9]

The twentieth century was packed with regular antidelinquency campaigns that were based on inaccurate information and deeply held prejudices about the scope and causes of crime. During and after World War II, for example, newspapers and magazines regularly carried stories about the alarming rise of crime rates and the "shock-filled world of the Juvenile Delinquent." This was mostly based on anecdotal evidence or on arrest statistics, both of which are inadequate barometers of the actual incidence of crime. Researchers do not know if the crime rate went up or down in the 1940s and 1950s. Historians do know, however, that public anxieties about crime were linked to concerns about changes in family life and, in particular, the growing economic independence of women. "If the drift of normal youth toward immorality and crime is to be stopped," wrote J. Edgar Hoover, then head of the FBI, in the *Woman's Home Companion* in 1944, "mothers must do the stopping."[10]

Given the persistent view that working-class youth are at the center of the crime problem—whether they had an "absentee mother," came from "broken families," or suffered "cultural deprivation"—it is important to be clear about the evidence for this claim.

We are used to reading sensational media accounts about crime rates going dramatically up or down, usually up. These stories typically cite year-to-year statistics about major crimes reported to the police and arrest data compiled by the FBI. The Uniform Crime Reports (UCR) system, a crude measure developed in 1930 by the International Association of Chiefs of Police, remains the primary way to assess the amount and scope of crime. Most crimes, however, are not brought to the attention of the police, and arrests address only a fraction of harmful behavior.

Not much has changed since the 1970s, when sociologists estimated that fewer than one in five people reported theft to the police; that perhaps only 10 percent of all rapes were reported; and that most crimes committed by youth were not reported. Today the majority of victims of sexual assaults, theft, and violence at school do not report their experiences to the authorities. Most people do not make an official complaint about being victimized because either they think the police are incompetent, unresponsive, or untrustworthy or that their lives will get worse if they get involved with the criminal courts.[11]

So-called increases in crime may reflect higher rates of reporting, technological improvements in data processing, better record-keeping systems, and political manipulation by local officials. Moreover, because the police are concentrated in poor and working-class communities or in downtown and commercial districts, crime statistics tend to reflect what the police do rather than overall levels of crime. Thus the UCR both grossly underestimates the amount of crime and skews what the public is told about the crime problem.[12]

More accurate information about the scope of everyday crime is available in the National Crime Victimization Surveys, initiated by the federal government in 1973. They are conducted by the Bureau of Justice Statistics and are based on interviews with households, businesses, and individuals in which respondents are asked to anonymously report whether they have been victimized by personal violence or economic crime. Because people are more likely to admit victimization than criminal behavior, the surveys are more reliable than the UCR.

Drawing upon the victimization surveys in the 1970s, sociologists found little difference in rates of delinquent behavior between working- and middle-class or black and white youth. Illegal use of drugs and alcohol, sexual violence, and theft were equally distributed across socioeconomic groups. In fact white middle-class teens were more likely than their working-class counterparts to commit theft, steal cars, and commit assaults. Also, many acts of illegal behavior relating to the market in drugs, stolen goods, and other commodities cross class and racial lines, with producers, sellers, and consumers coming from all sectors of society. National surveys, from the 1970s to the present, report that white suburban youth and black urban youth have similar rates of using and selling illegal drugs.[13]

Yet wealthy or middle-class youth rarely are among the populations of juvenile detention centers or reformatories. By the mid-1970s nationwide studies reported that African Americans comprised one-third of incarcerated youth and that patterns of racism and sexism accounted for who was referred to juvenile court, who was detained before trial, and who did time after trial. In the 1980s media and political images framed the cocaine crisis as white suburban addict-victims versus minority ghetto predator-criminals, with urban pushers and ghetto hustlers preying on impressionable middle-class youth. Meanwhile the reality was that whites made up the majority of cocaine users and African Americans 80 percent of defendants.[14]

In Chicago's juvenile court in the late 1990s, despite a staff of more than six hundred and an annual budget exceeding $20 million, on any given day each judge had fifteen hundred to two thousand cases pending and dispensed with an average case every twelve minutes. Of the nearly thirteen thousand youth who were held in detention annually before their cases were heard, the overwhelming majority were poor, African American (80 percent), Latino (15 percent), and male (90 percent).[15]

By 1996 young African Americans nationwide accounted for 44 percent of all cases referred from juvenile to criminal courts and 68 percent of incarcerated youth. In two states studied, one in seven African Americans, compared with one in 125 whites, was likely to be in a juvenile facility before the age of eighteen. By 1997 two-thirds of all incarcerated youth were African Americans, Latinos, and Native Americans. Girls of color made up half of all incarcerated young women; African Americans had a one in 188 chance of being incarcerated by age eighteen, compared with odds of one in 1,000 for white girls.[16]

Class resources determine which young people are tracked into carceral identities and who gets second and third chances. Working parents hustling low-paying jobs with erratic hours so they can pay the bills cannot hire tutors, counselors, and psychiatrists or turn to private schools or programs when their children are accused of breaking the law. Parents who live in middle-class suburbs, gated communities, and private estates can tell their hired security forces to deliver their children to their homes rather than to juvenile detention. And when cases are referred for official action, police and judges are much more likely to divert delinquents to informal and community programs when families can demonstrate that they have resources to pay restitution to victims or can put their children in private rehabilitation programs or military schools.

TOO BIG TO FAIL

In contrast to government responses to juvenile delinquency that are saturated with a rhetoric of moral righteousness and social obligation, an attitude of laissez-faire prevails in regard to corporate crime. Most federal prosecutors responsible for investigating high-level economic crimes regard criminal prosecution as the last resort.

As FBI director, James Comey gained notoriety twice, first by helping to derail Hillary Clinton's presidential campaign by announcing the reopening of an investigation of her use of a private email server eleven days before the 2016 elections and then by being fired by President Trump in May 2017, presumably because Comey was unwilling to curb the FBI's investigation of whether the Trump presidential campaign colluded with Russian intelligence agencies.[17]

Long before Obama appointed Comey head of the FBI in 2013, he was an upwardly mobile lawyer who moved easily, as did many of his colleagues, between jobs in government and the corporate sector. After receiving his law degree from the University of Chicago in 1985, he clerked for a federal judge, joined the prestigious firm of Gibson, Dunn and Crutcher, then worked his way up the bureaucracy as a federal prosecutor in U.S. Attorney's Offices in Virginia and New York. President George W. Bush's 2002 nomination of this churchgoing, lifelong Republican as U.S. attorney to head up the Southern District of New York was no surprise. In this capacity Comey chided his staff of hot-shot criminal prosecutors for belonging to the "chickenshit club" and urged them to take on tough cases of corporate crime, to "be righteous, not careerist," according to a reporter who documented the briefing.[18]

Comey's lecture had little impact on his staff, nor did he himself take it to heart. In 2005 he left the Justice Department to become general counsel for Lockheed Martin, the government's largest defense contractor. A few years later he joined an investment management company before taking a job with HSBC to help the company recover from its money-laundering scandal. By the time he returned to the Justice Department in 2013 to head the FBI, he was a full-fledged member of the club in good standing. In his bestselling memoir that selectively sums up his professional accomplishments, published after Trump ended his FBI career, Comey takes pride in his "higher loyalty . . . to lasting values, most important the truth," but conveniently omits any reflections on the years he spent serving corporate interests.[19]

The focus of criminal justice institutions is overwhelmingly on working-class people, especially racial minorities, who for the most part are arrested and incarcerated for relatively minor economic crimes, drug-related offenses, and violations of public order. In contrast businesses, organizations, government agencies, and wealthy individuals who engage in acts of extraordinary social harm are either diverted to civil resolutions or fined or admonished or, in some cases, rewarded. When he worked as a federal prosecutor, James Comey says that he was "stymied in [his] efforts to prove criminal intent [by] those who had bankrupted companies, destroyed countless jobs, and defrauded billions from investors." The idea that some "banks are too big to fail" and should not be subjected to criminal prosecution has a long history.[20]

In the 1930s and 1940s the serious crime of embezzlement, for example, was rarely prosecuted. Most cases were settled informally through a negotiated process because employers did not want bad publicity and prosecutors wanted to avoid the cost of a trial. Instead of condemnation and incarceration, notes the law professor Jerome Hall, embezzlers were "treated sympathetically by those in control," as if they were "models of success to be imitated." Prosecutors engaged in "wholesale avoidance of legal coercion." Instead "restitution pervades and defines the entire meaning of embezzlement."[21]

In the 1940s corporations that engaged in antitrust activity, false advertising, and violations of labor and copyright laws were regularly found guilty of criminal behavior but punished with civil fines. Why did the law have "a differential implementation for white-collar criminals than for others?" asked the sociologist Edwin Sutherland in a famous 1944 essay. "Most of the defendants in antitrust cases," responded a spokesperson for the Justice Department, "are not criminals in the usual sense. There is no inherent reason why antitrust enforcement requires branding them as such." Sutherland argued that selective media accounts of crime waves generated public "fear and resentment" about crime and that the means of communication were "owned or controlled by the business men who violate the laws and . . . are themselves frequently charged with violations of the same laws."[22]

In the 1960s President Johnson's Crime Commission devoted only seven pages of its massive investigation to corporate crime, concluding that "it is often extremely difficult even to discover the existence of white-collar crimes; it is similarly difficult to secure evidence of criminal guilt . . . Where corporate defendants are involved, the only criminal sanction available is the fine." The commission had numerous recommendations for dealing with inner-city street crime but did not think that criminal law was "an appropriate means of dealing with all kinds of white-collar misconduct." Thus no one expressed alarm in the 1970s when United Brands was only fined $15,000 for bribing the president of Honduras to reduce the export tax on Chiquita bananas.[23]

A few powerful people have done time in prison. In 1990 Michael Milken, known as the "junk bond king," received a ten-year sentence for insider trading and tax evasion. Patty Hearst, daughter of a ruling-class family who was kidnapped by the Symbionese Liberation Army and subsequently participated in a violent bank robbery, served only twenty-two months after Jimmy Carter commuted her sentence; Bill Clinton subsequently issued a full pardon. "That is a lesson in the value of wealth and privilege," says the legal commentator Jeffrey Toobin.[24] Martha Stewart, the television celebrity and entrepreneur, got off with only a five-month prison sentence for securities fraud in 2004. Jeff Skilling, the CEO of Enron Corporation, is serving fourteen years for his 2006 conviction on fraud and insider trading. Most notoriously in 2009 Bernie Madoff was sent to prison for the rest of his life after he was convicted of a brazen Ponzi scheme that defrauded individual investors, foundations, charities, and banks of billions of dollars. These cases of elite criminals being tried and convicted are well known because they are exceptional.

The record contains occasional examples of the federal government's attempts to hold corporations criminally liable. Following the savings and loan scandal of the 1980s, when hundreds of banks failed as a result of dubious real estate loans, the Justice Department prosecuted about eight hundred individuals, including top bank executives. In the 2000s high-level executives from Enron, Quest Communications, and Tyco International were prosecuted for financial crimes.[25]

But for the most part corporate criminals do not face either time in prison or the legal and social consequences of a criminal record. In the 1980s the Department of Justice brought only forty-four cases of corporate crime to court, and these resulted in only three prison sentences. Federal prosecutors typically rely on "deferred prosecution agreements" in cases against financial firms—they agree not to file criminal charges if perpetrators agree to stop their illegal conduct and pay fines.

In 2002 Purdue Pharma, a pharmaceutical company, hired Rudy Giuliani, the former mayor of New York who in 2018 would work as President Trump's personal attorney, to help the company stem negative publicity about one of its drugs, OxyContin, a powerful addictive painkiller that had reportedly killed hundreds of users. Purdue was in trouble for aggressively promoting the drug to general practitioners who lacked specialized knowledge and for understating the drug's addictive properties. Giuliani was well connected: a former federal prosecutor with close ties to the policing establishment, he was helping to raise money for a Drug Enforcement Administration museum, and his firm had part of a $1 million contract with the Justice Department. One of his associates who was working with Purdue Pharma was Bernard Kerik, the former

New York City police commissioner. Purdue's investment of millions of dollars for public relations, lobbyists, and lawyers paid off. In 2004 it received a $2 million fine for record-keeping improprieties and in 2007 another fine of $600 million for fraudulently misrepresenting the drug's long-term effects. Later that year, according to a *New York Times* investigation, federal prosecutors gathered sufficient evidence for the Justice Department to indict company executives on felony charges, including conspiracy to defraud the United States. Such a decision, said a former Drug Enforcement Administration official, "would have sent a message to the entire drug industry." Instead, despite proof of the key role of OxyContin in the opioid epidemic, which by then had killed more than two hundred thousand addicts, officials in the George W. Bush administration accepted guilty pleas to misdemeanor misbranding, and a federal judge sentenced three Purdue executives to only three years' probation and four hundred hours of community service. Meanwhile, according to the U.S. Centers for Disease Control and Prevention, 145 people in the United States die every day from opioid abuse.[26]

In 2008, following the worst financial crisis since the Great Depression, the federal government did not criminally prosecute a single major bank or high-level banker, although the crisis was fueled by predatory and fraudulent practices in the mortgage-lending industry. Despite reports of widespread criminal behavior, the number of FBI investigations and federal prosecutions of corporate crime declined in the aftermath of the Great Recession. By 2011 the federal prosecution of financial fraud had dropped to a twenty-year low. In its economic inquest the Financial Crisis Inquiry Commission, appointed by Congress, described a "systematic breakdown" in accountability and ethical behavior that amounted to fraud. "If you do prosecute—if you do bring a criminal charge—it will have a negative impact on the national economy, perhaps even the world economy," Attorney General Eric Holder rationalized to Congress. According to a *Wall Street Journal* investigation of 156 cases initiated by the federal government against the largest Wall Street banks between 2009 and 2016, no charges were brought in more than 80 percent of cases. Of the rest, no high-level executives were charged.[27]

After the attacks of September 11, 2001, the Justice Department shifted resources to investigations of terrorism, and the number of prosecutions for corporate crime fell. By 2007 only 120 FBI agents were assigned to review more than fifty thousand allegations of mortgage fraud. In 2012, following an exposé by the *New York Times*, the federal government investigated whether Walmart had bribed Mexican executives in exchange for market advantages. Similar allegations were made about Walmart operations in India, China, and Brazil. The company spent $700 million on legal advice, changed some of its internal procedures, and retired a few executives, thus avoiding criminal responsibility. The same pattern of procrastination, financial penalties, and avoidance of criminal prosecution occurred in cases involving British Petroleum following the 2010 Deepwater Horizon explosion in the Gulf of Mexico that killed eleven workers and caused the largest oil spill in U.S. history.[28]

To Jed Rakoff, a federal judge and gadfly, this failure to apply the law equally to rich and poor is disturbing. The unwillingness of the federal government to prosecute "colossal fraud" makes a mockery of justice for all. "No one that I know of has ever contended that a big financial institution would collapse if one or more of its high-level executives were prosecuted," says Rakoff, one of the few senior judges willing to speak out about the hypocrisy of a legal system that treats corporate executives engaged in systematic crimes as though they are minor first offenders who deserve the benefit of the doubt.[29]

TWO-TRACK WELFARE

The carceral state is typically characterized as a masculine institution because mostly men populate police cells, jails, detention centers, and prisons. This minimizes the significant sector of poor women, disproportionately women of color, who are snared by criminal justice operations. With the exception of Thailand, the forty-four jurisdictions with the highest rate of incarcerated women in the world are individual U.S. states.

The U.S. rate of women's incarceration, which tripled in a decade, was 127 per 100,000, compared with 8 per 100,000 for Norway and 6 per 100,000 for France in 1990. In 1970, 8,000 American women were in jail. By 2014 the number had increased fourteenfold, to 110,000, with African Americans and Latinas comprising almost 60 percent. Both the number and percentage of women incarcerated in jails and prisons has been edging up in recent years: from 164,200 (8.1 percent) in 2000 to 205,300 (8.7 percent) in 2010 to 213,700 (9.3 percent) in 2013. By 2016, 1.2 million women were either incarcerated or on probation and parole.[30]

Poor women are trebly victimized: by a state that ignores their needs, by abusive men both before and after incarceration, and by a society that treats women's poverty as though it is a personal failing. As victims of personal violence by men whom they know, poor women are underserved by social service agencies and routinely ignored by the police. When their abusers are detained, they emerge from prison dehumanized, often abused themselves, and more likely to be violent.[31]

A significant number of women are directly and deeply affected when men in their families are arrested, detained, and jailed. In prominent cases involving social causes, from the Scottsboro Boys' murder trial in the 1930s and Du Bois' treason trial in the 1950s to the arrest of civil rights and black liberation activists in the 1960s and 1970s, men are usually in the headlines, but the organizers of public campaigns for justice, who are usually invisible, are overwhelmingly women.

In routine criminal cases women are also the ones primarily responsible for scraping together money for bail and lawyers and for providing safe spaces for men on the run. Even trying to maintain a friendship with men facing arrest puts the women at risk. Relationships that are fragile to begin with quickly unravel. Law enforcement agencies psychologically and physically threaten women with eviction and loss of child custody if they refuse to snitch while their sons, brothers, and partners are dodging the police. "The great paradox of a highly punitive approach to crime control," Alice Goffman notes in her closely observed ethnography of a Philadelphia neighborhood, "is that it winds up criminalizing so much of daily life." Women who regularly visit or support family members doing time take on the identity of quasi-inmates, as they become enmeshed in the fallout of prison life, from providing psychological and material resources to taking on the duties of absent fathers.[32]

Public welfare is the primary way in which millions of poor women are subjected to social control and a status that parallels and incorporates many assumptions of criminalization.

The media tend to describe public welfare and criminal justice operations in binary terms, as separate and opposite. Encouraging this is the division of intellectual labor between academic disciplines that are rarely in conversation, such as social work and criminology, and by fractured social movements in which feminist, antiracist, and labor organizations are pitted against each other. Occasionally, as in the case of the Poor People's Campaign and the grassroots activism of the National Welfare Rights Organization in the late 1960s, the organizations make efforts to bridge this divide, but too often struggles for social justice in the United States are divided and conquered.[33]

Public welfare and criminal justice operations are complementary instruments of power, with jails and prisons primarily containing and punishing unemployed men and welfare agencies primarily regulating and punishing poor women and their children. Being on welfare is similar to having a criminal record: both carry a social stigma, both impede people's ability to find a decent job, and both are saturated with moralistic judgments.

Welfare is itself a double system that starts with the different language used to describe what it means to depend on the state and on employers for help and resources. The middle class and a small sector of the working class regard the generous benefits of job-related health coverage, pension plans, tax breaks, and property rebates as a hard-earned right. The language of welfare is not used to describe them, and beneficiaries are not depicted as scroungers or morally deficient. For the poor and irregularly employed, especially those in communities of color, welfare is a humiliating experience, from its punitive terminology to its begrudging programs hedged with unreasonable expectations.

Welfare is also a highly gendered process. Middle-class men and women enjoy all the benefits of welfare, mostly through employer-led schemes that subsidize health care and pensions. For poor men with erratic work histories and arrest records, welfare is rarely available. One in three African American men has a felony conviction that makes him ineligible for many social services at a time in his life when he most needs help. For impoverished women and children, many of whom are denied cash payments, welfare has become, in the words of Frances Fox Piven, an expert on the subject, "a lesson about the moral imperative of work and the fate that would befall those who shirked." Middle-class recipients are regarded as worthy beneficiaries of rightful benefits, the poor as unworthy exploiters of the public trust.[34]

More than half of the U.S. population benefits from one of the most privileged systems of welfare in the West: a regressive system of taxation, generous government rebates to businesses, and employer-subsidized pension and health plans. "In no other nation," the political scientist Jacob Hacker observes, "do citizens rely so heavily on private benefits for protection against the fundamental risks of modern life." This massive system of privatized welfare depends extensively on government interventions in the form of tax breaks, credit subsidies, and legislative regulations.[35]

For the rest, the United States has the most regressive system of welfare among developed nations, and in recent decades it has become increasingly begrudging and punitive. Public welfare has always been selective and racialized. Before the 1960s the limited beneficiaries of social insurance, public assistance, and other entitlement programs were typically white working- and middle-class men. A historical perspective helps to explain how welfare's double system emerged and developed.

During the period from the end of the Civil War in 1865 to the 1920s, the federal government created a postwar pension system that reached more than a quarter of the nation's elderly men. The federal Freedman's Bureau (1865–72), which implemented programs in the South to reverse the ravages of slavery, was short-lived and locally sabotaged. Women were excluded from Civil War pensions as noncombatants, and most African Americans were denied pensions because of outright racism in the South and Jim Crow practices throughout the country.[36]

In the 1910s and 1920s states authorized mothers' aid benefits for about fifty thousand widows with children. These programs conditioned welfare on the moral propriety of recipients and used a racialized means test: whites regularly received more money than blacks, and Mexican Americans in California were excluded as undeserving.[37]

As a result of the convergence of the interests of a militant labor movement and reform-minded capitalism in the wake of the Depression, New Deal leaders in the 1930s instigated old-age insurance, unemployment insurance, workers' compensation, and a variety of public initiatives to alleviate poverty. The New Deal was the first national program of social insurance in the United States, designed to protect individuals from the vicissitudes of a chaotic labor market. Yet Roosevelt's program contained no specific measures to prevent racism in their application, other than the promise that economic renewal would benefit everybody. In practice, however, universal policies reinforced the racial divide by functioning primarily as an affirmative action program for white men. The Social Security Act of 1935, for example, excluded African Americans and Latinos de facto by denying benefits to servants and agricultural workers. During the 1930s, 90 percent of black women worked in these two occupations. Only about 10 percent of black women derived any benefits from new federal policies relating to minimum wages, hours of employment, and Social Security. In New Mexico welfare workers rationalized discrimination by arguing that Latinas, unlike Anglo women, needed to stay at home to care for their families because of their "cultural traditions."[38]

Similarly the New Deal's public works programs, which provided millions of jobs for the unemployed, primarily benefited white men. Of the 1.6 million people collecting work relief in 1934, only 11 percent were women. Those who managed to get hired were typically assigned to low-paying factory jobs, while African American women and Latinas were lucky if they could find janitorial work. In some areas of the country local functionaries in the federal Works Progress Administration took women and men off the rolls when demand for domestic servants or agricultural workers increased. During a glut in the labor market in the 1930s the United States sent thousands of Latinas and Latinos, mostly Mexicans, back to Mexico to save on welfare costs.[39]

Other New Deal legislation and subsequent amendments operated within the assumptions of gender and racial discrimination. The 1935 Wagner Act was in effect "the Magna Carta of white labor" because it permitted racial exclusion in labor contracts, a policy that continued well into the 1970s. The 1934 National Housing Act created social policies that justified and perpetuated segregated and inferior residential policies. Housing legislation through the 1950s, backed up by redlining banking practices that limited loans to black families, ensured that residential segregation was enforced and only whites benefited from suburban subsidies and tax breaks. A survey of real estate agents in Chicago reported that 80 percent of realtors refused to sell property to African Americans in white neighborhoods. Federal public housing policies in the 1960s further reinforced segregation by locating projects within ghettos and barrios and by refusing to enforce integration.[40]

At the end of World War II, millions of returning soldiers benefited from a GI Bill that subsidized education, job training, housing, and child care. The legislation primarily propelled Irish and other ethnic Americans into stable working-class and public-sector jobs and Jews into academia and other professions. The few thousand African American men who went to college were mostly tracked into segregated, third-tier colleges. And when African Americans, Latinos, and women entered the military in large numbers during and after the Vietnam War, the preferential treatment accorded older veterans was drastically reduced, leaving the majority of servicemen and servicewomen in the 1990s close to the poverty line, with little possibility for upward mobility.[41]

In the 1960s, in response to the civil rights movement and urban rebellions, Johnson's War on Poverty included Medicare, Medicaid, community-based antipoverty initiatives, and affirmative action programs designed to redress the damage done by decades of racist and sexist employment and educational policies. For the first time poor women and men of color began to gain access to entitlement programs that gave people a chance of getting out of poverty and into work. Affirmative action opened up access to predominantly white colleges, public-sector jobs, and previously closed unions. But these reforms were short-lived. Legislation enacted in the 1960s incorporated tough, punitive measures of social control in the expanded welfare state, in particular by expanding muscular policing in inner cities.[42]

In 1965 the United States ranked twenty-first out of twenty-two Western nations in per capita welfare expenditures. Even in the 1970s, after national efforts to expand benefits provided by the New Deal, the United States spent only about 14 percent of the total federal budget on welfare, compared with 24 percent for other Western democracies. By 1995 public social expenditures represented 17.1 percent of the gross national product, the least of ten comparable nations and a little more than half the average level of other nations'.[43]

Gains made by poor women during the War on Poverty were erased in the 1970s and 1980s and reversed in the 1990s. During the Ronald Reagan and George H. W. Bush administrations, Congress and state legislatures made major cuts to programs such as Supplemental Security Income, Medicaid, food stamps, school food programs, nutrition programs for women, Aid to Families with Dependent Children (AFDC), energy assistance grants, public-service jobs and training, community grants, and low-income housing subsidies. In the 1960s people like Lynn Woolsey, who later represented California's Sixth Congressional District, were able to go on AFDC and get help with health care and child care for their children. "I was certain that I deserved it," she said at a public conference many years later. "It never entered my mind that I wasn't going to get everything that was available to us."[44]

Being against welfare was an ideological as well as a policy shift. In his campaign for the presidency in 1976, Ronald Reagan popularized the myth of the welfare queen—the undeserving, work-shy, African American woman who "has eighty names, thirty addresses, twelve Social Security cards and is collecting veterans' benefits on four non-existing deceased husbands," Reagan told crowds that lapped up the racial and mostly fictitious message. "Her tax-free income alone is over $150,000." This kind of demagoguery both legitimated and stoked cuts in working-class welfare.[45]

Between 1970 and 1996 California reduced public welfare benefits by 18 percent, New York City by 48 percent, Tennessee by 58 percent, and Texas by 68 percent. From March 1984 to October 1996 the number of AFDC recipients nationwide dropped 18 percent, from 14.3 million to 11.8 million. This trend accelerated throughout the 1990s: New York City reduced its welfare rolls by 30 percent; from 1997 to 1998 California reduced the number of families on public assistance by 12.2 percent, the largest decrease in the state's history. In two decades the purchasing power of an average welfare check was reduced by 45 percent, and most families on welfare lived well below the federal poverty line. Meanwhile profit-making human service corporations (nursing homes, hospitals, and child-care facilities) dramatically increased their access to public funds, benefiting from the contracting out of essential programs by local and state governments, a development that later came to dominate the funding of public security.[46]

In August 1996 President Bill Clinton signed into law the Personal Opportunity and Work Responsibility Act, which replaced AFDC with Temporary Assistance for Needy Families (TANF). This legislation limited aid to sixty months in a lifetime, required recipients to work, prohibited documented immigrants from receiving food stamps and Supplemental Security Income (for the disabled, aged, and blind), required teen parents to live at home or with adult supervision, and restricted food stamps for able-bodied single, unemployed adults. This reform in effect ended efforts to guarantee welfare assistance to people in need by imposing a time limit on welfare eligibility and punitive work requirements on recipients and by giving states more authority to substitute services for cash payments. By 2015, 43.1 million citizens were classified as officially poor—defined as a family of four earning about $24,000 a year—with welfare no longer a route out of poverty.[47]

The 1996 legislation included a statutory innovation called "charitable choice" that enabled states to delegate welfare programs to religious institutions. Previously religious organizations were required to set up separate, secular agencies to administer federally funded programs and to ensure the separation of church and state. When George W. Bush became president, he made religiosity the centerpiece of his "compassionate conservatism" by establishing the White House Office of Faith-Based and Community Initiatives and increasing federal grants to religious groups. Under Bush faith-based policies accelerated the trend toward the privatization of welfare by expanding tax breaks for charitable donations and promoting spiritual personal solutions to material public problems. Moreover, under the cover of religious freedom, the Bush administration enabled right-wing religious organizations to receive federal funds while practicing employment discrimination against gay and lesbian employees. In sum, a longtime welfare scholar notes, "charitable choice represents a fusion of the neoliberal urge to privatize and the hard Right's urge to moralize."[48]

As a result of TANF and bipartisan political support for massive cuts in public welfare, from 1994 to 2001 the nation's welfare caseload was reduced from 5 million to 2.1 million families, with poor single-parent women coerced into competition for jobs with public-service workers. Compulsory work for welfare recipients does not include the right to a minimum wage or unemployment insurance. TANF tracks women into low-paid drudgery, backed up by intrusions into their personal life and by morality tests that police their sexuality and living arrangements. In recent years the cuts in public welfare have continued, with TANF reduced from 1.9 million families in 2012 to 1.5 million families in 2016, while economic inequality deepened, as evidenced by the more than forty-four million individuals who use food stamps through what is now known as SNAP, or the Supplemental Nutrition Assistance Program.[49]

As public welfare became more and more punitive in its assumptions and practices, the number of African American and Latina recipients increased, and by 1998 they outnumbered white recipients by about two to one. The law professor Patricia Williams eloquently captured the situation in New York, where "the poor—many of whom are the descendants of hard-working enslaved people, or the grandchildren of hard-working sharecroppers, or the children of coal miners, dirt farmers and sweatshop laborers—are to be uplifted from their purportedly lazy ways through the rehabilitative effort of cleaning the subways. Subways in which some of them are living."[50]

The divide between employer-subsidized and public welfare has never been greater. The tax benefits received by the top one percent are not dependent on their meeting expectations of monogamous, heterosexual marriage. Employees' health care and pension plans do not require beneficiaries to sign pledges that they do not use drugs illegally. The United States subjects the poor to behavioral tests that are not required of any other class-based entitlement programs. For poor women welfare is not about ensuring the well-being of families but about deterring people from applying for welfare. The so-called social safety net is based on the assumption that economic need is rooted in personal pathology and latent criminality and that the motivation and honesty of recipients are suspect. It puts considerable resources into aggressively prosecuting fraud.[51]

The Trump administration came to power committed to doubling down on welfare policies initiated by the Clinton administration. Donald Trump had long been on record as favoring the replacement of government programs with private charities and volunteers, cracking down on food stamp fraud, and getting rid of "free welfare checks and health care" for illegal immigrants. "It's time," he told the Conservative Political Action Conference a few weeks after becoming president, "for all Americans to get off welfare and get back to work." Trump also delivered on his promise to the Right that he would "vigorously enforce Federal law's robust protections for religious freedom" by ordering the Departments of Justice and Health and Human Services to roll back rules that penalize employers who deny their workers the right to birth control services as part of their health insurance.[52]

This approach resonated with Republican Party leaders, who have called for devolving more welfare policies to the states, increasing privatization of welfare services, and, in the words of the social welfare professor Tina Sacks, leaving the poor more "vulnerable to the vagaries of the market instead of being a shelter from them."[53]

According to academic critics of welfare's double system, "the 'left hand' of the welfare state and the 'right hand' of the carceral state now work together." Welfare reformers emphasize the importance of recipients taking personal responsibility for their economic situation, learning skills of self-discipline, and enthusiastically entering a labor market crowded with younger, childless competitors; such exhortations also are hallmarks of current programs for former prisoners. The federal government, from Clinton to Trump, no longer regards poor women's work, rearing children and taking care of family members, as a public virtue. The mother on welfare is depicted as a "civic failure, not just for dodging her own work obligations, but also for presenting her children with a bad role model."[54]

Meanwhile the boys and men in impoverished families negotiate the everyday humiliations of the criminal courts.

MIRAGE OF JUSTICE

"I was lucky," said Bryan Stevenson, an African American criminal defense lawyer with a degree from Harvard Law School, about the day police stopped him near his home, searched his car illegally, and threatened him with guns. When a computer check confirmed his identity, they let him go with a taunt. He *was* lucky. Most police stops of young black men presume guilt.[55]

In the fictional adversary system of criminal justice, the burden is on the state to prove its case, and the state and accused supposedly battle it out in a fair contest. In reality the overwhelming majority of criminal justice personnel work against the interests of defendants. In 2008 the American Bar Association estimated that states and local governments spent only 2.5 percent of their criminal justice budgets on lawyers for the poor. The Sixth Amendment's guarantee that defendants receive a speedy public trial by an impartial jury of their peers and have the assistance of counsel is, as Judge Rakoff put it bluntly, a mirage.[56]

Theoretically the innocence of defendants is assumed before trial. In practice about 2.5 percent of criminal justice personnel (public defenders, probation and parole officers) nominally work on the side of defendants, while 97.5 percent (police, prosecutors, and guards) work on the side of the state. It is not a fair fight.

About 80 percent of employees in criminal justice institutions—more than three million—work in some kind of policing operation: urban police departments, private security, homeland security, counterinsurgency, criminal investigation, and immigration control. About 17 percent (701,000) work as guards and support staff in prisons and jails. The rest hold jobs in probation, parole, community corrections, courts, and juvenile justice. While police and guards have increased their share of overall carceral employment, the ratio of judges per 100,000 citizens declined 23 percent, from 13.2 in 1980 to 10.2 in 2011, another indication of the disparate allocation of resources.[57]

The criminal courts' double system does not depend on a grand conspiracy or suspension of the rule of law. Instead it operates through the normal, everyday minutiae of administrative practices and bureaucratic operations, carried out by professional functionaries.

For adults the first contact with the carceral state typically takes place in the lower courts after they have been arrested or given citations for noncriminal infractions, criminal misdemeanors, and "quality-of-life" offenses. In the town of Ferguson, Missouri, where eighteen-year-old Michael Brown, Jr., was shot six times and killed by Officer Darren Wilson on suspicion of stealing a packet of cigarillos in August 2014, the police that year issued 11,800 traffic violations and 11,900 nontraffic violations, about one violation for every resident, with the resulting fines and fees making up 22 percent of the municipal budget. In nearby Pine Lawn, which is also predominantly African American, the police issued eight violations for every one resident, generating 48 percent of the city's budget. In North Saint Louis County, violations that were routinely cited included wearing saggy pants, playing loud music, barbecuing in the front yard, loitering in a park, owning a barking dog, and leaving trash unsecured. In Sumter, South Carolina, Larry Marsh, who has a long history of homelessness and mental illness, has been arrested at least 270 times for trespassing.

An investigation of the Baltimore Police Department by the Civil Rights Division of the U.S. Department of Justice similarly found that between January 2010 and May 2015 the police stopped and frisked more than a quarter of a million people on the streets, mostly in African American neighborhoods; the police hassled hundreds of black men at least ten times each and seven men more than thirty times each. Police arrested

African Americans so often without cause or evidence for the so-called crimes of trespassing and loitering that prosecutors were forced to dismiss eleven thousand cases during the five-year period.[58]

These daily inconveniences and humiliations should not be minimized. They affect millions of people, and for many represent the beginning of a process that constricts job possibilities and whittles away civil rights. Police make three times as many arrests for misdemeanors and infractions as for felonies: in 2009 that meant 5.9 million misdemeanor arrests compared with 1.9 million felony arrests. Misdemeanor charges require resources that most poor people do not have, and diversion into community service and self-improvement programs takes away time from work, child care, and education. Misdemeanor convictions can mark people with an official record and rap sheet, and they enter a disciplinary process that requires defendants to demonstrate their capacity for self-governance—"arrive at court on time, sit and wait quietly, go to a program, arrive at community service on time—and earn either leniency or sanctions depending on how they perform."[59]

Those arrested for subsequent minor offenses or more serious misdemeanors and felonies are at a fatal disadvantage if they cannot make bail or hire private attorneys. People in jail have a high incidence of mental health and substance abuse issues, compounded by miserable conditions and skimpy services that increase their chances of premature death. Between 2000 and 2014 nearly fifteen thousand people died while in custody; 31 percent were suicides, the leading cause of death. The suicide rate in jail has increased in recent years, climbing to 35 percent of all inmate deaths in 2014. Doing time is not only punitive but also extremely unhealthy.[60]

In 1959 the law professor Caleb Foote first drew attention to a compelling statistic: in New York and Philadelphia as many as three-quarters of defendants arrested for felonies could not make bail and therefore remained in custody pending trial, thus undermining the spirit of the presumption of innocence. Backing up Foote's investigation was the Vera Institute's 1961 Manhattan Bail Project, which advocated, as an alternative to cash bail, the release of defendants on their own recognizance (OR) if they could demonstrate ties to the local community. Foote's research and the Vera Institute's pilot project influenced Congress in 1966 to pass the Federal Bail Reform Act, which authorized the granting of OR release to federal defendants in noncapital cases.[61]

Like many liberal reforms of the 1960s, this one was short-lived. Critics argued that bail reform likely meant the release of dangerous offenders who would commit more crimes before trial. In 1969 and 1970 President Richard Nixon proposed a law that would detain "dangerous hard core recidivists" before trial. Although the preventive detention bill stalled in Congress, it approved a similar law for the District of Columbia in 1970, despite the warning by Senator Sam Ervin (D-N.C.) about "what happens when politics, public fear, and creative hysteria join together to find a simple solution to a complex problem."[62]

By the time of Ronald Reagan's two-term presidency, bail reform was dead. Reagan's Task Force on Victims of Crime advocated policies that would deny bail to defendants "posing a danger to the community." The 1984 Bail Reform Act, the U.S. Supreme Court, and many state legislatures authorized denial of release on OR in cases in which release of a defendant "will endanger the safety of any other person or the community." With dangerousness broadly interpreted to include drug-related and nonviolent behavior, the demands of so-called public safety made the excessive bail clause of the Eighth Amendment empty rhetoric.[63]

In the 1990s and 2000s the percentage of federal defendants detained before trial increased considerably as a result of the growth of immigration-related cases. Meanwhile an occasional defendant with income in the top one percent was permitted to avoid jail by paying for an elaborate home confinement system, including twenty-four-hour security and GPS monitoring. "The rich are different from everyone else," a *New York Times* reporter observed, "even those accused of crimes."[64]

Between 1992 and 2009 the average bail set by local courts increased by 46 percent, to $61,000, resulting in, according to the White House Council of Economic Advisers, detention of "the poorest rather than the most dangerous defendants before trial." The number of women of color in jail awaiting trial or sentencing, or who were serving time for petty misdemeanors, increased fourteenfold since the 1970s. In 2013 the Vera Institute, which had led the fight for substantial bail reform in the 1960s, was still fighting the same fight, albeit now as a rearguard action: of the 731,000 people in jail on a single day nationwide, 62 percent were awaiting trial; more than one-third were African Americans; 47 percent had not graduated from high school; and a majority suffered from mental illnesses. As of 2015, 63 percent (435,500) of people in jail (693,000) had not been convicted. For them the presumption of innocence does not exist.[65]

In some regions of the country, such as New Orleans in 2016, the situation is worse; there, 90 percent of people in jail were awaiting trial. In a racially stratified city in which the poverty rate is almost twice the national average, and 85 percent of defendants cannot afford to hire an attorney, four in every five people in jail are African Americans.[66]

Sitting in jail because of an inability to make bail not only is punishment before trial but also increases fourfold a defendant's chances of being incarcerated after a case is decided. Most defendants choose a guilty plea rather than serve dead time awaiting trial. An extensive review of bail practices in New York City reported that defendants jailed before disposition of their cases had a conviction rate of 92 percent, compared with 50 percent for defendants who could make bail in nonfelony cases. In felony cases pretrial detention raised the likelihood of both conviction and postconviction incarceration. Defendants who were detained before trial were incarcerated in 87 percent of cases posttrial, compared with 20 percent of defendants who had made bail.[67]

The 1963 U.S. Supreme Court decision in *Gideon v. Wainwright*, which requires states to provide attorneys to defendants in criminal cases if they cannot afford counsel, certainly was an important victory. Some activists, such as the Socialist organizer Kate Richards (1876–1948), had been fighting since the 1920s for a public defender system "to assist in securing justice for citizens who come into court" and "to preserve individual rights before the law, if there are any such rights." She hoped that "a public defender might, though it is not certain he would, minimize the advantages of wealth over poverty in the courts. At any rate, it would be worth trying." Du Bois took up the same cause in 1951: "Thousands of innocent victims are in jail today because they had neither money, experience nor friends to help them. They daily stagger out of prison doors embittered, vengeful, hopeless, ruined. And of this army of the wronged, the proportion of Negroes is frightful. We protect and defend sensational cases where Negroes are involved. But the great mass of arrested or accused black folks have no defense."[68]

The right to an attorney was an important formal victory for defendants, and occasionally individual clients receive a vigorous and effective defense. Some counties around the country provided public defenders before 1963, but doing so was not obligatory. By 1967, 270 large cities had a public defender system in place, handling about one-third of all defendants. But overall the introduction of public defenders in the criminal courts helped to speed up the production of guilty pleas and reduce the number of trials.

Idealistic young lawyers who joined the Alameda County Public Defender's Office in Oakland, California, in the late 1960s and early 1970s quickly learned that they were expected to "represent cases not causes" and churn out their caseload without complaint. "I told everybody who came to work for me," the chief public defender instructed new recruits, "'if you're riding some hobby-horse and some kick, then you're not going to work for me.' I wanted no zealots, no person who had a philosophy of this, that and the other thing." When a small group of assistant public defenders in 1967 signed a "Lawyers Against the War in Vietnam" petition that appeared in local newspapers, they were reprimanded for "unprofessional conduct" and encouraged to resign. Those who remained developed immunity to the daily sorrows of their clients, even becoming somewhat callous and jaded.[69]

Four years after the *Gideon* case, 90 percent of all criminal convictions were obtained by guilty pleas. When the U.S. Supreme Court in 1967 decided that juveniles, too, are entitled to legal representation—"the condition of being a boy does not justify a kangaroo court," in the words of Justice Abe Fortas—the result was the same: administrative cooperation rather than legal advocacy prevailed because judges, prosecutors, and court officials exert enormous pressure on public defenders to resolve cases quickly in the name of efficient management. What in theory is supposedly adversarial is in reality a bureaucratic process.[70]

As the American Bar Association complained in 1982 and again in 2004, the lack of sufficient funding means that public defenders are overwhelmed by their caseloads, do not have time or money to do competent investigations or hire expert witnesses, and encourage more than 90 percent of their clients to plead guilty. In Nebraska two lawyers handled about twelve hundred cases a year, while the public defenders in one Louisiana parish did not even meet with their clients out of court in more than 80 percent of their cases. In Louisiana, where 80 percent of criminal defendants cannot afford an attorney, getting help from harried public defenders means adding your name to a waiting list. In South Carolina homeless men like Larry Marsh do time in jail and prison without ever conferring with a lawyer.[71]

To work in criminal justice on the side of defendants is wearing. When James Forman, Jr., was a public defender in Washington, D.C., 95 percent of his clients were African American and held in cells close to the courtroom. "No majesty here, no wood paneling, no carpeting or cushioned seats," he writes. His inability to give his clients the legal help they needed often made him want to cry with frustration. "It wasn't an unusual feeling," he says. "Sometimes the only thing that stopped the tears was another case or client who needed me right then."[72]

Today all but 3 percent of federal cases and 5 percent of state cases are settled before trial. Of the 2.2 million people in prison, Judge Rakoff claims, "well over two million are there as a result of plea bargains dictated by the government's prosecutors, who effectively dictate the sentences as well." He estimates that at least twenty thousand defendants who plead guilty because they were pressured to do so are in fact innocent.[73]

In theory the millions of people who come into contact with police, courts, and administrative bodies every year, from receiving citations in their neighborhoods for petty infractions to being assigned to solitary confinement in a supermax prison for violations of prison rules, have two ways to change these conditions: legal activism and political organizing. In reality they have only one choice. Aside from getting help from a small number of hard-pressed, underfunded, private, nonprofit legal service organizations, the subjects of the carceral state are barred from taking collective legal action. How did this happen?

The 1964 Economic Opportunity Act, part of Lyndon Johnson's War on Poverty programs, included for the first time the provision of federally funded legal services for the poor. Although the program focused primarily on helping individuals with claims against landlords, employers, and government agencies, and was criticized by activists for its timidity, by the late 1960s the Right was attacking it for provoking class warfare. It was "a systematic effort to redistribute societal advantages and disadvantages, penalties and rewards, rights and resources," Vice President Spiro Agnew argued in 1972. With passage in 1974 of an act that created the Legal Services Corporation (LSC), the Nixon administration's views prevailed. The measure moved federal legal services programs to the new agency, whose board of directors was appointed by the president; most significantly the legislation barred the LSC from taking on most abortion rights, desegregation, and class-action litigation. During the Reagan administration the Heritage Foundation and other right-wing think tanks' attacks on the toothless agency resulted in cuts in funding and even the appointment of a director who advocated its abolition. In response to claims from the Right that the LSC was impeding "the deportation of criminals" and defending "homosexual activists," the Clinton administration gutted what was left of the LSC by barring its participation in any class-action suits; prohibiting appeals of restrictions on, or denials of, welfare benefits; and barring LSC-funded agencies and lawyers from participating in litigation related to abortion, prisoners' rights, drug-related evictions from public housing, and undocumented immigrants' claims. The Trump administration continued this hostility to legal services for the poor, threatening to eliminate all funding for the LSC. Meanwhile Attorney General Jeff Sessions closed down the Access to Justice Initiative, a small department in the Justice Department established by his predecessor to provide legal resources to indigent litigants in civil, criminal, and tribal courts.[74]

"In the face of our nation's worst economic downturn since the Great Depression," New York State's chief judge observed in 2013, "millions of vulnerable, low-income individuals navigate our state civil justice systems without lawyers." In sum, if you are poor and snared in an ever-expanding criminal justice net, the most you can expect from a public defender is a speeded-up guilty plea and, if you are lucky, a modified punishment. And if you want to join with other suspects and defendants to challenge illegal police practices or unfair sentencing laws or inhumane conditions in jails and prisons or mass deportations, expect minimal help from public legal services.[75]

The economic, racial, and gendered prejudices of the carceral state are not occasional and erratic but its lifeblood. The double system of justice is so pervasive and routine that its consequences appear to be natural and inevitable. A historical exploration reveals, however, that crime and justice are highly mutable social categories, the result of social and political interventions and therefore subject to challenge and transformation.

II

3

EXCEPT FOR

*On grappling with the centrality of race in the
history of incarceration in the United States and
the relationship between exceptional measures of
exclusion and everyday criminalization.*

Neither slavery nor involuntary servitude, except as a punishment
for crime whereof the party shall have been duly convicted, shall exist
within the United States, or any place subject to their jurisdiction.
—Thirteenth Amendment to the U.S. Constitution

HUGE SWATH

"Our systems for maintaining the peace and our criminal justice systems
generally work," President Obama said in September 2015, "except for this
huge swath of the population that is incarcerated at rates that are unprecedented in world history."[1]

The huge swath to which Obama was referring was the high incarceration rate of African Americans, a fact well documented and publicized
by the time he made this statement. Putting aside for the moment Obama's
claims about the unprecedented rate of black imprisonment and the other-
wise benign functioning of criminal justice institutions, the intertwining
of racism and criminalization is well documented and ironclad.[2]

However you do the math (by rates, proportions, or percentages), the
number of African Americans entangled in the criminal justice system
today is staggering: about 766,000 in prison or jail on any given day. The

statistics are numbing but must be faced to appreciate their enormity and significance.

By 2010 African Americans were not underrepresented in the prison population of a single state—from 26 percent of the population and 54 percent of prisoners in Alabama to 6 percent of the population and 38 percent of prisoners in Wisconsin. African American men's national rate of imprisonment is more than five times that of the white rate—2,306 to 450 per 100,000—and black women's rate is twice that of white women.

By 2014 African Americans made up more than half the incarcerated population in twelve states and 72 percent in Maryland. The disparity is evident in every region of the country, not just the South: the rate of African Americans' incarceration (per 100,000 in the larger population) is, for example, much higher in West Virginia (7,360) than in Louisiana (2,749) and higher in California (3,036) than in Mississippi (1,788). As the law professor Jonathan Simon bluntly notes, "California is to incarceration what Mississippi was to segregation."[3]

The racial disparity in the incarceration rates of African Americans and whites permeates the carceral state. African Americans account for 13 percent of the U.S. population and 45 percent of felony defendants in the seventy-five largest counties; 36 percent of people in jail, which is twelve times the white rate; 33 percent of all deaths in jail; and 40 percent of all people held in prison between 2000 and 2012. African American youth are 4.3 times more likely than white youth to be incarcerated. One in every three black males is likely to be incarcerated at some point in his life, and an estimated 8 percent (or more than 2.2 million) of African Americans are disqualified from voting because of a felony conviction.[4]

Everywhere we look—police making arrests, defendants lining up in criminal courts, men and women filling jail and prison cells, and media covering criminal justice issues—we see compelling, palpable evidence of what appears to be ubiquitous black criminality. No wonder it is widely believed that the high rate of black incarceration is deserved and an appropriate response to African Americans' abnormal deviancy.

Years before Donald Trump made law and order a centerpiece of his presidential campaign, he raised the specter of a "population of adolescent males" roaming the streets like "wolf packs." Undoubtedly this highly racialized image of degeneracy links anxieties about crime and disorder with black and brown youth. "I actually have a theory," Trump asserted in 2011 without a shred of evidence, "that Mexico is sending their abso-lute worst, possibly including prisoners, in order for us to bear the cost, both financial and social. This would account for the fact there is so much crime and violence."[5]

Trump's language is crude and demagogic, but he was backed up by academics who framed their prejudices in more polite terms. "We must get our priorities clear," two leading criminologists wrote in 1977. "Vio-lent and predatory crime are what matter most." They did not have in mind war crimes, bank fraud, or corporate theft that resulted in destroyed lives and widespread economic hardships; rather, they were thinking of street crimes that "harm particular individuals and represent the citizens' prime fears, . . . threaten our cities and destroy our sense of community." Simi-larly a book that had far-reaching political influence in the 1980s asserted that "predatory street crime" is a "far more serious matter" than consumer fraud, antitrust violations, and other "white-collar crimes" because it "makes difficult or impossible the maintenance of meaningful human communities."[6] These prestigious authors did not think it was necessary to explain why corporate and state crimes also do not rip apart the social fabric.

This kind of linguistic trickery, which, as George Orwell says, makes "lies sound truthful" and gives "an appearance of solidity to pure wind," is more than a successful exercise in propaganda. It is deeply embed-ded in institutions, legal custom, and commonsense assumptions about the meaning of *criminal*. The combination of a judicial system that for the most part whitewashes crimes in high places and of police forces that make impoverished working-class communities their primary targets helps to solidify the assumption that street crime is responsible for the most serious social harm.

Meanwhile illegal drug dealing, rape, violence, and everyday theft are mostly dealt with informally in suburban communities and ignored or handled privately in the corporate world. Only after investigative journal-ists exposed the Hollywood producer Harvey Weinstein as a longtime sexual predator did his criminal behavior have social consequences. What the African American sociologist E. Franklin Frazier observed in 1935 is true today: the police "practice aggressions and brutalities upon the Har-lem citizens not only because they are Negroes but because they are poor and therefore defenseless."[7]

Criminal justice functionaries might carry out the day-to-day tasks of criminalization, but larger political, social, and cultural forces also are at work. To imagine and feel that a particular group of people is criminogenic—that they are inherently different, abnormal, and somehow predestined to crime—the ground has to be prepared. American history includes several long moments when the heft of government and public opinion was weighted against a whole group of people on the basis of their perceived collective dangerousness, foreignness, or expendability, irrespective of their actual behavior. In these periods victims were transformed into perpetrators, people going about their everyday lives suddenly became a threat to national security, and fighters for social justice were remade as enemies of the people. "Racism," Angela Davis notes, "has always relied on the conflation of the individual and the group."[8]

This kind of alchemy is at work, for example, in recent government efforts to discredit African American groups organizing to defend communities from unlawful police violence. As in the 1950s and 1960s, when the civil rights movement in the South mobilized African American communities to protect themselves against attacks by local sheriffs and the Klan, so in the 2010s the Black Lives Matter movement responded with militant street protests against the routine killing of black men and women by police and guards throughout the country. The Obama government's Department of Justice responded by investigating out-of-control police departments and initiating reforms through consent decrees, that is, an agreement to make changes in policy and training under federal supervision. The Trump government's Department of Justice moved quickly to undo these agreements on the grounds that they "can reduce morale of the police officers" as well as "push back against being out on the street in a proactive way." Meanwhile the FBI's Counterterrorism Division whipped up alarm that "perceptions of police brutality against African Americans spurred an increase in premeditated, retaliatory lethal violence against law enforcement and will very likely serve as justification for such violence." Acting on this assumption, in December 2017 the FBI arrested Christopher Daniels in Dallas and charged the African American antipolice activist with being a threat to law enforcement and an illegal gun owner. After Daniels was denied bail and spent five months locked up, during which time he lost his job and home, a judge ordered him released and dismissed the case. "This has been a nightmare for my entire family," said Daniels.[9]

The post–September 11 registration and monitoring by the Department of Homeland Security of about eighty thousand law-abiding people from majority-Muslim countries, and the widespread surveillance of mosques, schools, and Muslim associations by local counterterrorism units in New York and New Jersey, echo the incarceration without trial of 120,000 people of Japanese descent in the 1940s. "We have been down similar roads before," said the Third Circuit Court of Appeals in Philadelphia that decided in favor of plaintiffs in *Hassan v. City of New York*. "Jewish-Americans during the Red Scare. African-Americans during the civil rights movement and Japanese-Americans during World War II are examples that readily spring to mind." This decision prodded the New York Police Department in 2018 to settle monetary claims with mosques, groups, and individuals that had successfully made the case that Muslim religious identity should not be treated by the police as "a proxy for criminality."[10]

The routine processing of individuals through criminal justice institutions and extraordinary actions against groups are mutually reinforcing: those targeted for collective denunciation are invariably demonized as contaminated and perceived as hotbeds of criminality.[11]

African Americans have always been a significant component of the huge swath of people subject to criminalization—in the South in the 1870s, the arrest and persecution of thousands of individuals for trumped-up crimes under the Black Codes were accompanied by lynchings and other acts of terror aimed at all African Americans—but their experience is not unique or unusual. Race plays a decisive but not exclusive role in this process. Exceptional practices of group repression, it turns out, are not exceptional.

Consider, for example, how in the late nineteenth century local elites targeted white working-class neighborhoods, immigrant workers, and labor organizations for surveillance and corralling. Between 1880 and 1910 they built massive armories throughout northern and midwestern cities that were staffed by state militia armed for class warfare and battling strikers. Police and private security forces assumed the problem of labor militancy and criminal behavior were indistinguishable, when in fact working-class organizations were fighting for an adequate wage, an eight-hour workday, and the right to form and join unions. In 1880, at the height of campaigns against the labor movement, more than one in five prisoners nationwide was an immigrant from Europe.[12]

Another example of group repression and criminalization took place in the mid-nineteenth century during the shift in American policy from removal to confinement of Native Americans, when prison-like reservations in the far West became a model for a new kind of carceral institution that simultaneously contained native peoples, exploited their labor on local farms and ranches, and criminalized their resistance. Later, efforts were made to forcibly purge their children and grandchildren of cultural and linguistic traditions in boarding schools that were modeled on punitive reformatories. In California indigenous victims of genocide were treated as though they were a biologically inferior race predestined to extinction, while the architects of the genocide were heralded as founding fathers of the Golden State. The reservation and boarding school are as much a part of the carceral history of the United States as the jail and prison.[13]

Native peoples who survived war, displacement, theft of lands, forced labor, and breakup of families are overrepresented in the prison populations of Alaska, Arizona, Idaho, Minnesota, Montana, Nebraska, New Mexico, North Dakota, South Dakota, Utah, Washington, and Wyoming. Today they account for one in five arrests in Montana yet comprise only 7 percent of Montana's population.[14]

The U.S. carceral state extends beyond the nation's borders. In the 1900s, during the war in the Philippines, American forces rounded up thousands of Filipinos fighting for national liberation and political independence, first from Spain and then from the United States, on suspicion of disloyalty and subversion. Forcibly removed from their communities, they were herded into what were called "reconcentration camps." Contrary to President Teddy Roosevelt's claim in 1902 that any cruelties practiced by American soldiers against a "very cruel and very treacherous enemy" were "wholly exceptional," the murder and torture of Filipino soldiers and civilians were so routine that an American soldier composed a tribute to the "water-cure" (sung to the tune of the "Battle Hymn of the Republic"):

> Get the good old syringe boys and fill it to the brim
> We've caught another nigger and we'll operate on him
> Let someone take the handle who can work it with a vim
> Shouting the battle cry of freedom.
> Hurrah Hurrah We bring the Jubilee

Hurrah Hurrah The flag that makes him free
Shove in the nozzle deep and let him taste of liberty
Shouting the battle cry of freedom.[15]

The relocation and containment of what the historian Alfred McCoy calls "suspect populations" drew upon the model of the Indian reservation. At about the same time as the war in the Philippines, Germany created its first concentration camps (*Konzentrationslager*) in colonial Namibia. The reservation and concentration camp can be understood as relatives of the prison and ghetto, and an early predecessor of today's policed enclaves used throughout the world, such as refugee camps in Europe, immigrant detention centers in the United States, and the entire Gaza Strip, whose nominal independence as a Palestinian territory is subject to Israel's military control.[16]

The history of Chinese and Mexican immigrants to the United States provides yet more examples of how the political construction of collective dangerousness is linked to everyday criminalization. During the second half of the nineteenth century, government agencies collaborated with vigilante organizations to carry out pogroms against Chinese workers in the rural Pacific Northwest, forcing them to seek safety in urban ghettos known as Chinatowns. Their only crime was being Chinese. In California in the 1870s race-specific laws targeted them: living in a tenement without sufficient space was a crime, local police had license to cut off men's queues, and carrying baskets on sidewalks and running laundries from wooden buildings were illegal. By 1881 Chinese immigrants comprised almost one-fifth of California's convicts. The criminalization of opium use and construction of images of the "yellow peril" helped to consolidate legal and political actions against the Chinese.[17]

Mexicans were routinely targeted by mob violence from the Gold Rush through the 1920s, and subsequently they, along with Central Americans, have been subjected to large-scale importations and deportations: the so-called repatriation campaign of the 1930s, Operation Wetback in 1954, the post–World War II bracero program, and the millions swept up by the Department of Homeland Security since September 11. Between 1848 and the 1920s, 547 documented cases of lynchings of Latinos occurred, a per capita rate equivalent to that for the lynchings of African Americans. In the early twentieth century federal and state authorities regularly linked crime and marijuana use with "the Mexican problem." As a result, by the 1930s Mexican and Mexican American youth accounted for as much as one-third of the residents of a California reformatory.[18]

From 1950 to 1960, under a contract ratified by the Mexican and U.S. governments, almost 3.5 million braceros were recruited to temporarily work as a migrant labor force in Texas, California, New Mexico, Arizona, and Arkansas. Although they were integrated into the economy, they were socially isolated and politically marginalized, housed in barns, stables, warehouses, garages, mosquito-infested bogs, and fetid camps. Local contractors price-gouged these workers for food and other services; travel outside camps and workplaces was restricted; those who complained were likely to be labeled communists and sent home. "The picture of the ideal worker drawn by managers of migration was that of the man of the barracks, the man in a camp who spent all of his time under supervision if not under surveillance," Ernesto Galarza notes in his groundbreaking investigation of the bracero program. "Outside the barracks the limits of freedom were prescribed, and they were also the limits of the job."[19]

The experiences of the millions of Mexicans who have been subjected to deportation without due process and victimized by mob violence, detention, and incarceration are comparable in rate and proportion to the experiences of African Americans.

Like European immigrants in the nineteenth century, and African Americans and Native Americans throughout the nineteenth and twentieth centuries, Latinos in the United States have always been disproportionately arrested and incarcerated in local jails and state prisons. Today they are disproportionately detained and prosecuted for violations of immigration law. In 2010 Mexicans accounted for nearly three-quarters of all deportations, with nationals from Guatemala, Honduras, and El Salvador accounting for another 15 percent. The majority of almost 420,000 deportees in 2012 had either no criminal record or had committed traffic and minor drug offenses. "When you have more than a thousand people deported every day," the sociologist Tanya Maria Golash-Boza observes, "that's a policy of mass deportation."[20]

Latinos are also overrepresented in the state prisons of Arizona, California, Colorado, Mississippi, Nebraska, New Jersey, New Mexico, Oregon, Pennsylvania, Utah, and Washington. They are jailed at five times the rate of white defendants in New York, and they are about 35 percent of all federal prisoners and almost 50 percent of all federal defendants. In 2012 Latino men accounted for about 88 percent of all immigrants sentenced for immigration-related crimes. By the end of 2015 more than 425,000 Latinos were incarcerated in jails and prisons. This took place before President Trump gave "clear direction" to the Department of Homeland Security to step up arrests and deportations.[21]

The use of extraordinary legislation and emergency laws to identify problematic and potentially dangerous populations long preceded the counterterrorism measures inaugurated in the aftermath of September 11. The liberal rule of law has always coexisted with authoritarianism. Now it has become a normal practice. A closer look at the experiences of African Americans illustrates how exceptional and everyday repression became twinned.[22]

BLACK CODES

The rate of African Americans' incarceration saw a "stunning increase" during the last thirty years of the twentieth century, from 368 per 100,000 in 1973 to 1,860 in the 1990s, a fivefold increase. From 1926 to 1976 black-to-white admission rates held steady at a three-to-one ratio, then dramatically increased to six to one. Even as the incarcerated population declined in recent years, the proportion of prisoners of color was unchanged.

It is questionable, however, as some experts claim, whether this kind of racial disparity is unprecedented, that it "broke from its historic norm" or that "for the first time in national history, African Americans make up a majority of those walking through prison gates every year."[23] Again, a long-term historical perspective is useful for exploring and complicating these claims.

Accounts of the origins of incarceration in the United States usually begin with the rise of the modern prison and leasing of prisoners to private contractors in the nineteenth century, but understanding how carceral measures do not rely only on walls and guards requires going back to even earlier periods. Under slavery millions of Africans were forced into a system of production that relied on repressive regulations, not only in the form of punishment for infractions (whipping, shackles, mutilation) but also through daily disciplining of the personal space of enslaved

Africans. The power of slave owners was absolute, the historian Walter Johnson observes, organized as a permanent "counterinsurgency campaign to which there could be no end." To be enslaved on a nineteenth-century cotton plantation was to be embedded day and night, at work and off work, in a carceral system that stretched far beyond the fields. Constant surveillance and coercion denied enslaved people sufficient clothing, bedding, and food, even forbade them to learn to swim, making escape an extraordinary challenge. State legal codes backed up the power of slave owners by requiring absolute obedience and authorizing vicious punishments for any behavior that could be read as insolence.[24]

Not surprisingly, as long as slavery lasted and slave owners exercised complete authority over their human property, hardly any African Americans were in the South's penitentiaries: convicts in Alabama were 99 percent white; and of Georgia's entire population of ninety thousand in 1850, a mere forty-three were prisoners. The South's only experiment with large-scale incarceration took place during the Civil War, when the Andersonville Prison, built in 1864 by enslaved Africans, housed more than 33,000 Union prisoners of war. By the end of the war 12,920 had died of malnutrition and illnesses.[25]

Even after slavery was outlawed and industrial systems of production took over work once done by the enslaved, the owners of factories and plantations retained the power to brutally punish recalcitrant workers on the job, backed up by laws that proscribed protests and work stoppages. A strike for higher wages on Louisiana's sugar plantations in 1887 met with the massacre of more than one hundred African Americans by the state militia; a strike by Arkansas cotton pickers in 1891 led to the killing and lynching of its leaders. Formerly enslaved people who quit their jobs could be arrested for criminal breach of contract. What Michel Foucault calls "the perfect continuity of the punitive and the penal," as in the use of the legal system and governmental power to enforce contracts that openly sided with capital against labor, is well illustrated by what happened in the South after the defeat of Reconstruction (1865–77).[26]

For more than a decade following the Civil War, Reconstruction offered the promise of full political emancipation. It was, according to Eric Foner's definitive account, "a massive experiment in interracial democracy without precedent in the history of this or any other country that abolished slavery in the nineteenth century." By 1875 the South had managed to undermine and reverse progress achieved under Reconstruction, and southern states quickly moved to impose on about four million freed African Americans a racial hierarchy that combined hybrid elements of the past and future: the ideas and cultural assumptions of slavery and new brutal forms of economic exploitation suitable to the accelerated industrial development of the region. For almost forty years the legal system and criminal punishment played a significant role in constructing and defending this new order.[27]

In the aftermath of civil wars, when the victorious and defeated face each other on a daily basis, even in the best of circumstances the transition to a peacetime economy is fraught with tensions. For black southerners the end of Reconstruction meant the worst of circumstances, "the crash of hell," as W.E.B. Du Bois said.[28]

By 1877 every former Confederate state except Virginia had adopted the convict leasing system. The process had two steps: criminalization of noncriminal behavior followed by coerced exploitation of a criminalized labor force. Legislation known as the Black Codes created new categories of race-specific crimes, including vagrancy, idleness, mischief, insulting gestures, keeping guns, migration, and violations of work contracts, all explicitly designed to replace slavery with new forms of subordination. The codes, as Du Bois put it, were an "astonishing affront to emancipation." South Carolina required workers to be licensed; Mississippi required written proof of residence or employment; Louisiana made disobedience on the job a crime; Alabama limited workers' ability to change jobs; Florida prohibited ownership of guns and bowie knives by African Americans; and Georgia targeted "all persons wandering or strolling about in idleness."[29]

The arrest today of young men in places like Ferguson, Missouri, for "manner of walking" has its echo in places like Savannah, Georgia, where, at the beginning of the twentieth century, "walking on the grass, expectorating upon the sidewalk, going to sleep in a depot, loitering on the streets, or other similar misdemeanors which could not by any stretch of the imagination be called a crime" resulted in "trumped-up charges."[30]

This innovative form of legalized coercion, which made citizenship for people of color into a precarious status, was new to the South after the Civil War, but had many parallels and predecessors in other parts of the world. As capitalism replaced feudalism, the use of ferocious punishments was a foundational component of the labor process, backed up by legal and moral codes designed to keep workers working and powerless. One of the first houses of correction, established in Amsterdam in the sixteenth century, forced the unemployed, beggars, and tramps to work under conditions that combined elements of the poorhouse, workhouse, and prison.[31]

The roundup of Native Americans in California after the Gold Rush and criminalization of African Americans after the defeat of Reconstruction recall what happened in England between 1688 and 1820, when the rising capitalist class criminalized all kinds of new offenses against property, creating one of the most vicious criminal codes in Europe. As John Locke wrote in 1690, "Government has no other end but the preservation of property." By the nineteenth century contract law had replaced feudal relations, and long-held rights to land, water, and timber became illegal, making vagrancy commonplace and widely criminalized. "A plain enough case of class robbery" was how the historian E. P. Thompson describes efforts to transform formerly public land into private holdings. The vagabond, as Foucault observes, was reconstituted as a "social enemy," that is, "any person hostile or opposed to the rule of the maximization of production."[32]

The 1823 Master and Servant Act in Britain enabled employers to send workers to houses of correction for hard labor for violations of terms of employment. Between 1857 and 1875, in England and Wales alone, about ten thousand workers were prosecuted annually for breach of contract.[33]

Similarly in California the brutal exploitation of Native Americans who had survived the genocidal policies of the Spanish missions and Gold Rush reminded a local newspaper of "cottondom." From the beginning of American occupation, Indians were "required to obtain employment and not permitted to wander about in an idle and dissolute manner," as a military commander ordered in 1846. "If found doing so, they will be liable to arrest and punishment, by labor on the public works." This proclamation, the historian Benjamin Madley notes, "made Indians either captive laborers or outlaws, thereby criminalizing Indian freedom."[34]

Legislation passed in 1850 and 1860, paternalistically titled "An Act for the Government and Protection of Indians," enabled California to arrest and lease out to private employers perhaps as many as ten thousand Indians found guilty of vagrancy, "strolling about," or "leading an immoral or profligate course of life." Children were bound out to white families, young women to household service and rape, and men to hard labor. The new state received revenue, while employers had access to a labor force that was cheap, without rights, and recovering from extermination campaigns. Because Native Americans could not testify in court against whites, the law in effect encouraged entrepreneurs to kidnap and sell Indians as apprentices to white farmers, ranchers, and miners. According to one estimate made in 1862, children fetched a market price of $30 to $200. As a result of being excluded from the rights of citizenship, California Indians were victimized at will. The laws of so-called protection facilitated crimes against humanity because, like the Black Codes, they were reinforced by a regime of terror. "Exterminationists were thick on the ground," as the writer Larry McMurtry writes bluntly. "Indians were killed as casually as rabbits."[35]

Beginning in the mid-1870s policy makers and politicians decided that separating Native American children from their families was the best means to break the bonds of tribal cultures and indoctrinate a new generation with the values of individualism, capital accumulation, Christianity, and U.S. citizenship. The Indian boarding schools combined the worst elements of a forced labor camp and an orphanage, with harsh punishments for such infractions as "talking Indian," going barefoot, and running away. At the Sherman Institute in California the lesson plan included unpaid backbreaking labor: harvesting melons and oranges for local farmers. "Our girls learned to sew and set Emily Post's table," a Yurok-Karuk activist and poet recalls, "while our boys were taught to weed and manicure lawns to prepare for great futures in menial labor." In 1928 a national survey of boarding schools reported "unmistakable evidence of malnutrition" and so-called teaching programs that were geared "for production and not for education." In some schools, as the federally commissioned Meriam Report noted, "the child must maintain a pathetic degree of quietness."[36]

LEGAL RACISM

The nineteenth-century penal system was a hive of industry and productivity. To be convicted of a crime meant being put to work without any of the meager benefits of labor achieved by free people and often meant being worked to death. In regions of the country with a serious shortage of labor and a potential labor force that lacked the full rights of citizenship, the legal system made sure that race- and class-specific sanctions were followed to the letter of the law and facilitated without trial the transfer of large groups of people into the hands of brutal regimes administered by and for private overseers. The profits generated by this convict lease system, an early-twentieth-century prison activist observed, "curse everything they touch—the machinery of enforcing the court decrees, state politics, the prison staff, the inmates, the press, and the public. They breed an atmosphere of cynicism and moral decay."[37]

In the New South judges sent free African Americans either back to their former plantations or into the convict lease system. The exception was Virginia, where, by 1871, 609 of the 828 prisoners in the penitentiary were African American men and 63 were African American women. Elsewhere in the South, rather than build an archipelago of penitentiaries to house this newly criminalized population, legislatures created a pass-through system under which convicts were immediately leased out to employers at a cost below that of labor by free people but high enough to provide much-needed revenue for a region of the country recovering from war and defeat. This system recalls the transportation of more than 100,000 convicts from England to Australia between 1787 and 1857, a policy that also was driven by the need for highly exploitable labor in the colonies.[38]

What was essentially the sale to private interests by the state of prisoners' productive labor power was not specific to the South but was characteristic of penal systems throughout the country from the 1820s to the end of the nineteenth century. The anarchist Alexander Berkman, who served fourteen years in Western Penitentiary in Pennsylvania, beginning in the early 1890s, was subjected to the same "grinding and pulverizing" work routine as convicts in the South, but racism added a level of vindictive cruelty and disregard for human life far beyond what took place in the North.[39]

The convict lease system privatized penal control and the form of incarceration traveled with the convicted. The Black Codes in the South enabled white employers to exercise domination of workers that was "as great as that which slaveholders had exercised," the historian John Hope Franklin observes. "This was White Supremacy."[40]

As in the North, where convict labor was also highly profitable, in southern states it was a boon to the rising capitalist class, but it also played an important role in facilitating the shift from an agrarian to an indus-

trialized economy. Tens of thousands of prisoners worked on Texas' sug-
arcane plantations and for TCI, a precursor to U.S. Steel; in North
Carolina in the 1870s and 1880s convicts laid most of the thirty-five
hundred miles of new railroad track; by 1888 all of Alabama's able-
bodied male prisoners had been leased to the state's two major coal-mining
companies; and African American women and men in Georgia were
put to brutal work in coal and iron production, railroad construction,
the turpentine industry, and brick manufacturing.[41]

Convict leasing played a significant role in the region's economic re-
suscitation and modernization. Major companies such as U.S. Steel,
Wachovia Bank, Georgia Power Company, and Coca-Cola, as well as
Atlanta's business and civic elite, significantly profited from leased labor.
First Atlanta Bank, later acquired by Wachovia, benefited from doing
business with James English, whose labor force included a large number
of convicts. Their work was key to the development of the South's public
and private infrastructure. The forced labor of prisoners made Georgia into
one of the most prosperous states in the Southeast. The economic system
of the New South recalled the racial hierarchy of slavery, but it was not a
nostalgic effort to revert to the agrarian past. Rather it embodied many of
the tenets of progressivism, such as the use of technology and science, that
were in effect throughout the country. The rise of the New South, the historian David Oshinsky argues, "can be traced by the blood of its prisoners."[42]

In the latter part of the nineteenth century, reformers and the labor
movement combined efforts to end the lease system, citing humanitarian
concerns, scandals relating to corruption and escapes, unfair competition
with free white workers, and the states' own need for a cheap labor force.
The legal relationship may have changed, but not the degradation of prisoners' everyday lives. Judges now assigned most convicts to government-run
mobile units and dispersed labor camps; they worked primarily on the
development of states' transportation infrastructure throughout the
United States. The shift from private to public administration of criminal
justice did not ameliorate working conditions because, according to the
sociologist Thorsten Sellin, governments were just as eager as beneficiaries of the lease system "to have the labor of the convicts yield maximum
financial profit."[43]

In 1908 Georgia established chain gangs to replace the leasing of convicts to private companies, changing the relations of power but not the

murderous conditions under which convicts worked. Black women convicted of crimes ended up working either with men on public projects or
as servants in white middle-class homes. Between 1908 and 1938 nearly
two thousand black women—but only four white women—were sent to
build and surface roads throughout the state. When the State of North
Carolina needed laborers to build roads, a study of chain gangs reported,
"the mill of criminal justice grinds more industriously."[44]

Convict leasing and state-run chain gangs were not based on the same
legal-economic relationship as chattel slavery, but its human damage was
devastating, more so than slavery, according to most historians. "We go
from can't to can't," one convict in Florida observed about a typical
workday—"can't see in the morning to can't see at night"—and their work
was enforced by brutal beatings and malign neglect. Corporal punishment
was so elaborate, from whipping to water torture, from sweat boxes to
punishment stools and bucking machines, that it required specialists
known as "whipping bosses" to supervise its implementation. Black women
were routinely raped, abused, medically mangled, and beaten, with every
stroke and stripe meticulously documented in bureaucratic reports. According to the African American activist Mary Church Terrell, in 1907
thousands of men, women, and children were forced to endure "a bondage, in some respects more cruel and more crushing than that from which
their parents were emancipated forty years ago."[45]

The convict lease system in the North, where the victims were primarily
white immigrants, was comparably brutal. Injuries on the job and from
elaborate physical punishments, which included slugging, stringing up
by the thumbs, and immersion in ice, were common.

In California a prison labor force that included Chinese and Mexicans
played a significant role in the state's rapid economic development: by
producing cheap jute bags for the nineteenth-century wheat industry, by
building roads in the early twentieth century to transport lumber from
the Northwest, and by digging the Folsom Dam, which would supply elec-
trical energy. Prison authorities routinely used elaborately vicious punishments on recalcitrant prisoners: hanging them for hours from a hook,
placing them in cells coated with a bleaching powder that damaged their
nasal passages, and tying them into straightjackets.[46]

The mortality rate of northern and western prisoners, however, was
considerably below the mortality rate of black prisoners in the South,

where the vast pool of available coerced labor made human life cheap, expendable, and easily replaced. If convicts died on the job, no problem: more were always available. In Mississippi in the 1880s the annual prisoner mortality rate ranged from 9 to 16 percent, with convicts dying from exhaustion, pneumonia, malaria, frostbite, consumption, sunstroke, gunshot wounds, and infections resulting from shackling. "Not a single leased convict," the historian David Oshinsky concluded in his study of Jim Crow justice, "ever lived long enough to serve a sentence of ten years or more."[47]

In 1870 Alabama prison officials reported that more than 40 percent of their convicts had died on the job. In North Carolina convicts sentenced to laying track for the Western North Carolina Railroad were lucky to survive more than two years of working conditions that routinely included out-of-control explosions, landslides, and floods. In South Carolina between 1877 and 1879 the Greenville and Augusta Railroad had a death rate of 45 percent. In the 1880s, at one mine owned by the Georgia Pacific Railroad, about 30 percent of its workers died annually. By 1918 almost four thousand convicts had died in Texas, and many others were maimed.[48]

For about forty years, from the defeat of Reconstruction to World War I, black lives in the South were constantly at risk. Behind the legalisms of the Black Codes, and bureaucratic regimes of convict leasing and chain gangs, stood a campaign of terror that was as intrusive and pervasive as the most finely constructed panopticon.[49]

White mob attacks on black communities—Wilmington in 1898, New Orleans in 1900, Atlanta in 1906, to name some of the most notorious incidents of mass violence—were by no means rare. An estimated four thousand lynchings of African Americans took place in twelve southern states between 1877 and 1950. From 1882 to 1930 Mississippi was the site of more lynchings (463) than executions (239). The historian Leon Litwack conservatively estimates that from 1890 to 1917 two to three black southerners were "hanged, burned at the stake, or quietly murdered every week." In addition to the "voyeuristic spectacle" of extralegal lynchings, "as many if not more were victims of legal lynchings (quick trials and executions) and private white violence and 'nigger hunts,' murdered by a variety of means in isolated rural sections and dumped into rivers and creeks."[50]

It is not hyperbolic to characterize the death rates of black convict laborers as comparable to those of the concentration camps under Nazism, and before the 1920s the daily life of African Americans in the South was a constant struggle for survival. "Probably in no country in the civilized world did human life become so cheap," Du Bois concluded.[51]

NORTH, EAST, SOUTH, AND WEST

The journalist and author Isabel Wilkerson characterizes the Great Migration, the exodus of about six million people from the South in search of political asylum, as "the first mass act of independence by a people who were in bondage in this country for far longer than they have been free." The threat of daily deadly violence was not as ubiquitous in New York, Philadelphia, Chicago, and San Francisco, but the newcomers found no lack of injustices in the Promised Land: ghettos, substandard schools and health care, a two-tiered job market and deep poverty, and urban police with a penchant for brutality and an affinity for racism.

Black communities saw eighteen major eruptions of mob violence between 1915 and 1919. In the North, James Baldwin later observed, "Negroes do not escape Jim Crow: they merely encounter another, not-less-deadly variety." They may have left behind the whipping bosses, but plenty of jailers and guards filled the void.[52]

For those who stayed in the South, a run-in with police could result in time in jail where "stocks, dungeons, to say nothing of just plain filth, were by no means unique," according to a survey prepared in 1940 for the Carnegie Corporation's study of American race relations. When prisoners in Georgia's convict camps were classified as incorrigible, they faced solitary confinement and worse: iron shackles on their ankles, iron bands about their necks, sweat boxes, and stretching. The sociologist Arthur Raper did not expect conditions in prisons, jails, or camps to improve "as long as the police, courts, and dominant public feel that the Negroes and poorest whites are unfitted for responsible roles in the community. Why try to help a man who is preordained to dependency?"[53]

In the first decade of the twentieth century, the newly created juvenile justice system, a product of Progressive reformism that promised rehabilitation and diversion from the criminal courts, for the most part excluded

African Americans. In the South little changed for black youth, who always had done time alongside adults in the fields or on chain gangs. Jim Crow juvenile justice carried on as usual, with severe punishments—including executions, whippings, commitment to adult prisons, and forced labor—the norm.[54]

As early as 1903 Du Bois' accusation of southern racism had broadened: "When you [southern gentlemen] fasten crime upon this race as its peculiar trait, they answer that slavery was the arch-crime, and lynching and lawlessness its twin abortion; that color and race are not crimes, and yet they it is which in this land receives most unceasing condemnation, North, East, South and West."[55]

By the time that Du Bois railed against the "double system of justice," racism was already well established in criminal justice. In the early nineteenth century, African American women in Philadelphia, for example, were already more likely than white women to be convicted of larceny, receive long sentences, and be assigned to solitary confinement. With the inclusion of prison statistics in the 1890 U.S. Census and later publication of the federal *Uniform Crime Reports*, compelling evidence existed for what was already obvious. By 1890 African Americans, who comprised 12 percent of the population, were 30 percent of prisoners nationwide. In 1923 their proportion of the general population declined to less than 10 percent, while their share of the prison population increased to more than 31 percent.[56]

During World War I Cleveland's jail population reached a high of 87 percent black. In the mid-1920s African Americans composed 7.4 percent of Philadelphia's population and 24.4 percent of arrestees; their arrest rate in Detroit was almost four times higher than whites'. A 1927 survey of prisoners in Pennsylvania's Western Penitentiary reported that black prisoners outnumbered white prisoners by more than thirteen to one. In the South, as states shifted from convict leasing and mobile chain gangs to penitentiaries, African Americans filled the cells, accounting for about 85 percent of Georgia's state prisoners in 1899 and about 90 percent of prisoners held at Parchman Farm in Mississippi in 1917.[57]

By 1928 a mainstream sociologist, writing in a highly respected journal, had documented and discredited the widespread belief that "the Negro in our country is more criminal than the white." Thorsten Sellin made the case that the high rate of black incarceration was in part explained by "a decided discrimination against the Negro on the part of our agencies of criminal justice, particularly the police and courts," amplified by a press that "is almost certain to brand him." Du Bois found this position illuminating and endorsed it.[58]

Sellin's observation about branding, like Du Bois' observation about the fastening of race to crime, anticipated by decades the now routine observation that blackness is so culturally associated with "phantasms of criminality" that it has assumed the status of a quasi-biological trait. In *The Condemnation of Blackness* the historian Khalil Muhammad traces how racialized criminality became normalized in scientific discourse early in the twentieth century: "The statistical rhetoric of the 'Negro criminal' became a proxy for a national discourse on black inferiority." Decades before the war on drugs, state police in the South warned of the danger of African Americans going on crime sprees "crazed by cocaine." In 1910 Hamilton Wright, the U.S. opium commissioner, tied black drug use to sexual attacks on white women when he identified "the use of cocaine by the Negroes of the South [as] one of the most elusive and troublesome questions which confront the enforcement of the law."[59]

About sixty years later the Nixon administration followed the same path. "We knew we couldn't make it illegal to be either against the war [in Vietnam] or blacks," John Ehrlichman recalled, "but by getting the public to associate hippies with marijuana and blacks with heroin, and then criminalizing both heavily, we could disrupt those communities. We could arrest their leaders, raid their homes, break up their meetings, and vilify them night after night on the evening news. Did we know we were lying about the drugs? Of course we did."[60]

The overrepresentation of black Americans in jails and prisons continued throughout the twentieth century, with fluctuations in numbers and proportions depending on wartime mobilizations and regional variations. In 1937 young African American men made up more than 80 percent of the inhabitants of Lorton Reformatory in Washington, D.C. In 1940 they accounted for less than 2 percent of California's population but 10 percent of the incarcerated. Nationwide they were 34 percent of state and federal prisoners in 1950, 37 percent in 1960, 41 percent in 1970, and 44 percent in 1980.[61]

PUNITIVE TURNS

The lives of African Americans have taken so many punitive turns that their post-1980s experience as "a huge swath of the population" incarcerated beyond reason is not so much a rupture with the past as another moment in a long zigzagging history of racist violence and social exclusion that stretches from seventeenth-century slavery through twentieth-century legal and de facto segregation. Certainly slavery's racial hierarchy has echoes in today's mass incarceration: you can hear it in assumptions about black inferiority and sense it in fears of black dangerousness and contamination. But today's race relations have different economic, political, and legal underpinnings than chattel slavery. Contemporary racism is not only a legacy or residue of slavery, debris that needs to be cleaned up, as President Bush put it in 1991.[62] The war on communities of color disguised as a war on crime is not so much a regression to the rural caste system of the South or its Jim Crow successor as it is a revitalized racism, renewed by legal and then de facto segregation, and anchored in specifically urban innovations in social control.[63]

"The entire narrative of this country," the writer-activist Ta-Nehisi Coates says, "argues against the truth of who you are." His righteous anger at "the warehousing of black bodies" is rooted in his generation's expectation that, with the successes of the post–World War II civil rights movement, institutionalized racism might gradually wither away under the impetus of modernity's triumvirate: reason, science, and progress.[64]

This initial optimism had some basis in history. "I have seen the impossible happen," Du Bois exulted when he heard the news in 1954 that the U.S. Supreme Court had overturned school segregation in *Brown v. Board of Education*.[65] The 1950s are generally recognized as the starting point for the second wave of the civil rights struggle, but its roots go much deeper. Between Reconstruction and the movement that resumed after World War II were many false starts. The successes that were finally achieved through national legislation and legal decisions were the culmination of a long struggle, a changing political climate, and an expanded economy fueled by two world wars. But the socioeconomic changes were short-lived. What endured were ingenious new forms of social control and an expanded and refined carceral state.

The American social-democratic liberal tradition, from Progressivism through the New Deal to the War on Poverty, has always been ambivalent about racial equality, subordinating it to economic reforms in the 1930s and turning it into a problem to be managed by technocrats in the 1960s. Yet Cold War advocates of liberalism, motivated by a concern that the U.S. model could not be exported around the world so long as white supremacy was the law of the land back home, opened the door to the rights of citizenship for African Americans. In the period between World War II and the Vietnam War, liberalism was not the only source of public ideas about race. The dominant political discourse was pulled left by political and ideological pressures coming from powerful civil rights and black liberation movements that emphasized the constitutive and structural role of racism in American society.[66]

Once the 1954 Supreme Court decision opened the door, there was no holding back a movement that was the broadest and most inclusive this country has ever witnessed. "What did our kids actually fight for?" the activist Fannie Lou Hamer asked about the thousands of black men who expected that a willingness to die for their country in war would be rewarded with full equality. "They would go in the service and go through all of that," she said, explaining how raised expectations can embolden a struggle, "and come right out to be drowned in the river in Mississippi." This kind of embittered hope created the conditions for a mass movement that forced a liberal government to concede much more than it had bargained for.[67]

The result of this political ferment was pioneering legislative, legal, and regulatory victories, as well as the formal repudiation of a segregated public life. In 1961 President John F. Kennedy's Executive Order 10925 for the first time linked the phrase "affirmative action" to civil rights enforcement policy; it was bolstered three years later by passage of the Civil Rights Act of 1964 and subsequent legislation pushed through Congress by President Lyndon Johnson, with Supreme Court decisions ordering tough remedies to undo institutionalized racism. These were followed by the establishment of hiring goals and timetables during the Nixon administration.[68]

Affirmative action was a hard-won redistributive measure based on the same kind of preferential group policies that in the past had benefited mostly white retirees and the unemployed during the New Deal, mostly white GIs returning from the war, and mostly white male workers in racially exclusive unions. With the brief exception of Reconstruction, for the first time in sixteen generations, or 280 years—190 years of slavery, 40 years of Jim Crow in the South, and another 50 years of separate and unequal treatment throughout the country—African Americans were no longer forced by law to live in slavery or officially sanctioned segregation. Affirmative action policies generated concrete gains by empowering activists in the Democratic Party, significantly increasing the number of black judges and politicians, and opening up jobs in federal contracts, skilled trade unions, and the public sector. Elite universities, which had been largely a white old boys' club until the 1960s, began the process of becoming more democratic institutions, not only by diversifying students and faculty but also by diversifying cultural life on campus.[69]

No one should forget or underestimate the profound material changes that took place in one generation of American race relations. True, the civil rights movement was not revolutionary, but it accomplished much more than a palliative reform. In addition to generating responsive government policies and legal decisions, the struggle also educated millions of people about the history and consequences of racism, and the movement mobilized the powerless to make the most of their newly won rights. Moreover, it helped to create an antiracist political culture that resonated with popular support and brought many activists into the machinery of government to ensure that official decisions were put into practice. The era gave us "hope for tomorrow," the author Alice Walker recalled, and "called us to life."[70]

At the same time, however, the material, political, and cultural gains made in the 1960s were uneven and precarious. In 1968 the National Advisory Commission on Civil Disorders, chaired by Governor Otto Kerner of Illinois, issued a much anticipated report that provided seemingly unassailable moral authority for the proposition that "our nation is moving toward two societies, one black, one white—separate and unequal." The Kerner Report's call for racial justice and a national program of reforms, comparable to the GI Bill after World War II, was heard and then shelved, while its lesser-known recommendations for how to improve "public safety forces" prevailed.[71]

The high point of restorative policies and entitlements lasted at most fourteen years, from the Civil Rights Act of 1964 to the Supreme Court's decision in the 1978 *Bakke* case, which began the process of dismantling affirmative action. The political mood changed quickly in the 1980s with the rise to power of the Reagan wing of the Republican Party, the marginalization of liberalism within the Democratic Party, the collapse of mass antiracist activism, and the deepening economic polarization in the United States.

By the time the backlash against racial equality was initiated, the United States had just about reached the crawling stage in addressing institutionalized racism in poor and working-class communities. The urban rebellions of the 1960s, from Harlem in 1964 to the nationwide response to the murder of Martin Luther King, Jr., in 1968, represented the voices of the disenfranchised and disillusioned whose lives were mostly bypassed by affirmative action reforms. For urban African American communities, segregation in public housing and public education remained firmly in place. Organizations that represented this forgotten constituency, such as the Black Panther Party, were targeted for destruction by the state, and tens of thousands of young men and women who took to the streets in fury ended up in jails and with criminal records: 4,000 in Watts in August 1965; 7,800 in Detroit in 1967; 13,000 in Washington, D.C., and Baltimore; and more than 3,000 in Chicago after King's death. As many people were arrested and legally processed in Detroit in six days in July 1967 as normally would be charged in six months.[72]

For the majority of African Americans, even during the most successful moments of the civil rights movement, chronic unemployment and high arrest and incarceration rates remained the norm, with good odds of ending up on death row, in jails and prisons, and in the trenches of war. By 1975, according to the National Urban League, official black unemployment reached 1.5 million out of 15.7 million African Americans nineteen years old and older, a number not seen since the 1930s. Between 1970 and 1990 African Americans almost doubled their participation in the military, partly as a way to escape segregation and make a commitment to public service, and partly as a way to escape jail and the unemployment line. Still, one-third of the black population remained mired below the poverty line.[73]

The Kerner Report's plea for a national commitment to end racial inequality—"to turn with all the purpose at our command to the major unfinished business of this nation"—was eclipsed by the rise of neoconservative and neoliberal think tanks that tapped into popular discontent about race and revitalized long-held attitudes about black inferiority.

Influential rightist intellectuals and think tanks articulated a coherent worldview that blamed affirmative action for promoting a "culture of victimization" and undermining meritocratic "standards of excellence," revived eugenic theories of racial difference to explain structural inequalities, and argued that "tribal identity politics" was undermining a common national culture. The struggle against racism, President George H. W. Bush argued in 1991 in what was now a common refrain, had "replace[d] old prejudices with new ones."[74]

In *The Closing of the American Mind* (1987) Allan Bloom made the case that racism in academia was no longer a problem, that black students "have, by and large, proved indigestible . . . They continue to have the inward sentiments of separateness caused by exclusion when it no longer effectively exists. The heat is under the pot, but they do not melt as have all other groups." In *The Bell Curve* (1994) Richard Herrnstein and Charles Murray argued that "trying to eradicate inequality with artificially manufactured outcomes has led to disaster. It is time for America once again to try living with inequality, as life is lived."[75]

From the 1970s on, the linking of criminality and race was central to cultural attacks on ideas about equality. In his popular and influential book, *Thinking About Crime* (1975), the political scientist James Q. Wilson dismissed the search for root causes of crime, arguing instead for feasible programs aimed at controlling "lower-class" African Americans who are "preoccupied with the daily struggle for survival" and are "inclined to uninhibited, expressive conduct." The sociologist Jackson Toby, writing in the *New York Times* in 1973, proposed that people deemed incorrigibles should be subjected to "internment, a long-lasting deprivation of liberty without duration fixed in advance." A leading sociological journal published an article claiming that "IQ is more important than race and social class" in determining delinquency. A study of "criminals killed by police officers" blamed the victims, concluding that they "generally are responsible for their own deaths." Another academic's supposedly serious book was devoted to debunking the relationship between racism and incarceration as a myth. In a widely read polemic a cantankerous right-wing criminologist advocated "post-punishment incapacitation," banishment, and increased use of the death penalty in the "war against crime." By the end of the decade Wilson's views represented the new common sense: "We know that confining criminals prevents them from harming society, and we have grounds for suspecting that some would-be criminals can be deterred by the confinement of others."[76]

During the 1980s, according to a Harvard Law School study, the U.S. Commission on Civil Rights, which at one time had been a "credible and independent critic of injustice in our society," became a "public-relations firm for a presidential administration determined to roll back advances in civil rights." President Ronald Reagan packed the commission with conservatives who opposed antidiscrimination programs, women's equality, and gay rights. Its chair, Clarence Pendleton, derided comparable worth as the "looniest idea since Looney Tunes" and dismissed affirmative action as a "bankrupt public policy." In a revealing slip of the tongue to the International Association of Chiefs of Police in 1981, Reagan acknowledged that "only our deep moral values and strong institutions can hold back that jungle and restrain the darker impulses of human nature."[77]

Neoconservative ideas about criminality that became canonical in leading political and cultural circles not only justified the punitive turn but also articulated a rationale for the continuing overrepresentation of those indigestible African Americans in police and prison statistics. "The whole problem is really the blacks," Nixon said in an aside to his chief of staff in 1969. "The key is to devise a system that recognizes this while not appearing to." The Nixon administration gave grants to university architects and business professors to design new prisons, authorized experiments in behavior modification and sensory deprivation at the Federal Medical Center in Missouri, and initiated federal funding of state prisons that led to what became known as mass incarceration.[78]

By 1979, fifteen years after passage of the civil rights legislation that had ended legal apartheid and before the prison boom of the 1980s, black Americans already comprised a majority of prisoners in several states: 60 percent in Delaware, 62 percent in New Jersey, 64 percent in Mississippi, 71 percent in Louisiana, 77 percent in Maryland, and 97 percent in Washington, D.C.[79]

In 1971 William Nagel, who had worked as a prison administrator in New Jersey for many years, evaluated more than one hundred institutions. He reported that prisoners were "mostly black, brown, red, and urban." Of the twenty-three "new and shiny" prisons he visited, he found a majority of "minority inmates" in eleven, and 40 percent or more in six institutions. He was so alarmed by the experience that he recommended an immediate moratorium on prison construction. Nagel's advice was ignored. Instead the United States embarked on the largest prison-building expansion in its history, and the huge number of impoverished prisoners of color got even larger.[80]

This phase of mass incarceration was facilitated by police forces and private security operations that took seriously their mission to engage in a war on crime by looking and acting like a military campaign operating in hostile territory. While policing has become much more battle ready since the late 1970s, its combative mission has deeper roots.

4

ON GUARD

*Why militarism is central to the roots
and development of modern policing,
and how everyday and political
policing became entangled.*

If the show seems familiar, it is because the show has been running a
very long time . . . and you will hear the same old piano, playing the
same blues.
—James Baldwin, preface to *The Negro in New York*

ROUGH RIDE

Freddie Gray, Jr., was only twenty-five years old when he died from a devastating injury that he suffered in April 2015 while being transported to
a police station in Baltimore. He had been arrested for supposedly running
away from police, who during a search found an illegal switchblade in his
pocket. Gray had a long history of petty arrests, mostly drug related, as
he tried to hustle a living in the shadow economy of West Baltimore. He
had graduated from a vocational high school, described by UCLA researchers as an "apartheid school" with its 98.7 percent black student
body, and once aspired to becoming a brick mason, but no jobs were available to a young black man with a record. Also, he and his twin sister, Fred-
ericka, had longtime health problems caused by lead poisoning when
they were children. His family's landlord, Stanley Rochkind, owned
several properties that were involved in lawsuits, including one that he
settled with Freddie's family. Freddie received hospital treatment for lead

poisoning. His parents put him on a special diet and constantly cleaned the house to remove peeling and flaking paint.

Freddie probably suffered long-term neurological damage from the lead exposure. According to a 2009 housing survey, twenty-three million units in poor neighborhoods nationwide contain one or more lead-based paint hazards and seventeen million have a high exposure to indoor allergens. These conditions have a significant impact on people's health and serious social consequences, such as poor educational performance and asthma-related emergency room visits. As with corporate crimes, the government takes a laissez-faire attitude toward unsafe and unregulated housing conditions that cause or exacerbate diseases and contribute to social inequality.[1]

The circumstances of Freddie Gray's arrest were similar to the more than 300,000 street arrests made by Baltimore police during the previous five years that overwhelmingly involved African Americans and petty or nonexistent crimes, according to a major investigation carried out by the Justice Department's Civil Rights Division during Obama's second term. Police routinely used "excessive force" and "heavy-handed tactics" while carrying out arrests, especially against people with mental health disabilities.[2]

When six Baltimore cops arrested Freddie Gray, they put him in handcuffs and leg irons but did not strap him into a seat belt for the ride to jail in a van, as required by the department's regulations. Such informal extralegal punishment exposes helpless passengers to being hurled around and is so widespread that it is known as a rough ride. Records of its use go back at least to the 1960s when southern sheriffs wanted to give civil rights activists a taste of what they could expect in jail and prison. By the time the Baltimore police van reached its destination, Freddie Gray's spinal cord was permanently damaged, and he was in a coma. He died a week later at a nearby hospital.

The situations vary, but the killing of African Americans by police or their surrogates is quite commonplace, about one in four of all police-related deaths. A study of 1,217 fatal police shootings from 2010 to 2012 found that black boys aged fifteen to nineteen "were killed at a rate of 31.17 per million, while just 1.47 per million white males that age were killed by police"—that is, the black youth were twenty-one times more likely than their white peers to be killed. Among the most notorious cases in recent years was that of seventeen-year-old Trayvon Martin, shot by a neighborhood watch volunteer, George Zimmerman, in the Retreat at Twin Lakes, a gated community in Sanford, Florida, where Martin and his father were visiting a friend in February 2012. Martin was walking back from a nearby convenience store when Zimmerman told a police dispatcher, "The guy looks like he is up to no good or he is on drugs or something," conjuring up a generic black criminal. He described Martin as wearing a "dark hoodie, like a gray hoodie." By the time the police arrived, Zimmerman had shot and killed Martin.[3]

In 2014 the usually anonymous African American victims of police killings became human beings with names and biographies: Eric Garner, choked to death in New York; Michael Brown, Jr., shot by Officer Darren Wilson in Ferguson, Missouri; Akai Gurley, shot by police on "vertical patrol" in a New York housing project; and twelve-year-old Tamir Rice, shot to death by Cleveland police, who claimed they mistook the boy's toy gun for a real one.

The legal consequences of police shooting civilians form a familiar pattern: criminal prosecutions of officers are rare and convictions are exceptionally rare. In thousands of "justifiable homicides" voluntarily reported by police departments over a decade, only fifty-four officers were charged with crimes and eleven convicted. To their credit Baltimore prosecutors charged six police officers with crimes relating to the death of Freddie Gray, and the city settled a civil case with his family for $6.4 million. But all the defendants were acquitted of criminal charges in circuit court in Baltimore, and in September 2017 U.S. Attorney General Jeff Sessions, a law-and-order Republican who once described the NAACP as un-American, announced that the Justice Department had insufficient evidence to charge the police with a violation of civil rights laws.[4]

Unlike the Trump administration, which made clear it was not in the business of investigating or regulating local police departments, even in cases of gross malpractice, the Obama administration was prompted by widespread grassroots protests to try to initiate a national conversation about policing. Public events forced Obama to do what previous administrations had done when they needed to buy time and move an unruly debate from the streets and into the corridors of power: appoint a commission.[5]

In December 2014, responding to "recent events that have exposed rifts

in the relationship between local police and the communities they protect and serve," Obama created the Task Force on 21st Century Policing,
composed of eleven members, a majority of whom had a background in
law enforcement and prosecution, with only one experienced in civil rights
law. "There have been commissions before, there have been task forces,
there have been conversations, and nothing happens," Obama said. This
time, he promised, it "will be different," not just "an endless report collecting dust on the shelf."[6]

The recent events that prompted the investigation were the publicized
killings in Florida, New York, Missouri, and Cleveland. While the task
force was working on its report in April 2015, Walter Scott was shot in
the back in North Charleston, South Carolina, and Gray died in a Baltimore hospital. But it was not so much the killing of black men that motivated the president to create a blue-ribbon commission, for such deaths
are a regular by-product of modern American policing, and more recently
they have been a predictable spectacle on social media. "There is a legacy
of inequity that did not just appear overnight," said Eric Adams, cofounder
of 100 Blacks in Law Enforcement Who Care. Rather, he said, "nightstick
and quick-trigger-finger justice" has been "carved into the culture of law
enforcement over decades."[7] What had sparked the president's attention
was the spread of large and often furious protests proclaiming "I can't
breathe" and "Black lives matter," just as urban riots and antiwar protests
of the 1960s had triggered President Johnson's National Advisory Commission on Civil Disorders and President Nixon's National Commission
on Campus Unrest.

The nationwide months of rage began in July 2013, when a jury acquitted Zimmerman of killing Trayvon Martin in Florida, sparking protests
across the United States that condemned the verdict and made the hoodie
a symbol of resistance. Zimmerman's successful defense relied on Florida's "stand-your-ground law," which justifies the use of lethal force when
someone believes that their personal safety is at risk, whether at home
or in a public place.[8]

In 2014 many local police killings of African Americans became national events. Spontaneous rallies and street marches erupted in Milwaukee after Dontre Hamilton's death; in New York after publication of a video
of Eric Garner's being choked to death; in Dayton, Ohio, after the killing
of John Crawford III in a Walmart after he was reported carrying an air

gun that he had picked up off a shelf in the store and intended to buy; in Los Angeles after police killed Ezell Ford, a mentally ill man; in New York after the accidental shooting death of Akai Gurley by police; in Cleveland after Tamir Rice's death; in Phoenix, after Rumain Brisbon was shot and killed by a cop who mistook a vial of pills for a gun; and again in New York, when protesters staged a "die-in" at Grand Central Terminal during rush hour after a special grand jury refused to bring charges against the officers involved in the death of Eric Garner.[9]

In the same way that *Attica* in 1971 became synonymous with the dehumanizing brutality of prisons, so too *Ferguson* became widely equated with police brutality and racism. In August 2014 eighteen-year-old Michael Brown, Jr., got into a dispute with police involving allegations that he had stolen a box of Swisher cigars from a local market in the Missouri township close to St. Louis. Brown, who two days later was scheduled to start a technical training program for heating and air-conditioning repair, ended up dead, shot six times by Officer Darren Wilson, who told a reporter that he felt intimidated and unprepared to work in a community where 90 percent of the people are black and poor. "I've never been in an area where there was that much poverty," the twenty-nine-year-old white cop said.[10]

As Michael Brown lay dead in the street for more than four hours in the sweltering Midwest heat, his body testified to callousness and disrespect and generated a local movement that became globally recognized. In response to widespread outrage at his death, Governor Jay Nixon declared a state of emergency and a curfew. He mobilized the National Guard against protesters, and the police deployed tear gas and rubber bullets. Solidarity marches took place in New York, Oakland, and Seattle. A few weeks later, when a grand jury declined to indict Wilson in Brown's death, the governor again had to call out the Guard.[11]

"History simmers beneath the surface in more communities than just Ferguson," Attorney General Eric Holder said a few days after Brown died. "As the eyes of the nation turned to events in Ferguson, Missouri, we cannot—and must not—allow tensions which are present in so many neighborhoods across America, to go unresolved." The problem was not unique to Ferguson, echoed Obama, as he, too, described "a simmering distrust that exists between too many police departments and too many communities of color."[12]

"I don't think there has ever been this level of attention being paid to [police in] communities all over the country," Vanita Gupta, head of the Justice Department's Civil Rights Division, said. The highly localized street protests became nationally prominent through social and commercial media and, in some cities, were channeled into electoral campaigns for political office. "They are much better organizers than I was when I was their age," Obama said when he met later with Black Lives Matter activists at the White House.[13]

Obama's task force on policing worked fast, taking only five months to complete a final report that called for symbolic changes in police culture from a warrior to a "guardian mindset." Its primary concern—a "foundational principle"—was "nurturing legitimacy" and restoring "confidence in law enforcement." A blue-ribbon commission assembled by the National Academy of Sciences expressed a similar concern that the U.S. prison system "risks losing its legitimacy, particularly in the communities where its effects are felt most deeply."[14]

Restoration of a sense of legitimacy implies that criminal justice agencies once enjoyed the trust of the majority of people in the communities they policed and in which they made arrests, a claim that is not supported by historical evidence. Moreover, to make the police responsive and accountable requires structural changes in the governance and organization of criminal justice institutions. Yet nothing in the task force's report addressed the long history of police militarism or the undemocratic governance of policing or the intimate ties between policing and institutionalized racism. The term *guardian*, with its suggestion of a sentinel standing watch and serving as a custodian of other people's business, is not the best metaphorical choice to replace *warrior*. It may be less explicitly martial, but it still assumes that communities cannot be trusted to run their own police departments.

The task force proposed a variety of sensible but toothless midrange policies and did not tackle the most important issue, namely how to overcome resistance to even the most modest reforms, including training police in multicultural sensitivity, ensuring transparency in the processing of complaints, appointing independent prosecutors to investigate officer-involved killings, and better use of technology to "fully engage and educate communities."[15]

On the policy front Obama's White House announced a $263 million program to provide police with fifty thousand body cameras that would, it was hoped, reduce extralegal violence. The administration also called for tighter standards for transferring surplus military equipment to local police departments, a $5 billion program that had been in place since 1990. Between 2006 and 2014 police acquired Iraq War hardware, including 435 armored vehicles, 44,900 night vision devices, 533 aircraft, 93,763 machine guns, and almost 200,000 magazines of ammunition. Obama's executive order prohibited the Pentagon from redistributing tracked armored vehicles, grenade launchers, and bayonets, but drones, tactical vehicles, "breaching apparatus," and weapons less lethal than .50-caliber remained on the approved list. This order resulted in police departments returning 126 armored vehicles and 138 grenade launchers to the Pentagon.[16]

Obama's task force and executive orders provided some modest encouragement to reformers but had almost no impact on police practices even before the November 2016 election. Requiring officers to wear cameras on their uniforms may have opened up a new niche market for technology companies, but according to an eighteen-month study in Washington, D.C., cameras made no difference in the rate of civilian complaints against police.[17]

Rhetorical calls to demilitarize the police lacked political and popular support, and they did nothing to change what had become established orthodoxy. By 2005 nearly 90 percent of police departments in U.S. cities with at least fifty thousand residents already boasted paramilitary units (known as SWAT teams) and close ties to military special operations experts. Private companies, such as CQB (Close Quarters Battle) and Trojan Securities, received lucrative contracts to train police in "battle-proven tactics" and surveillance operations. In the wake of mass killings by terrorists in Paris in November 2015 and San Bernardino, California, in December 2015, the task force's critique of a warrior mind-set quickly became a dim memory. By the time of the Super Bowl in San Francisco in February 2016, despite the lack of credible threats, no one was voicing opposition to the massive show of police and military force and the omnipresent surveillance operations that had been two years in the making, supposedly to deter terrorism.[18]

After the November 2016 election the rhetoric of reform quickly disappeared from political discourse about policing. Among Trump's first acts as president was to make "Standing up for our law enforcement community" one of his six political priorities; one of his first executive orders called for all levels of government to protect the police, to "back the blue," as it was known. "We will not participate in anything," Trump's attorney general told a gathering of police, "that would give comfort to radicals who promote agendas that preach hostility rather than respect for police."[19]

In August 2017 Trump reversed his predecessor's efforts to restrict police use of military surplus. Obama's restrictions on police "went too far," Attorney General Sessions explained. "We will not put superficial concerns above public safety." The use of military materiel and other "life-saving gear," as Sessions described tactical vehicles and grenade launchers, was necessary for the police to protect themselves. This meant that Keene, New Hampshire, with a population of twenty-three thousand, could resubmit its request for an armored vehicle to patrol its annual pumpkin festival, and the fourteen-member police department of Snoqualmie, Washington (population about thirteen thousand), could get the three bomb robots it said it needed.[20]

Although Obama's reform efforts were too cautious and therefore easily rolled back, he was right to point out that police violence is a deeply rooted problem, its precarious foundations continually sending rattling reminders into the present. Models of professional policing in the early twentieth century looked to the military and corporate security sectors, not to democratic institutions, for inspiration. Policing has always been an undemocratic and hybrid affair in the United States, a combination of private and public operations, of national and local initiatives, and international and national relationships. Before addressing the significant ruptures with the past that are transforming policing into a complex security operation in the twenty-first century, I want to explore how the late-nineteenth- and early-twentieth-century roots of modern policing shaped its mission.

HALF-MILITARY

The police have never been effective at reducing social harm. Law enforcement and crime control are not their forte. Their main priority, as even the conservative political scientist James Q. Wilson conceded, is "maintaining order." Most theft is neither reported nor punished; most sexual assaults and rapes are not prosecuted; most interpersonal violence is settled privately; most corporate crime is referred to civil settlement. And as for so-called consensual crimes that involve the sale and purchase of illegal or unprescribed drugs, consumption of off-the-books alcohol, and the sale of sexual services, policing mostly takes a hands-off approach. The United States may have the largest, most complex, and most expensive criminal justice institutions in the world, but it also promotes a high level of insecurity about crime and a realistic understanding that self-defense is the responsibility of each woman, man, and child.[21]

The risk of victimization is closely tied to the material conditions of everyday life. Women of color suffer a higher rate of sexual attacks than white women because women of color are more exposed to the insecurities of nighttime work and public transportation, live in unsafe public housing, and have less economic independence and limited access to crisis intervention programs. The elderly who live on fixed incomes in downtown hotels are much more physically vulnerable than their counterparts in suburban leisure communities. Small businesses that cannot afford the protection of private security are more likely to be burglarized, and working-class and poor parents do not have resources to divert their delinquent children from the juvenile court and into private rehabilitative programs.[22]

The best way to reduce chances of victimization is to learn techniques of "target hardening" and, if you can afford it, buy an insurance policy and create a defensible space around your home or business with private guards, gated walls, and high-tech surveillance systems. If you are poor, less-expensive security comes in the form of walls topped with claws, spikes, and razor wire, fenced-in roofs and bolted doors fronted by iron gates, guard dogs, and inexpensive guns. The police acknowledge their own impotence when they advise communities to organize neighborhood watches, look out for suspicious intruders, and, if you are a woman, carry a whistle and Mace, take classes in martial arts, and stay off the streets after dark. In other words, take personal responsibility, and good luck!

There were no good old days when friendly urban police patrolled local neighborhoods, developed personal relationships with communities they policed, and made crime reduction a priority. The only places that have truly democratic, responsive policing today are in middle-class suburbs, gated communities, and business parks—what Robert Reich, Clinton's secretary of labor, calls the "secession of the successful," where police are under community control and serve the people who employ them.[23]

For poor and working-class communities policing has never been a reciprocal relationship. From the beginning it was conceived as what Theodore Roosevelt, then the New York Police commissioner, in 1895 called a "half-military," with rank-and-file police trained as "soldiers of peace," ready for a war on crime.[24]

The modern model of policing is built on three interrelated foundations. First, its organizational structure is derived from the military, with an emphasis on a hierarchical chain of command, internal discipline, esprit de corps, and a code of secrecy. "Like all military and semi-military organizations," the President's Commission on Law Enforcement and the Administration of Justice observed in 1967, "a police agency is governed in its internal management by a large number of standard operating procedures."

Second, the formal governance of policing is as far removed as possible from popular control, relying instead on an ethos of professional independence and oversight by political elites. Policing has never been a democratic operation.

Third, the police are trained for a war on crime, not only in terms of uniforms, equipment, and weaponry but also in cultural assumptions about the dangerousness and inherent criminality of the communities in which they are deployed. "For years, ever since Spanish-American War days," reflected August Vollmer, the former head of Berkeley's police department and a founder of American criminology, "I've studied military tactics and used them to good effect rounding up crooks. After all we're conducting a war, a war against the enemies of society, and we must never forget that." This attitude of us against them is most apparent in the twentieth-century history of policing African American and Latino communities, but it also characterized policing of white working-class communities during the heyday of the labor movement.[25]

Modern American policing as we know it—professionalized, bureaucratic, and nominally insulated from political cronyism—did not become organized until the early twentieth century. By the 1870s most large cities had organized police departments, but they were small, locally run, ineffective, and corrupt. In 1880 only New York City and Philadelphia had a force of more than one thousand men. With bribery and payoffs rampant, the police did not so much try to eradicate crime as selectively regulate and benefit from it.[26]

The first reform efforts, led by civic and business groups as a state-building project during the Progressive Era, were modeled on corporate and military organizations, with an emphasis on centralized power, a chain of command, and scientific methods of management. Reformers pushed for more careful selection of recruits, an emphasis on brains as well as brawn, and public relations efforts to overcome widely held views of the police as, in the words of a New York Police commissioner, Arthur Woods, a "natural enemy."[27]

In 1883 New York's police department came under civil service regulations, as did a majority of urban police departments by World War I. St. Louis was the first city, in 1904, to use fingerprints to solve crimes. The first university-based law enforcement program was set up in Berkeley in 1916. And big-city police departments did not adopt two-way radios, communications systems, and crime labs until the 1930s.[28]

Despite the emphasis on the police as politically neutral and impartial defenders of public order, inside the velvet glove of community relations and technical proficiency was an iron fist of considerable ferocity. The militarization of professional urban policing drew upon two important models: private security forces that throughout the nineteenth century and well into the twentieth century were much larger and better organized than public police; and state militias that had been actively engaged in battling the labor movement and urban disorder since the last quarter of the nineteenth century.

The first organized police forces in the United States were privately run: Pinkerton National Detective Agency opened in 1850 and Brink's in 1859, followed by the William J. Burns International Detective Agency in 1909. Allan Pinkerton's career was typical of what the criminologist Jean-Paul Brodeur describes as the "interpenetration of public and private policing," which reached "an unprecedented scale relatively early in the history of the United States." Pinkerton started his career as Chicago's first detective, then started his business, returned to government to head up the Union Intelligence Service during the Civil War, and after the war built Pinkerton's into a leading private security firm. Burns started his career in the Secret Service, then developed his security company, and returned temporarily to the federal government from 1921 to 1924 to head up the Bureau of Investigation, predecessor of the FBI. When James Comey moved easily from the Justice Department to the corporate world and back to the FBI many decades later, he was following a well-established career pattern.[29]

Before the Bureau of Investigation, and later the FBI under J. Edgar Hoover's direction, developed a capacity to infiltrate and disrupt radical organizations, private security agencies took the lead in covert surveillance, spying on labor and political organizations, and providing muscle to break strikes. They practiced, as Brodeur puts it, "an early form of counterterrorism."[30]

The most profitable contract for private security was in policing the labor movement. Pinkerton's worked for the railroad companies, first by vetting employees and then by policing their loyalty. Its agents infiltrated the Workingman's Benevolent Association in Pennsylvania and played a key role in the arrest and conviction of leaders of the Molly Maguires, a militant group that organized workers in the coal mines. Deputized as the infamous Coal and Iron Police, Pinkerton agents were given the power of government agents to investigate, arrest, and bring activists to trial. As a labor historian has noted, the state was required to provide only "the court and the hangman." In 1892 about three hundred Pinkerton operatives fought strikers at the Carnegie Steel Company in Homestead, Pennsylvania. In Maryland and South Carolina, as well as Pennsylvania, state legislatures authorized the deputation of private security to take on the labor movement. In the early twentieth century, when the federal government developed its own counterinsurgency capacities, it continued to work closely with the private sector, outsourcing operations that were, as Brodeur says, "of dubious legality and of obvious immorality."[31]

Private security remained an important part of policing throughout the twentieth century and has continued to grow and expand in the twenty-first. In the early twentieth century the Silk Association of America and the Jewelers' Security Alliance took the lead in combating widespread theft in their industries. They advised businesses on how to protect themselves, trained security personnel, employed their own detectives, and provided prosecutors with evidence to ensure guilty verdicts. In the

1930s these private associations, according to the law professor Jerome Hall, were "by and large, the most persistent and active group in our society for the repression of professional theft and criminal receiving."[32]

Railroad companies employed a private security force of ten thousand in 1929. At its peak in the 1930s, Ford Motor Company had thirty-five hundred roughnecks on the payroll, one of the largest private security forces nationwide. In the mid-1930s the leading steel companies acquired more tear gas equipment than any urban police department. Republic Steel's arsenal included hundreds of revolvers and rifles. As late as 1978 General Motors had forty-two hundred plant guards in the United States, a force larger than all but five city police departments'.[33]

Private security has always operated in the public sphere, engaging in the same work as city police and sheriff's departments—from investigation and arrests to spying and repression—but without the minimal legal and political restraints imposed on government employees.

For most of the nineteenth century local police were incapable of controlling urban riots and labor disputes, and the federal army was small and dispersed throughout the country. The police were not only poorly organized and equipped but also often unreliable as an instrument of effective force, given their familial and cultural ties to the communities in which they operated. Volunteer militias, composed of affluent men who could afford to pay dues and buy uniforms and weapons, were better suited to ceremonial and social functions than street fighting, and they could not be counted on to put down riots. Sometimes they were fiercely repressive, sometimes they did not show up for duty, and sometimes they fraternized with people they were supposed to police. On a few occasions the militia stayed neutral in labor disputes, but mostly they actively sided with employers and were willing to shoot to kill: attacking demonstrators calling for an eight-hour day in Milwaukee in 1866, firing on coal workers and repressing miners in Pennsylvania in the 1890s.[34]

Early policing was very much a joint enterprise in which private and public agencies shared information, collaborated on public order campaigns, and worked together to repress labor organizations and political leftists. This relationship was not so much based on a secret conspiracy as on what the sociologist Gary Marx describes as "a common occupational culture, informal networks, similar tasks, and the exchange of personnel." By the time urban police became professionally organized, they, too, with a few exceptions, were antilabor. "An army of the status quo [that] took the side of law and order" is how a leading legal historian characterizes their role. With "brutality and violations of civil liberties" is another historian's assessment of how police handled labor disputes in New York during the last quarter of the nineteenth century. In January 1874, when police attacked a demonstration in Tompkins Square calling for public works jobs, Police Commissioner Abram Duryée reveled in "the most glorious sight I ever saw. Their order was perfect as they charged with their clubs uplifted."[35]

The national railroad strike of 1877, during which President Rutherford B. Hayes mobilized the army to restore order after many workers were killed and injured, was the impetus for the professionalization of the militia into national guard regiments, the creation of paramilitary state police forces, and the modernization of public policing. Several states transformed their militias into bureaucratic organizations with a tight chain of command and staffed by regiments and brigades equipped with new weapons and uniforms. By the mid-1880s the National Guard, as it was now known, had grown to 112,000 men, committed to "maintaining order no matter who was disrupting it," according to the historian Robert Fogelson. Some units weeded out recruits sympathetic to union activism. "Are you connected in any way with any labor organization?" an officer in Brooklyn's Forty-Seventh Regiment asked each applicant.[36]

Between the late 1870s and 1910 local elites financed the building of physically imposing, fortified armories in working-class communities throughout the North and Midwest, a symbolic reminder of the state's repressive power and a practical site from which to begin military operations. At a ceremony to celebrate the new Seventh Regiment Armory in New York in 1879, a speaker welcomed the assembled troops: "In the last dire extremity, behind the policeman's club, glistens your bayonet."[37]

The U.S. Army was another source of influence on the professionalization of policing. From the 1870s to the 1920s the use of troops during industrial disorders became routine, with the restoration of public order always heavily weighted in favor of owners and manufacturers. The president sent in the army, for example, to break strikes on the railroads in 1877, in Chicago in 1894, and in the Coeur d'Alene mining region of Idaho in 1899. During World War I and the 1920s the army acted unilaterally in civil and labor disorders, "virtually unfettered by presidential or War

Department supervision," even when no danger of violence was present. The army occupied the copper-mining regions of Arizona and Montana, sent troops to Seattle, Washington, and quashed organizing in ten different states during the coal strike of 1919.[38]

In 1932 President Herbert Hoover and Army Chief of Staff Douglas MacArthur ordered George Patton to lead his cavalry regiment against fellow World War I veterans who were encamped in Washington, D.C., demanding their benefits. Patton believed that communists and revolutionaries had stirred up the Bonus Marchers and that they had crossed the line from protest to insurrection. He took pleasure in leading the charge and "had some nice work at close range" as he rode into the crowd; "sabers rose and fell with a comforting smack," he noted in his diary. On the basis of this experience he prepared a how-to manual, *Federal Troops in Domestic Disturbances*, in which he advocated preemptive strikes against public protests: "If they are running, a few good wounds in the buttocks will encourage them. If they resist, they must be killed."[39]

The military model of policing promoted the idea that police and working-class communities are combatants. It owes a great deal to the export and import of counterinsurgency operations, as well as to a fear that the Republic's political authority was under threat from disorder and uprisings. The New York antidraft riots of 1863 and the insurrection in Paris of 1871 stayed on the minds of politicians and professionals who wanted the police transformed into frontline defenders of public order. "In the judgment of one who has been familiar with our 'dangerous classes' for twenty years," the American reformer Charles Loring Brace observed in 1872, "there are just the same explosive elements beneath the surface of New York as of Paris." Leading newspapers and magazines stirred up popular anxieties by constantly reminding readers that Native American resistance in the West and a militant labor movement in the East shared the same goal of replacing civilization with savagery.[40]

The aftermath of the war in the Philippines in the 1900s provided an important testing ground for the extreme measures of curtailing civil liberties and employing censorship, surveillance, and mass relocations, all of which shaped the development of the U.S. security state during World War I. Following the U.S. occupation of territories formerly held by Spain, a nationalist anticolonial movement fought for full independence from the United States. The U.S. military quickly defeated the Filipino military, but the resistance movement, which relied on guerrilla warfare, necessitated a permanent garrison of about forty-seven thousand troops for more than a decade. Here the military first used the "water cure" to extract confessions, a method of torture later preferred by sheriffs against uppity African Americans in the South before World War II and by the U.S. military against prisoners during the occupation of Iraq. Under the leadership of General John Pershing, who had fought in the Indian wars, the United States used some of its most brutal tactics against the Moro Rebellion in the Philippines. In 2016, responding to a terrorist attack in Spain, the presidential candidate Donald Trump cited an apocryphal story about Pershing's effort to defeat the insurgency by executing Muslim rebels with bullets soaked in pigs' blood. "There was no more Radical Islamic Terror for 35 years," Trump tweeted, transforming fanciful myth into historical fact.[41]

Ralph Van Deman, who had led the field intelligence operation in the Philippines, was put in charge of the army's Military Intelligence Division in 1917. Lessons learned in putting down insurgency abroad were brought home. Working with about 300,000 members of the right-wing American Protective League, the division hunted for traitors and slackers, an effort that turned into a widespread attack on progressive organizations. It targeted radical unions, especially the International Workers of the World, for destruction.[42]

Routine cooperation between federal agencies and civilian organizations persisted throughout the twentieth century, particularly in moments of mass protests and political turmoil. During the 1910s the "great scout citizen" Theodore Roosevelt mobilized the Boy Scouts to stage massive operettas in celebration of "America First," and the Committee on Public Information worked with thousands of volunteers during World War I to brand antiwar sentiment as un-American and stir up a "white-hot mass instinct" for war. In his January 2017 inaugural address Donald Trump evoked what he termed a "new vision" of the country's role in the world, although it had been popular a century earlier: "From this day forward, it's going to be only America first. America first."[43]

In the 1930s the Los Angeles Police Department joined forces with the American Legion to harass the American Civil Liberties Union (ACLU), the Communist Party, and other leftist organizations; the head of the LAPD's Intelligence Bureau, who had previously worked as a labor spy for private employers, set up his office in the chamber of commerce to better coordinate attacks on strikers. In Detroit the police regularly broke up picket lines of striking workers, while its "red squad" kept files on local organizers.[44]

During the 1930s and 1940s the FBI's line on the dangers of subversion influenced local police departments. New York, Chicago, Philadelphia, Detroit, and Los Angeles had active units that infiltrated progressive organizations, collected information on thousands of activists, and broke up strikes and protests. African American activists were particular targets. In January 1946 the president of the Florida Peace Officers' Association referred to returning black veterans as "Eleanor's chosen children," whom he deemed "ready to attack policemen, sometimes with guns, if they are roughed up a little. These boys are coming back pretending to be heroes without even having seen a gun unless they stole one and smuggled it in. We've got to keep them in their place."[45]

The role of federal authorities in setting priorities and a tone for local police agencies persisted throughout the twentieth century. It was evident, for example, in the "social hygiene" crusade against prostitution near military bases during World War I, the role of the U.S. Treasury Department in leading enforcement of Prohibition in the 1920s, the national campaign against "sexual perversion" after World War II, and in Cold War efforts to destroy progressive Chicano organizations in the 1970s. When then-FBI director James Comey intervened in the 2016 presidential race eleven days before the election by raising the specter of Hillary Clinton's criminal misuse of her private email server—a decision that the Justice Department's Office of the Inspector General subsequently characterized as a violation of departmental "practice and protocol"—he continued a long tradition of using the national security apparatus for political and ideological purposes.[46]

DEFIANTLY ASSERTIVE

The association of criminal behavior and dangerousness with group identity is porous and easily shifted. In the aftermath of September 11, the New York Police Department (NYPD) targeted hundreds of Muslim organizations and associations and recruited "mosque crawlers" to infiltrate religious services. A suit initiated by the ACLU successfully exposed illegal police practices and put some limits on the NYPD's efforts to racially profile Muslim groups. During the Republican primary campaigns in 2016, aspiring presidential candidates associated undocumented Mexican immigrants with criminality, called for a ban on entry of Muslim immigrants into the United States, and defended the police against charges of racism by Black Lives Matter activists. In the wake of a terrorist attack in Brussels in March 2016, Senator Ted Cruz of Texas advocated policies to "empower law enforcement to patrol and secure Muslim neighborhoods before they become radicalized."[47]

By the time public policing became solidified in the early twentieth century, its militarism and racism were prominent lines in its pedigree. Professionalization incorporated hostility to social movements from below, a fear that revolution would be imported into the United States, and a deep distrust of communities targeted for policing. This tendency is evident in the long antagonistic history of policing in communities of color.

During slavery plantation owners organized patrols to catch runaways and terrify the enslaved into submission. Local courts, militia, and police were integrated into the machinery of control and backed up the plantation owners. Patrols were so brutal that enslaved people developed warning systems and elaborate subterfuges to avoid capture. "In some districts," the historian Eugene Genovese notes, "slave resistance to patrols reached high levels and produced alarm and emergency measures among the whites." If enslaved people were caught, their violations of local codes—being on the streets after curfew, refusing to step aside for whites on sidewalks, dancing in public places, exhibiting a "spirit of insubordination," and so on—were punished by branding, mutilation, and whipping. Alabama permitted as many as one hundred stripes on the bare back of an enslaved person who forged a pass or gave "seditious speeches."[48]

After the abolition of slavery the South did not completely abandon patrols, and in some southern states they served as a transitional model for modern policing. In the Southwest, organizations such as the Texas Rangers played a formidable role in brutally policing Native American and Mexican communities. The Ranger, according to a foundational text, was "a man standing alone between a society and its enemies . . . It has been his duty to meet the outlaw breed of three races, the Indian warrior, Mexican bandit, and American desperado, on the enemy's ground and deliver each safely within the jail door or the cemetery gate."[49]

In the early twentieth century national security agencies reinforced the assumption that communities of color were inherently subversive and susceptible to communist propaganda. When a young J. Edgar Hoover joined the Bureau of Investigation as head of its General Intelligence Division in 1919, he already had experience in the Justice Department's Alien Enemy Bureau, where he had ferreted out leftists and potential traitors. As director of the bureau and FBI for forty-eight years (1924–72), his long-standing loathing of the Left and deep-seated racism sent the message throughout law enforcement that black political militancy and black criminality were inextricably intertwined, a view he never changed.[50]

In 1919 Hoover initiated covert operations against every black political organization, including the NAACP. He suspected that African Americans were "seeing Red" and getting cozy with "the Bolsheviki," and he expressed the alarm that black men were a danger to white women. The bureau investigated the black press, which promoted, in Hoover's words, "defiantly assertive" ideas about "the Negro's fitness for self-government." Hoover was convinced that "the reds have done a vast amount of evil damage by carrying doctrines of race revolt and the poison of Bolshevism to the Negroes." In 1922 Hoover's boss at the bureau was William Burns, the founder of the Burns International Detective Agency, to which he would return two years later. He shared Hoover's assumption that the "Communist International" had targeted "Negroes, labor unions, and various social organizations" for recruitment to the cause of establishing a "dictatorship of the proletariat" in the United States.[51]

This worldview promoted, inspired, and legitimated racial violence. Policing in the South continued what slave patrols, convict leasing, and chain gangs had started. As a police captain told a researcher during World War I, "In this town there are three classes of homicide. If a nigger kills a white man, that's murder. If a white man kills a nigger, that's justifiable homicide. If a nigger kills a nigger, that's one less nigger."[52]

The first comprehensive national investigation of law enforcement, published by the Wickersham Commission in 1931, minimized the problem of police racism and regarded it as unique to the South. The commission was sympathetic to the "burden of crime placed upon police" because of "the present heterogeneity of the population, the high percentage of immigrant citizens and residents, the lack of a common tradition, the large number of Negro inhabitants." The commission had "no reason to think that the police used more discrimination in arresting colored boys than white boys." Whatever discrimination occurred, it supposedly was minimal in the North, where the police "do not have the same opportunity to oppress Negroes as the police down South." The Negro in the North "benefits [from the] greater respect for law and order." In the South, however, "any 'foreign' Negro without a job is by that fact alone a vagrant; and it takes the judges about a minute to dispose of him with instructions not to let sunset catch him in the county."[53]

The commission was clear in its condemnation of the widespread practice of "the third degree," notably the "cruel and illegal treatment and sometimes torture of persons accused of crimes," but it regarded such abuse as racially neutral. However, a careful search of the commission's *Report on Lawlessness in Law Enforcement* will reveal, buried in its discussion of appellate cases, clear examples of how African American defendants were subjected to the most vicious kinds of torture. "One of them was put in water and his head held in water until he was almost drowned . . . Another was laid across a log, his clothes were removed, and he was whipped by the officers with a switch . . . An 18-year old Negro [was] whipped over a period of six or eight days until he confessed to a murder. The warden who administered the whippings [said] he was a mean, hardheaded nigger." The threat of the water cure, which involved the forced consumption of water followed by beating the victim's stomach until he or she vomited, was used especially on black defendants, including a fifteen-year-old girl who was told she would be turned over to a mob if she did not sign a confession. "Finally our patience was about exhausted and the sheriff took her to the window and pointed out the water tower and asked her if she knew what it could be used for . . . It was soon after that or about that time she signed it."[54]

In an unpublished study commissioned by Gunnar Myrdal for *An American Dilemma*, an encyclopedic investigation of American race relations in the late 1930s, the sociologist Arthur Raper reports that the police "winked at or connived in" lynchings. Myrdal describes the "average Southern policeman" as a "weak man with his strong weapons, a promoted poor white with a legal sanction to use a weapon [against] Negroes whom he conceives of as dangerous or as 'getting out of their place.'" Of African Americans killed by whites in the South between 1920 and 1932, more than half died at the hands of police.[55]

Raper provided a detailed portrait of "crude and hard-boiled" police, continually "on the lookout for 'outside agitators,' 'communists,' and 'subversive influences.'" Racism was embedded in everyday practices: "The law is white. So too are the officials who administer it." The police "keep the Negroes intimidated, they maintain arrest quotas, they earn money for the police court, and sometimes they help preserve order." When the chief of police in Helena, Arkansas, was asked in 1930 if the department had any black officers, he replied: "We do not trust Negroes here unless they are in the graveyard." Raper's conclusion: "To hear the average policeman talk, a Negro is a sort of animal, but necessary to have around to do certain menial tasks, blame the city's troubles on, and flatter the white man's ego."[56]

Despite its prestigious reputation Myrdal's report had no impact on police violence in the South. President Harry Truman's Commission on Civil Rights reported in 1947 that "the incidence of police brutality against Negroes [was] disturbingly high," and "violent physical attacks by police officers on members of minority groups" were commonplace: pistol whippings, bullwhips, and rubber hoses extracted confessions.[57]

A few years later the Civil Rights Congress petitioned the United Nations for relief from "acts of genocide against the Negro people. Once the classic method of lynching was the rope. Now it's the policeman's bullet." The 1951 petition documented numerous cases of humiliations, brutality, and killings by law enforcement officers between 1945 and 1951. The record was incomplete, however, because suspicious "unrecorded deaths were the rule rather than the exception." Thirteen years later, in 1964, a similar petition was filed in federal court in Mississippi, based on 257 affidavits charging the state with "legalized injustice," and the police, in the words of the theologian Reinhold Niebuhr, with "a brutality . . . that frequently approaches sadistic cruelty and on occasion has resulted in actual murder." When the anthropologist Michael Banton visited the South in the summer of 1962, he was struck by the way in which white police still "did not see Negroes and themselves as being members of the same community" but referred "to Negroes as 'they.'" Sixty-seven years after the Civil Rights Congress sought relief from police violence at the United Nations, the nonprofit Sentencing Project similarly appealed to the international body for help in addressing "the racial disparity that pervades the U.S. criminal justice system" in violation of the right to equal treatment under the law.[58]

A LONG TALE TO TELL

Systemic state violence was not only a problem of the South and backward rural sheriffs, as Myrdal implied and as the Wickersham Commission claimed. Myrdal ignored evidence provided by Raper that police brutality was a national problem. In 1937 the Dallas city council rescinded an order to hire black police after seven thousand people signed a petition, a local court issued a restraining order, and white police threatened to strike; in Philadelphia, between 1929 and 1939, not one African American police officer was hired. In the 1930s Michigan's rate of African Americans killed by the police was higher than Tennessee's. Detroit, Raper noted, "stands out for police brutality," and Washington, D.C., "presented one of the worst pictures in the nation." In addition to police killings of fifty African Americans and ten whites from 1926 to 1938 in the capital were "many instances of severe beatings, petty discourtesies, abusive language, and epithets." A pamphlet published in 1937 by the Interracial Committee of the District of Columbia captured the problem in its title: *Brutality Enthroned*.[59]

Myrdal chose to ignore Raper's important observation that "people get killed by the police outside the South. We see that in the South, where scarcely one fourth of the population is Negro, over two-thirds of the police killings are Negroes; while outside the South, where the Negro is less than one twentieth of the population, he is the victim of nearly three sevenths of the killings by the police."[60]

"Now there is not a great American city," the Civil Rights Congress charged in 1951, "that is not disgraced by the wanton killing of innocent Negroes. It is no longer a sectional phenomenon." Racial segregation in housing, education, and jobs permeated the whole country, with the police assigned the job of enforcing a public order based on separate and unequal relations. "Out of the inhuman black ghettos of American cities, out of the cotton plantations of the South," the leftist William Patterson noted, "comes this record of mass slayings on the basis of race, of lives deliberately warped and distorted by the willful creation of conditions making for premature death, poverty, and disease."[61]

In the North, as James Baldwin sharply and eloquently observed in an essay first published in *Esquire* in July 1960, Negroes "do not escape Jim Crow: they merely encounter another, not-less-deadly variety." Baldwin's insight summed up half a century of persistent antagonisms since the early twentieth century.[62]

Official investigations into white violence against black communities in northern cities during the 1910s conceded that the police typically "shared the lust of the mob for negro blood," as a congressional committee noted in its report on the bloody East St. Louis pogrom of 1917. Following the 1919 racist riots in Chicago, the local Commission on Race Relations similarly reported "instances of actual police participation in the rioting as well as neglect of duty." In the wake of a day of protests and property destruction in Harlem in 1935, a commission appointed by the mayor found that the police had a reputation for being "persecutors and oppressors."[63]

The author of the Harlem report, the distinguished African American sociologist E. Franklin Frazier, paid a price for his frankness. He was hounded by the FBI, and later the House Un-American Activities Committee, for his leftist sympathies. Tagged by the FBI "for unresolved questions of loyalty," his file included every tidbit of innuendo agents could scrape up, including reports that he had once sent two dollars to the United States Spanish Relief Committee, subscribed to *New Masses*, and had purchased maps of Washington, D.C., during the war. One informant identified Frazier as a "crazy racialist," and Frazier's friendship with W.E.B. Du Bois convinced the intelligence agencies that Frazier probably was a target of "Communist infiltration of minority groups." During World War II, when the FBI began its most thorough investigation of "foreign inspired agitation [in] colored areas and colored neighborhoods," black intellectuals critical of American racism were fair game for red-baiting and slurs against their professional competence.[64]

Not surprisingly, given national campaigns against subversion, everyday policing made blackness itself suspect. In his ethnographic study of Chicago police in the late 1940s, the sociologist William Westley noted that it was routine for the police "to mock the Negro, to use some type of stereotyped categorization." The writer Richard Wright was more blunt in his assessment: "When they see one of us, they either smile with contempt or amusement. When they see two of us, they treat us as though some grave thought were on their minds. When they see four of us, they are usually silent. When they see six of us, they become downright apprehensive and alarmed. And because they are afraid of us, we are afraid of them. Life for us is daily warfare and we live hard, like soldiers . . . We are always in battle, but the tidings of victory are few." In the first sociology textbook focused on African American culture and institutions, published in 1949, Frazier observes matter-of-factly: "The police, who generally use brute force on Negroes, have little respect for the rights of Negroes as citizens or human beings."[65]

"Arrest first, then find a charge" was a common practice in Los Angeles in the late 1940s, according to a California branch of the Civil Rights Congress, which gave this example:

> Come to the Hall of Justice. Watch the parade. Note the
> numbers of Negroes, of Mexicans, of working people. All out of
> proportion. Listen to the wheels grind:
> [Defendant charged with being] Drunk.
> How do you plead?
> Guilty.
> Ten dollars or two days.
> Next case.
> Gambling.
> How do you plead?
> Guilty.
> Ten dollars or two days.[66]

In the 1950s the ultra-right-wing John Birch Society was estimated to have two thousand members among Los Angeles law enforcement organizations. The Birchers feted Chief William Parker (1950–66) for his anticommunist politics and denunciation of the courts as coddlers of criminals. Throughout the 1960s and 1970s police on patrol and in management positions nationally took their racial cues from intelligence agencies and political leaders. In the 1960s the FBI indiscriminately pursued the civil rights movement, from the Southern Christian Leadership Conference to the Black Panther Party. High-level officials encouraged local police departments to raid Panther offices, arrest and beat militants, and assassinate leaders. Vice President Spiro Agnew called the Panthers "a completely irresponsible, anarchist group of criminals," ignoring their efforts to defend black communities from state violence and to provide basic educational and health services to communities ignored by government agencies. To Jerris Leonard, an assistant attorney general who headed the Civil Rights Division, the Panthers were "nothing but hoodlums, and we've got to get them." J. Edgar Hoover spurred on the vendetta when he announced that the Black Panther Party (BPP) "without question represents the greatest threat to the internal security of the country [among] violence-prone black extremist groups."[67]

Following the election of Richard Nixon and in response to guidance from the FBI, local police and federal agents ransacked Panther offices in Indianapolis, Denver, Des Moines, Newark, and San Diego, and arrested Panthers all over the country. According to a recent in-depth study of the Black Panther Party, "no form of repression was more direct, more provocative, and more violent" than what was carried out by official agencies from 1968 to 1970. In Chicago in December 1969 police attacked the local Panther headquarters at dawn and fired more than eighty rounds that killed Fred Hampton and Mark Clark and seriously wounded four other people. A commission of inquiry, chaired by NAACP director Roy Wilkins and former U.S. Attorney General Ramsey Clark, concluded that the raid had been conducted "with wanton disregard of human life and the legal rights of American citizens."[68]

Under its counterintelligence programs (known as COINTELPRO), created in 1956, the FBI devoted considerable resources and personnel to undermine, discredit, and disrupt African American organizations. Some tactics used against the movement included disinformation campaigns that created fictitious memos and images to provoke internal conflicts, stories planted in the media, and leaks of private information; recruitment of informants and infiltration of agents provocateurs to create havoc within the groups; and encouragement of local police to arrest leaders on flimsy or manufactured evidence. For example, Hoover ordered agents in Baltimore to "submit imaginative and hard-hitting counterintelligence measures aimed at crippling the BPP." According to a former FBI agent, the bureau "itself created the threat" of the Panthers, then "set out to neutralize it." Robert Wall, who was assigned to work on racial matters, eventually quit the agency because "the appalling racism of the FBI on every level became glaringly apparent to me."[69]

Files liberated by activists in 1971 from the FBI's office in Media, Pennsylvania, revealed that Hoover had ordered investigations of black student unions throughout the country. One industrious agent reported that every black student at Swarthmore College was under surveillance. "To become targets of the FBI," notes a former reporter for the *Washington Post* who received copies of the Media documents, it "wasn't necessary for African Americans to engage in violent behavior. It wasn't necessary for them to be radical or subversive. Being black was enough." In the FBI's taxonomy of racial groups, according to the reporter Betty Medsger, African Americans were reduced to two categories: "Black people who should be spied on by the FBI and black people who should spy on other black people for the FBI." This meant that the moderate wing of the civil rights movement received as much attention as revolutionary organizations. Hoover pursued a particular vendetta against Martin Luther King, Jr., whom he considered a "security problem" because of his ties to leftists, as well as a "fraud, demagogue, moral scoundrel" and "tom cat with degenerate sexual urges." In 1964 Hoover authorized sending King an anonymous letter that encouraged him to commit suicide: "You are done. King, there is only one thing left for you to do." In 2018, a former director of the FBI admitted that Hoover had instigated "an unchecked, vicious campaign of harassment and extralegal attack on the civil rights leader and others."[70]

Organizations such as the Panthers on the west coast and Deacons for Defense and Justice in the South, which the FBI characterized as inherently violent, actually had emerged to defend black communities from white supremacist violence, typically involving local police and sheriffs, with the active or passive complicity of the FBI. The BPP's name and the symbol of a black panther were adapted from the Lowndes County Freedom Organization in Alabama, an organization working to register black voters. In 1964 African Americans had formed a clandestine, armed self-defense group in Jonesboro, Louisiana, that surfaced publicly the following year as Deacons for Defense and Justice. By the end of 1966 it had twenty-one chapters with several hundred members in Louisiana and Mississippi. According to the historian Lance Hill's definitive study of the Deacons, "they preached self-reliance rather than dependence on government for rights and freedom; they sought reform by force and coercion rather than by pacifism and moral suasion; and they repudiated the strategy of winning white approbation through suffering. Freedom was to be won through fear and respect, rather than guilt and pity."[71]

As she was growing up in Washington, D.C., Ericka Huggins would walk with her sister to a local grocery store to buy a bag of french fries. "Almost every time we did," she recalls, "we saw the police beating somebody to the ground." That was a motivating factor for her decision to join the Panthers. Its original name, she reminds everyone, was the Black Panther Party for *Self-Defense*. "We believe we can end police brutality in our black community," the Panthers declared in the party's 1966 program, "by organizing black self-defense groups that are dedicated to defending our black community from racist police oppression." This alleged mob of anarchists and hoodlums took time to draft proposals for "a citizens' peace force" to replace the militarized model of policing, and one of the BPP's cofounders called for a conscripted police force, civilian control, and "para-legal, para-medical, and civic techniques for solving immediate urban problems," with an emphasis on training to "respond to the variety of emergencies that constitute everyday life in the poverty community."[72]

Compelling evidence exists that self-defense groups during the 1960s actually reduced violence against black communities. In one city, according to the sociologist Harold Nelson, when activists organized a counter-police force, "Negro neighborhoods were now effectively closed to Klansmen," and the extralegal power of the police to arbitrarily beat and arrest African Americans was "to a great extent stripped from them."[73]

Urban protests and riots in the 1960s generated an unprecedented flurry of investigations and commissions, all of which emphasized the role of police in enforcing inequality and triggering revolts. Cops "come into the neighborhood aggravated and mad," a thirty-three-year-old resident told researchers for Harlem Youth Opportunities Unlimited in 1964. "They start more violence than any other people start." James Baldwin knew hardly anybody in Harlem, "from the most circumspect church member to the most shiftless adolescent, who does not have a long tale to tell of police incompetence, injustice, or brutality." Yet Baldwin made a distinction between the "blank, good-natured, thoughtless and insuperably innocent" police officer who every day faces "people who would gladly see him dead," and the social imperatives that shape policing as an institu-

tion: "The only way to police a ghetto is to be oppressive . . . like an oc-
cupying soldier in a bitterly hostile country."[74]

"Woe to the black man who is out very late in a white neighborhood,"
as expressed by a member of the Panther 21, was a widely shared sentiment that researchers confirmed. As late as 1968 a majority of rank-and-
file police surveyed in fifteen cities echoed Hoover's alarm of nearly fifty
years earlier about "defiantly assertive" Negroes when they complained
that African Americans were moving "too fast" in their demands for
equality, with nearly half of the cops surveyed also disgusted by "Negroes
socializing with whites."[75]

By the mid-1970s a mass of evidence documented the role of systemic
police violence as a major cause of anger, rebelliousness, and political protests in urban African American communities. "In city slums and ghettos," the Crime Commission (appointed by Lyndon Johnson) reported in
1967, "there is much distrust of the police," not surprising given "the
use of racial epithets, such as 'nigger,' 'coon,' 'boy,' and 'Pancho' [which]
appears to be widespread." Racist insults were so common in Oakland,
California, in the mid-1960s that the police chief had to issue a written
directive banning the use of "coon, spook, head hunter, jungle bunny,
burr head, ape, spick, and mau mau."[76]

In 1968 the Kerner Commission concluded there was a "widespread
belief among Negroes in the existence of police brutality and in a double
standard of justice—one for Negroes and one for whites . . . To many Negroes, police have come to symbolize white power, white racism, and white
repression." Sociological surveys sponsored by the commission confirmed
the "deep hostility between police and ghetto communities." Studies in
fifteen cities found that the majority of African Americans stopped and
frisked on the street "are innocent of any wrong doing," one in three
African Americans said the police "rough up people unnecessarily," and
the majority of police believed that "equality has been mainly achieved."
To a leading sociologist of policing, the response to urban disorders
had "no other apparent purpose in mind than to visit punishment on
the people they sought to subdue." Twenty years after publication of the
Kerner report, Jewelle Taylor Gibbs, a leading professor of social work,
lamented that "several Black males are killed each week in America in lethal encounters with police officers."[77]

A national study that I worked on in 1968–69 reported that "anger, hatred, and fear of the police are a major common denominator among black Americans at the present time" and that "the majority of rank and file policemen are hostile toward black people." Another study, carried out in the summer of 1966 in Boston, Chicago, and Washington, D.C., found that 38 percent of the cops expressed extreme prejudice and 34 percent considerable prejudice about black people. In Los Angeles cops routinely referred to their nightsticks as "nigger-knockers." Between 1987 and 1990, 41 percent of the forty-four hundred misconduct complaints against the Los Angeles Police Department were filed by African Americans, who made up only 13 percent of the city's population. A local investigative commission reported that members of the LAPD "repetitively use excessive force against the public."[78]

When prejudice turned to fatal violence, African American men were nine or ten times more likely than white men to be killed by the police. African Americans made up 10 percent of the U.S. population in the 1960s, but they accounted for almost 50 percent of the victims of police killings. From the 1960s until 2014, when widespread protests forced President Obama to establish an investigative task force, police homicides continued at a regular pace of an estimated three a day. The actual number is not known because no one had mandated reporting by police departments or established a national database. Scholars do know, however, that a disproportionate number of the victims are black, Latino, and Native American, that a high percentage of the dead suffered from serious mental illnesses, and that police who kill are rarely punished and even more rarely prosecuted.[79]

Even as Obama's attorney general, Eric Holder, spoke out against civil rights abuses by police, the Justice Department that he directed resolutely defended police officers charged with use of excessive force. U.S. Supreme Court decisions made it almost impossible to successfully pursue civil rights claims against police departments because petitioners carried an unfair burden of proof. "When the police kill or injure innocent people," Berkeley Law School dean Erwin Chemerinsky says, "the victims rarely have recourse."[80]

The report of Obama's Task Force on 21st Century Policing is already gathering dust, joining many others on the shelves, including the 1969 task force report that I coauthored and in which we warned that "this nation cannot have it both ways: either it will carry through a firm commitment to massive and widespread political and social reform, or it will develop into a society of garrison cities where order is enforced without due process of law and without the consent of the governed."[81]

I AM BLEEDING

The experience of Chicanos, Chicanas, and Mexican immigrants with policing has a different trajectory but similar outcome. National policies relating to labor, immigration status, and welfare have shaped actions and perceptions at the local level, in both rural areas and barrios. In 1931 President Hoover's secretary of labor encouraged the Los Angeles police to round up and deport thousands of undocumented immigrants to Mexico as a solution to the unemployment crisis. In the 1960s and 1970s an FBI-led campaign against the Chicano movement, including the Crusade for Justice in Colorado, emboldened local police to harass, infiltrate, and demonize activist organizations. In recent decades the enforcement of punitive immigration policies has in several states blurred distinctions between federal and local policing, and it has encouraged urban and rural law enforcement agencies to crack down on petty crimes in the hope that they will lead to federal violations. One of Trump's first executive orders called for local police agencies to strictly enforce immigration laws against "tens of thousands of removable aliens."[82]

The role of police in ensuring insecurity in immigrant communities is well established. In the 1920s, when antagonisms between Polish and Mexican immigrants in Chicago turned into violent confrontations, the police sided with the Poles, not unlike the way in which the authorities endorsed white mobs against northern black communities during World War I. "Conflicts with the police were so common," the historian Juan García says, that "Mexicans believed they were under siege and could not expect justice within the American legal system." Again, in June 1943, when tensions between white sailors and Chicano youth escalated into street battles, the Los Angeles police, judicial system, and media backed up the sailors. The police initially refused to intervene as the sailors went on a rampage, beating up Filipinos, African Americans, and young Chicanos. And when the police did intervene, they arrested hundreds of Chicanos, a decision applauded by the *Los Angeles Daily News*: "The time has come to serve notice that the City of Los Angeles will no longer be terrorized by a relatively small handful of morons parading as zoot-suit hoodlums."[83]

In Los Angeles in the 1930s, an era of high unemployment, county welfare agencies enforced the national campaign against providing services to "illegal aliens" by calling for their repatriation to Mexico. Federal immigration agents worked closely with the Los Angeles police to not only round up undocumented immigrants but also to send a chilling message to all Mexican Americans that "constitutional rights of Americans don't apply to them, no matter how remote they may be from Mexican nationality." In his definitive study of policing in Los Angeles before World War II, Edward Escobar could not "imagine a time when conflict was not the underlying theme in the relationship between Chicanos and the LAPD."[84]

In the postwar period Latino organizations, such La Associación Nacional México-Americana (ANMA), organized against "a nation-wide pattern of indignities, court injustices, and senseless killings suffered by the Mexican American people." In Los Angeles the ANMA chapter called on Chief of Police William Parker to end "police attacks on eastside Mexican-Americans under the guise of controlling 'wolf packs.'" About fifty years later Donald Trump would evoke the same animalistic imagery to depict black teenagers running wild in New York: "We're going to have wolf packs roaming the streets," he wrote in 2000.[85]

From World War II through the 1970s Chicano groups in California made everyday police brutality and repression of the movement a central theme of their political organizing, from the railroading of seven young men in a 1942 murder trial known as the Sleepy Lagoon case to the National Chicano Anti-War Moratorium in 1970 in Los Angeles, when police killed a leading journalist, Rubén Salazar, and "the whole barrio became a war zone." When the U.S. Commission on Civil Rights held hearings in Los Angeles in 1960, a representative of the local ACLU testified that "instances of police malpractice reported to us involve almost invariably Negroes and Mexican-Americans in the ratio of at least 50 to 1. That is a fairly conservative estimate."[86]

For those working in the fields throughout the Southwest, contact with law enforcement involved confrontations with sheriff's deputies who invariably sided with ranchers and growers. One farmworker in Texas in the early 1960s taught her children what to expect when the cops showed up in the fields: "The mere sight of them was enough to keep everyone in line for a good long time . . . They will call us 'suspicious.' They will say we are union troublemakers. That will be the end of us. Once they arrest you, they never leave you alone. They watch you. They keep scaring you."[87]

Tensions between police and urban Latino communities were so widely recognized in the early 1970s that U.S. senator Fred Harris, an Oklahoma Democrat, could publicly note, "If you are a Mexican American . . . you are discriminated against and stereotyped. You may live constantly in fear of the police, who are supposed to protect you, and of immigration officials, who can send you out of the country."[88]

In his ethnographic study of Chicano Los Angeles, *Ando Sangrando (I Am Bleeding)*, Armando Morales documented widespread police brutality and profound community distrust of policing, compounded by "dangerously overprotective" government agencies that refused to charge officers with illegal violence. The problem was so entrenched that in 1966 the American Civil Liberties Union opened a police malpractice center in East Los Angeles, and the Happy Valley Parents' Association established the Civilian Alert Patrol to keep an eye on police cars in the area.[89]

The sociologist Joan Moore estimated in the mid-1970s that 20 percent of men living in the East Los Angeles barrio had done time, in jail or prison. Like African Americans in places like Ferguson, Missouri, Latinos' involvement with criminal justice operations typically began with petty everyday issues: parking tickets, traffic warrants, trespass charges. "Traffic court and municipal court are a curious mob scene, a bureaucratized, time-consuming, Hogarthian madhouse," Moore writes.[90]

In the early 1990s in New York's East Harlem, people on the street were used to witnessing cops beating up suspects. "They do it with pleasure," one informant told the anthropologist Philippe Bourgois. "I don't even know why they have human police officers. They should just put animals out there patrolling the streets."[91]

IT'S STILL GOING ON

In April 2016 yet another task force, this time appointed by Chicago mayor Rahm Emanuel, issued what the *New York Times* called a "blistering, blunt" assessment of the Chicago Police Department. "A painful but necessary reckoning is upon us," the blue-ribbon commission said. "We arrived at this point because of racism." The U.S. Department of Justice reinforced this conclusion in its investigation of Chicago's use of force in black communities and the whitewashing of complaints filed against the police department. It was the same old blues, backed up with compelling statistics. In a city where African Americans comprise a third of the population, they account for about three-quarters of police shooting and taser victims.[92]

A few months later the Justice Department repeated the same litany of injustices, this time in Baltimore: unconstitutional stops by police in black neighborhoods, excessive force, failure to respond to victimization of African American women, retaliation against critics of the police, and so on. One of these stops had led to the death of Freddie Gray.[93]

"For generations," Justice Sonia Sotomayor wrote in her memorable dissent in *Utah v. Strieff* (2016), "black and brown parents have given their children 'the talk'—instructing them never to run down the street; always keep your hands where they can be seen; do not even think of talking back to a stranger—all out of fear of how an officer with a gun will react to them."[94]

Rudy Salas, Sr., a Latino artist who lived in Los Angeles, carried with him all his life "an insane hatred for white policemen," the result of a brutal beating he experienced as a young man in the 1940s. Four cops had kicked him in the head, fracturing an eardrum. "From that day on," he told the playwright Anna Deavere Smith in 1992, "I had a hate in me, even now." When his sons grew up, "I had a lot of anxiety. I told them, 'Cooperate.'" This did not stop the police from pulling over one of his sons, a student at Stanford, and pointing a gun at his head. "It drove me crazy," Salas said. "It's still going on, it's still going on."[95]

In 2018 it is still going on, but policing in the twenty-first century has also undergone some extraordinary changes.

5

THE INSECURITY SYNDROME

*How public and private policing in the twentieth century
became entangled and how American policing in
the twenty-first century became federalized, global,
corporate, and even more militarized.*

The illegality that is supposedly to be eradicated becomes the *raison
d'etre* of the security apparatus and enters into the "insecurity syndrome" that affects the entire state.

—Étienne Balibar, *We, the People*

PATRIOT ACTS

In November 2002, in a secret prison near Kabul, Afghanistan, code-
named Cobalt, CIA operatives tested the ideas that two American psychologists, Bruce Jessen and James Mitchell, had developed for extracting
information from al-Qaeda fighters. With doctorates from Utah State
University and the University of South Florida, respectively, Jessen and
Mitchell first worked together at Fairchild Air Force Base southwest
of Spokane, where they helped to teach military personnel how to resist
torture tactics if captured. The psychologists parlayed this experience
into a company that sold the CIA on a plan, endorsed by the Justice Department, for "enhanced interrogation techniques" that included sensory
deprivation, waterboarding, confinement in a small box, walling (slam-
ming the body into a wall), shackling around the clock, and extreme
cold. Some prisoners in Cobalt were deprived of sleep for as long as 180

hours, others immersed for hours in ice-water baths. One, Gul Rahman, died from hypothermia, the result of being fettered for days to a concrete floor while naked from the waist down. Many years later Rahman's family and two surviving prisoners, Mohamed Ben Soud and Suleiman Abdullah Salim, sued American officials and reached an undisclosed settlement as restitution for torture.[1]

At about the same time that the CIA was torturing prisoners in a black site in Afghanistan, a government official in Arizona had become the darling of right-wing advocates of law and order. Unlike Jessen and Mitchell, who operated under the clandestine shadow of national security, Joe Arpaio publicly celebrated his views and policies. Drawing upon his experience as a police officer in Washington, D.C., and as federal drug agent in Las Vegas, in 1993 Arpaio was elected sheriff in Maricopa County, where he developed a national reputation as "the toughest sheriff in America." He prided himself on creating all-female and all-juvenile chain gangs, forcing male prisoners to wear pink underwear, and managing to cut back the cost of feeding prisoners in jail to less than it cost to feed the department's dogs. When the jail became overcrowded, he built an open-air extension with surplus Korean War tents that at one time housed more than seventeen hundred prisoners, who were exposed to the region's extreme weather conditions.[2]

Arpaio's main claim to fame was not his ruthless treatment of prisoners but his anti-immigrant vendettas. He ordered his deputies to target Latinos and Latinas suspected of being undocumented, a policy that was so blatantly racist it drew the attention of even George W. Bush's Justice Department in 2008. When Obama became president the following year, Arpaio created a cold case investigative unit to try to prove that Obama's birth certificate was fake, and the sheriff intensified his crackdown on immigrants. In 2011 the Justice Department documented "wide-ranging discrimination" and illegal retaliation by Arpaio against Latinos and his political opponents. Two years later a federal judge confirmed that Arpaio had engaged in unconstitutional racial profiling and ordered him to stop using race as a basis for raids and traffic stops. When the sheriff ignored this order and was voted out of office, the Justice Department initiated criminal contempt charges that in 2017 led to his conviction for "flagrant disregard" of the judge's order.[3]

It took twenty-four years to bring Arpaio to justice. It took President

Trump a few weeks to pardon him while praising the former sheriff's "years of admirable service to our nation," describing him as someone who "kept Arizona safe" and is "an American patriot."[4]

In the 1960s and early 1970s there had been considerable talk of reducing incarceration and shifting from a punitive to a rehabilitative philosophy, as well as democratizing the police or at least making them more accountable to communities in which they worked by setting up civilian review boards and subjecting police to public scrutiny. By the time of George W. Bush's two-term presidency (2001–2009), the neoconservative regime had marginalized the liberal reform movement, making it much easier for security and criminal justice functionaries such as Jessen, Mitchell, and Arpaio to act with impunity.

During the Obama years (2009–17) no one was talking much about changing how police are organized and governed, but some put forward initiatives to change police culture, to make them less authoritarian and combative, more professional, and more attuned to the needs of a diverse society. By the end of Trump's first year, no longer was anyone making even a pretense of liberal reforms in national debates about policing.

In some ways it was back to business as usual, with the legacies of the early twentieth century continuing to shape policing in the new century: a warrior mentality, unregulated cooperation between public and private security agencies, and deeply rooted institutionalized racism.

But some significant innovations did qualitatively change the operations, organization, and governance of policing and security. In the 1960s the federal government began to play a much more influential role in the economics and cultural politics of regional and criminal justice policies, a trend that accelerated after September 11, 2001. This coincided with the increased involvement of corporations in selling weaponry, technology, and know-how to public agencies and with the carceral state increasingly contracting out day-to-day operations to the corporate sector. The public and private became inseparable, as did the national and international, with the increased globalization of U.S. criminal justice policies and growing interdependence of foreign and domestic security operations. Next to the vast reach and secrecy of today's national security state, the Machiavellian chicanery of the FBI under J. Edgar Hoover pales in comparison.[5]

BIPARTISAN WAR ON CRIME

The United States that emerged from the wreckage of World War II had an opportunity to overcome segregation, systematic injustice, and profound economic and social inequality by building a social democratic state. The postwar expansion of the economy, the GI Bill, and a revitalized civil rights movement made this aspiration credible. Unlike its European counterparts, the United States did not provide free health care or a guaranteed income, but with passage of civil rights legislation and the Economic Opportunity Act in the mid-1960s, and Lyndon Johnson's initial commitment to the War on Poverty, liberals in government made efforts to expand the promise of the New Deal. A policy of "maximum feasible participation," initially backed up by funding for education and job training in the most impoverished communities, was designed to empower residents in the governance of local agencies. It was a hopeful moment.

Quickly, though, the era of liberal reform turned hostile and mean-spirited. The fierce pushback that arrived with Richard Nixon's presidency in 1969 meant the defeat of the short-lived American experiment in a Western-style welfare state. Now the federal government would take much more refined and brutal measures of social control to hold back millions who had tasted freedom and knew that poverty and inferiority were neither predestined nor inevitable.

The most impoverished sectors of American society—notably urban African American and rural Latino and Native American communities—did not substantially benefit from the economic reforms of the 1960s, and the failure to integrate public education and housing projects during the brief reform era made segregation a continuing de facto reality for millions of people. Enduring poverty, as James Baldwin observed in 1960, was like being on a "treadmill forever."[6]

Keeping the machine going and keeping defiantly assertive communities running in place became the responsibility of the police by default. No surprise, then, that, beginning in 1964, police both triggered and were the targets of a series of rebellions that erupted in more than one hundred urban African American communities. The National Guard was mobilized twenty-five times in 1967, and about a hundred times in 1968, to deal with urban riots, as well as with vigorous campus protests and the antiwar movement. As the frontline guardians of public order, the police were poorly trained and ineffective at controlling what they were led to believe was an illegal insurrection rather than a cry of rage and demand for equality. More often than not, their efforts at riot control aggravated the situation, thus motivating the government to mobilize experts to study what had gone wrong, both with respect to efforts to reduce social inequality and the failure of the police to efficiently take back the streets.

Within five years a slew of national and local commissions, composed of political elites and professionals, and staffed by academics—California's 1965 McCone Commission, the 1967 President's Commission on Law Enforcement and Administration of Justice (the Crime Commission), the 1968 National Advisory Commission on Civil Disorders (the Kerner Commission), the 1969 National Commission on the Causes and Prevention of Violence (the Violence Commission, directed by Milton Eisenhower), and Nixon's 1970 Commission on Campus Unrest (appointed in the wake of killings at Kent State and Jackson State)—generated a mound of policy proposals calling for both the amelioration of unjust social conditions and more refined systems of social control.[7] The rhetoric may have been balanced, but the action was one-sided.

When Lyndon Johnson announced in July 1967 the appointment of the National Advisory Commission on Civil Disorders, chaired by Otto Kerner, the president made a distinction between "law-abiding Negro families [who] hope most fervently . . . to share in America's growth and prosperity," and "the apostles of violence, with their ugly drumbeat of hatred . . . and their miserable virus of hate." A year later the commission's blunt conclusion about the racial divide that permeated the United States took a backseat to its detailed riot contingency plans; a call for coordination of local police, the National Guard, and the army; and a recommendation that riot preparation become a standard part of police training. At about the same time the FBI drafted a manual instructing the police and National Guard about how to identify a "demagogue or professional agitator" and how an "impressive display of police power and resolve [can] promptly overcome resistance." The Republican Party, flexing its muscles after Richard Nixon's successful run for the presidency in 1968, equated social movements mobilized to end racism and the Vietnam War with extreme violence, just as right-wing ideologues in 2014 tried to discredit

Black Lives Matter as "radical extremists" who posed more of a threat to the United States than al-Qaeda and the Taliban.[8]

"Communists are in the forefront of civil rights, anti-war, and student demonstrations, many of which ultimately became disorderly and erupt[ed] into violence," J. Edgar Hoover testified to the Violence Commission in 1969. Police forces all over the country received the message that mass protests were inherently violent and illegitimate, as well as a site of Cold War confrontations. In fact, postwar social movements in the United States were remarkably and overwhelmingly nonviolent. In the South, African American organizations organized to defend communities against white violence; in the North members of the Black Panther Party were more often victims of police violence than instigators of violence against police.

The antiwar movement was boisterous, militant, and adopted tactics of civil disobedience but rarely advocated violence against public officials. When urban rioters in black communities turned to violence, they primarily targeted property—price-gouging stores, welfare offices, and banks—not people. Moreover, the police routinely initiated violence: government-run agents provocateurs infiltrated progressive organizations and encouraged activists to plan violent actions, and during street demonstrations the cops came looking for a good fight. "Nearly all the violence that has occurred in mass demonstrations," a task force of the Violence Commission concluded in 1969, "has resulted, not from the demonstrators' conscious choice of tactics, but from the measures chosen by public authorities to disperse and punish them." The phenomenon was so commonplace that sociologists gave it a name and Life magazine made it a cover story: POLICE RIOTS.[9]

The widespread demand for social justice was met with an unprecedented show of force, with professional organizations and academics involved as enthusiastic collaborators with the government. In the early 1970s several private think tanks, well funded by corporations and conservative philanthropists, instructed government forces how to respond to unruly social protests with "flexible response capability" and "instrumental escalation" of force. The Institute of Defense Analysis weighed in with suggestions for improving the "operational effectiveness of the collective forces"; the army prepared plans for setting up command posts during civil disorders; and a leading social scientist, concerned that riots reflected "a weakness in the system of social control," called for police to undergo "realistic training in sharpshooting and precision firing." Quickly abandoned was the Kerner Report's warning that "white society is deeply implicated in the ghetto. White institutions created it, white institutions maintain it, and white society condones it."[10]

The National Advisory Commission's advocacy of a two-pronged approach of "order and justice" was implemented politically as a mix of progressive rhetoric and repressive policies. From the Johnson to the Reagan administrations, the federal government reshaped local criminal justice priorities through unprecedented funding of day-to-day operations. In 1965 Johnson's Law Enforcement Assistance Act expanded the role of the Justice Department through its Office of Law Enforcement Assistance, which was designed to beef up local police operations. One of its largest grants went to the private Institute of Defense Analysis to study how scientific advances in defense and military operations could be applied to policing low-income communities. Another grant went to the Los Angeles County Sheriff's Department for helicopter patrols. The Defense Research Corporation of Santa Barbara, a military think tank, prepared an inventory of urban insurgent and counterinsurgent techniques, tactics, and doctrines, and the Pentagon's Project Agile added studies of "urban disequilibrium" to its counterinsurgency research program.[11]

With Johnson's characterization of the police as "frontline soldiers"— an upgrade from Roosevelt's "half-military"—combat metaphors dominated the federal reform movement. "The task of law enforcement agencies is really not much different from [that of] military forces," observed the chair of the Senate Judiciary Committee, Roman Hruska, a conservative Republican. In 1965 Chief William Parker of the Los Angeles Police Department compared putting down the Watts rebellion to "fighting the Viet Cong." By the time Reagan authorized the Department of Defense to cooperate with law enforcement agencies in the war on drugs, the line between civilian and military authority was blurred, and policing's main priority had become social control of urban unrest.[12]

The 1968 Omnibus Crime Control and Safe Streets Act provided financial incentives to urban police departments to meet federal expectations, while Johnson's Crime Commission and its various spin-offs generated detailed blueprints for policy and organizational reforms, as well as the logic of a war on crime. The Safe Streets Act expanded the Office of Law Enforcement Assistance, renaming it the Law Enforcement

Assistance Administration (LEAA), which lasted through several administrations until 1982 and pumped $8 billion into the states, with police departments the main beneficiaries. The agency played an influential role in efforts to standardize criminal justice policies nationwide. About three-quarters of LEAA's initial funding went to the police, including subsidizing the tuition of about fifty thousand officers who were enrolled in college programs, some of whom attended Berkeley's School of Criminology, where I was teaching, and reported me to the FBI for un-Americanism.[13]

The large-scale privatization of social control operations and outsourcing of public projects to corporations, both of which are now taken for granted, were rooted in initiatives of the Johnson administration. The increased involvement of Congress in local policing generated a police-industrial complex that took technical developments originally created for overseas warfare and the space program and, backed by generous government subsidies, applied them to problems of domestic disorder. The police in particular benefited from this largesse and were reorganized in the image of a military-corporate model that emphasized capital investments in technology, a specialized division of labor, communications systems, and managerial techniques of command and control.[14]

In 1967 the Crime Commission's Task Force on Science and Technology noted the paucity of scientists and engineers working on issues relating to crime control. The task force called for technology transfers from the aerospace and defense industries, as well as the increased involvement of university and private think tanks, in upgrading and reorganizing the police. Too many police departments, the commission's Task Force on Policing concluded, were "not organized in accordance with well-established principles of modern business management." With funding and subsidies provided under the Safe Streets Act, major U.S. corporations (including IBM, Sylvania, Rockwell, Motorola, Hughes Aircraft, Bell Helicopter, DuPont, and General Electric) for the first time took up the challenge of selling police departments everything from communications systems, helicopters, and weapons to "less-than-lethal" riot-control devices while helping to shape the rationale of policing as warfare. These were boom years for companies manufacturing breakaway nightsticks, stun guns, rubber batons, water-filled projectiles, water cannons, sound curdlers, stench grenades, foam generators, and smoke dyes.[15]

During the next twenty years whether Democrats or Republicans controlled the White House and Congress made little difference in criminal justice policies: the private sector became a full partner in the war on crime, the war on gangs, and the war on drugs. During the Nixon administration Ernst and Ernst, an accounting firm, received hundreds of thousands of dollars for designing manuals and surveys, while Motorola monopolized the sale of police radio equipment. Academics also profited from federal handouts. Nixon's LEAA gave grants to architects at the University of Illinois to create new prisons and to the Wharton School of Business and the University of Pennsylvania to design new juvenile facilities. During Jimmy Carter's presidency Westinghouse Corporation received the largest single competitive contract, to reduce crime in Baltimore "through environmental design." On Reagan's watch in 1984 the Corrections Corporation of America opened the first private prison in Texas.[16]

From the 1960s through the 1980s impoverished communities were the primary targets of the revitalized carceral state. Whatever it was called—Johnson's police saturation of "high crime" neighborhoods, Nixon's "High Impact" policy of preventative detention and expansion of imprisonment, Ford's focus on "career criminals," Carter's Urban Initiatives Anti-Crime Program, or Reagan's war on drugs—the targets were African Americans and Latinos. Sometimes the language was thinly coded, as in a former Harvard president's reference in 1961 to unemployed black youth as "social dynamite," piled up like "inflammable material in an empty building," or as in the widespread use in the 1970s of racially tinged terminology about "violent gangs," predators, and "amoral youth" to describe the "crime problem."

Even Carter's attempt to shift some anticrime funding from the Justice Department to the Department of Housing and Urban Development ended up expanding, not replacing, punitive measures. With its innovative use of barriers, walls, and gates to make sure the poor remained segregated and confined, the architecture of public housing came to resemble the architecture and assumptions of prisons. Reagan may have represented the rise of neoconservative thinking and neoliberal economics, but his policies regarding the carceral state were "the outgrowth of a process that liberals themselves had developed within a broad bi-partisan political consensus," as the historian Elizabeth Hinton astutely notes, and a "commitment to crime control as a viable response to socioeconomic inequality and institutional racism."[17]

Early-twentieth-century public policing was built upon a militaristic and corporate model of organization and ideology, governed by elite politicians and functionaries and marked by close ties to private security operations and by deeply racist assumptions about the meaning of criminality. The idea of policing as a democratically accountable public service, committed to equitably enforcing the rule of law, remained an aspiration but never became a reality. With the reorganization of policing that took place in the 1960s and 1970s, the aspiration became faint, kept alive only by social movements demanding community control of police. In the wake of September 11, 2001, it dissipated altogether.

HOMELAND SECURITY

Attacks on the World Trade Center and the Pentagon provided the rationale for an extraordinary piece of legislation and the largest expansion and reorganization of federal agencies since President Truman created the Department of Defense to fight the Cold War in 1947. The result was a huge boost to budgets and personnel in jobs related to immigration, national security, and U.S. criminal justice projects around the world. The size and cost of this sector can only be estimated because of government secrecy and lack of transparency.

In October 2001, after two days of debate and in an atmosphere of political hysteria, Congress passed the USA Patriot Act (Uniting and Strengthening America by Providing Appropriate Tools Required to Intercept and Obstruct Terrorism), which loosened the constraints on the government's ability to conduct searches, deport suspects, eavesdrop on internet communications, and crack down on violations by noncitizens. Democratic safeguards that Congress had put in place in the aftermath of the Watergate scandals of the 1970s were eviscerated and replaced by draconian measures. The White House authorized the revival of military tribunals and gave broad powers to intelligence agencies; the Department of Justice approved widespread FBI surveillance and roundups of thousands of suspects.[18]

President George W. Bush authorized a policy of "extraordinary rendition," that is, the transfer of terrorism suspects to prisons around the world. The CIA ran the operation, providing more than $300 million in seed money for the construction of black sites and millions of dollars in cash payments to foreign government officials. "Unlawful combatants" were sent to the U.S. prison in Guantánamo, Cuba, and other secret facilities, where they were routinely tortured.[19]

Budget and employment data for most national security agencies are shrouded in secrecy. Thanks to Edward Snowden, a former subcontractor for the National Security Agency who leaked classified information, we have some idea about the 2013 black budget, but getting accurate information about detention camps in war zones (Abu Ghraib in Iraq, Bagram in Afghanistan), extraterritorial prisons (Guantánamo Bay), and CIA off-the-books prisons in Poland and Romania is difficult. As Vice President Dick Cheney revealed in 2005, "We've got to spend time in the shadows in the intelligence world."

The CIA alone, according to a former agent who wrote a tell-all book in 1975, is "the biggest and most powerful secret service that has ever existed." Philip Agee reported that the agency then had 16,500 employees and an annual budget of $750 million (equivalent to $3.4 billion in 2016). This did not include its mercenary operatives or its commercial subsidiaries. Altogether the agency employed or contracted with hundreds of thousands of people, with an annual cost running to billions of dollars. In 2006 John Negroponte, then the director of national intelligence, estimated that 100,000 people worked in the "intelligence community" but did not provide any documentation. In 2010, according to an investigation by the *Washington Post*, 1,271 government organizations and 1,931 private firms were working on programs related to counterterrorism and homeland security in about ten thousand locations across the country, and about 854,000 employees held top-security clearance.[20] This number represents about two-thirds of all people employed by police departments in the United States.

In 2002 the newly created U.S. Department of Homeland Security (DHS) absorbed the Immigration and Naturalization Service, the Transportation Security Administration, Coast Guard, and other agencies to become the fastest-growing cabinet department, charged with defending the United States from acts of terrorism and guarding the borders. Between 2005 and 2013, the number of DHS employees increased by 31 percent, and those of the Department of Defense by 22 percent, while the Department of Education stagnated, and the Department of Housing and Urban Development reduced its personnel.

Homeland Security has about 250,000 employees that the public knows of. That is more than half the number of primary care physicians in the United States.[21]

DHS now has a more significant role than the Justice Department in shaping carceral priorities through the provision of grants and subsidies. In 2015, for example, it distributed $1.6 billion to government agencies and the private sector to fund responses to "weapons of mass destruction terrorism incidents," "terrorism prevention," and other catastrophic events.[22]

Endorsed by both political parties, the policies of the DHS dramatically expanded an already punitive crackdown on undocumented immigrants and documented immigrants charged with crimes. Until the 1980s the deportation of permanent residents, even those convicted of crimes, was quite rare. From the Reagan to the George W. Bush administrations, the Border Patrol grew from a small force to the federal government's largest policing operation. Beginning in 1988 Congress expanded the range of deportable crimes to include "aggravated felonies"; in 1990 Congress added any crime of violence for which the sentence was at least five years, and in the mid-1990s, during the Clinton administration, Congress added several nonviolent crimes and "moral turpitude" to the list.

In 2004 alone the United States ordered more deportations—eighty-eight thousand—than in the seventy-two years between 1908 and 1980 (fifty-six thousand).[23]

Immigration policy also became an important site of increased privatization of public programs. The Immigration and Naturalization Service, forerunner to DHS's Immigration and Customs Enforcement, or ICE, gave CoreCivic (formerly Corrections Corporation of America) its first "design, build, and manage" contract in 1983 and contracted with the GEO Group (formerly Wackenhut Corrections) in 1987. By 2011 contracts with ICE accounted for 20 percent of CoreCivic's revenue and 14 percent of the GEO Group's.

The number of U.S. citizens held in private prisons is quite low, and in fact declined between 2008 and 2010, but the number of immigration-related prisoners held in private institutions has steadily increased. The punitive turn in immigration policy increased the number of detainees in private prisons by 259 percent between 2002 and 2010.[24]

During the Obama years Congress expanded the criteria by which individuals who are lawfully in the country may be "delegalized." Immigrants convicted of relatively minor crimes, including misdemeanors and nonviolent felonies, are routinely deported, typically with speed and without due process. For every forced deportation there are an estimated four "voluntary deportations" of family members and relatives. The number of noncitizens, mostly Mexicans, formally removed from the United States increased from 25,000 in 1986 to a high of 419,000 in 2012. In 2013 immigration-related prosecutions reached an all-time high of nearly 100,000.

Two years later deportations declined to 253,000, partly as a result of a reduction in the number of undocumented immigrants trying to get into the United States. Still, during his two terms Obama authorized 2.4 million deportations, more than all previous administrations combined. Also, in recent years tens of thousands of unaccompanied minors from Central America have been stopped at the border and referred to nonprofit and religious organizations as a holding action.[25]

The Justice Department now prosecutes more immigration-related offenses than all other federal crimes combined. In 2005 President George W. Bush authorized Operation Streamline to speed up the prosecution of, and increase penalties for, undocumented migrants crossing the U.S.-Mexico border. Special courts located near the border held mass hearings of as many as eighty immigrants at a time, handing out routine sentences of as long as 180 days for "improper entry" and two years for "improper re-entry." The Obama administration intensified prosecutions. In 2015, 49 percent of all federal prosecutions involved border violations, mostly by Mexicans. As a result 23 percent of people currently incarcerated in federal prisons are noncitizens, overwhelmingly Latinos. The Trump administration shuttled batches of judges to courts on the border to address a chaotic backlog of hundreds of thousands of cases and to process immigrants, who have no right to government-appointed lawyers. It is not unusual for immigrants seeking asylum to wait for months in one of CoreCivic's privately run detention centers. Since 2005 the United States has carried out three-quarters of a million prosecutions at a cost of about $7 billion. The United States currently spends an estimated $1.7 billion annually to run a vast immigrant detention system of more than five hundred facilities.[26]

The federal government continues to be deeply involved in subsidizing the expansion of local policing. According to a report issued by President Obama's staff, in the five years between 2009 and 2014 the federal government provided nearly $18 billion in funds and resources to state and local law enforcement agencies. This annual subsidy of $3 billion was in addition to the $84.1 billion spent on the police by all local governments in 2012.[27]

The transfer of surplus equipment and weaponry facilitates the close cooperation between military and law enforcement agencies. The National Defense Act enables police agencies to purchase drug enforcement, homeland defense, and emergency response materials and equipment at a discount through the federal government. The Department of Justice's Edward Byrne Memorial Justice Assistance Grant Programs, established in 2005, disbursed $290 million in 2014 to state and local law enforcement for everything from radios to explosive devices. Since 2009 the federal government has passed on to the police about $2.7 billion in funds acquired through its civil forfeiture program. The High Intensity Drug Trafficking Areas program provides money to local police for a variety of projects. In 2014 Homeland Security gave more than $1 billion in grants to public and private agencies.[28]

The events known as September 11 transformed the entire U.S. political system, not only criminal justice operations. The war on terror is much more substantial than previous federal campaigns because it made carceral issues a priority of government, was the occasion for a reorganization of federal bureaucracies, and reshaped regional and local policing and security operations. It justified expansion of the national security state into the mundane and everyday, from personal bank accounts and travel habits to our emails and associations.

Unlike the red scare of the 1950s, which conjured up the imaginary threat of foreign enemies boring from within, attacks on the Twin Towers and the Pentagon demonstrated that small extremist groups could target the United States, using tactics of asymmetrical warfare against an enemy with military bases all over the world and an unprecedented arsenal of nuclear weapons. But the postmortem on September 11 did not explain why an already bloated national security state had not been able to identify and prevent such crudely planned attacks.

The rhetoric of the war on terror emphasizes the vulnerability of the

United States and its need for constant preparedness. The reality, however, is that the United States and the West are rarely targets of jihadist-inspired violence. The nearly three thousand people killed on September 11 represent a fraction of the more than 383,000 people killed by terrorist violence worldwide between 1970 and 2016. At home the government puts most of its resources into identifying and combating "Islamic extremism," yet the main danger of political violence comes from right-wing extremists, especially those associated with white supremacist organizations. Between 2007 and 2017 they committed seven out of every ten politically inspired murders in the United States.[29]

Multiple killings involving four or more victims are a serious problem in the United States, but violence in the name of global terrorism is rarely their cause. With 5 percent of the world's population, the United States had 31 percent of world's mass shooters between 1966 and 2012; most were killed for reasons ranging from personal vendettas to right-wing extremism, rarely in the name of Muslim extremism. Of eighty-one mass killings between 1990 and 2010 that ended in the suicide of the shooter, only twelve were linked to terrorism.[30]

From a public health standpoint, deaths and injuries caused by guns are a much more serious national problem than mass killings. In 2013, gun-related deaths in the United States included 21,175 suicides, 11,208 homicides, and 505 accident-related deaths, more than ten times the number killed on September 11. Each year since 2013 guns have killed or injured 35,000 to 45,000 people.[31]

The United States ranks first globally in rates of gun-related mortality and in gun ownership, at 88.8 firearms per hundred people, far ahead of its closest rival, Yemen. The chances of being killed by a gun in this country are thirty times greater than in Australia, England, France, or Spain. Yet effective lobbying by the National Rifle Association and right-wing politicians in the United States not only makes it easy to acquire and use guns but also shields gun manufacturers from lawsuits and restricts government-sponsored research on the public health implications of gun-related deaths and injuries. In 2005 Congress passed the Protection of Lawful Commerce in Arms Act, which protects companies that make and promote guns from litigation in the same way that tobacco companies were able for many years to avoid responsibility for smoking-related cancers. Between 1973 and 2012, when more than four million injuries were caused by guns, the National Institutes of Heath funded only three research grants on this issue, while research on rabies—with sixty-five reported cases—was funded eighty-nine times.[32]

CORPORATE SECURITY POLICING

In addition to the increased role of the federal government in shaping local carceral policies and the unprecedented expansion of homeland security measures, the third significant transformation of the carceral state in the twentieth century was the extraordinary growth and expansion of private security, from its previous role as an appendage of public policing to an indispensable component of governance.

As the class and racial divide widened in the 1980s, security firms forged an important niche for themselves in "target hardening" suburban communities—protecting the boundaries of businesses and malls and policing urban centers after dark. Many wealthy communities now provide and control their own policing, whereas public policing is primarily imposed on urban enclaves and protects city centers. The brave new world of downtown has become a complex, multifaceted operation, combining a hybrid mix of public and private police, architectural barriers, technologies of omnipresent intrusion, and new forms of instrumental discipline adapted from malls, sports stadiums, and rock concerts. From entertainment venues such as Disney World, public security learned how to use round-the-clock surveillance and a variety of manipulative and seemingly noncoercive techniques for observing and regulating crowds. When a show of force is needed, public officers and private agents stand side by side.[33]

Private policing, notes the criminologist Les Johnston, "does anything that public police do, and rather more besides": patroling industrial, commercial, and office facilities; recreational complexes; nighttime entertainment hubs; shopping districts; and residential neighborhoods. Internal corporate policing replicates public policing as security for customers and employees, first responders, undercover investigators, and defenders of commercial interests. By the 1990s almost half of all local governments were contracting out some of their security needs. As an industry executive observed in 1993, "The plain truth is that today much of the protection of our people, their property, and their businesses, has been turned over to private security."[34]

The intimate ties between and within the public and private sectors are evident in how easily police and prison functionaries acquire second careers in the security business or transfer into other government agencies. Ever since Allan Pinkerton and William Burns moved back and forth between their public responsibilities and private for-profit organizations, police in management positions routinely retire into second careers as consultants and in-house security operatives or start their own companies. After the federal Office of Public Safety was dismantled in 1974 in the wake of disclosures of its complicity in human rights abuses around the world, former employees moved on to lucrative jobs in the private sector, including an engineering firm in Brazil, Gallo Winery, and PacEx in Hawaii. Many members of the Society of Former Special Agents for the FBI have senior positions in the private security industry. Two former directors of the Federal Bureau of Prisons were hired by CoreCivic (Corrections Corporation of America), which later gave large contributions to the Trump campaign and inauguration. According to the sociologist Gary Marx, the leadership of the private security industry is composed of thousands of former military, national security, and police managers "for whom public service [is] a revolving door."[35]

Typical of this cozy relationship are the examples of former high-level prison officials who were hired as consultants by Science Applications International Corporation in 2003 to design the notorious Abu Ghraib prison in Iraq; the retired detective who applied his knack for extracting confessions from African Americans in Chicago's police cells to working over prisoners in Guantánamo's interrogation rooms; and the former New York City narcotics detective with a reputation for throwing his weight around who became Donald Trump's chief of security.

Bernard Kerik is the personification of a career officer who made public service a stepping-stone to a profitable hustle. He went from the U.S. Army Military Police Corps to working as a security consultant in Saudi Arabia, then returned to the public sector as the commissioner of corrections and, later, police chief in New York City. After that he went to Iraq in 2003 as George W. Bush's interim interior minister, assigned to train Iraqi police, before joining former New York City mayor Rudy Giuliani's firm as a counterterrorism expert hired by foreign governments. Even after serving three and half years in a federal prison for tax evasion—including failing to pay taxes on the $250,000 bribe he took from an Israeli defense contractor while in Iraq—he returned to a career as a criminal justice and counterterrorism consultant.[36]

The professional relationship between private and public sectors was cemented in the early 1980s when the National Institute of Justice set up the Joint Council of Law Enforcement and Private Security Associations as an umbrella organization to share information and facilitate cooperation of the International Association of Chiefs of Police, the National Sheriffs Association, and the American Society for Industrial Security. Since then corporate involvement in policing, immigration control, and intelligence operations has become routine and unquestioned, with many hybrid organizations now straddling the public and private sectors. The Law Enforcement Intelligence Unit, a private nonprofit organization created in 1956, swaps intelligence data with public agencies and was funded in part by the Justice Department in the 1970s.

In 2002 the Jewish Institute for National Security Affairs inaugurated the Law Enforcement Exchange Program to bring American officials and law enforcement personnel to Israel for training programs. As of 2015, more than ninety-five hundred police have participated in conferences organized by the institute. Similarly, since 2004 the Anti-Defamation League has brought 175 police executives to Israel for a counterterrorism seminar. In 2013 New York City police commissioner Bill Bratton delivered the keynote address at the National Conference on Personal Security in Jerusalem. Today the U.S.-based International Association of Chiefs of Police, with more than twenty thousand members, has meetings and offices in Europe. At its 2015 annual conference AT&T, Motorola, and Taser each paid a fee of $75,000 to showcase and hawk their wares.[37]

From the early days of the modern alarm industry and convict leasing in the mid-nineteenth century to today's niche market for body cameras and the $52 billion national intelligence budget, of which an estimated 70 percent is contracted out to the private sector, criminal justice has always been a profitable commodity. Today activists and critics draw attention to the ways in which a prison-industrial complex benefits from the carceral state through bail bond companies that annually retain $1.4 billion in fees from defendants; a $1.6 billion per year business of selling products to prisoners at inflated prices; the outsourcing of the housing of prisoners and immigrant detainees to private corporations, such as the GEO Group and CoreCivic; price-gouging prisoners for access to medical resources, phone calls, and care packages; paying prisoners much less than the minimum wage for work done for private companies; and lobbying for law-and-order policies to justify privatization of programs as well as more jobs and higher wages for criminal justice functionaries. As Ta-Nehisi Coates observes, the warehousing of prisoners has become a "lucrative investment."[38]

Profits are indeed being made from incarceration, as they are from any public institution with ties to the private sector. But exploiting prisoners by making them work for a pittance or buy goods and services at exorbitant prices is not the cause of the extraordinary growth of the American carceral state. Prisoners' labor is no longer profitable in the way it was in the nineteenth and early twentieth centuries because most prisoners either do not engage in productive work or work only on maintaining the institutions in which they are incarcerated. For a long time now prisons have become repositories of surplus, not exploited, labor—resembling "human landfills," to use Angela Davis' imagery.

Moreover, private prisons represent a relatively small share of the criminal justice market and seem to be in decline. In 2016 the Federal Bureau of Prisons, in response to a reduced number of prisoners overall and the Inspector General's criticisms of poor practices in private prisons, announced its decision to phase out the relationship. As of 2015 private firms owned or managed only 9 percent of all prison beds in the United States. Although President Trump's attorney general rescinded the Obama administration's decision to reduce the use of private prisons at the federal level, state and local governments show little inclination to change the status quo. In 2013 the private prison industry (including immigration-related detention centers) brought in about $5.47 billion, a little more than half of California's annual corrections budget.[39]

Profits from prison labor, construction, and services are quite modest when compared with the extraordinary growth in recent years of the corporate security sector and the increased blurring of public-private boundaries in policing. Since the late 1970s security has become a global transnational operation, with the private sector playing a decisive role, not only in feeding the state's huge appetite for equipment, technology, and weaponry but also in shaping national priorities, stoking cultural anxieties about insecurity, and developing a global reach. The Pinkerton Vigilance Network, now part of the multinational company Securitas, has offices around the world, including China, Germany, Indonesia, and Mexico. Dwight Eisenhower's warning in 1961 about the dangerous "acquisition of unwarranted influence" by the "military-industrial complex" in "the councils of government" presaged the rise of the corporate security complex, which is now a fait accompli.[40]

The massive phenomenon of private security, including companies that provide know-how and technology, overshadows the extraordinary growth of public policing and state guard jobs in recent decades. The number of private security firms increased from an estimated 4,000 in 1967 to almost 10,000 in 2010, and the number of employees from 960,000 in 1980 to 1.7 million in 2010, outnumbering public police by more than 25 percent. There are now five times as many private security employees as there were in 1969.[41]

The public and private spheres of policing do much more than exchange information, security-related services, and employees. The relationship is symbiotic and cooperative. This is evident in large-scale operations, such as the coordinated effort to defend the Dakota Access Pipeline against tribal protests at the Standing Rock Indian Reservation in 2016. This project involved coordination of thousands of personnel from the local sheriff's department, public police personnel from nine states, the North Dakota Highway Patrol, the National Guard, Silverton Security, TigerSwan Security, 10-Code Security, G4S, and the Security Resource Group.[42]

"Big Brother is increasingly outsourced," the political scientist Reg Whitaker notes. Private firms now stimulate the huge appetite in the public sector for equipment, surveillance systems, and data mining. Today markets for security services and technologies are a growth industry. These are indeed "golden days for the electronic industry," as the then-FBI (and later CIA) director William H. Webster predicted to participants at a 1994 conference, Law Enforcement Technology for the 21st Century.[43]

In the wake of September 11 the right-wing Manhattan Institute envisioned how the "trillion-dollar infrastructure of semiconductor and software industries, with deep roots as defense contractors," could quickly provide the technology needed "to watch and track everything that moves."

The private sector quickly delivered the goods at taxpayers' expense. Tyco, UTC, Honeywell, and GE, for example, are deeply involved in the electronic surveillance industry, and military defense corporations, such as Dyncorp, Boeing, Northrop Grumman, Lockheed Martin, and General Dynamics, dominate the homeland security sector. Immigration and counterterrorism operations have been a boon to companies that produce radio frequency identification chips, biometric identification systems, screening databases, and all the related technologies of surveillance. An "alliance between public practitioners and private providers of technology," a leading authority on policing speculated in 2010, "may be the driving force in the transformation of policing" and much more consequential "than changes in policing workforce and its governance."[44]

The evidence is in, there's no need to be so cautious anymore: the contracts are huge, the private sector leads as well as follows, and the fusion of criminal justice and security operations is inseparable. For example, in 2004 Accenture, a private company, was awarded $10 billion to develop the "United States Visitor and Immigration Status Indicator Technology" system to screen visitors at a virtual border. Private research firms (such as the Rand Corporation, Securitas, and Jane's Information Group) innovate policy proposals and mine massive databases for public intelligence agencies. It is no longer a one-way migration of public officials to the private security sector but rather a convergence of strategic interests between corporations seeking global markets and states preoccupied with governing through insecurity.[45]

This does not mean, however, that corporate security policing operates as a unified, centralized operation. Didier Bigo, an academic who also serves as director of the Center for the Study of Conflicts, Liberty and Security, imagines it is not a coherent integrated network but an often fractious and heterogeneous "archipelago of policing, or a mosaic that holds together national police, military police, customs control, immigration, consulates, and even intelligence services and the military." Yet a convergence of interests produces the material artifacts of policing and security, from uniforms to weapons and communication systems, and a whole field of professionals specializes in articulating, identifying, predicting, and framing the discourse of unease. Just as applied criminology emerged in the late nineteenth century to articulate a domestic need for managing disorder and inequality, today's globalized security offers its services in the analysis of numerical data, development of technologies of biometrics, and social and cultural profiling.[46]

The intermingling of private and public security gives the corporate sector a decisive role in determining what constitutes the general welfare. What is good for companies that profit from making and selling everything from advice, research, training, and evaluation to uniforms, guns, tasers, body cameras, high-tech gadgets, and data-mining systems is not compatible with equitable law enforcement, the rule of law, and service-oriented criminal justice agencies. To make the public sphere into a marketplace of products and commodities erodes the idea of government of, for, and by the people. The term *conflict of interest* does not capture the calamity and absurdity of our government's willingness to pay multinational corporations billions of dollars for goods and expertise required to manage millions of people who are unable to find permanent, adequately paid work or dignified welfare programs under a global corporate economic system that benefits from inequality.

BOOMERANG

In addition to the consolidation of bipartisan political support for a politics of law and order, the central role of the federal government's war on terrorism in shaping local law enforcement priorities, and the symbiotic relationship of public policing and private security, the fourth important development in recent decades is the increased interdependency of domestic and foreign security operations. The United States has always exported ideas and policies around the world, but it also imports what it has learned in other countries, bringing back not only weapons and techniques of social control but also ideas about dangerousness and otherness. In the 1970s Congress put these policies under scrutiny and held them in check, but not for long.

Since the U.S. war in the Philippines at the beginning of the twentieth century, the ties between the American military and American policing, between the U.S. government and foreign police forces, between foreign governments and American police agencies, and between paramilitary operations and everyday policing have been close. In the twentieth century transnational policing became normalized.[47]

During the Cold War the Office of Public Safety (OPS), a department within the U.S. Agency for International Development (USAID), funneled money, equipment, and personnel to governments friendly to, or economically reliant on, the United States. "[The] mission [of OPS] was explicitly ideological," aimed at countering the spread of communism, according to an expert on international conflict resolution. During its thirteen years of operation (1962–75), OPS trained more than one million police around the world, including seventy-five hundred senior officers, and distributed $200 million worth of weaponry and equipment in forty-seven countries. Between 1961 and 1972 total aid in training and equipment amounted to $308.6 million, of which about two-thirds was allocated to Southeast Asian countries.[48]

The war in Vietnam and counterinsurgency against social movements in Latin America received most of OPS's attention. The police in Latin America, as the head of USAID testified to a U.S. Senate committee in 1964, were "close to the focal points of unrest, and more acceptable than the army as keepers of order over long periods of time." Policing was conceptualized as an integral component of military operations. "We appreciate now that every young, emerging country must be constantly on the alert, watching for those symptoms which, if allowed to develop unrestrained, may eventually grow into a situation such as that in South Vietnam," General Maxwell Taylor told police cadets from around the world in 1965. "We have learned the need for a strong police force and a strong police intelligence organization to assist in identifying early the symptoms of an incipient subversive situation." After a trip to Latin America in 1969, New York governor Nelson Rockefeller advocated increased American training of foreign military and police as a way to combat "growing subversion, mounting terrorism, and violence."

As their colleagues did back home, U.S. government representatives equated social movements for justice and political power with terrorism and smeared activists as criminals. Projects nominally designed to upgrade records and identification facilities essentially were used to create data banks about activists and leftists. By 1970, for example, OPS enabled South Vietnam's National Police Force to amass fingerprints, biographies, photographs, and political data on millions of people, and OPS supported the CIA-funded Operation Phoenix, which detained more than 150,000 suspects in prisons, including the "tiger cages" of Con Son, where political prisoners were tortured. OPS funds and projects supported the construction of a national police academy in Brazil, expansion of the South Vietnamese prison system, and installation of a "war room" in the Caracas police department in Venezuela. OPS also was involved in training right-wing death squads in Guatemala, Argentina, Uruguay, and Brazil.[49]

In the late 1960s and early 1970s a series of political crises, mass protests, journalistic exposés, and congressional investigations for the first time revealed the inner workings of intelligence agencies and generated legislative reforms. A quick succession of events turned deep secrets into a public debate.

A 1967 *Ramparts* magazine essay exposed the role of the CIA in funding the European anticommunist Left, trade unions, and the National Students' Association (NSA) in the United States. At NSA's peak in 1960, more than four hundred universities were associated with the organization, whose substantial annual budget was funded by the CIA through nonprofit fronts and secret conduits. When the NSA became involved in international student organizations, the CIA made sure that it toed the line of U.S. foreign policy. "The best way to understand the CIA's motives," wrote Marcus Raskin in an afterword to the *Ramparts* article, "is to see it as primarily a commercial institution which deals in buying, renting and selling people." Later, the public would learn in more detail how a CIA-created organization, the Congress for Cultural Freedom, deeply influenced a wide variety of cultural organizations, events, and publications throughout the West from 1950 to 1967.[50]

In January 1970 ABC News carried a story about the U.S. Army's spying on civilians. The director Costa-Gavras' popular, thinly fictionalized film *State of Siege* (1972) exposed the counterinsurgent role of OPS in Uruguay and helped to turn popular and political opinion against the agency. The Watergate hearings in 1973 detailed the role of the White House in authorizing illegal break-ins at the offices of political opponents and led to the resignation of President Nixon the following year. In 1974 the investigative journalist Seymour Hersh broke a story in the *New York Times* that documented how the CIA, from the 1950s through the Nixon era, consistently violated its charter mission by carrying out massive illegal domestic operations against activists and dissidents. Despite the advice of William Colby, head of the CIA, that "family skeletons are best left where they are—in the closet," Hersh outed the CIA for keeping files on ten thousand U.S. citizens and for engaging in clandestine break-ins, wiretaps, and mail tampering.[51]

In 1975 this changing political climate emboldened a publisher to release the former CIA agent Philip Agee's documentation of the everyday workings of the country's most secretive intelligence agency. Agee made a persuasive case that the "CIA is one of the great forces promoting political repression in countries with minority regimes that serve a privileged and powerful elite." *Inside the Company* included a shocking twenty-three-page list of the names and affiliations of CIA agents, informants, and unwitting stooges around the world.[52]

From 1975 to 1976 a Senate committee, chaired by Senator Frank Church, an Idaho Democrat, carried out a fifteen-month investigation of intelligence agencies. The committee released a series of reports that documented a wide variety of abuses by intelligence agencies, including attempts to assassinate foreign leaders, interception of more than two hundred thousand pieces of mail, the destabilization of the Allende government in Chile, electronic surveillance of activists, and burglaries of leftist organizations.[53]

The Church Committee represented the first time that the CIA's activities had been closely investigated, publicly debated, and subjected to congressional oversight. As a result of the spotlight focused on international security operations, many politicians expressed concern about "the use of program funds to support repressive regimes that committed human rights abuses." After Congress voted in 1973 to prohibit USAID from conducting police training and other activities in foreign countries, OPS was phased out and some of its operations were transferred to other agencies. In 1974 Congress added a rider to the Foreign Assistance Act that emphasizes that U.S. funds should not be used to underwrite training, advice, or equipment for police or prisons abroad.[54]

The exposés and publicity generated by the Church Committee interrupted, but did not stop, the globalization of U.S. policing operations. The ban on funding foreign police operations was eroded, first by exempting the FBI and Drug Enforcement Administration (DEA) from the 1973–74 legislation, then by waivers and amendments granted by the Reagan administration. In the late 1980s the Department of Defense trained and equipped El Salvadoran and Honduran police "to counter urban terrorist activities."[55]

One of the beneficiaries of the demise of OPS was the Justice Department's DEA, previously known as the Federal Bureau of Narcotics. In 1973 it expanded from a budget of about $3 million and staff of 300 agents six years earlier to a budget of $74 million, 1,446 agents, and offices in thirty-three countries. By 1976 its budget was $200 million, and the DEA had 2,141 agents and offices in forty-three countries. An investigation by Jack Anderson documented a close working relationship between the DEA and CIA. By the early 1990s the DEA had a presence in seventy countries. The DEA had effectively repackaged itself as a terrorism-fighting agency by finding tenuous connections between the global drug trade and so-called narcoterrorism.[56]

Another conduit for U.S. support for foreign police forces was the Justice Department's LEAA. Narcotics trade and terrorism concerns enabled the government to circumvent prohibitions on assistance to domestic police forces. In 1997, before it became part of the Department of Homeland Security, the U.S. Immigration and Naturalization Service already had agents stationed in forty offices abroad, under its Operation Global Reach, which supplemented FBI projects in at least seventeen countries, including military operations in Afghanistan and Pakistan.[57]

The post–September 11 legislation and governmental reorganization erased the memory of the 1970s scandals and massively increased funding and personnel for global police and security operations. From 2002 to 2008 training and equipping the Afghanistan National Police alone cost $6.2 billion. This did not include the $200,000 spent by the CIA in Afghanistan in 2002 to build a black site where it could carry out waterboarding, sleep deprivation, and shackling in painful stress positions of suspected terrorists.[58]

These operations paled in comparison with the size and reach of the Department of Homeland Security, with its initial budget of $37 billion, more than 170,000 employees, and personnel assigned to seventy-seven countries. In the aftermath of September 11 all policing and security agencies took on counterterrorism operations as a central function, even when the chances of terrorism were remote or criminal investigations had nothing to do with terrorism. In 2003 the Southern Command's General James Hill referred to trafficked drugs as "weapons of mass destruction." A General Accounting Office report on the Department of Justice found that 46 percent of cases identified by the FBI as "terrorism-related" in 2002 were misclassified to boost confidence in the agency's effectiveness. Between the late 1960s, when the State Department started to keep records of the number of deaths attributed to terrorism worldwide, and the first decade of the twenty-first century, more people in the United States died annually in bathtub drownings than at the hands of terrorists.[59]

The latest iteration of U.S. involvement in global criminal justice operations is the International Criminal Investigative Training Assistance Program (ICITAP). Authorized by Congress in 1986, ICITAP is located in the Justice Department, funded by USAID, and gets its marching orders from the State Department. Although the law still prohibited direct training of foreign police forces, a General Accounting Office study reported in 1992 that 125 countries received $117 million in various kinds of police assistance through ICITAP and the Departments of State and Defense.

ICITAP set up field offices and subcontracted projects to private companies in countries all over the world, from Ukraine and Bosnia to Panama and El Salvador, led by personnel drawn almost exclusively from the FBI and DEA. Gauging the effectivness of ICITAP is difficult because the agency does not evaluate its own programs or make public its personnel and budgets. Its approach, according to the Georgetown law professor Allegra McLeod, "is analogous to that of Cold War foreign internal security training programs, and similarly dominated by U.S. law enforcement officers."[60]

Mismanagement and scandals have plagued ICITAP. A congressional investigation in 2000 reported "a history of turmoil," including security failures, improper use of funds, and overcharging by contractors. Figuring out how budgets are authorized, routed, and implemented is a challenge because funding for international police projects is fragmented and comes from several federal departments (State, Justice, Defense, Treasury, Homeland Security) and USAID. "Reliable estimates of the amount of money being spent annually on police assistance [globally] or the nature of the programs being supported are difficult to come by," a specialist in international criminal justice operations concluded in 2011.[61]

In 2003, after the defeat of the Saddam Hussein regime, ICITAP sent a team of experts to Iraq to help transform the Abu Ghraib facility into a U.S. military prison that became synonymous with torture. The project was requested by the Department of Defense, funded by the State Department, and subcontracted to a private consultancy firm that in turn hired four retired corrections officials who had run prisons in Texas, New Mexico, Utah, Arizona, and Connecticut. As head of Arizona's Department of Corrections (1995–2002), Terry Stewart had authorized the routine use of pepper gas and Israeli foggers on recalcitrant prisoners as well as attack dogs for "cell extractions." As first revealed by *60 Minutes* and a Seymour Hersh investigation for the *New Yorker*, Abu Ghraib was where the U.S. military systematically abused prisoners, including by intimidating detainees with dogs.[62]

Even as the American carceral state came under widespread criticism at home from conservatives, libertarians, the federal courts, liberal academics, progressive think tanks, and community activists seeking to reverse overimprisonment, wasteful spending, torturous use of solitary confinement, racial profiling, and a callous disregard for human rights, the United States continued to export its worst practices around the world in the guise of the "rule of law," "professional policing," and "corrections." By early 2017 ICITAP had operations in thirty-one countries and the support of the new administration. Similarly, the Department of Homeland Security had more than two hundred agents stationed in seventy countries.[63]

What the United States does globally has a boomerang effect, with ideas and practices tested on populations abroad applied back here. The war in Southeast Asia and the Watts rebellion provided the occasion for private and public think tanks to apply their expertise in war to domestic conditions. "Vietnam had come home," Mike Klare, an expert on global security, observed. Now this is a routine phenomenon. Baltimore, for example, uses aerial surveillance equipment, originally used to track roadside bombs in Iraq, to supplement "hot spot" policing. Foreign and homeland security operations now collaborate, borrowing each other's ideas, equipment, and strategies, ranging from the use of nonlethal weapons against protesters and fortified sites to contain problematic populations to techniques for tracking and profiling individuals, groups, and locations.[64]

Ideas about dangerous and potentially dangerous populations abroad—terrorists, drug traffickers, jihadists—segue into images of populations at home as transgressive, contaminated, and criminogenic—African Americans, Mexican immigrants, Muslims, urban youth. The cultural anthropologist Allen Feldman argues that Americans are witnessing the rise of a "nomadic order of public safety," seamlessly moving back and forth between here and there, inside and between nation-states.[65]

This "nomadic order" is apparent in a dystopian scenario imagined by two senior fellows at the right-wing Manhattan Institute shortly after the September 11 attacks:

> Step by step, cities like New York must now learn to watch and track everything that moves . . . We are destined to fight a never-ending succession of micro-scale battles, which will require us to spread military resources across vast expanses of empty land and penetrate deep into the shadows of lives lived at the margins of human existence. *Their* conscripts dwell in those expanses and shadows . . . It is a horrible vision. It gives us no joy to articulate it. But at home and abroad, it will end up as their sons against our silicon. Our silicon will win.[66]

When Yale professor David Bromwich writes about how "the suspect becomes a rightless subject and not a person who bears the inalienable rights of a citizen," he could be referencing migrants in refugee camps, military detainees at Guantánamo, or prisoners held in solitary confinement in California's Pelican Bay State Prison, a supermax facility.[67]

What has been happening to American policing in recent decades draws upon and echoes long-standing practices and assumptions. But today's security state, as it is sometimes called, has become a normalized and indispensable part of governance, organized to manage displaced, disposable, and redundant populations. Its implementation did not require emergency legislation or special measures, the sociologists Simon Hallsworth and John Lea say, because its protocols simply became standard practice: "There is no formal abolition of civil rights, just their hollowing out." Campaigns for public safety are now "de-territorialized," operating beyond borders, on the lookout for the dangers of contamination and transgression, and as preoccupied with political and ideological warfare as with the practicalities of national defense. As one critic observes, "Security works like a virus," spreading from government agencies to civil initiatives and self-policing.[68]

Policing-as-security increasingly is no longer about investigating crimes, arresting suspects, and collecting evidence for prosecution. As its

military functions prevail, it emphasizes preserving the existing public order, taking preemptive action in anticipation of dangerousness, and targeting whole populations and neighborhoods deemed collectively suspect.
The exceptional state mobilized in extraordinary circumstances—riots,
political protests, global events, natural disasters—has become the new
normal in many countries. The following description could refer to any
urban American ghetto or barrio: "Instead of enforcing the law, as they
would describe their activity, officers patrolling in the disadvantaged
neighborhoods are actually enforcing a social order characterized by swell-
ing economic inequality and expanding racial discrimination." It is a
description of the French police in Paris' *banlieues* in the 2010s.[69]

In the early twenty-first century we are witnessing the increasing de-
tachment of policing and guarding from democratic political governance
and their consolidation as security organizations rather than public-
service institutions. The partnership of private and public sectors in formu-
lating and carrying out policing strategies is now a matter of established
policy. The globalization of security operations promotes a blurring of national security, counterinsurgency, antiterrorist, crime-control, and anti-
immigrant operations. It is no longer sufficient to say that militarism
influences policing but rather that policing has become an important component of militarism.

During the late twentieth and early twenty-first centuries, the government's iron fist of social control became more formidable, much more
likely to act preemptively than reactively, no longer reluctant to display
its symbolic and material power. But the exercise of power in the United
States has always relied on much more than brute force. It also takes considerable political, cultural, and social resources to preserve inequality and
stability, to win hearts and minds without resorting to explicit force. The
United States has a long history of this kind of coercive benevolence.

III

6

THE PERILS OF REFORM

On the history and legacies of carceral reforms,
with particular attention to the pitfalls of do-gooding
and the tough underside of liberal crusades.

I was glad when George Pataki came to the governorship of New York promising to restore the death penalty. George took a lot of heat, but he's doing civilization's heavy lifting.

—Donald J. Trump, *The America We Deserve*

HARDER AND HARDER

During World War I the federal government led a campaign to round up thousands of women suspected of infecting American soldiers with venereal disease and morally sapping their preparedness for war. "Everywhere delinquent women and girls must be made to feel that the government is interested in them," a spokeswoman said while emphasizing that the War Department intended to "come down harder and harder upon them as they prove a menace to our efficiency, and the program we offer must be constructive but firm."[1]

This mixture of benevolent rhetoric and punitive measures of coercive intervention typifies the liberal reform tradition in the United States.

The United States has a long and varied legacy of reform movements, including organizations that provide services to impoverished communities, political efforts to make government responsible for the general welfare, and radical proposals for redistributing wealth and power. For the most part, though, reformism has been closely linked to strategies of social control and to reinforcing, rather than transforming, unequal relations of power.

The history of the carceral state is inescapably linked to reforms that purport to reduce suffering and better people's everyday lives but often do the opposite. The first houses of correction in late-sixteenth-century Europe, and the first penitentiaries in nineteenth-century United States, were innovations framed as dramatic improvements on previous methods of physical punishment, such as mutilation, flogging, and capital punishment. But the earliest prisons were fiercely brutal. City fathers forced Amsterdam's beggars, unemployed, and petty thieves into the exhausting work of scraping dyewoods for textiles. Here, pairs of men pulled a seventy-pound saw back and forth over a log until it produced a quota of sawdust, the work often resulting in hernias and pulled muscles. Anybody caught cursing or fighting was subject to eating nothing but bread and water for as long as eight days. More serious infractions, such as insubordination or attempting to escape, were punished with confinement in a dungeon for up to six months or being beaten with a switch while clamped to a bench with a vise. Repeat offenders could end up in the water cellar.

Centuries later Pennsylvania's Quaker reformers were convinced that putting prisoners to work in enforced silence during the day and into solitary confinement at night was a more humane alternative to stocks, flogging, and irons. When Charles Dickens asked a prisoner in Eastern State Penitentiary in 1842 how he felt at the prospect of being released after doing twelve years inside, the man answered that "he didn't care, that it was all the same to him now, that he had looked forward to it once, but that was so long ago, that he had no regard for anything." Successful reformation, Dickens concluded, meant a living death.[2]

Not all reforms are punishments in disguise. The philanthropic tradition, typically couched in the religious imagery of compassion and benevolence, is based on providing services to individuals. Today it is represented by nonprofit organizations that do their best to ameliorate the most debased kinds of poverty, alleviate pain and suffering, and compensate for what government should and does not provide: food for the hungry, job training and care for millions not covered by unemployment and health insurance, help for the beaten and abused, and transitional programs for the formerly incarcerated.

Occasionally efforts to make government meet these needs, to transform charity into a right, succeed. After the Civil War survivors and their families fought for, and gained, pension rights for veterans and their dependents. In the 1930s the New Deal meant basic economic benefits for millions of workers. In the 1960s an alliance of civil rights and antipoverty groups managed, briefly, to expand the New Deal to communities of color and poor women. But these gains were meager and short-lived because the constituencies that benefit from these reforms generally lack ongoing, institutionalized political representation. Unlike other countries in the West, the national political system of the United States is hostile to a multiparty democracy and has not welcomed organizations with roots in labor and progressive movements.

This dynamic helps to explain why so many grandiose schemes for substantial change deliver less than they promise, big on rhetoric and small on real change. For example, reform of policing in the early twentieth century was intended to replace corruption and cronyism with a model of civil service professionalism. Two decades later the Wickersham Commission (1929–31) documented the persistence of systematic corruption and third-degree tactics nationwide, and the Myrdal report drew attention to everyday racism in the criminal justice operations in the South.

Similarly, California's postwar experiment with the "rehabilitative ideal" was supposed to replace the punitive exploitation of prisoners' labor with diagnosis and treatment, analogous to hospital care for the sick and contagious. Instead corrections administrators used the indeterminate sentence as a cudgel to depoliticize prisoners' grievances and encourage mindless submission to authority. The Economic Opportunity Act of 1964 planted the seeds of upward mobility and community empowerment, but the Johnson administration also planted the seeds of repression. A fierce pushback against African American rebellions in Watts and other cities resulted in new carceral strategies, from manipulative techniques of co-optation and management to counterinsurgency operations tested in Vietnam.[3]

Another tradition, which I call managerial reform, is unambiguously part of the carceral apparatus. It is more preoccupied with initiatives to respond to real or perceived threats to national identity and stability than with helping individuals or addressing systemic inequities. Typically tough-minded and strategic, and not at all reluctant to use muscular force as necessary, it draws upon narratives and techniques of medicine, psychology, science, and education.

Many programs associated with top-down reforms that profess public-spirited goals of benefit to the nation—to save children from a life of crime, make schools into engines of patriotism, defend family values, combat so-called social evils, and better the human race—result in widening the net of social control and diminishing the civil and legal rights of a large swath of people. We need to be aware of both the unintended and sometimes intended repressive consequences of reforms, how the best of intentions often leads to reproducing or deepening, rather than alleviating, inequalities and injustices. Today's advocates of reform need to know this history and make sure the velvet glove does not cover an iron fist.

CHILD SAVING

In 1948 the African American photographer Gordon Parks gained unprecedented access to seventeen-year-old Leonard "Red" Jackson, a leader of a Harlem gang called the Midtowners. Parks captured his subject in all aspects of daily life—hanging out on the streets, in fights, doing chores at home, playing with kids—and turned over hundreds of pictures to editors at *Life* who made all the decisions about which images to include and how to crop and caption them. Parks destroyed one negative to prevent the magazine from using an image of Red with a gun on its front cover, but he had no control over the final piece, which sensationally emphasized how "Red Jackson's life is one of fear, frustration and violence," by using images that reduced a complex young man to an emblem of black dangerousness. "Damn, Mr. Parks," Red Jackson said, "you made a criminal out of me."[4]

Two decades later popular images still erased corporate criminals and middle-class delinquents from discussions of the "problem of crime," focusing instead on what the sociologist and future U.S. senator Daniel Patrick Moynihan called the "tangle of pathology" that "seriously retards the progress" of black communities, which he claimed was rooted in the breakdown of the patriarchal family. Lyndon Johnson's Crime Commission similarly concentrated on youth crime in "deprived areas" where "life is grim and uncompromising" and "the slum child arrives at school in the habit of being his own master . . . accustomed to autonomy and averse to assertions of authority."[5]

The year after the *Life* photo essay was published, the general secretary of the National Probation Association acknowledged the fiftieth anniversary of the U.S. juvenile court system by heralding it as "one of the greatest advances in child welfare that has ever occurred," a triumph of progressive liberalism over the forces of reaction. "No single event," Charles Chute wrote, "has contributed more to the welfare of children and their families. It revolutionized the treatment of delinquent and neglected children and led to the passage of similar laws throughout the world."[6]

Social reformers had created the new court system at the end of the nineteenth century in response to what they perceived as an alarming rise in urban delinquency and breakdown of traditional institutions of social control. "By some cruel alchemy," a leading Chicago activist in 1905 noted, "we take the sturdiest of European peasantry and at once destroy in a large measure its power to rear to decent livelihood the first generation of offspring on our soil." The problem with the criminal courts was not their punitiveness but their ineffectiveness: they accomplished too little, too late.[7]

To address this failure the child-saving movement, led by middle-class and elite women, created a new legal institution, the juvenile court, that became a global model of modern jurisprudence. It substituted paternalism for due process and expanded the definition of delinquency to include a variety of offenses, including drinking, begging, public displays of sexuality, curfew violations, and rowdy behavior. It replaced the right to a trial and legal defense with an administrative process that emphasized the importance of removing young people from the decadence of urban life to rural reformatories, where they would be both protected and corrected. For the first half of the twentieth century, professionals and academics shared Chute's assessment that the juvenile court was the best way to deal with young men such as Red Jackson.[8]

The combination of an obsession with poor communities as hotbeds of criminality and uncritical praise for juvenile justice operations persisted until the 1960s. Then, the civil rights and black liberation movements forced an acknowledgment of the humanity and diversity of communities of color, the U.S. Supreme Court reconsidered the apparent benevolence of juvenile courts, and a new generation of historians, deeply influenced by postwar social movements, took up the challenge of revising accounts of the past with a more critical eye.

In 1965 a young Claude Brown reached a wide audience with his vivid memoir of time in a northern reformatory, not a southern prison, where "everybody was under guard, all the time, and everybody had a job to do . . . Work gangs were a lot like chain gangs, minus the chains." During the summer Brown "busted rock and threw sledgehammers and picked onions and stuff like that." In the winter he shoveled coal and snow. Malcolm X's popular autobiography, published the same year as Brown's *Manchild in the Promised Land*, gave millions of readers a sense of how an anonymous prisoner—"you never heard your name, only your number"— became, in the words of Alex Haley, a widely recognized leader with "that shocking *zing* of fire-and-be-damned-to-you."[9]

Just as John Howard Griffin's *Black Like Me* (1961) and Michael Harrington's *The Other America* (1962) exposed many people for the first time to the pervasiveness of racism and poverty, so, too, Claude Brown and Malcolm X demolished the myth of a benevolent system of criminal justice and complicated binary perceptions of African Americans as either victims or monsters.

Social scientists confirmed what poor communities knew from experience: that the United States imprisoned about one million juveniles annually at a rate unmatched by Western countries and that youth of color comprised more than 40 percent of those arrested and incarcerated. Lyndon's Johnson's Crime Commission declared in response that it is "urgent and imperative" that "wherever coercive action is a possibility," young defendants should be provided with legal advice "as a regular matter."[10]

In an important 1967 case the Supreme Court recognized that juvenile courts did not always represent the best interests of youth. It reinstituted the right to counsel and other legal protections, with Justice Abe Fortas warning in the court's majority opinion that "unbridled discretion, however benevolently motivated, is frequently a poor substitute for principle and procedure . . . However euphemistic the title, a 'receiving home' or an 'industrial school' for juveniles is an institution of confinement in which the child is incarcerated."[11]

The roots of the liberal wing of the American carceral state lie in the Progressive Era (1890s–1920s): the creation of a separate, welfare-oriented justice system for youth; the implementation of probation, parole, and what would become "community corrections" as a supplement to incarceration; the professionalization of policing and social work; and the introduction of scientific methods of crime control. The Progressive tradition, in the words of a distinguished historian, was supposed to "first broaden the numbers of those who would benefit from the great American bonanza and then to humanize its workings and help heal its casualties."[12]

When the failures of Progressive reforms were finally acknowledged in the 1960s—overcriminalization of youth, racial disparities from arrest to incarceration, and harsh conditions in reformatories—Johnson's Crime Commission blamed the "grossly overoptimistic" expectations of nineteenth-century reformers and the "community's continuing unwillingness to provide the resources—the people and facilities and concern—necessary to permit [the juvenile courts] to realize their potential."[13]

This assessment of the Progressive movement as too impractical, naive, and overly ambitious, its good intentions undermined in practice, misses the point that the child savers were highly practical, tough-minded social engineers who deprived urban youth of legal safeguards and increased the role of the state in regulating the daily lives of working-class families. The child-saving movement was in reality quite conservative. It was part of a larger movement to rescue capitalism from ongoing economic instabilities and counter political and labor activism of the late nineteenth century. It represented a victory for the liberal wing of the corporate sector over the laissez-faire sector of business and for greater involvement of government in education, public health, recreation, and criminal justice operations. Managerial reforms, the historian Lisa McGirr observes, came loaded with "strong doses of coercive moral absolutes."[14]

The rhetoric of child saving emphasized measures to incorporate working-class youth into the economic and social mainstream, and many immigrant families turned to child-saving institutions for help in controlling their wayward children and in asserting their authority as parents. They received little help. Instead tens of thousands of European families had their children taken away or diverted into institutions that marked them as delinquent or incorrigible. By 1899 one reformatory in New York alone crammed fifteen hundred young men into five hundred cells. Meanwhile African American and Latino communities had their children placed in segregated or adult institutions, or the families were forced to find resources from their own beleaguered professional, religious, and social networks.[15]

During the Progressive Era carceral measures for the first time incorporated the language and ideas of medicine and science. The child savers thought of themselves as comparable to doctors and social workers rather than police and guards. Their worldview was optimistic and utopian. The new penology emphasized the importance of identifying adolescents in need of saving and intervening in their lives at the first sign of trouble. "When an individual actually enters upon a criminal career," the sociologist Charles Cooley observed in 1896, "let us try to catch him at a tender age, and subject him to rational social discipline. The criminal class is largely the result of society's bad workmanship upon fairly good material." Prophylaxis was the key to anticipating and preventing delinquency in working-class children. "They are born to it, brought up for it," a leading reformer wrote. "They must be saved."[16]

Backed by big business and wealthy philanthropists, and supported by the emerging professional class, privileged white women led and staffed the national child-saving movement. Many were genuinely concerned about alleviating human misery and improving the lives of the poor, and they devoted their lives to public service. This work also enabled them to break out of the cloistered, suffocating world of their own middle-class families, free themselves from the total domination of fathers and husbands, and become creative participants in the world beyond their homes. At the same time, as the historian Sheila Rowbotham points out, middle-class reformers who imagined themselves as liberators of poor women and children "frequently ignored the economic and sexual realities of working-class life. The rescuers persisted in seeing the values of their own class as universal and in seeing the state—their state which enforced their class interests—as a neutral body." They were both agents of their own ideas and personal freedom and defenders of structures of inequality.[17]

Although the child savers framed the reformatory as an alternative to punitive force, it was from the beginning an institution of coercion and regimentation. Military drills, "training of the will," and long hours of labor constituted its core program. "The reformatory," recalled a New York leader of the new penology at Elmira, "became like a garrison of a thousand prison soldiers. Vigorously and thoroughly the grand object of the reformatory was pursued; every incipient disintegration was promptly checked and disinclination of individual prisoners to conform was overcome. The regime was planned to both arouse and restrain."[18]

The Fifth International Prison Congress, held in Paris in 1895, welcomed efforts of authorities to deprive "unworthy parents of the right to rear children" and as a corrective advocated manual labor in "institutions of preservation," particularly "agricultural labor in the open air for both sexes." "To make a good boy out of a bundle of perversities," a reformatory superintendent noted at a meeting of the National Conference of Charities and Correction, "his entire being must be revolutionized. He must be taught self-control, industry." This took time, agreed Enoch Wines, a leading child saver, so the longer young men and women were kept in institutions, the better the chance of reformation. The sentences should not be "absurdly shortened as if they signified only so much endurance of vindictive suffering."[19]

Yet, when Mary Carpenter, a British reformer, toured American institutions, she found "an entire want of family spirit" at the Massachusetts Reform School and hundreds of young people locked up in Philadelphia. And had she visited the Illinois State Reformatory at Pontiac, she would have witnessed a seriously overcrowded small penitentiary where prisoners worked ten hours a day making shoes, brushes, and chairs.[20]

By the 1940s the reformatory operated much like a prison stripped of benevolent rhetoric. The Preston School of Industry in California, for example, was "organized like the military into companies, and these companies were used to divide the races as well as to divide the more troublesome boys from the comparatively docile. We marched everywhere, and were always on 'Silence,'" a former prisoner recalled. "We were easier to manage on Silence."[21]

While the child-saving movement practiced malign neglect in African American communities, it ruthlessly carried out good works in Native American territories, promoting cultural erasure over mass annihilation. Field matrons generally viewed the objects of their reformation as living in "the throes of savagery," just as urban social workers imagined themselves immunizing immigrant families against the seductive dangers of urban life. A few women did not subscribe to a narrative of cultural uplift and moral superiority and instead learned from their experience in Indian country and admired the power and independence of

Indian women. But most social workers, such as participants at the 1892 conference organized by Friends of the Indian, plunged into Native American communities with the fervor of missionaries dedicated to spreading "a contagion of home-making on the reservation" and removing indigenous children from their parents. They saw no contradiction in seeking their own independence and fulfillment outside their homes while trying to regulate the most intimate and personal spaces of Native American families and bodies: how they cared for their children, furnished their homes, engaged in relationships, and decided what to wear.[22]

The federal Indian Services (which became the Bureau of Indian Affairs) believed that forcibly removing Indian children from their communities and sending them to faraway boarding schools was a humanitarian way of breaking the bonds of tribal cultures and indoctrinating a new generation in the values of individualism, Christianity, and subservience as maids and agricultural workers. Native Americans resented coercion wrapped in the language of benevolence. "None of us wanted to go and our parents didn't want to let us go," Lone Wolf said, recalling how soldiers took him and other children from the Blackfeet tribe to a school in Fort Shaw, Montana, where teachers burned all their belongings, including medicine bags packed by their mothers to protect them from harm. "They told us Indian ways were bad," recalled Sun Elk, who spent several years in the Carlisle Indian School in Pennsylvania. "He is not one of us," a Taos Pueblo chief concluded when Sun Elk returned to his tribe and was rejected by his parents. Sun Elk said he "walked out of my father's house and out of the pueblo."[23]

By the early 1900s several boarding schools throughout the country were committed to stamping out Native American languages, customs, clothing, and beliefs. The operation was not in any way benign: they meted out harsh punishment for marching out of time, walking on the grass, going barefoot, and "talking Indian." Yet this form of repression was not effective: arson and running away were common problems, and young people from disparate tribes plotted what decades later would become a pan-Indian resistance movement.[24]

The unsentimental interventionism of the child-saving movement, framed in the language of maternalism, characterized managerial reformism from the Progressive Era through the twentieth century and has its echoes in the criminal justice discourse of today.

MORAL ZONES

The child savers' tough-mindedness and emphasis on bringing order to a changing world were replicated in a variety of institutions and locales. Progressivism, as the historian Margot Canaday succinctly puts it, had "a coercive edge."[25]

In 1881 a Chicago politician introduced legislation that would "abolish all street obstructions." He did not have in mind inanimate objects but rather "any person who is diseased, maimed, mutilated, or in any way deformed, so as to be an unsightly or disgusting object." Other cities, first in the West, then throughout the country, passed one or another version of these "ugly laws," as a later generation of disability activists named them. The intention was to criminalize the "unsightly beggar" and contain what Susan Schweik calls "civic contagion." The legislation may have been enforced only occasionally, but it revealed a great deal about Progressive preoccupations with purity and order, and the law laid the cultural basis for unforgiving cruelty against the physically and mentally disabled in the 1920s.[26]

In public schools reformers forged rituals of patriotism, aimed at inculcating an unquestioning loyalty in immigrant students. A popular primer, written by a New York educator in 1898, emphasized the importance of "ready obedience to rules and instruction." In the wake of the Spanish-American War and later, during World War I, patriotism increasingly reflected militarist and nationalist ideas. The Pledge of Allegiance—"I pledge allegiance to my flag and to the Republic for which it stands, one Nation indivisible, with liberty and justice for all"—was introduced at the first Columbus Day celebration in 1892 and was gradually adopted throughout the country. A few years later "my flag" became "the flag of the United States of America" to make sure that fifth columnists did not secretly swear loyalty to another country.[27]

Right-wing nationalists quickly co-opted the pledge, which its author, Francis Bellamy, had once imagined as a living principle of equality and liberty. At Columbus Day parades and celebrations around the country, millions of children marched with "drilled precision" as "one army under the sacred flag." Daily rituals aimed at reaching children's hearts were backed up with new civics curricula to secure their minds with heroic images of virile soldiers honored to die for their country. A typical children's primer, published in 1903, taught "B stood for battles" and "Z for the zeal that has carried us through / When fighting for justice / With the Red, White and Blue."[28]

When these efforts at political socialization failed, the power of the state was invoked. In Chicago in 1916 a young African American boy was arrested because he refused to respect a symbol that stood for Jim Crow and lynching. "I am willing to salute the flag," Hubert Eaves explained, "as the flag salutes me." Between the world wars, campaigns for "100 percent Americanism" led to the persecution of thousands of Jehovah's Witnesses and the expulsion of their children from school when they refused to participate in patriotic rituals. What began as a movement to encourage loyalty to a nation "with liberty and justice for all" was hijacked by jingoists who promoted government policies that suppressed dissent and demanded unquestioning homage to what the historian Cecilia O'Leary describes as a "militarist, racist, and exclusive brand of patriotism."[29]

The combination of techniques of persuasion, tough measures of control, a rhetoric of moral panic, and scientific-medical rationales that characterized the child-saving movement persisted and shaped the contours of reformism throughout the twentieth century. This was particularly evident in campaigns against gays, lesbians, and sexual nonconformists. The well-known crackdown on homosexuals in government jobs and the military during the 1950s linked disloyalty to the nation with threats to the nuclear family, and the repression built on decades of homophobic and restrictive sexual policies, often initiated by federal efforts to root out "pederasts and sodomites" among immigrants and welfare applicants.[30]

In the early twentieth century, when young, urban, working-class women began to express their independence from the family by spending wages earned in factories and domestic service on dance halls, amusement parks, and movie theaters, reformers became alarmed and obsessed by what they regarded as an avalanche of promiscuity and immorality in the city. Whether they regarded the new urban woman as an unwilling victim of lecherous men on the prowl or a promiscuous agent of her own pleasure, middle-class crusaders and professionals did everything they could to sublimate sexual desire through wholesome leisure activities based on what the historian Kathy Peiss calls "orderly sociability." When these efforts failed, as they usually did, evangelicals were on hand to disappear white "fallen women" into maternity homes, while the growing profession of social work sought to interpret young women's sexuality in the language of psychological deviation or inherited pathology.[31]

By the late 1910s campaigns against women's sexual independence had taken a nastier and much more punitive turn, accelerated by American participation in World War I. "The Constitution of the United States," as Kate Richards O'Hare observed in 1923, "was the first casualty of the war."[32] Nationalism typically flourishes during wars and rigorously punishes nonconformity, leaving its mark for a long time.

In April 1917 President Woodrow Wilson created a new federal agency, the Commission on Training Camp Activities (CTCA), to prevent the spread of venereal diseases among American troops, especially in the South, where about half a million soldiers and sailors were stationed. The commission was led by men and chaired by Raymond Fosdick, a lawyer and philanthropist who later played an influential role in the Rockefeller Foundation. Soldiers in camps received movies, recreation, lectures, a sanitized reading list (Alexander Berkman's *Prison Memoirs of an Anarchist* was banned), and the *Official Army Song Book*, which plugged "All Hail the Power of Jesus' Name," "Dixie," and "Onward, Christian Soldiers." Women who lived close to the camp were regarded as contaminated instigators of sex outside of marriage.[33]

White, middle-class women, both volunteers and professionals, were the CTCA's ground troops, pursuing a two-pronged strategy of "uplift and distraction" for men, "coercion and repression" for women. According to the historian Nancy Bristow, they did not target only women working as prostitutes or in brothels. "Single, working-class women, caught alone on the street, or engaging in what progressive reformers considered suspect recreation, such as improper dancing, drinking, or visiting cafes unchaperoned" were fair game for CTCA enforcers. The focus was primarily on heterosexual women, but the commission also went after "male perverts," "fairies," "muff-divers," and "women pervertors." Stanford University's leading psychologist, Lewis Terman, tested his ideas about inborn traits of masculinity and femininity on soldiers imprisoned for sodomy.[34]

The basis of the campaign against venereal diseases was the assumption that prostitutes were "in large measure responsible for dissemination of the disease" and that "the prostitute is not a local or regional but rather a national liability." More than fifteen thousand women were incarcerated in forty-three federally funded institutions during a period of twenty-seven months, for an average of seventy days in detention centers and one year in reformatories. According to the U.S. Interdepartmental Social Hygiene Board, this policy was necessary because the majority of "inmates under care would, if free, be a menace to the health of soldiers, sailors, and the civilian population." Barbed wire and guards were preferred "both as a protection against intrusion and to insure time for effective work." According to doctors working in the institutions, "better results are obtainable, from the point of view of health, when patients are literally held in quarantine."[35]

The program for protecting the "health and morals of our men in training" required "holding women on long-term sentence," with "suitable places provided for their custody and training." There they would be cured of diseases and trained in "domestic work involved in the conduct of a house, including the laundry work." Special attention, a representative of the War Department noted, should be paid to "the menace of the immoral colored girls and women."[36]

While military brass encouraged the troops to participate in chaperoned dances, organized sports, and cultural events, CTCA enforcers targeted for arrest, quarantine, and humiliation women accused of prostitution and "charity girls" suspected of lax morality. "If we are to safeguard the health of soldiers and sailors," the secretary of the New York Probation and Protective Association said in 1918, "we must free the communities from the delinquent and the diseased women, who are the greatest menace." Freedom meant providing men with medical care and entertainment and incarcerating perhaps as many as thirty thousand women in federal and local institutions.[37]

The federal government played an active role in the campaign. It authorized a civilian quarantine and "isolation fund" that was used to build or expand dozens of detention centers and reformatories for women, led a national educational program that primarily blamed women for venereal infections, and encouraged local authorities to eliminate red-light districts and construct "moral zones" around training camps. Police arrested more than one thousand women in St. Louis and raided brothels from Charleston to Los Angeles; in California the State Enforcement and Protective League boarded up dance halls.[38]

In the 1920s reformers shifted their moral zeal to the scourge of alcohol. The Eighteenth Amendment was, according to McGirr, "the boldest effort to remake private behavior in the nation's history." Again, working-class, poor, and immigrant drinkers were the primary victims of repressive do-gooding, with the federal government leading the charge. The Treasury Department's Prohibition Unit (later called the Prohibition Bureau) hired 1,550 field agents supported by a staff of equal number, almost five times more than the staff of the FBI. By the late 1920s the Prohibition Bureau had four thousand employees. Its budget in 1930 was $13 million, compared with a little more than $2 million for J. Edgar Hoover's operation. Treasury agents and local police selectively enforced the law against the poor and unlucky, while the wealthy drank in protected clubs or bribed their way out of arrest.[39]

A generation later the Cold War provided the context for another sexual crusade. This time the government made no effort to balance repression with persuasion and education. In 1947, after President Harry Truman established a loyalty program to root out disloyalty among federal employees, its main victims were suspected communists and homosexuals. "One homosexual can pollute a Government office," a Senate committee reported in 1950. President Eisenhower included "sexual perversion" and "notoriously disgraceful conduct" as grounds for firing in his 1953 executive order. In the years between the end of World War II and the mid-1950s, thousands of mostly gay men either lost their federal jobs or were refused a position on the basis of their suspected sexual preference. At a rate of about one thousand per year in the 1940s and two thousand in the early 1950s, men and women were similarly discharged from the military. As had occurred during the campaign against sexually independent women during World War I, local authorities took their cues from the federal government. "The widespread labeling of lesbians and homosexuals as moral perverts and national security risks," the historian John D'Emilio writes, "gave local police forces across the country a free rein in harassment. Throughout the 1950s gays suffered from unpredictable, brutal crackdowns."

Everyday life, at work and play, became a source of perpetual anxiety and a "gnawing insecurity." In the early 1950s police arrested more than one thousand people every year in Washington, D.C. In Philadelphia misdemeanor charges against gay men and women averaged about one hundred per month. Thousands lost their jobs, and many more fretted that they would be exposed. In surveys conducted by the Kinsey Institute in the 1940s and 1950s, one in three gay men reported that he had had run-ins with the police, comparable to the experience of African American men today. Those who managed to avoid arrest and public humiliation could not escape the prevailing psychiatric and medical view of homosexuality as a pathological deviation from normality. As he set out on his career as a distinguished historian and playwright, Martin Duberman lived a closeted double life on campus, exploring his sexuality while accepting "the culture's verdict that I was defective [and] crippled in my affective life."[40]

HUMAN BETTERMENT

While Progressive Era reformers emphasized that, in the struggle over "nature versus nature," profoundly changing human behavior to turn delinquents and unruly young women into orderly, law-abiding citizens is possible, the more pessimistic view also persisted that in many instances biology determines behavior and certain groups of people are predestined to inferiority. This perspective, known as eugenics, was influenced by nineteenth-century developments in genetics, medicine, and public health. It played a significant and varied role in public policies around the world: endorsed by Fabian socialists in England and racial scientists in Germany; linked to birth control and economic reforms in Denmark and to racial policies against itinerant Roma in Sweden; served as an expression of fascist ideology in Germany and Argentina, and of cultural hybridity in Mexico; and was closely associated with the sterilization of those defined as feebleminded in Germany, the United States, and Scandinavia.[41]

In the 1930s Nazi Germany made eugenics an official state policy, first openly sterilizing hundreds of thousands of women, then secretly murdering most of its disabled and mentally ill patients whom it judged to be leading "lives unworthy of life." Until the onset of World War II, when selective killing turned into organized butchery, Nazi racial scientists were appreciated in many countries, notably the United States.

Right-wing hard-liners ideologically dominated the American strand of eugenics; their focus was on reformation of the social order rather than individuals. In addition to promoting utopian visions of a brave new world and exploiting cultural anxieties about racial degeneracy, supporters of eugenics were hands-on activists who campaigned against race mixing and miscegenation, defended policies of segregation, promoted ideas about inherent intelligence in education, and lobbied for immigration and welfare restrictions. At the core of eugenics was a belief in the central role of heredity in both determining and explaining social inequality.

In the mid-1930s a California philanthropist returned from a visit to Germany with the good news for a Sacramento audience that the Nazi regime had "cross-indexed her people until she has located all her probable weaklings" and planned to "eliminate all low-powers to make room for high-powers, and thereby also save taxes." The speaker, Charles M. Goethe, was not a crank on the margins of American political life. He had made his fortune in banking and real estate, was appointed to the advisory board of a state university that honored him in 1965 as "Sacramento's most remarkable citizen," was awarded an honorary doctorate by the University of the Pacific, and was made an "Honorary Chief Naturalist" by the National Park Service. Lyndon Johnson described Goethe as a national leader of "distinction, integrity, and unceasing energy," while Chief Justice Earl Warren recognized Goethe's "remarkable career of public service." His defense of Nazi Germany's "honest yearnings for a better population," as he put it in his presidential address to the Eugenics Research Association in 1936, was not an aberration or side interest. It was his life's work, publicly and proudly proclaimed.[42]

Goethe was a key member of an independent Pasadena-based think tank with the Orwellian name of the Human Betterment Foundation. Founded in 1929, the foundation included in its ranks some of the best and brightest representatives of an intellectual elite that shaped public debates about race, gender, and social policy through the 1950s: Stanford's chancellor, David Starr Jordan, and the psychologist Lewis Terman; Harry Chandler, publisher of the *Los Angeles Times*; the Caltech physicist and Nobel Prize winner Robert Millikan; and professors from Berkeley, the University of Southern California, and Huntington Library.

The foundation's most prolific writer, Paul Popenoe, a self-made expert on biology, was the coauthor of a popular textbook, *Applied Eugenics*, first published in 1918 and reprinted into the 1930s. When Popenoe submitted to the *Journal of Heredity* an article about Germany's 1933 Law for the Prevention of Genetically Diseased Offspring, which authorized the eventual sterilization of 400,000 women without their consent, he included a large photograph of Hitler and several favorable quotations from *Mein*

Kampf. In return, when the German government published the Nazi law in its legal journal, it included flattering references to the foundation, including its assertion that sterilization was "a practical and essential step to prevent racial degeneration."[43]

Popenoe was an outspoken supporter of white supremacy, attributing differences in "racial temperament" to inherited biological tendencies: "The Negro lacks in his germ-plasm excellence of some qualities which the white race possesses." His solution to what he perceived as the unregulated birthrate of African Americans was to use them as fodder in war. "In the United States," Popenoe and a coauthor declared, "are millions of negroes who are of less value than white men in organized industry, but almost as valuable as the whites, when properly led, at the front."[44]

The foundation promoted "positive eugenics" to increase the birthrate of Nordic families and discourage white women from professional careers, and it promoted "negative eugenics" to reduce the birthrate of the "socially inadequate." For organizations such as the Human Betterment Foundation, sterilization was not so much a technical medical procedure to enhance physical and mental health as it was a means to cleanse the body politic of racial and sexual impurities and put a halt to the "evil of cross-breeding."[45]

Whereas men led the eugenics movement and dominated its public discourse, middle-class women were its enthusiastic practitioners. In its efforts to be taken seriously as a discipline based on scientific norms and a distinct body of knowledge, social work embraced eugenics in the 1920s. Its foundational commitment to social justice was subordinated to the "talismans of professionalization—objectivity, efficiency, rationality." Through "pedigree studies" social workers documented the "direful chain of hereditary pauperism" in the poor's inability to compete in industrial society. In his presidential address to the National Conference of Charities and Corrections, the University of Chicago professor C. R. Henderson called for "closing out the stock of a hopelessly degenerate line." To social workers who asserted a link between what was then called feeblemindedness, unregulated sexual appetite, pregnancy, and dependent children, the solutions were to be found in early diagnosis, segregation, surveillance—preferably in locked institutions—and, successively, through sterilization, birth control, and population control. Even the well-known reformer Jane Addams, who generally advocated social solutions to personal problems, welcomed eugenic insights into "the inheritance of well-born children" and the "evil heritage" that prostitutes transmitted to their children.[46]

Between 1907 and 1937 thirty-two states authorized their institutions to sterilize patients considered unfit for reproduction. Under California's eugenic laws medical superintendents of nine state homes and hospitals had the power to sterilize patients classified as mentally ill, feebleminded, epileptic, syphilitic, or with other conditions "likely to be transmitted to descendants." Under the banner of "national regeneration" tens of thousands of mostly poor women were subjected to involuntary sterilization in the United States between 1907 and 1940. California carried out one-third of all sterilizations nationwide.[47]

Those sterilized included people with conditions we would identify today as psychiatric disorders or intellectual disabilities, as well as poor women and juveniles deemed antisocial, who did not have the resources or social connections to hire attorneys or fight back. Eugenicists primarily targeted women considered feebleminded and promiscuous, including those who had one or more children out of wedlock. Some middle-class women were also sterilized because of their sexual activity or after being designated mentally ill.

Quite a few men were sterilized against their will. Six hundred men at San Quentin prison in the 1930s received vasectomies. In 1933 the Oklahoma legislature passed the Habitual Criminal Sterilization Act, which made prisoners convicted of two felonies involving "moral turpitude" subject to sterilization. The state senate made sure that government functionaries and their cronies would preserve the right to have children by exempting from sterilization those convicted of "offenses arising out of violations of the prohibitory laws, revenue acts, embezzlement or political offenses." Most prisoners were white migrant workers, day laborers, and sharecroppers who for the most part had committed economic crimes of desperation. As the warden of Oklahoma State Penitentiary in McAlester admitted, the Depression had turned "honest laborers to crime."

In 1934 prisoners organized to lobby against the state sterilization law. The odds were heavily stacked against them. In the infamous Supreme Court decision of 1927, *Buck v. Bell*, Justice Oliver Wendell Holmes had justified the forced sterilization of seventeen-year-old Carrie Buck on the ground that "three generations of imbeciles were enough." Public opinion overwhelmingly supported sterilization of "habitual criminals," and leading criminologists, such as Harvard's Sheldon Glueck and Eleanor Glueck, advocated similar measures to "reduce the reproduction" of a criminal class. Yet, in a case that took years to reach the Supreme Court, the prisoners prevailed. "The power to sterilize, if exercised, may have subtle, far reaching and devastating effects," Justice William O. Douglas wrote in the unanimous decision in *Skinner v. Oklahoma* (1942). "In evil or reckless hands it can cause races or types which are inimical to the dominant group to wither and disappear."[48]

Poor women, however, had no legal relief from the devastating, life-changing effects of involuntary sterilization. Before World War II most sterilizations took place in hospitals and institutions, justified as a public health measure and designed to relieve government of the responsibility of taking care of dependent children. The grounds for sterilization included the vague categories of feeblemindedness and idiocy, as well as "excessive masturbation," immorality, and "hereditary degeneracy."

In California in 1926 the superintendent of Riverside's Bureau of Welfare and Relief advocated the sterilization of feebleminded unmarried women as a means of halting the "menace to the race at large." At the Sonoma State Home authorities perceived sexual activity as evidence of a mental defect, whether a patient met medical or psychological standards of mental illness or disability or not. Women committed to mental hospitals and homes for the feebleminded were required to acquiesce to sterilization as a condition of release. The director of the Sonoma State Home "has always had a strong weapon to use in getting consents for sterilization," Paul Popenoe wrote to the eugenicist John Randolph Haynes in 1930, "by telling the relatives that the patient could not leave without sterilization."

Haynes, a member of California's State Board of Charities and Corrections and of the University of California's board of regents, had in 1918 anticipated the Nazi regime's murder of 100,000 mentally ill patients with these chilling words: "There are thousands of hopelessly insane in California, [and] the condition of those minds is such that death would be a merciful release. How long will it be before society will see the criminality of using its efforts to keep alive these idiots, hopelessly insane, and murderous degenerates? Of course the passing of these people should be painless and without warning. They should go to sleep at night without any intimation of what was coming and never awake."[49]

Race, as well as class and gender, played a central role in medical decisions to sterilize. The historian Alexandra Minna Stern and her colleagues researched sterilization orders in California institutions from 1922 to 1952 and found that Spanish-surnamed patients, predominantly of Mexican origin, were sterilized at rates ranging from 20 to 30 percent, far surpassing their proportion of the general population. Of more than seventeen thousand patients recommended for sterilization from 1920 to 1945 in the state, on average Latinas were sterilized at 2.65 times the rate of non-Latinas, were more frequently flagged as having "criminal tendencies," and were more likely to be labeled "sexually delinquent." Hundreds of Latinas younger than eighteen were sterilized, many on the basis of their supposed promiscuity and immorality. Another study confirmed that in the late 1930s, at the height of sterilization policies, Mexican American youth accounted for about 21 percent of those sterilized in California institutions.[50]

Terman, Stanford's leading psychologist, sent his doctoral student J. Harold Williams to the Whittier State School for Boys, where he confirmed his mentor's assumptions about the racial differences in intelligence. Williams classified as feebleminded 60 percent of youth of Mexican background, 48 percent of African Americans, and 6 percent of whites. "While Mexicans are usually classified as white," Williams recommended, "it seems best here to make the distinction on account of intelligence differences probably due to the intermingling of Indian blood." Terman agreed, saying that feeblemindedness was "very, very common among Spanish-Indian and Mexican families of the southwest and also among negroes." He added that the feebleminded should be "segregated during their period of reproduction in order to extinguish the defective strains which now encumber our prisons, reform schools, jails, courts, and public schools." In his influential 1916 book, *The Measurement of Intelligence*, Terman concluded that there were "enormously significant racial differences" in "Indians, Mexicans, and negroes," that "children of this group should be segregated in special classes and given instruction which is concrete and practical. They cannot master abstractions, but they often can be made efficient workers."[51]

ENOUGH'S ENOUGH

The Progressive roots of the eugenic tradition continued to shape the American carceral state long after Nazi racial science was discredited. The carceral state's defining characteristics—a managerial worldview implemented by a cadre of professionals and bureaucrats and legitimated by a medical and scientific discourse, with a mix of soft and repressive techniques of persuasion—thrived in the second half of the twentieth century. Eugenic assumptions were revived in post–World War II initiatives to promote marriage and motherhood as women's primary goal in life, to justify the systematic sterilization of poor women of color in the 1950s and 1960s, and to search for the biological roots of sexual orientation in the 1990s.[52]

Before World War II advocates of sterilization focused primarily on poor women and men in mental institutions and prisons. After the war government authorities targeted poor women of color in their communities and increasingly used public health and welfare incentives to induce, trick, and coerce their consent. In Puerto Rico between the 1930s and 1970s social workers were enthusiastic supporters of eugenics, eager "to protect the United States from too many of 'them,'" according to the feminist scholar Laura Briggs. In a forty-year period one-third of Puerto Rican women of childbearing age were sterilized. During the early 1970s, with funding mostly provided by the U.S. Department of Health, Education, and Welfare, approximately one million women were sterilized annually, primarily African American and poor white women in the South, Puerto Rican women in New York, and Chicanas and Native American women in the Southwest.[53]

An influential social work book, published in 1950, defended "selective sterilization as one approach to a happier world where all people will be truly 'well born.'" Moya Woodside called for a focus on African Americans in North Carolina, given their tendency to "perpetuate former ways of behaving" and to be "less responsive to new ideas." Her recommendation apparently was followed. Between 1929 and 1940, 78 percent of people approved for sterilization were women, 21 percent of whom were African American. By 1964 black women constituted 65 percent of all women sterilized by the state. "Contrary to common belief," an extraordinary piece of investigative journalism by the *Winston-Salem Journal* in 2002 concluded, "many of the thousands marked for sterilization were ordinary citizens, many of them young women guilty of nothing worse than engaging in premarital sex. The sterilization program ended in 1974, but its legacy will not go away. Many of its victims are still alive and they bear witness to a bureaucracy that trampled on the rights of the poor and the powerless."[54]

For about forty years, beginning in the 1930s, the Eugenics Board of North Carolina sterilized more than seventy-six hundred people. Despite revelations about eugenic malpractice in Germany, the rate of sterilization increased after World War II. According to a review of the case records, acceptable reasons were given for surgery in only 446 cases; these patients or their families consented to the decision. For the most part the medical rationale was flimsy, the moralistic bias explicit: "Pauper, needs close supervision, hypersexuality . . . She wears men's clothing all the time . . . She seems lazy and unconcerned . . . While in school attempted to write love letters to boys she imagined were interested in her."[55]

Social workers, who had the unique authority in North Carolina to authorize sterilization, were committed to eugenic practices. They received no training, no consideration of ethical issues, a former director of a county welfare agency told the Journal. "It was just something you picked up." Welfare workers in the 1960s routinely imposed birth control decisions on their clients: "Enough's enough, she's already had one or two children, let's put a stop to it."[56]

While California's eugenics leaders quietly closed down the Human Betterment Foundation and later destroyed incriminating correspondence with Nazi racial scientists, their counterparts in North Carolina created the Human Betterment League in 1947. As in California wealthy right-wing philanthropists bankrolled the nonprofit institute, academics and scientists endorsed its practices, and its leaders promoted aggressive sterilization policies, primarily against African American women.[57]

Not surprisingly, political opposition to government-sponsored sterilization emerged initially from communities of color during the 1970s, led by Puerto Rican organizations in New York, the Committee to End Sterilization Abuse, and the National Women's Health Network. The Black Panther Party, following in the tradition of Du Bois, who had warned African Americans in 1936 to keep a sharp eye on "so-called eugenic sterilization," educated African American women about the abuses of sterilization policies and campaigned to separate sterilization from welfare rights.[58]

California's sterilization policy was not repealed until 1979, after it was revealed that about 140 women, mostly of Mexican heritage, had been sterilized without their consent at USC/Los Angeles County Hospital. The leading obstetrician at this hospital had strong convictions about the need for population control, which he practiced by coercing women during labor or immediately after birth to undergo tubal ligations. And even after repeal of the policy, unauthorized sterilization persisted. Between 2006 and 2010 at least 148 women in California's prisons were sterilized without informed consent and in violation of state regulations.[59]

CIVILIZATION'S HEAVY LIFTING

The eugenic preoccupation with the biology of ability returned in intellectual debates about inequality in the 1980s, with neoconservative and neoliberal intellectuals promoting ideas associated with biological determinism that repudiated government efforts to address structural inequalities of class, gender, and race.

"The egalitarian ideal of contemporary political theory underestimates the importance of the differences that separate human beings," the authors of The Bell Curve assert in a 1994 book that had a significant influence on educational and welfare policies and helped to reverse the modest gains generated by affirmative action. "It fails to come to grips with human variation. It overestimates the ability of political interventions to shape human character and capacities."[60]

Richard Herrnstein and Charles Murray's polemic resonated in policy circles, reinforcing ideas about the genetic roots of inequality and making a case for limiting government's role in social engineering, except as an agent of enforcement and punishment. According to James Q. Wilson, a "variety of public problems" could best be understood as "arising out of a defect in character formation." Liberalism was to blame, the conservative author Shelby Steele argues, for producing a "narcissism of victims." Too much emphasis on structural determinism, the historian Gertrude Himmelfarb claims, "has the effect of belittling the will, ideas, action, and freedoms of individuals." William Bennett, who served as President Reagan's secretary of education, believed that "government, even at its best, can never be more than an auxiliary in the development of a free people's moral disposition and character." Marvin Olasky, an author and editor whose ideas about "compassionate conservatism" and faith-based charity influenced Republican welfare policies in the twenty-first century, yearned for the good old days when social services relied on "small-scale, personal involvement, rather than large-scale administered relief" and when "enforcing work among the able-bodied was not seen as oppressive."[61]

This revival of right-wing ideology, which shaped Donald Trump's emerging public views in the 1980s, had much more in common with the coercive interventionism of early-twentieth-century nation building than with George W. Bush's era of "compassionate conservatism" or the efforts of today's libertarian reformers to reduce the scope of the carceral state. Trump's ideas about the uniqueness of "American civilization" echo Teddy Roosevelt's argument in 1902 that the U.S. military in the Philippines represented "the triumph of civilization over forces which stand for the black chaos of savagery and barbarism." Trump's mantra of "America First"—"from this day forward," he announced in his inaugural address, "it's going to be only America first"—was articulated during World War I when the national security state was forged and the Right made dissent unpatriotic. His attack on "welfare dependency," "an explosion of out-of-wedlock births," a "food stamp crime wave," and the "nanny-state agenda" was lifted from the politics of Margaret Thatcher. Trump's assertion that American detention centers are "resort-like accommodations" that "coddle illegal aliens" is rooted in a long history of nativist xenophobia.[62]

Trump revealed his eugenic impulse in his views about the "big social issue" of crime and how he framed carceral policies as a matter of national defense. Whether he is ranting about "wolf packs roaming the streets," the "overwhelming amount of violent crime going on in the inner cities right now," or "crime-infested" neighborhoods responsible for "this American carnage," he leaves no doubt that the "crazed misfits" he evokes are primarily African American and Latino youth who, in his view, either regress to animal-like behavior or deliberately break the bonds of civilized society. "Sadly," Trump noted in 2013, "the overwhelming amount of violent crime in our major cities is committed by blacks and Hispanics—a tough subject, must be discussed."[63]

When Trump linked himself with "civilization's heavy lifters," he was carrying on a long tradition of carceral liberalism, from the Progressive reformers who rounded up uppity working-class kids and came down harder and harder on wayward women to the nativists who pursued ethnic cleansing through selective sterilization and right-wing criminologists in the 1980s who described black and brown "habitual offenders" in apocalyptic terms as "public enemy #1."[64]

While this tendency has dominated the ideology of top-down reform, a leftist tradition rooted in a grassroots politics fights for structural reforms and recognizes that a society in which inequality rules will not easily bend to the arc of justice.

7

RADICAL VISIONS

How the arrested, incarcerated, and humiliated find
solace in each other, make do under the worst of conditions,
and contribute their ideas and imagination to the world.

While there is a lower class I am in it, and while there is a criminal element I am of it, and while there's a soul in prison I am not free.
—Eugene Victor Debs, "My Prison Creed"

GRAY ZONE

Social control institutions in the United States, as I have shown, can be a
brutalizing experience, authoritarian and relentless in their drive to cat-
egorize, separate, and demoralize large groups of people on the basis of
their class origins, citizenship status, sexual preference, gender, and racial identities. These institutions produce and organize a prodigious waste
of human ability and potential, and they embody "things unbelievable and
monstrous," as Jack London summed up his experiences in New York's
Erie County Penitentiary in 1894.

Many of the millions of people who have been on the receiving end of
brutal police tactics, red-baiting and blacklisting, petty arrests and stream-
lined judicial injustice, dehumanized jails and prisons, deportation and
detention, coercive medical interventions, humiliating welfare policies,
and sexual banishment never recover from what the Socialist Party leader
Eugene V. Debs once described as "a vast sepulcher in which the living
dead had been sequestered." From loss of jobs and premature deaths to

loss of sanity and unquenchable rage, contact with criminal justice operations leaves a deep wound on the human body and body politic.[1]

At the same time the carceral state can be extraordinarily ineffective and counterproductive, and in the areas it overlooks or ignores, in its "in-between spaces," all kinds of surprising creativity, opposition, and resistance grow. Even under the most totalitarian conditions of a concentration camp, as Primo Levi revealed, doomed petty functionaries tried to make lives worth living within a gray zone as "sweepers, kettle washers, night-watchmen, bed smoothers (who exploited to their miniscule advantage the German fixation about bunks made up flat and square), checkers of lice and scabies, messengers, interpreters, assistants' assistants."[2]

In American prisons, where time is watchfully measured and daily routines meticulously prescribed, and where, you would think, there is no room for independent thinking and social action, many people make something out of nothing, manage to survive "in a shaking bad environment without being personally destroyed," in the words of Paul Goodman, and dare to shout out against injustice, organize themselves in protest and resistance, and tackle the nuts and bolts of policy proposals. There are thousands of examples of ingenious resourcefulness, such as the young men in a California reformatory who circumvented the silence rule by learning the "deaf-and-dumb alphabet, formed on the fingers of one hand, and rapped over dinner without making a sound."[3]

This does not mean that all who are arrested and incarcerated are blameless victims or that ideas and actions emanating from grassroots and political activists are inevitably radical or wise. Some people in prison, albeit a small minority, have committed dreadful acts against other citizens. Some parrot and reproduce the assumptions of their keepers, and some have a blind spot when it comes to issues of race, gender, and sexuality. But more often than not they have a point of view and life experiences that enable them to dig deeply into root causes, see human connections between them and us, and imagine a much more egalitarian world. "Beyond these bars," Debs wrote in prison, "I see the stars." To find these perspectives requires excavation and rethinking what constitutes resistance, following Alice Walker's insight about how "our mothers and grandmothers, more often than not anonymously, handed on the creative spark, the seed of the flower they themselves never hoped to see."[4]

MAKING SOMETHING OUT OF NOTHING

The history of social movements—from the revolts by enslaved people and workers who put their bodies on the line for the right to join unions to civil rights activists risking death to gain the right to vote—teaches us that people find ways of organizing themselves, resisting, and fighting back when the odds are heavily stacked against social justice. Nowhere is this more evident than in the totalitarian confines of the prison.

American literature would be greatly diminished if not for the extraordinary contributions of women and men who make carceral institutions into a site of relentless imagination.

Austin Reed's account of his experience as a young African American incarcerated in New York's House of Refuge and Auburn State Prison in the antebellum United States set a high literary standard. This "very unpromising child," according to a reformatory superintendent's assessment, captured what it was like to "pass through the iron gates of sorrow and trouble" and become an exploitable body stripped of rights. "Hard, hard indeed is the convict's allotment. Hard is his food, and hard and rough is his bed, and cold is his cell when he returns to it on a cold winter's night. Ill is his treatment, and hard is his usage."[5]

The prison memoir is such a widespread phenomenon, from dozens of Civil War accounts to Alexander Berkman's *Prison Memoirs of an Anarchist*, Piri Thomas' *Seven Long Times* in Sing Sing, and George Jackson's letters from a *Soledad Brother*, that a book is devoted to a bibliography of the genre and another contains the work of jailhouse journalists who write for in-house prison publications and public media.[6]

Writing in and about the prison experience, an expert in American literature claims, is not a "peripheral cultural phenomenon but something close to the center of our historical experience as a nation-state." The nineteenth-century lyrics of African Americans on chain gangs and plantations were sung well into the twentieth century: "I say get up dead man / Help me carry my row," went the refrain of "Go Down Old Hannah." As one "long-time" man told Bruce Jackson when he visited Texas prisons in the 1960s, "You get worked to death or beat to death. That's why we sang so many of these songs. We would work together and help ourselves as well as help our fellow man."

Prison lyrics permeate popular and commercial culture, articulated in the blues by Leadbelly, Lightnin' Hopkins, Billie Holiday, Bukka White, Bessie Smith, and many others. "Easy Rider" bequeathed us a memory of the guard on horseback in plantation prisons: "I hate to see the rider, when he rides so near, / He so cruel and cold-hearted, boy, these twenty year." Women's blues, Sarah Haley tells us in her history of southern prisons after the defeat of Reconstruction, was a form of "sonic sabotage . . . that provided alternative visions of community and freedom." It was also a statement of defiance, as expressed by Bessie Smith in "Sing Sing Prison Blues": "You can send me up the river or send me to that mean old jail / I killed my man and I don't need no bail."[7]

As for fiction, nonfiction, and poetry, a slew of authors, from the already established to novices, regularly reached mainstream audiences. "They write well," Goodman observes, "these pacifists, blacks, anarchists, free speakers, fighters for justice." Jack London drew upon his experiences in the penitentiary in 1894, after being convicted of "having no fixed abode and no visible means of support," to write stories for *Cosmopolitan* magazine. Agnes Smedley, who did six months in 1918 in New York's Tombs for advocating women's access to birth control information and devices, recalled her experiences in the Sunday supplement to *Call Magazine* in 1920. "In America," she wrote, "we have been carefully taught that we live in a democracy, and we are still waiting for some one to feed us democracy. While waiting, we starve to death or are sent to prison, where we get free food for 15 or 20 years." Kate Richards O'Hare, who served fourteen months in 1919–20 for her antiwar activism, wrote a book based on her experiences in Missouri State Penitentiary that became influential in the penal reform movement.[8]

The anarchist Alexander Berkman did fourteen years for the attempted assassination of the businessman Henry Clay Frick. Berkman's memoir of prison life captured what it was like in 1906 to leave a regimented world—the last year spent in a workhouse where "the slightest motion of the lips is punished with the blackjack or the dungeon"—for anarchic city streets where "eyes are turned on me from every side." Today's survivors of solitary confinement can relate to Berkman's angst when he was around friends and how he got some temporary relief in the anonymity of crowds and in the countryside. When he was indoors, he felt "a sense of suffocation, . . . and I dread the presence of people. It is torture to talk; the sound of voices agonizes me."[9]

When H. L. Mencken became editor of *American Mercury* magazine in 1924, he invited contributions from writers inside. Jim Tully, who was in and out of jail for about five years on vagrancy charges, published fourteen stories in the magazine. "If Jim Tully were a Russian, read in translation," Mencken said, "all the professors would be hymning him." Ernest Booth, who did time in San Quentin, contributed to *American Mercury*, published an autobiography with Alfred A. Knopf, and wrote a play that was turned into a Hollywood movie, *Ladies of the Big House* (1931). Chester Himes, one of the most important African American writers of the twentieth century, "grew to manhood" while in Ohio State Penitentiary: "I was nineteen years old when I went in and twenty-six when I came out." While still a prisoner, he got his earliest stories published in *Esquire*, alongside Ernest Hemmingway and William Faulkner. "To What Red Hell?" was based on a 1930 fire that killed 317 prisoners.[10]

During the Depression authorities cracked down on writers, trying to stop prisoners from earning money from publications and reaching a wide audience with their critiques of prison life. At San Quentin the regular cell searches were "not for narcotics or knives but for manuscripts," a correspondent for *The Nation* reported in 1930. Yet writers kept writing. Robert E. Burns' *I Am a Fugitive from a Georgia Chain Gang* became a popular book and a movie starring Paul Muni in 1932. Malcolm Braly arrived at a young men's reformatory in California in the early 1940s carrying the *Oxford Book of English Verse*, a decision that was as dangerous, he said, as if he had shown up wearing a dress. James Cannon, the head of the Socialist Workers Party, was imprisoned for sixteen months in 1944–45 for violating the Smith Act, which made it illegal even to be a member of a group that advocated the violent overthrow of the government. He made use of his enforced seclusion to send detailed instructions to his comrades, learn German and Spanish, and catch up on his reading of Aristotle, Plato, Thucydides, Euripides, the *Iliad*, and *Odyssey*. During her twenty-eight months in a federal women's reformatory in the early 1950s for her communist politics, Elizabeth Gurley Flynn penned sentimental poetry—"It is early evening; the sun sets in a red-gold glow, / From my prison window I drink in its beauty"—and took notes for her prison memoir published a decade later.[11]

About 120,000 Japanese immigrants and Japanese Americans, rounded up during World War II without trial on suspicion of potential subversion, were sent to special federal institutions, euphemistically called relocation camps, where many prisoners channeled their sorrow into art and literature. Itaru Ina, who seriously considered renouncing his American citizenship, chose haiku as his genre: "I live in a country / without love, / where the roses are red."[12]

When the prison literati were not writing, they were reading, talking, and testifying. Federal prisoner number 21669 acquired a personal library of several hundred books and decorated her cell with artwork. Kate O'Hare complained about the lack of library books for the other prisoners and successfully lobbied the authorities to permit women to get one book a week from the men's library. At Norfolk Prison Colony in Massachusetts in the early 1950s, an almost illiterate Malcolm Little learned how to write to the Nation of Islam by copying every single item and definition from a dictionary that he transformed into an encyclopedia. Through what he called "prison studies," he became a prolific letter writer, articulate speaker, and relentless reader. "Between what I wrote in my tablet, and writing letters, during the rest of my time in prison I would guess I wrote a million words . . . Until I left that prison, in every free moment I had, if I was not reading in the library, I was reading on my bunk. You couldn't have gotten me out of books with a wedge."[13]

In the late 1960s five prisoners in California's Soledad Prison formed the Saturday Morning Study Group, which met for seven weeks and then issued its "Report on a Study of the Central Facility Library." It is a serious investigation, documenting a systematic lack of professionalism: "If a determined effort were under way to suppress reading and to ferment resentment against the library program, it could not be handled in any better manner than present actual library functioning." The group made twenty-six recommendations, from maintenance of an inventory and creation of a waiting list for books in demand to keeping the library open for more hours during evenings and weekends and broadening the scope of books to "include reading material for men whose taste does not run to Westerns, Tarzan adventures, etc." Prison officials ignored the report.[14]

Of course activists talked up their politics while inside. "We talked war and profits, war and profits, war and profits, until the administration was compelled in sheer self-defense to make some attempts to silence us," O'Hare recalled. Yet their talking reached "a wider and more sympathetic audience than ever before." But not only people convicted of political crimes found their voices. In the early 1960s black residents of Mississippi, like Annell Ponder, testified in court about being beaten for trying to register to vote: "I could barely walk. My body was real hard, feeling like metal."[15]

In 1961, when Freedom Riders deliberately filled Mississippi's jails and prisons, they drove their guards crazy with their talk. They took every opportunity in "America's first organized jail-in," a participant recalled, "to explain, to argue, to make jokes about Ol' Jim Crow, to preach philosophy and morality to their jailers, and to sing their never-ending songs about such upsetting subjects as equality and freedom and love."[16]

Elaine Riddick Jessie, an African American woman who was sterilized against her will as a teenager in 1968, not only told her story for a book about North Carolina's sterilization program—"I hide. I hid. I'm sort of still hiding"—but agreed to have her photograph on the front cover and testified about her experience to an investigative committee appointed by the governor: "I'd just turned fourteen, so I didn't know nothing. What was a fourteen-year-old kid going to know about sterilization?" More recently women who experienced harsh medical treatment and abuse in prison also went public with their testimony: Olivia Hamilton shackled as she went through labor and delivery; Maria Taylor raped by a guard; Irma Rodriquez developing a drug habit inside—"I went in for angel dust, but I came out actively using heroin."[17]

RAISING HELL

For seventeen years, from age fourteen until his release from a California prison in 1975, Willie Tate spent less than one hundred days on the streets. His time in juvenile hall, reformatories, and prison made him tough, angry, and apolitical until he came into contact with George Jackson in Tracy. "He knew a lot of things, so I looked up to him. Always studying, always," Tate recalled. From Jackson and other activists Tate learned about racism and the need for unity of prisoners across the color line: "We can all live and bloom in the sun."[18]

Contemporary political activism in prison usually is associated with political rebellions led by African Americans such as Willie Tate during and after the civil rights movement. Muslim prisoners in the 1950s demanded the right to hold religious meetings, study the Koran, and receive visits from ministers. From his jail cell in Alabama, Martin Luther King called for nonviolent, direct action against segregation, urging activists to be "extremists for the cause of justice." The killing of George Jackson by guards in San Quentin on August 21, 1971, triggered his subsequent commemoration by the prison movement as a martyr of liberation, and his demonization by prison authorities as the epitome of criminal dangerousness. The rebellion in Attica a few weeks later led to a slaughter and political cover-up that still resonates as a historical turning point. "Attica! Attica!" shouted Al Pacino's character in the 1975 movie *Dog Day Afternoon*.[19]

These strikes, protests, and rebellions in U.S. prisons in the 1960s and 1970s echoed events a century earlier. The mostly white Civil War veterans who made up the majority of prisoners in the North in the 1870s "did not check their memories of war, or their war-making skills, at the prison gates," the historian Rebecca McLennan writes. They brought "a robust sense of themselves as citizen-soldiers who had risked life and limb in the causes of freedom and national reunification," and they believed that, even in prison, their service to the country "had earned them the full dues of republican manhood and citizenship." As prison contractors tried to squeeze every last bit of profit from prisoners working in mines, factories, and mills, prisoner-laborers put up a fierce fight: protesting poor food and taking hostages in Missouri State Prison in 1874, then striking against labor conditions in Sing Sing in 1877, the Massachusetts state prison in 1882, and in Trenton, New Jersey, in 1890. Large-scale riots sparked by inadequate food, beatings, and efforts to increase the rate of production were widespread, with prisoners often acting like a labor union: forging solidarity, issuing a list of demands, and appointing negotiators.[20]

Black men and women leased out to mines and plantations in Florida, Georgia, Alabama, Mississippi, and South Carolina cleared a gray zone in their autocratic environment and regularly struck for better food and against the whip. In response to a strike at Rising Fawn Mines in Georgia in 1884, the governor dispatched the militia to starve the prisoners into submission. At the Milledgeville State Prison in Atlanta in 1900, prisoners burned down the women's camp quarters. Sabotage, arson, and attempting to escape were common in women's convict camps. "Disobeying

1. Social control takes many forms: Carlisle Indian School, 1884, is designed to forcibly strip thousands of Native children of their tribal identities.

2. Carlisle Indian School, 1892, bans Native languages, ceremonies, and clothing in effort to carry out cultural erasure.

ONLY *HEALTHY* SEED
MUST BE SOWN!

CHECK THE SEEDS OF
HEREDITARY DISEASE AND
UNFITNESS BY EUGENICS

ISSUED BY THE EUGENICS SOCIETY 69 ECCLESTON SQUARE LONDON SW1

3. International poster, c. 1930, promotes eugenics. In the name of "human betterment," hundreds of thousands of women in the United States are sterilized without consent.

4. Tule Lake Segregation Center, California, 1945: one of ten institutions where 120,000 Japanese immigrants and Japanese Americans are "relocated" without trial during World War II.

5. Border Patrol detention center, McAllen, Texas, June 2018. During the last decade, millions of immigrants have been detained, incarcerated, and deported.

6. Detroit, 1937. Local police all over the country take the side of factory owners against striking workers.

7. Police confront social worker Guadalupe Marshall and kill ten striking steelworkers at the Memorial Day Massacre in Chicago, 1937.

8. Activists who protest anti-Japanese repression during World War II are rousted by federal agents at Tule Lake Segregation Center, c. 1945.

9. Chicago police in 1969 carry the body of Black Panther Party leader Fred Hampton, a killing that was part of a nationwide campaign to destroy the African American political organization.

10. U. S. military uses the "water cure" (waterboarding) to torture prisoners during Philippine-American War, c. 1900s.

11. "Tiger cages" in Con Sao, Vietnam, where political activists are incarcerated and tortured in underground prison cells during the Vietnam War, 1964-1973.

12. Abu Ghraib prison, Iraq, c. 2004, where U.S. military routinely humiliated and tortured prisoners.

13. A corporal abuses a prisoner at Abu Ghraib, c. 2004. She is later convicted of a crime, while her superiors go free.

14. Mexican braceros being trucked to work camp in Hidalgo, Texas, 1956.

15. Civil rights activists being trucked to jail in Jackson, Mississippi, 1965.

16. Cotton pickers at Huntsville, Texas, prison farm, 1968, part of a hundred-year-old system of brutal exploitation.

17. Prisoner worked to exhaustion in Huntsville, 1968.

18. Teenage civil rights activists incarcerated without trial in Leesburg Stockade, Georgia, 1963.

19. Waiting for food stamps, 1939.

20. Waiting for unemployment benefits, 2007.

21. Waiting for court to open, 2015.

22. "Let us not be guilty of maudlin sympathy for the criminal, who . . . counts upon the compassion of our society and the laxness or weakness of too many courts to forgive his offense." (Dwight D. Eisenhower, July 15, 1964)

23. "For all of our people, we will set as our goal the decent order that makes progress possible and our lives secure." (Richard M. Nixon, January 20, 1969)

24. "There is crime to be conquered, the rough crime of the streets." (George H. W. Bush, January 20, 1989)

25. "There is work to do: . . . coming out from behind locked doors and shuttered windows to help reclaim our streets from drugs and gangs and crime." (Bill Clinton, January 20, 1997)

26. "The proliferation of prisons, however necessary, is no substitute for hope and order in our souls." (George W. Bush, January 20, 2001)

27. "The American carnage stops right here and stops right now." (Donald J. Trump, January 20, 2017)

28. President Trump, with leaders of Fraternal Order of Police, 2017, promises to "back the badge."

29. Voter rights activists arrested for lawful protest in Atlanta, 1963.

30. Elise Greene confronts an officer in Charlotte, North Carolina, 2016, after the killing of Keith Lamont Scott by police.

31. Police take back the streets in Charlotte, North Carolina, 2016, after protests of police killing.

rules and impudence," Sarah Haley observes, "were frequent charges leveled against black women."[21]

Activists, such as the journalist Ida B. Wells and Mary Church Terrell, took up the cause of the lynched, and of women and men being worked to death or close to death on plantations, in mines, and on chain gangs, spreading the word that the free and unfree had good reason to join forces: there but for the grace of God go we. Terrell crossed the color line by pointing out how poor whites were also being forced into exploitation. "The connection between disenfranchisement and peonage," she wrote in 1907, "is intimate and close."[22]

Young Native American women and men forcibly removed to boarding schools also found all kinds of ways to resist, subvert, and disrupt the authorities. When roundups took place on reservations, they would hide or leave the area, often with the complicity of their families. Once in the schools, they had, in the words of a superintendent in 1886, a "pernicious habit of running away" and heading home. Mysterious fires were so commonplace that arson, as well as shabby construction, was suspected. Passive resistance in the form of work slowdowns, silence, and pranks drove some teachers away. When the superintendent of Keams Canyon School locked Hopi boys in a dormitory at night without toilets, they decided, as one former student remembered, to "just crap all over the floor." In violation of regulations students secretly spoke their birth languages and passed on stories and folktales. What teachers considered nonresponsiveness actually disguised the students' active efforts at cultural preservation. "Maybe you think I believe you," wrote a Navajo boy in the 1930s. "But always my thoughts stay with me / My own way."[23]

In the early twentieth century, labor organizers, anarchists, pacifists, socialists, and feminists went to jail and prison in significant numbers, mostly for prohibited speech and trumped-up charges of disorderly conduct and violations of public order. Many organized themselves and other prisoners while doing time and sharpened their commitment to the causes that brought them to prison. Ernestine Hara Kettler, who was arrested in 1917 with other members of the Woman's Party for picketing the White House during the suffrage campaign, recalled how her group "cooked up our political prisoner demands," including refusing to work in the Occoquan Workhouse in Virginia. Their resistance was contagious, spreading to nonpolitical prisoners in the sewing room. The activists, the *New York*

Times noted, "gave their custodians a lively time." When they were moved to another jail, the protests continued. "We raised so much hell. We had all kinds of notoriety," one told the paper.[24]

In another prison Kate O'Hare was so disgusted by the "dead, rancid odor" in the dining room, having to share tables with "well established cockroach families," and having to tolerate the encrusted filth in the bathrooms that she smuggled out a letter of protest to the local press. As a result of this publicity the dining room was cleaned and given a coat of paint, and showers were installed in the bathrooms.

Prisoners are not saints. O'Hare revealed class snobbery when she touted her political comrades as "superior [to] the common mass." Socialists, she claimed, brought with them to prison their "education, culture, scientific knowledge of human psychology, a clear understanding of the economic forces that so largely shape human life, and a saving sense of humor. So, for the first time in the history of our country, our penal system has been studied by convicts enduring it who had intellectual background, sympathetic understanding, scientific training, and actual experience on which to base conclusions."[25]

Some activists, however, found that their background and training were their undoing. O'Hare, who proudly identified herself as a committed socialist and went to prison in 1917 for speaking out against U.S. involvement in the war, was also a committed racist, standing with "the defeated Southerners" who during Reconstruction felt "the stinging disgrace of having ignorant blacks placed in positions of power and authority over them." O'Hare assured her readers that socialism did not mean "Nigger Equality" and that the only solution to the "race question" was segregation. Moreover, incarceration did not in every case fortify activists' ideological convictions. Some political prisoners were so intimidated by witnessing other feminists being badly beaten in prison that they questioned their own commitment. Kettler acknowledged that she "just wasn't courageous enough to go back again. I felt horrified by the different things that could happen to you in prison."[26]

Many political activists used their time inside to think and write about penal issues, often with sharp insights and an observant eye for detail. To O'Hare prisons combined "the slave, the feudal, and the capitalist systems at their worst" and were characterized by "stupidities, cruelties, and barbarities." After leaving the Missouri penitentiary she remained active in the prison reform movement and in 1938 became the assistant director of the California Department of Penology. In 1943 Governor Earl Warren recognized her contribution to the field and appointed her to join the state crime commission, on which she served until her death in 1948.[27]

Of all the leftists who were imprisoned before World War II, Gene Debs was among the most thoughtful and most engaged by his experience. His four years in county jails, a state prison, and a federal penitentiary on a variety of charges—from labor activism and contempt of court to seditiously advocating resistance to the draft—gave him a deep understanding of the carceral state. A lifelong socialist, he ran four times for the presidency on the Socialist Party ticket. He waged his 1920 campaign from the Atlanta Federal Penitentiary and received nearly 920,000 votes. He developed a close affinity with his fellow nonpolitical prisoners whom he regarded as "not the irretrievably vicious and depraved element they are commonly believed to be, but upon average they are like ourselves." He never forgot his first incarceration in the Cook County Jail, where he heard women sobbing and screaming in their cells; he declared, "I was not one whit better than they." He made a point of listening to prisoners' grievances, helped them when he could, and in return he experienced nothing but "personal kindliness" from men who demonstrated "an unselfish desire to give rather than receive," setting "an example that might well be followed by some people who never saw the inside of prison walls."

When Debs left prison in Atlanta in 1920, the prisoners staged a massive, spontaneous demonstration of solidarity. He was deeply touched. "I had shared with them on equal terms in all things and they knew it and loved me as I loved them." As he walked out of the prison, he heard a "roar of voices" cheering him on his way, "an overwhelming, bewildering scene, without a parallel in prison history." After his release he not only wrote about his experiences in prison but also spoke out against society's "burning shame" and developed some innovative suggestions, which he set out in a chapter, "How I Would Manage the Prison," in his 1927 book, *Walls and Bars*.[28]

During the postwar McCarthy era, dozens of leading communists were incarcerated. A few years later they were replaced by thousands of activists from the civil rights, black liberation, and antiwar movements, most of whom had been arrested for nonpolitical crimes and became politicized while incarcerated. Malcolm X was originally arrested for burglary, George

Jackson for robbery. A literary outpouring reminiscent of the 1920s and 1930s began in the early 1960s. Memoirs and political critiques reached millions of readers with a message that Debs had tried but failed to get most people to heed: the need to create close ties between prison and community and to understand that those inside and outside the carceral state share a common humanity.

An older generation of activists continued to write about their experience as political prisoners. Elizabeth Gurley Flynn, who did twenty-eight months in the 1950s under the Smith Act, was a well-known Communist Party cadre. After her release, getting prison out of "her heart and mind" took a long time. She remembered the parting words of her sister prisoners: "Don't forget us. Tell the world about this place." And she did, writing a book about her time in Alderson, a federal prison in West Virginia, that was published in 1963. Long before solitary confinement became a commonplace punishment in American prisons, Flynn called for its use only in exceptional circumstances. "Seclusion seemed as about effective as putting a child in a dark closet," she wrote. Flynn felt uncomfortable around lesbians in prison and worried that dormitories had become "seedbeds of degeneracy," but she was particularly insightful about the dynamics of race, how "the tragedies of Negro Americans were keenly felt even in prison: segregation, discrimination, racist ideas of white supremacy, a lack of equality. Like a cancer it gnawed at their lives everywhere." The black women she got to know were "from farms or workers from cities, hard-working women, more solid in character and sober in mind than many of their Northern city sisters." When a young white woman objected to sharing a cell with a black woman, Flynn intervened and mediated the conflict. "When I returned home I missed the many Negro women, who were my friends in Alderson," she said.

Like Debs, Flynn regarded penal institutions as an archaic relic of the backward past, unscientific as well as unnecessarily cruel. She called for closing down Alderson prison, built in 1927 as the first federal women's prison, declaring, "The women there, in the main, need hospitals, sanitariums, rest homes, training schools, psychiatric treatment—not a prison." Here Flynn shared reformist ideas about the need to develop medical and psychological programs, but, unlike her liberal colleagues, she was not so much interested in expanding as replacing prisons.[29]

Another communist, Mort Sobell, was convicted of conspiracy to commit espionage in 1951. Unlike his codefendants, Julius and Ethel Rosenberg, who were executed, he was sent to prison for more than eighteen years, including five years in Alcatraz. On his release he felt paralyzed, as had Alexander Berkman, by the "freedom which lay within my grasp—but was not yet mine. A prison mentality cannot be discarded overnight; a slave is not freed by a proclamation." For years he felt "tight inside" and a need to keep his everyday life under "absolute control." But, unlike most former long-term prisoners, he was lucky to return to a loving family and friends and to have skills and contacts that enabled him to write a book about his years inside. Moreover, as he put it, "1969 was a good year in which to come back to free society." By then civil rights, antiwar, feminist, and student activists were on the march, shedding the anxieties and fear that permeated the Left in the 1950s. On his first ride on the New York subway, Sobell was surprised and glad to see that African Americans no longer "held their heads bowed, as if in perpetual submission. Now they all rode heads erect, proudly looking ahead. It made me feel better than anything else could, to be a part of this scene."[30]

A new generation of activists emerged, expressing their rage and critiques in a much more eclectic and anarchic form, eclipsing the voices of the Old Left, with whom they had little dialogue. No longer bound by political and organizational dogma, the new prison movement was "a coalition of the unruly." As participants in the social movements of the 1960s battled police and troops, joined nonpolitical prisoners in the jails and prisons, and exposed the political bias of the legal system, the esoteric field of criminology became the subject of news headlines, television specials, literary critiques, bestselling autobiographies, and investigations by reporters. The prison once again became a central site of this literary renaissance.[31]

Martin Luther King's *Letter from Birmingham Jail*, in which he made a case for nonviolent resistance to racism, was first published in 1963 and later reprinted in hundreds of editions and anthologies. Several white northerners who went to the South as part of Freedom Summer in 1964 told their tales of first-time imprisonment. Sally Belfrage, who had grown up with "a child's faith in law," quickly learned about what it was like to feel "immobilized, responsibility gone, at the mercy of someone's tender sadistic care." Barbara Deming was jailed in 1963, also in Birmingham, for walking on the sidewalk with a sign around her neck proclaiming ALL

MEN ARE BROTHERS. Later she was jailed for a few weeks in Albany, Georgia, where she tested her belief in nonviolent, civil disobedience by joining other activists on a fast. With Debs her inspiration, she, too, did not feel free while a single soul was in prison. Deming returned home to the east coast a few weeks later and committed herself to the politics and tactics that had propelled her into the civil rights movement. "We tried in Albany, however clumsily," she recalled in an eloquently written, introspective memoir, "to act out the truth that all men are kin to one another. As the drama ended it was we ourselves, inevitably, who felt the truth of it most sharply—and felt it hard to simply take our leave."[32]

Bob Martinson, who would become my colleague at Berkeley's School of Criminology, also traveled across the country to put his body on the line and ended up, to his surprise, in Mississippi's Parchman prison rather than a local lockup. His rough ride from the Jackson city jail to the state penitentiary was similar to the one that killed Freddie Gray, Jr., in a Baltimore police van in April 2015, except Martinson did not die. "Our trip was a nightmare of jolts, sudden stops, and screaming sirens." In the penitentiary he put his research skills to use, doing an informal survey of his comrades' backgrounds and keeping notes for an article that was published in *The Nation*. He reported that even under the "almost hopeless conditions" of Parchman, a democratic spirit prevailed among the prisoners: they set a regular time for debates and arguments about tactics, passed motions laboriously from cell to cell, took votes, and unanimously agreed to engage in acts of resistance, from violations of petty rules to grand acts of defiance. When they took time to relax, they fashioned chess pieces out of bread. Rather than destroy the Freedom Riders, their stay in Parchman emboldened them—"it educated the ignorant and trained the naïve"—and taught them "the only chain a man can stand / Is the chain of hand in hand."[33]

Movement leaders, intellectuals, and journalists reached millions of readers with radical ideas about prisons, crime, and justice. Malcolm X's autobiography was issued as a paperback soon after his assassination in 1965, the same year that Claude Brown's account of his experience in juvenile reformatories was published. In 1968 Eldridge Cleaver and Bobby Seale recounted the history of the Black Panther Party in, respectively, *Soul on Ice* and *Seize the Time*. George Jackson's letters from prison were first published in the *New York Review of Books* in 1970 in the same month that his *Soledad Brother* came out. Its introduction was by Jean Genet, the formerly imprisoned French writer, who recognized a kindred spirit of rebellion and "the special odor and texture of what was written in a cell, behind walls, guards, envenomed by hatred." The revolt at Attica generated a flurry of books, including Samuel Melville's correspondence, published in 1971, a year after he was killed in the prison massacre. *Kind and Usual Punishment* (1973), by the well-known writer and activist Jessica Mitford, effectively translated the demands of the prison movement for a broad audience.[34]

The prison letter became a popular literary genre: James Blake's correspondence was published in the *Paris Review* and *Esquire* before it became a well-received book; the journalist Eve Pell edited letters written to lawyers from California's maximum-security prisoners, including James Ralph Williamson's pledge "to do our bit—writing, drawing, talking—coming out from under *our* way, in whatever way we can." Piri Thomas, who did "seven long times" in Sing Sing and Comstock prisons, where he got too used to the "monotone sounds" of guards beating prisoners, wrote a powerful memoir of how he transformed himself from "once a con, always a con" to "once a human, always a human."[35]

In 1971 the collective autobiography of the New York Twenty-One, members of the Black Panther Party who had been tried and acquitted of planning attacks on police stations, was published as *Look for Me in the Whirlwind*. That same year an influential anthology of "voices of resistance" reached a huge audience with statements from and about political prisoners, including James Baldwin's memorable "open letter to my sister, Angela Davis," which expressed solidarity "with the numberless prisoners in our concentration camps" and called upon readers to defend political activists: "For, if they take you in the morning, they will be coming for us that night." A decade later Norman Mailer helped another "state-raised convict" get his letters into print—"I love Jack Abbott for surviving and for having learned to write as well as he does"—and supported his short-lived release from prison. Abbott was convicted of manslaughter and returned to prison in 1982, where twenty years later he committed suicide.[36]

Although African Americans were the most prominent authors to draw upon their experiences in prison, others made important contributions. John Irwin, who did five years in Soledad Prison for armed robbery in the 1950s, received his doctoral degree in sociology from Berkeley in 1968, drew upon his experiences inside for his first book, coauthored an important policy report for the American Friends Service Committee, and became active in educational programs for former prisoners. As New Left antiwar activists increasingly found themselves in court and prison, they, too, wrote about their experiences. On any given day in the late 1960s, about three hundred Vietnam War resisters were in federal prisons for evading the draft and acts of civil disobedience. Howard Levy, a physician in the army who served twenty-six months in prison for refusing an order to train Special Forces, and David Miller, who did twenty-two months for burning his draft card, documented their experiences and spoke up for all prisoners' rights, as did many other activists who for the first time in their lives experienced incarceration.[37]

The movement exposed every aspect of criminal justice operations to scrutiny and debate. What usually happens in secret, such as everyday prison life, or in the decorous atmosphere of a courtroom that "demands an absolute conformity to its rules," was fair game for critiques and ridicule. A defendant in the Chicago Seven case, Tom Hayden wrote one of many influential accounts of the sensational 1969 trial (they were charged with conspiracy to riot), during which the Black Panther leader Bobby Seale was bound, gagged, and chained to a chair in the courtroom for demanding the right to defend himself. The defendants wanted to be recognized as political prisoners in much the same way that a decade later Bobby Sands and other IRA hunger strikers challenged British rule in Northern Ireland.[38]

Not only the arrested and convicted told their stories. Several state functionaries committed professional suicide by documenting exposés of government malpractice. Arkansas governor Winthrop Rockefeller hired Tom Murton, with whom I had attended graduate school at Berkeley, to reform the brutal Cummins State Prison Farm, but Murton was quickly fired when he took the job too seriously, doing his best to abolish corporal punishment and investigate suspicious deaths of prisoners that occurred before his appointment. According to Murton, Rockefeller "tried to lend credence to the fiction that reform has really taken place without the agony of revolution. It can't be done." According to Rockefeller, Murton was "totally incapable of and insensitive to the requirements of operating in harmony with his associates in a governmental structure." Murton never worked in corrections again, but he spoke out against life imprisonment as a slow death sentence, and his 1969 memoir inspired the film *Brubaker*.[39]

An ex-FBI agent, William Turner, went public with his inside stories about J. Edgar Hoover. Another ex-agent, Robert Wall, explained in the *New York Review of Books* how the FBI operated as a "relentless guardian of orthodoxy" and was "all too effective in harassing legitimate political activity." In 1975, long before Edward Snowden brought light to the shadowy world of American intelligence operations, Philip Agee published an exposé about his work in the CIA.[40]

Some longtime criminal justice functionaries fought the inevitable disengagement and cynicism that became part of the job. William Nagel used his experience as a corrections administrator to call for a moratorium on the building of new prisons in the 1970s. Carroll Bud Picket, a prison chaplain in Texas, witnessed ninety-five executions, which changed his attitude toward the death penalty. "People don't realize that you never get over it, unless you're just cold and calculated. I'll never forget it. Not a day goes by. Not a day goes by."[41]

Poets, too, seized the moment to capture the dread, monotony, and sweetness of prison life. Paul Mariah became a leading figure in gay literature after his release from prison, and Norma Stafford's poems drew upon her roots in rural Tennessee and a California prison, where "I earned my Ph.D. from Hell." William Wantling's experience under San Quentin's "sun-stricken gun-towers" figured prominently in his published work, and Jimmy Santiago Baca made use of his four years in solitary, additional years in maximum security, and shock treatments to bring readers face to face with men inside—"the young eyes scared and the old eyes / tarnished like peeling boat hulls." Etheridge Knight survived his impoverished childhood in Mississippi and years in Indiana State Prison to win the American Book Award for poetry and a nomination for the Pulitzer Prize. "I died in Korea from a shrapnel wound and narcotics resurrected me," he reflected. "I died in 1960 from a prison sentence and poetry brought me back to life." Gwendolyn Brooks, who received a Pulitzer in 1950, greeted Knight's prison poems as "freed and terrible and beautiful."[42]

In the early 1970s young men at the Norfolk Prison Colony wrote essays, fiction, poetry, and plays, and directed and performed two productions inside the prison. There, two decades earlier, Malcolm Little became Malcolm X as he was exposed to group discussions, debates, lectures from university professors, and a massive library in which "I read aimlessly, until I learned to read selectively, with a purpose." By 1971 African Americans constituted 3 percent of Massachusetts' population and almost 40 percent of Norfolk's. "They are my brothers, they are my sons, they are my students, and in a very real sense, they are also my teachers," wrote their drama instructor, Elma Lewis, founder of the National Center of Afro-American Artists in Boston (she was named a MacArthur Foundation Fellow in 1981). She thanked her prisoner-students for teaching her to imagine "the development of alternatives."[43]

ALTERNATIVES

People have a tendency to think of the subjects of the carceral state as either aberrant monsters or pitiable victims, beaten down into nothingness or salvageable only if uplifted by agents of good works. This one-dimensional view hides other experiences that tell a different story. How, for example, Chinese laborers, driven out of their communities by ruthless campaigns of ethnic cleansing in the late nineteenth century, and reduced to a faceless mass in twentieth-century popular literature, hired lawyers to pursue criminal complaints and file civil cases against local and regional governments and their former employers. How, in the early twentieth century, a small Indian tribe in northern California, missing from the history books, enlisted a high-powered law firm to successfully defend their right to own land, force the University of California to return human remains it had plundered, and make a public school admit Native American children. How impoverished rural white prisoners faced down forced sterilization in Oklahoma in the 1930s by successfully pleading their case before the U.S. Supreme Court. How an Indian coalition that occupied Alcatraz from November 1969 to June 1971, triggering the rise of the Red Power movement, took time to develop a proposal for turning the island into a museum that would tell a history of genocide and resistance and depict "cultural contributions we have given to all the world." How poor black, Puerto Rican, and white women joined forces to create the Welfare Rights Organization in the 1960s and demand welfare as a political right rather than a rite of degradation.[44]

The carceral state has been the site of extraordinary creative output, riots, and protests, as well as an opportunity for the politically committed to deepen their dedication to social justice. It also has generated a wide variety of ideas about how to change, and in some cases eliminate, penal institutions. This perspective tends to be neglected and overshadowed by the professionals and philanthropists who dominate the discourse of reform. Unlike managerial reforms, which are designed to enforce inequality more effectively, and liberal reforms, which are designed to either expand networks of socialization beyond the prison or smooth power's rough edges, structural reforms are ground-up initiatives that seek to both improve conditions of everyday life and challenge established political-economic systems. They call for decentralization of decision-making authority, restrictions on existing institutions of governance, and expansion of popular power. This radical tradition not only draws attention to existing inequalities but also imagines utopian forms of justice and social relationships. It, too, has a long history and is associated with proposals that range from the incremental and mundane to the ambitious and visionary.[45]

Early-twentieth-century socialists gave considerable thought to how to change prisons as well as raising the desirability of their abolition. O'Hare took herself seriously as a prison reformer. She did interviews with other prisoners and compiled an extensive file of case histories that prison officials did not allow her to keep when she was released. This did not stop her, however, from speaking publicly about prison conditions and advocating a variety of specific proposals. She recognized that the prison as an institution is "a violation of every normal urge of human life," that "social justice is never handed down from above by a ruling class," and that it is not possible to reform what she labeled a cesspool. She nevertheless felt a responsibility to "patch up what we have so that it will operate with as little friction and waste of human life as possible, while we are building the machinery of the new order." With this in mind she proposed ending the leasing of prisoners to "vampires that suck dry the vitality of our prison population"; hiring professionally trained and well-paid staff to replace the "human misfits and failures, and generally illiterate human scrubs" who work in prisons because they are "too worthless for other employment"; replacing most prisons with hospitals, farms, and factories regulated by the state; and setting up a national prison commission to develop alternative programs. "The prison as we know it today," she wrote in 1923, "must go."[46]

When Debs got out of prison, he, too, wrote a book on the topic and weighed in with his ideas about prison reform. He took what today we would call an abolitionist stance, associated with the exploration by Angela Davis and grassroots activists of "new terrains of justice," namely an ideal society in which prisons do not play a significant part. "The prison as a rule, to which there are few exceptions, is for the poor," comparable to the mills and mines that grind up human labor, Debs wrote in 1926. "It ought not merely to be reformed but abolished as an institution for the punishment and degradation of unfortunate human beings."[47]

Debs was a practical man who knew that abolition was a journey that first required small and then bigger steps. He questioned the absurdity of regulations that required prisoners to "cheerfully obey all rules" and refrain from singing or whistling. He objected to the prison's poor management—"there is little method and no system"—and observed how "the guard and inmate cease to be human beings when they meet in prison." He called for removing prisons from political control, turning over governance to civil service appointees, and not only disarming the guards but replacing them with prisoners who would take care of everyday operations on the "basis of mutuality of interest and self-government." Decades later the Black Panther Party would make a similar proposal for how the police should be governed. Debs conceded that it might be necessary for the prison to hire a few professionals and specialists, but for the most part jobs "could and should be filled by inmates," accountable to a democratically controlled prisoner council. He volunteered to implement his ideas without pay, promising to return prisoners to society "in a different spirit and appreciably nearer rehabilitation than is now done or possible." Nobody took him up on his offer.[48]

Socialists and the next generation of activists shared some common ground with liberal reformers, especially in demands to alleviate suffering and defend legal rights. But, unlike liberal reformers, they were more likely to link the everyday with the systemic, the practical with the ideal, the short term with the long term, and appreciate that a truly humane carceral system is an oxymoron. This rift between liberal and radical politics widened in the 1960s.

For a decade the prison cell was an outpost of a broader agenda for social and economic equality. Southern jails and prisons, as exemplified in Martin Luther King's 1963 call to action, had long been a site of civil disobedience and protest. "Injustice anywhere is a threat to justice every-where," King wrote from Birmingham's jail. "Freedom is never voluntarily given by the oppressor; it must be demanded by the oppressed." Through-out the rest of the country many prisoners incarcerated for nonpolitical crimes followed Malcolm Little's example as he transformed himself from a "ghetto-created Negro" to Malcolm X, a "black man something worth-while," determined to "destroy the racist cancer that is malignant in the body of America."[49]

What is popularly known as the sixties actually began quite a bit ear-lier. The civil rights movement had its roots in the determination of Afri-can American veterans of World War II to make racial democracy a reality in the United States, not just in postfascist Europe. The prison revolts of 1971, now associated with the death of George Jackson and with Attica, had been simmering for about twenty years. Between 1950 and 1953 riots occurred at more than fifty prisons. "Crowding, communism, lack of work, [and] sex repressions" were to blame for prisoners' activism claimed the *U.S. News & World Report.* Mostly spontaneous and triggered by a specific incident, prisoners protested against intolerable long-term conditions re-lating to food, work, and health care. During a takeover at Jackson State Prison in Michigan in April 1952, prisoners made modest demands: humane guards to work with the mentally and physically disabled; an end to brutal restraints used on prisoners; decent dental care; and a much di-luted version of what Debs had called for, an elected prisoners' council to confer periodically with prison officials. All these demands were rejected, and prison officials also reneged on their promise not to carry out reprisals against strike leaders.[50]

The new cadre of activists owed a great deal to Malcolm X's example, whereas Debs was mostly forgotten. An eventual success for some pris-oners in the 1950s was the demand for religious freedom made by Afri-can American Muslims. Although it was a one-issue campaign, their discipline, organization, and purposefulness served as a model for radi-cal organizing in the 1960s, even after Muslims' influence inside prisons waned following the assassination of Malcolm X and the split within the Nation of Islam.[51]

Until the Attica revolt in 1971, California was the center of prison and antipolice activism. Prisoners at San Quentin, Soledad, Folsom, and the California Institution for Women protested poor food, unpaid labor, harassment by guards, and the use of strip cells as a prison-within-a-prison where activists were denied clothes, books, and recreation and were forced to sleep on a thin mattress. "The mass of convicts both black and white," a local newspaper reported in February 1967, "were seething with grievances that crossed race lines." Many of these grievances involved the ideology and practice of rehabilitation, both in its failure to deliver on promises and in how it was manipulated to treat social protests as a matter of individual pathology.[52]

By the 1950s California had little use for the prison labor that about seventy years earlier had played a significant role in the state's rapid economic development. With the creation of the California Department of Corrections in 1944 and construction of the California Medical Facility in Vacaville in 1950, the state reorganized its penal system and developed a new rationale for imprisonment, adjusting to the reality that prisons were no longer productive factories. Prisoners were transformed from workers without rights into objects of diagnosis and treatment. What were once dungeons became "adjustment centers." Psychiatric screening, group counseling, and behavior modification supposedly replaced forced, profitable exploitation. The logic of California's indeterminate sentence law was that prisoners, like patients in hospitals, should not be released until healthy or no longer contagious. But rehabilitation was largely a sham. A defining characteristic of the twentieth-century prison, as Michel Foucault mordantly observed, was "not one of teaching prisoners something, but rather to teach them nothing."[53]

Though rehabilitation figured prominently in post–World War II corrections rhetoric, in reality rehabilitative programs reached a small minority of prisoners, and most prisoners regarded with suspicion and hostility what passed for treatment. California's model medical prison in Vacaville experimented with tranquilizers, aversion therapies, and psychosurgery and encouraged prisoners to volunteer as guinea pigs for untested and dangerous drugs. As one critic noted, the result was that treatment was in fact a "more profound mode of punishment" because it cloaked "its repressive practices under the mantle of dispassionate professionalism." An activist prisoner such as George Jackson was unlikely to get released until, as he said, "they see that thing in his eyes, and you can't fake it, resignation and defeat. It must be stamped clearly across the face."[54]

At Soledad Prison in 1967 about one thousand prisoners went on strike to gain improvements in everyday conditions. According to one participant, the guards in the towers responded by shooting around the prisoners until "bedlam struck" and the strikers were "thoroughly impressed." But instead of intimidating prisoners, this show of force emboldened them. For about a year prisoners at San Quentin researched and wrote a lengthy report that they presented to the California State Assembly Criminal Procedures Committee in February 1969. The report begins its analysis of the failure of rehabilitation with philosophical asides and Shakespearean quotes: "What is a man's significance when he must exist in a wallow-hole of almost total frustration? If you prick us, do we not bleed? The villainy you teach me, I will execute." It then goes on to make a lengthy list of proposals, such as ending the indeterminate sentence, implementing due process in disciplinary hearings, and creating an office of ombudsman to investigate prisoners' complaints.[55]

The Folsom Manifesto, issued by striking prisoners in November 1970, similarly raged against the "façade of rehabilitation" and initially demanded that political prisoners be given asylum in progressive and socialist nations. This demand was quickly dropped, and the focus shifted to better health care, more family visits, the right to dissent, working wages for prison labor, abolition of indeterminate sentencing, and an end to teargassing of prisoners in their cells.[56]

Cooperation between longtime and newly politicized activists generated a flurry of prison-related proposals. In 1971 two rival activist organizations in California each published a broadsheet and a list of demands. "We are the first to be accused and the last to be recognized," the California Prisoners' Union said. "Prisons should no longer be dim, gray garrisons designed to isolate human waste," the United Prisoners' Union said. "In that spirit, we demand the restoration of our constitutional and human rights."[57]

The revolt at Attica in September 1971 built upon and incorporated demands made by California prisoners, including application of minimum-wage law, the right to free expression, effective rehabilitation programs, and adequate medical treatment. Politically active prisoners also demanded transfer to "non-imperialist nations." The repression that followed was bloody and unrelenting, but it was also a public spectacle that revealed the world inside to millions who had never so much as visited a prison. For the first time reports by television and print journalists shifted public opinion about prisoners and prisons in a progressive direction, with the men inside revealed as human and courageous and the authorities as inhuman and callous. "We were willing to pay whatever price was necessary," said Frank Smith, a leader of the revolt. "Attica is all of us. Attica is everything."[58]

Revelations about other prisons followed. Danny Lyon, the civil rights photographer, produced a memorable book of photographs about Texas prisons: "I tried with whatever power I had to make a picture of imprisonment as distressing as I knew it to be in reality." While serving a forty-year sentence at the Louisiana State Penitentiary at Angola, Wilbert Rideau started writing poems—"that's what the average prisoner does"—then wrote for magazines (including *Penthouse*) and with coeditor Billy Sinclair transformed the prison newspaper, *The Angolite*, into a widely respected publication that received national awards. Thus they were able to "chip away at the monstrous image the public has conceived of us."[59]

Based on their experience as conscientious objectors during the Vietnam War, Howard Levy and David Miller called for a variety of reforms that would benefit all federal prisoners. Some proposals were modest demands that would enable prisoners to make use of rights already on the books or humanize the prison experience: encourage college students to teach remedial courses to prisoners who did not make it through high school, end censorship of books and magazines, expand vocational training programs. Other proposals were aimed at expanding rights or increasing the power of prisoners in governance: a federal minimum wage for prisoners' labor, the election of political councils run by prisoners, and parole as a right rather than a privilege. On the east coast Sam Melville organized white prisoners to support black prisoners' demands in Attica, and David Gilbert, imprisoned in the early 1980s for political violence, became an AIDS activist in New York prisons, organizing for programs to combat "a social epidemic of neglect based in bias."[60]

New ideas about policing also emerged in the 1970s. Liberal reformers emphasized the importance of diversifying the racial composition of police forces, reducing the level of militarization, training police in cultural sensitivity, and getting officers out of their cars and back into the streets. Activist organizations focused on ways to democratize policing through proposals to shift governance to local neighborhoods, require police to live where they work, and establish civilian review boards to adjudicate complaints against the police. The Black Panther Party introduced the idea of a "citizens' peace force." In 1974 Huey Newton recognized that "as control slips visibly away from traditional urban institutions, panicky, poorly trained police shoot to kill in the ghetto." He argued for structural solutions to this problem, including replacement of professional police with a citizens' peace force composed of local residents under civilian control. The ideal recruit would have the personality profile of a conscientious objector, someone committed to serving the community. Training would emphasize paralegal and paramedical skills as well as an ability to mediate conflicts. The peace officers would be required to live locally and have knowledge of the community. "We will not have mercenary armies, but community Peace Officers in a face to face relationship with their own, . . . cross-trained to respond to the variety of emergencies that constitute everyday life in the poverty community," Newton wrote.[61]

With the success of efforts to maintain ties between activists inside and outside prison, the movement made some significant political and legal gains. The U.S. Supreme Court ruled in 1963 that states were required to provide lawyers for indigent defendants in criminal cases and in 1967 that young people also were entitled to be represented by counsel in cases in which they risked loss of freedom. Between 1967 and 1977 the United States had a moratorium on executions. Many cities established civilian review boards to monitor police misconduct, and prison officials all over the country cracked open their gates to let in educational programs run by community activists. Between 1969 and 1973 Massachusetts removed all youth from the state's juvenile institutions.[62]

By the early 1980s the prison was no longer the site of a creative storm or organizing, and efforts to curb police violence were blocked. In response to the rebellions of the 1960s and 1970s, prison authorities made a coordinated and effective effort to break up political groups, isolate leaders, make learning into an obstacle course, limit ties with outside groups, and boost racial animosities as a management strategy. Even when postmortems at Attica revealed governmental malfeasance and cover-ups, the government endlessly litigated righteous claims of prisoners and their families.[63]

The widespread demand to end indeterminate sentencing on the grounds that it kept prisoners permanently insecure and powerless was met, only to be replaced by determinate sentences that were longer and more punitive, giving rise to what became known as mass imprisonment. The spaces created by prisoners for political study, political expression, and creative writing were mostly closed. Literary journals committed to publishing the work of prisoners went out of business. When he walked out of prison for the last time, having done nearly seventeen years inside by age forty, Malcolm Braly had to deal with a parole officer who tried to censor the manuscript of what would become Braly's most successful novel, *On the Yard*.[64]

Today the few incarcerated writers who make a living from their work risk losing that income in the more than forty states where prisoners can be compelled to pay for the cost of their imprisonment. In 2018 Michigan sued Curtis Dawkins to recover most of the $150,000 that he received from a publisher for *Graybar Hotel*, a book of short stories, money that the author intended to use for the education of his three children.[65]

The attack on prisoners' rights initiated in the 1970s recalled a comparable moment in the early nineteenth century when authorities in New York segregated the most rebellious prisoners from the rest of the prison population and created a separate physical space to house them, a precursor to today's "special housing units," or SHUs.[66] Now academics and journalists, such as Michelle Alexander and Ta-Nehisi Coates, and nonprofit organizations, such as the Sentencing Project, American Civil Liberties Union, and Prison Policy Initiative, have taken up the cause, but they lack the power and persuasive ability of a movement.

What happened in the 1980s was an extraordinary defeat, not just for activists and creative people inside the carceral state but also for civil rights, black liberation, antiwar, and student movements that had developed close ties to the damned and the deprived and had demonstrated the common humanity of the criminalized and oppressed. Not everything was lost. The Black Lives Matter movement later revived a much more moderate version of the Black Panthers' program and backed up its militant street protests with a set of concrete demands. And even under the harshest conditions of solitary confinement and tense segregation, a group of prisoners in northern California's Pelican Bay State Prison organized themselves into the Short Corridor Collective, and in 2012 called for a cessation of "all hostilities between our racial groups" in order to "focus our time, attention, and energy on mutual causes beneficial to all of us."[67]

Danny Murillo, doing five years in Pelican Bay's SHU, tried to ward off the madness that comes from sensory deprivation and seclusion by seeking relief in reading mostly fast-paced popular novels, not unlike how Jack London and a long line of resourceful predecessors had tried to survive inside. One day the invisible prisoner in the enclosed exercise pen next door told Murillo that he needed to read more seriously and started him off with Voltaire's *Candide*, then urged him to put *The Grapes of Wrath* and books about Mexican history on his reading list. This literary grounding served Murillo well when, years later and against all odds, he was admitted to the University of California at Berkeley, where he helped to establish an organization of former prisoners who were building bridges between the free and unfree. And so the creative spark and seeds of a new movement were planted.[68]

This time, however, unlike the 1960s, it would be much more of a challenge to take on a carceral state that had expanded its operations and refined its techniques in a political climate that celebrated rather than challenged law and order.

IV

8

THE DISTANT PRESENT

*After decades of enduring a political monologue of law
and order, suddenly we were surrounded by a volatile argument
about justice and injustice, followed by a glimmer of hope,
then a serious setback that changed everything.*

Crime is a national defense problem.

—Senator Joe Biden

Tough crime policies are the most important form of national defense.
—Donald J. Trump, *The America We Deserve*

NO FRILLS

When news spread that guards had killed George Jackson in San Quentin State Prison on August 21, 1971, prisoners at Attica demonstrated their solidarity at the noon mess: "Not a man ate or spoke—black, white, brown, red. Many wore black armbands," wrote Sam Melville, a white leftist doing time for a series of politically motivated bombings. "No one can remember anything like it here before." A few weeks later the bloody quelling of a revolt at Attica that resulted in the deaths of dozens of guards and prisoners, including Melville, sent a clear message to politically active prisoners throughout the country. It also inaugurated the rise of supermax, high-tech prisons designed to isolate troublemakers and enforce the Jim Crow–style racial segregation that persists today.[1]

The modest reforms of the late 1960s and early 1970s were quickly rolled back, almost as though they had never occurred, and the strong links between community and prison were broken, as were efforts to build racial unity among prisoners.

The often-acrimonious debate between liberals and radicals about whether treatment was punishment in disguise became irrelevant, as the ideological discourse about crime shifted far right with rehabilitation dismissed as softhearted sentimentality. With the decline of mass movements for social justice, and the increasing sophistication and repressive capacity of government agencies, the criminal became racially demonized and politically isolated, fair game for politicians stoking populist anxieties. In his run for the presidency Richard Nixon devoted seventeen speeches to law and order. By the time Bill Clinton became president in 1993, the New Democrats had also taken the low road to demagoguery, abandoning a traditional liberal agenda on crime prevention, community development, and rehabilitation. The consequence of this political consensus was an orthodoxy unchallenged for almost forty years: unprecedented expansion and increased militarization of policing, a boom in prison construction and mass imprisonment that gave the United States the distinction of being "the world's warden," and the gutting of public services in poor communities.[2] How did this happen?

While the Nixon government (1969–74) made law and order a central plank of its politics, a shift that the Democrats later would enthusiastically replicate, the previous administration of Lyndon Johnson (1963–69) was not exactly soft on crime. Johnson took a tough stand on the widespread urban riots, beginning in 1965 with the roundup of more than four thousand African Americans during the Watts uprising, one of many mass protests against police brutality and the broken promise of desegregation. Johnson's vow that the War on Poverty would expand the New Deal to communities of color and poor whites was quickly supplanted by the war on crime. For forty years the federal government siphoned massive resources from social services and pumped them into boosting prisons and police, throwing a carceral net far beyond the prison. The punitive turn in the 1980s accelerated the shift from an incipient social democracy to a mean-spirited neoliberalism that, in addition to accelerating privatization of public services and deregulation of the economy, expanded the role of the state in meeting demands for social equality with beefed-up security. The result was an extraordinary expansion of carceral operations.[3]

In Europe the sociologist Stuart Hall located the punitive turn in what he called Thatcherism, identifying a profound shift in political ideology associated with the rise to power of the neoconservative wing of the Tories under Margaret Thatcher's leadership. The American equivalent of Thatcherism might be called Nixonland, to use Adlai Stevenson's pejorative, for it was Richard Nixon in his 1968 campaign for the presidency who appealed to that brilliant political construct, the silent majority, in order to criminalize and push back against the struggle for racial justice.[4]

In Nixon's rhetoric "unprecedented racial violence" and "unprecedented lawlessness" were interchangeable. "Our founders," Nixon claimed at the Republican National Convention in August 1968, "recognized that the first requisite of progress is order." But Nixon was neither the first nor the last politician to whip up a fear of crime as a central preoccupation of the federal government. At least since 1929, when Herbert Hoover in his inaugural presidential address identified "the failure of our system of criminal justice" as a "malign danger" facing the nation, politicians have politicized crime.

Nixon owed a great deal to the presidential candidate Barry Goldwater's call in 1964 for "security from domestic violence" and recognition of "the growing menace to personal safety, to life, to limb and property." Other speakers at the Republican National Convention, notably former president Eisenhower, echoed Goldwater's racial views about law and order. "Let us not be guilty of maudlin sympathy for the criminal, who roaming the streets with switchblade knife and illegal firearms seeking a helpless prey, suddenly becomes upon apprehension, a poor, underprivileged person who counts upon the compassion of our society and the laxness or weaknesses of too many courts to forgive his offense."

Nixon's perspective also had much in common with Lyndon Johnson's insistence that "one of the most legitimate functions of government is the preservation of law and order" and with Ronald Reagan's campaigns against the "odd philosophy of permissiveness" and "those who foster racial tensions and incite class warfare." Reagan, the former Hollywood actor, embarked on his political career at the 1964 Republican National Convention, where he advocated "the maximum of individual freedom consistent with order." His brand of freedom, however, did not embrace the "sexual orgies" that apparently were the rage, sadly without my knowledge, at the university where I was a graduate student. Reagan made a centerpiece of his campaign for California governor a "peace trip" dance at Berkeley in May 1966 that, according to police reports, was the devil's workshop, with its strobe lights, nudity, wafts of marijuana, and "indications of other happenings that cannot be mentioned." As the governor-to-be told a rally of supporters, "a small minority of beatniks, radicals, and filthy speech advocates have brought such shame to a great university." Reagan paved the way in the West, but Nixon made the most effective use of law and order as a national political slogan and rallied his supporters to turn back "the wave of crime" and restore "freedom from fear in America."[5]

During the 1988 presidential campaign George H. W. Bush drew upon Nixon's racial playbook to attack the Democratic candidate, Michael Dukakis, for being soft on crime. As governor of Massachusetts, Dukakis had opposed the death penalty and supported a weekend furlough program for longtime prisoners. A few weeks before the election the Bush campaign ran an effective attack ad that accused Dukakis of allowing "Willie Horton," an African American doing time for murder, to leave prison for a weekend and commit more crimes. An image of a disheveled, bearded William Horton, Jr., was followed by the tag line, "Weekend Prison Passes: Dukakis on Crime." The ad even distorted Horton's name. "The fact is, my name is not 'Willie,'" Horton said a few years later. "The name irks me. It was created to play on racial stereotypes: big, ugly, dumb, violent, black—'Willie,' I resent that. They created a fictional character who seemed believable, but who did not exist."[6]

By the end of Bill Clinton's second term in 2001, the Democratic and Republican platforms shared fundamental premises about policing and prisons and disagreed only on minor details. "The rise of punitive federal policy over the last fifty years is a thoroughly bipartisan story," the historian Elizabeth Hinton says. "Indeed, crime control may be *the* domestic policy issue in the late twentieth century where conservative and liberal interests most thoroughly intertwined." This united front was in place for several years. "You're in as much jeopardy in the streets as you are from a Soviet missile," Senator Joe Biden said in 1982 during the Reagan era. The 1984 Comprehensive Crime Control Act, which passed 406–16 in a Democratic-majority House, authorized the federal death penalty and preventive detention, increased the length of sentences for serious crime, and enabled police to keep a large chunk of drug dealers' assets.[7]

Unlike Dukakis four years earlier, Bill Clinton made sure in 1992 that he would not be labeled a "card-carrying member of the ACLU" or represented as the kind of politician who would release a "Willie Horton" into a work-furlough program. On Clinton's watch as governor of Arkansas throughout most of the 1980s, the number of prisoners increased by 83 percent, and in January 1992 he approved the execution of Ricky Ray Rector for killing a police officer. Rector had survived a self-inflicted shot to his brain that left him severely impaired. He put aside the slice of pecan pie that came with his last meal, saying that he would eat it after he returned to his cell. "You can't law-and-order Clinton," said the Arkansas head of the American Civil Liberties Union. "If you can kill Rector, you can kill anybody." The National Association of Police Organizations endorsed Clinton over Bush in 1992.[8]

By the 1990s it was hard to tell the difference between Republicans and Democrats on criminal justice issues. In the 2000 campaign they echoed each other's positions. Clinton and Gore "fought for and won the biggest anti-drug budgets in history. They funded new prison cells, and expanded the death penalty for cop killers and terrorists. But we have just begun to fight the forces of lawlessness and violence," the Democrats asserted. "We renew our call," the Republicans responded, "for a complete overhaul of the juvenile justice system that will punish juvenile offenders" and for "no-frills prisons" for adults.[9]

In his first run for the presidency even Barack Obama, who once described Clinton's attitude toward capital punishment as "frighteningly coldhearted," meekly called for "more cops on the street" and reform, not abolition, of the death penalty. "I don't want to wake up four years from now," Obama said in 2007, "and discover that we still have more young black men in prison than in college." Four years later Obama woke up to find the situation essentially unchanged.[10]

KNOWN UNKNOWNS

The result of this political consensus from the Nixon presidency to the Obama years was a boom in prison construction, expansion of the criminal justice workforce, and a spending bonanza at the public's expense. But precisely how big and how expensive is not known.

If it were not for print media and nonprofit organizations no one would be able to estimate how many people the police kill or what it costs to incarcerate more than two million people every day.[11] Given how much inflammatory rhetoric, political grandstanding, and policy debates are devoted to "the crime problem," a responsibility of government should be to keep us informed and current. The government does neither.

The chaos of statistical information about the carceral state evokes the observation by Donald Rumsfeld, George W. Bush's secretary of defense, about how governmental policy decisions are often based on partial knowledge and total ignorance: "There are known knowns; there are things we know. We also know there are known unknowns; that is to say we know there are some things we do not know. But there are also unknown unknowns—the ones we don't know we don't know."[12]

Researchers know that we lack critically important information, such as how many people work in private security, how much it costs to export American criminal justice programs around the world, and to what extent the federal government subsidizes local and state criminal justice operations through grants and the transfer of equipment and technology. We also know that a great deal of information to which we do have access is typically outdated, such as the number of criminal justice employees, because of a significant lag in how information is reported. Not to mention the shadowy territory of the "unknown unknowns," such as how intelligence agencies function and spend taxpayers' money and the terms under which large-scale projects involving surveillance, data management, and technologies of social control are outsourced to the corporate sector.

What do we know? At least we know more than the sociologist Stan Cohen did in 1979 when he complained that we have "surprisingly little information." We can say with certainty that since the 1970s the expansion and diversification of carceral institutions has been unprecedented, and we know a great deal, albeit belatedly, about specific aspects of criminal justice agencies, such as how many people work as public police and how much states budget for incarceration.[13]

While it is an exaggeration to claim, as some do, that criminal justice agencies now employ more people than any other sector of the labor force, unquestionably that sector has grown considerably since the 1960s, and its growth is dramatically skewed in favor of occupations involved in policing and guarding.[14]

I estimate that at least 4.3 million people are currently employed in carceral operations, about 400,000 more than work as nurses. This is a conservative figure because some data are a few years old, official statistics mostly do not count part-time employees, the figure for intelligence agencies is undoubtedly too low, and the numbers do not include the vast knowledge industry and the private contractors that service the carceral state.[15]

The number of people employed in carceral operations is larger than that which government agencies typically report for criminal justice employees because it includes private security, national security, and immigration and counterterrorism agencies. They need to be included because they articulate national definitions of dangerousness and criminality, and they shape local criminal justice priorities through economic incentives. Trying to figure out exactly how many people work in these sectors is a challenge because the information is incomplete, inconsistent, or, in the case of national security operations, hidden from public view.

The largest increase in criminal justice employees since the 1970s took place in policing and guarding. For example, from 1971 to 2012, while the U.S. population increased by almost 150 percent, the number of people employed in all capacities by police departments more than tripled, to 1.25 million. Meanwhile occupations such as probation, legal services, and social work, which serve people on trial, in jail or prison, and the formerly incarcerated, have stagnated or declined.[16]

Today about 2.95 million employees work for police departments or private security firms, another 452,000 for national security agencies, and 701,200 work as guards in prisons and jails. Less than 5 percent of carceral employees work in the interests of defendants and prisoners, thus making a mockery of the notion that criminal justice is an adversarial system in which both sides, prosecution and defense, command the same level of resources.[17]

The increase in public policing in recent decades is modest when compared with the growth of the private security sector, in terms of both numbers and influence. Private security forces should be included in any assessment of the scope of policing because they do much of the same work in corporate workplaces that regular police do in public spaces. Moreover, a significant number of government agencies contract out police services to private organizations, and many sites of policing—recreational and sporting events, concerts and festivals, malls and entertainment districts—involve joint operations. The number of private security personnel almost doubled in the three decades from 1980 to 2010 and they now outnumber regular cops by about half a million. Yet the federal government does not keep or require annual statistics on private police.

The last half of the twentieth century was also a boom time for the prison industry. When Malcolm Braly was first sent to a reformatory in California in the 1940s, the state had only a handful of prisons. By the time he became a free man in the mid-1960s, California had thirteen in operation and several in the planning stage. This meant "more guards—more sergeants, more lieutenants, more captains, more program administrators, wardens, associate wardens and superintendents. More correctional counselors, clerks and storeroom keepers. More vocational instructors, teachers, doctors, dentists and medical techs. More psychologists, psychiatrists, sociologists and psychometricians. More chaplains, librarians, stewards, cooks, and recreational supervisors. And," Braly concluded, "always more and more prisoners."[18]

In the 1970s state governments initiated a frenzy of prison construction. California built another twenty-three prisons, at a cost of $280 to $350 million each. Florida, Texas, and Arizona tried to keep up with California, while city and county jail admissions throughout the country nearly doubled, from 6 million in 1983 to 11.7 million in 2013.[19]

Not surprisingly, the workforce in jails and prisons underwent a significant expansion. Guarding has always been more labor intensive than policing, although in 1950 only one-thirtieth of today's staff was required to run prisons nationwide. With significant growth in the number of prisoners—from 302,000 in 1980 to more than two million in 2010—in a fourteen-year period beginning in 1971, the number of state prison, federal prison, and county jail employees doubled. State prison employment in 2012 was about 422 percent higher than it was in 1971.[20]

What these figures starkly demonstrate is not only the extraordinary growth of jobs in policing and guarding but also how the carceral workforce increased at the expense of jobs that serve the needs of the poor and disenfranchised and of efforts to reduce or ameliorate the effects of social inequalities that widened and deepened in the 1980s.

The gross disparity between public-service and social control jobs is a matter of grave concern: by the second decade of the twenty-first century, the United States had more carceral employees (4.3 million) than teachers in public and private schools (3.5 million).

Almost three times as many state workers in California are employed in corrections as in health and human services.

There are more public and private police nationwide (2.95 million) than workers in agriculture and food-related employment (1.8 million).

More people work in private security (1.7 million) than as lawyers (1.2 million).

More than twice as many guards work in local and county jails (213,000) than as probation and parole officers nationwide (90,000), and the United States has more than twice as many prosecutors (33,000) as public defenders (15,000).

Many more people work in jails and prisons (740,000) than as primary care physicians (430,000).

State prison employees (448,000) outnumber firefighters (307,000); police (2.95 million) outnumber social workers (607,000) by almost five to one.[21]

These disparities show that American society attaches far more material importance to security than it does to education, public health, and job training. However, this is only part of the story and not its most important part. The funding and governance of the carceral state reveal more than employment data about how national priorities are determined and how power is exercised.

FOLLOW THE MONEY

When it comes to figuring out carceral budgets, researchers operate mostly in the dark. Reckoning the cost of social control operations is even more of a challenge than accounting for the number of employees.[22]

Since the mid-1950s, when criminal justice expenditures at all levels of government constituted about one-half of one percent of the gross national product, the carceral state has persistently increased its share of the public coffers, with policing and security the primary beneficiary. In 1974 the police received 57 percent of the country's $15 billion criminal justice budget, eight times the amount they received a decade earlier. The cost to cities of police protection per individual officer almost tripled from the 1980s to the 2000s. Similarly, spending by states on prisons, adjusted for inflation, rose from $9.7 billion in 1982 to $37.3 billion in 2010, and per capita expenditures on corrections increased by almost 250 percent between 1980 and 2010.[23]

In recent years, with states facing fiscal crises and increased demands for public services, many legislatures are trying to cut prison costs, and cities and towns are looking to outsource police operations. The economics of criminal justice operations, however, is not only a regional and local matter.

Official budgets significantly undercount actual costs because they do not include federal subsidies and transfers of equipment, which make up a sizable proportion of state and local budgets. Since the 1920s, when the federal government enforced Prohibition and the Wickersham Commission tried to rein in police corruption, national agencies have been actively involved in shaping and funding regional and local law enforcement priorities. The scope of this involvement increased dramatically in the 1960s, when the federal government and the White House began to play a decisive economic and policy role in state and urban criminal justice policies.[24]

Congress now significantly shapes carceral operations. For example, the annual appropriation by Congress for immigration custody grew from $49.3 million in 1982 to more than $2 billion in 2013, increasingly to the benefit of private corporations that contract with government agencies to build and run detention centers.[25]

In addition, the Department of Homeland Security sends billions of dollars to regional and local governments for "terrorism prevention." The U.S. Senate's vote in June 2013 to "secure the border" included an allocation of $30 billion to double the number of Border Patrol agents, a "staggering figure," according to the political scientist Marie Gottschalk, "roughly equal to what all fifty states together spend on corrections each year, or approximately seven times the annual budget of the federal Bureau of Prisons."[26]

The White House also has a significant impact on criminal justice funding. With the support of Lyndon Johnson, the Law Enforcement Assistance Administration was the fastest-growing federal agency in the 1970s, with three out of every four dollars going to urban policing.[27]

During the presidency of Ronald Reagan, who had a long and cozy relationship with the FBI from his days as an informant in Hollywood, the agency's budget more than doubled, from $622 million in the 1980s to $1.3 billion in 1987.

When he became president in 1994, Bill Clinton's eagerness to wave the banner of law and order directly over the Democratic Party influenced Congress to pass a $30.2 billion crime bill that funded 100,000 new police and $8.8 billion in state prison construction.[28]

Some important parts of federal funding are a mystery. Because of multiple funding sources and a lack of transparency, fathoming the extraordinary cost of U.S. criminal justice operations around the world is difficult. Budgets are often concealed and originate in several government departments. The funding process mystifies even experts with access to internal data. What is known, though, suggests unrestrained, cavalier spending.

In 1992 Congress asked the General Accounting Office, a government watchdog agency, to assess how much the United States was disbursing for training foreign police forces. The GAO reported that it could not provide an adequate answer and "could not determine the total extent or cost of U.S. assistance to foreign police because some agencies do not maintain such data." If Congress today were to ask the GAO to investigate how the Department of Justice's International Criminal Investigative Training Assistance Program dispenses criminal justice funds around the world, it would be similarly frustrated because ICITAP does not publish its budget.[29]

By any standard—numbers, rates, and cost—criminal justice institutions are considerably larger and more complex than they were during the last four decades of the twentieth century. Many specifics may be murky, but what is clear is that the United States invests far more public resources in social control than in social welfare. In 1980 the United States invested three times more in food stamps and welfare grants than in prisons and jails. By 1996 the policy was reversed.[30]

A NATIONAL ARGUMENT

The criminal justice juggernaut that was created in the distant present, in the last five decades from the Nixon through the Obama administrations, is not only a network of well-funded institutions and operations with a sizable workforce.[31] It is also a set of powerful ideas that successfully transformed law and order into widely accepted common sense, propagated the impression that crime is a natural rather than a social phenomenon, and made the need for authoritarian measures appear necessary and inevitable. Politicians from Richard Nixon to Donald Trump understand that maintaining order and stability is an ideological as well as a hands-on project, that language and images are as central to social control as riot police and prison walls because they foment as well as respond to popular anxieties about disorder and justify antidemocratic policies and curbs on civil liberties.[32]

At least since 1948, when *Life* magazine reduced the young African American Red Jackson to a one-dimensional street thug, the media have had a great deal of experience conflating criminality with race. By March 1981, when *Time* and *Newsweek* published cover images of guns and lead stories about the contagion of dangerousness, neoconservative framing of the "crime problem" was the new normal. "How can the sociopaths be weeded out?" *Newsweek* asked. "A pervasive fear of robbery and mayhem threatens the way America lives," *Time* agreed.[33]

For a brief moment during the Johnson presidency, politicians actually had a national debate about criminal justice policies, pressed to do so by social movements. The academic fields of criminology and criminal justice opened the canon to critical thinking and interdisciplinary scholarship from history, sociology, economics, and the new disciplines of ethnic and feminist studies. But the "new criminology" met the same fate as the prison movement, as radical intellectuals were either shunted to the hinterlands of academia or lost their jobs.

In the 1970s the federal government began spending about $20 million annually on police education, with more than 750 colleges and universities offering degrees in "police science" and related topics. By 2007 about nine hundred bachelor degree programs were offered in criminal justice, and doctoral programs in criminology and criminal justice had increased from a handful in the 1960s to thirty-two. Criminology became a technical and specialized adjunct of government, no longer a site of vigorous debate and competing ideas.[34]

Federal subsidies helped to create an extensive knowledge sector that trained personnel for a growing criminal justice job market, hired retired police functionaries for teaching positions, and produced mountains of research for government agencies. Many academics, co-opted by government funding or cowed into compliance, retreated into technocratic research and made sure big ideas and uncomfortable thoughts were swept out of the journals and textbooks. Heads down again, blinders back on.

"Have you ever read any criminology texts?" Michel Foucault asked in 1977. "They make you gasp." Foucault was exasperated not only by the narrow administrative focus of criminology and its tendency to train cheerleaders for criminal justice agencies but also by its shallow historical perspective. In his 1977 book, *Thinking About Crime*, James Q. Wilson, who influenced Donald Trump's ideas about criminal justice policies, touted programs he deemed feasible for controlling everyday crime and dismissed efforts to search for root causes of social problems. Wilson echoed the argument made by another political scientist, Edward Banfield, a few years earlier—that cultural and familial, rather than structural and economic, factors were mainly responsible for a high crime rate in African American communities. Wilson's highly influential "broken windows" essay, coauthored with the criminologist George Kelling in 1982, became the defining policy statement of late-twentieth-century urban policing. It provided a rationale for the police to get involved in regulating quality-of-life issues in poor communities in order to "elevate, to the extent they could, the level of public order." It was a mistake, Kelling and Wilson argued, to decriminalize "disreputable behavior," for "a score of drunks or a hundred vagrants may destroy an entire community." As the sociologist George Lipsitz observes, this approach not only substitutes policing for social services, it also "treats symptoms rather than causes. It is not the windows that have been broken, but rather the promise of full citizenship and social membership."[35]

For decades a political monologue, representing a triumph of law and order, saturated the public discourse. In the early 1990s a leading authority on the history of U.S. criminal law concluded his encyclopedic treatise on a defeatist note. "Crime," he wrote, "is part of the American story, the American fabric . . . It is a cost that is badly and unfairly distributed. But for now, at least, there may be nothing to do but grit our teeth and pay the price." In 2009 Senator Jim Webb was a lone voice in Congress calling the U.S. prison system a "national disgrace."[36]

A few years later Webb's idiosyncratic position became mainstream. By 2015 Obama was urging Congress to "reform America's criminal justice system so that it protects and serves all of us."[37] In the first half of the second decade of the twenty-first century, a national argument erupted about the state and future of U.S. criminal justice institutions, notably prisons and urban policing. The debate was surprisingly fierce, given that, from the Nixon years through the turn of the century, governing institutions had reached a political consensus on these issues. No one was publicly airing differences, which had been commonplace in the late 1960s and 1970s. Since the publication in 1977 of Wilson's right-wing policy tract, *Thinking About Crime*, no criminology literature had caught the public imagination until 2010 when *The New Jim Crow*, a radical critique of the racist underpinnings of criminal justice by Michelle Alexander, a little-known law professor at Ohio State University, became a bestseller.

By then politicians, academics, and pundits from the Right, Left, and center had unclenched their jaws, called themselves reformers, and mobilized us to action. Everybody, it seemed, suddenly became an expert on criminal justice issues. By June 2013 an influential right-wing organizer was calling other conservatives to join the reform movement and get "tough on failed, too-expensive criminal justice programs."[38] Liberal think tanks, nonprofits, and advocacy organizations suddenly received a receptive hearing after years of the silent treatment. What accounted for this extraordinary shift in public and political opinion?

First, after an almost forty-year binge, the American penal system halted its expansion, the result of a combination of factors: fiscal necessity, declining political credibility, and grassroots activism. "The climate has definitely shifted," Marc Mauer, executive director of the Sentencing Project, said. The overall growth of incarceration slowed considerably, reaching a plateau in some states and declining nationwide by almost 5 percent since 1999. In 2009, for the first time since 1982, the U.S. jail population declined. The number of African Americans incarcerated for drug offenses dropped significantly. Also in 2009 twenty-seven states, from Rhode Island to Mississippi, reduced their prison populations. State and local governments, feeling the long-term effects of the economic crisis and declining tax revenues, decided to cut back their investments in expensive penal projects. In 2014 and 2015 forty-six state legislatures considered prison reform measures, from reducing the number of prisoners to creating reentry programs. Between 2011 and 2016, twenty-two states shuttered ninety-four state prisons and youth institutions. Seven states

(Alaska, California, Connecticut, New Jersey, New York, Rhode Island, and Vermont) reduced their prison population by more than 20 percent.[39]

Second, the fiscal crisis generated a multifaceted reform movement that reflected the growing influence of libertarianism in national politics, with its emphasis on fiscal accountability, individual rights, and reducing the power of government in social matters. The enormous cost of policing and guarding, aggravated by the devolution that passes the economic burden down to states, counties, and cities, is at odds with a political philosophy that, with the exception of the military and national security, calls for less government. The conservative wing of the Republican Party, not liberal Democrats, initially promoted alternatives to imprisonment that are cost effective and "protect public safety." Around 2008, the right-wing American Enterprise Institute invited politicians and think tank policy makers to an informal discussion, hosted by Newt Gingrich, about how to introduce a criminal justice reform agenda. In 2010 a group of influential political leaders began a new national organization, Right on Crime, to lobby for reforms nationally and at the state level. One of its key principles is this: "Criminal law should be reserved for conduct that is either blameworthy or threatens public safety, not wielded to grow government and undermine economic freedom." Before the 2016 presidential campaign, U.S. senator Rand Paul of Kentucky, a leading conservative in the Republican Party, spoke to African American audiences, arguing that the inequities of the criminal justice system were "something like segregation" and calling for reforms that would send fewer people to prison and make it easier for former prisoners to vote and get jobs.[40]

The Republican National Convention moved the party to the extreme right, with Donald Trump channeling Nixon's 1968 campaign—"There can be no prosperity without law and order"—and the Republicans adopting one of their most socially conservative platforms—against same-sex marriage, for teaching the Bible in public schools, against gun control, for building a wall to "cover the entirety of the southern border." The party's platform also included a call to modify the policy of "mandatory minimum sentencing" in the case of "nonviolent offenders and persons with drug, alcohol, or mental health issues." Legislation that would have reduced sentences for about twelve thousand federal prisoners even won bipartisan support in the Senate's Judiciary Committee before being shelved after Republican hard-liners complained that the United States suffered from an "under-incarceration" problem. Jeff Sessions, the Alabama senator who would become Trump's attorney general, was a leading opponent of federal reforms.[41]

The political initiative from the Right opened up space for civil libertarian and nonprofit groups and for liberal academics who were glad to be back inside the corridors of power, albeit in a subordinate role. The left-of-center equivalents of Right on Crime are the Brennan Center for Justice, a law and policy institute based at New York University that is committed to "ending mass incarceration" and "preserving Constitutional protection in the fight against terrorism," and *The Marshall Project*, a nonprofit news organization founded in 2003 to "create and sustain a sense of national urgency about the U.S. criminal justice system." In 2016 it won a Pulitzer Prize for its reporting.

These liberal tendencies are represented on investigative task forces (such as Obama's Task Force on 21st Century Policing and the National Research Council's report on mass incarceration) composed of professionals and academics who call for more accountable policing and a significant reduction of the prison population. Its watchwords are *sensible, legitimate, evidence based, empirically verifiable, cost effective*, and *public safety*. The shared language of conservatives and liberals even produced some joint projects. In 2015 the right-wing Koch brothers joined the American Civil Liberties Union and Tea Party–oriented groups in the Coalition for Public Safety. The former community activist Van Jones and Gingrich, the former speaker of the House of Representatives, welcomed an array of government officials, establishment politicians, and nonprofit administrators to the Bipartisan Summit on Criminal Justice Reform in Washington, D.C. "The current system is broken beyond repair," Gingrich and Jones agreed.[42]

Third, another concern of the governing class and motivation for reform was the declining political support for criminal justice institutions in the communities that they police and guard. "Incarceration is an awesome state power," a prestigious task force observed in 2014. Its overuse and misuse were "threatening the republican values that underpin the legitimacy of the prison and the state." Obama's policing task force similarly emphasized the importance of "building trust and nurturing legitimacy on both sides of the police-citizen divide." The global notoriety of the U.S. carceral state, especially its overuse of prisons, widespread practice of solitary confinement in violation of international standards of human rights, unregulated access to guns, and everyday police killings of citizens, became a political embarrassment for a country that claims an exceptional right to export freedom and liberty around the world. Advocates of government-led reforms promoted a mix of persuasion and force, warning that state violence by itself is counterproductive if not balanced with efforts to win the hearts and minds of the governed.[43]

Fourth, the rise of a militant grassroots activism all over the country, proclaiming "Black lives matter," "I can't breathe," and "Stop deportations," challenged police racism, advocated for immigrant rights, and organized to end mass incarceration and stop or slow down the building of new jails. This decentralized, locally based movement pushed the more genteel, top-down reform agenda of political elites to the left, in much the same way that urban rebellions in the 1960s radicalized the civil rights struggle. What once seemed far away—the Arab Spring and rise of insurgent parties in Europe that were expressing a wide sense of disillusionment and anger at the established order—was now in the heart of the homeland. As the Occupy Wall Street movement dispersed, new forms of struggle emerged, from the Bernie Sanders presidential campaign to spontaneous protests, sending a message that one spark could set the public prairie ablaze.[44]

In the wake of publicized police killings of African Americans, protesters regularly took to the streets, for the most part peacefully but with an edge of deep anger and militancy not seen in years. Since 2006, when Latino groups mobilized an unprecedented wave of protests, they have been steadily campaigning to stop the detention and deportation of hundreds of thousands of undocumented and documented immigrants. Prisoners in remote prisons in northern California and Guantánamo went on hunger strikes to protest the torturous conditions of solitary confinement. Single-issue campaigns were in full swing to "ban the box" (prohibit employers from initially asking former prisoners about their record) and end prison gerrymandering (that is, require the U.S. Census Bureau to count people in their home community rather than place of confinement). And millions of people were reading and discussing powerful critiques of the U.S. injustice system, such as *The New Jim Crow* and Ta-Nehisi Coates' *Between the World and Me*, just as my generation read George

Jackson and Malcolm X in the 1970s. Coates' ideas also spread through a graphic magazine, *Black Panther*, that reached a younger generation of activists.[45]

Protests generated some modest results. In April 2016 Virginia's governor, Terry McAuliffe, used his executive power to restore voting rights to more than 200,000 former prisoners in response to campaigns to end felony disenfranchisement. "I remain committed to moving past our Commonwealth's history of injustice to embrace an honest process for restoring the rights of our citizens," the governor said. "The struggle for civil rights has always been a long and difficult one, but the fight goes on." Other states explored changes in voting rights, especially for people on probation and parole. A blue-ribbon commission in Chicago, in recognition of a "significant and historic public outcry," called for a variety of reforms in the city's police department, including the creation of a "fully transparent and accountable Civilian Police Investigative Agency," and, after years of organizing, activists in Chicago forced the city to pay reparations to the victims of police violence.[46]

Government reports about police abuse, judicial interventions in the management of prisons, and journalistic exposés of criminal justice scandals became commonplace. In 2012 the U.S. Department of Justice initiated an investigation of allegations of "unreasonable and unnecessary" use of force by police in Cleveland, as exemplified by the militaristic message on a large banner hanging in one of the city's police stations: FORWARD OPERATION BASE. In New York a federal judge characterized the police department's stop-and-frisk tactics as racial profiling. The Obama administration, in response to widespread criticism, started the process of asking police departments and coroners' offices to report incidents of death while in police custody to the U.S. Justice Department.[47]

Three hunger strikes in California prisons between 2011 and 2013 drew attention to the twenty-five thousand prisoners around the country held in solitary confinement under conditions that, according to human rights organizations, are "legalized torture." The *New York Times* condemned the practice as "bestial treatment." Legal challenges in 2013 on behalf of prisoners and their families exposed the unlawful segregation of HIV patients in Alabama and degrading conditions in which the mentally ill were locked down in Mississippi. In response to suits filed by California prisoners, federal judges and the U.S. Supreme Court persistently intervened to reduce overcrowding in California's prisons and draw attention to the systematic violations of prisoners' human rights.[48]

IDEAS MATTER

Early in 2016, given the resurgence of grassroots activism, an openness to debate in political forums, and concrete efforts to fashion a reform program, it appeared that the long run of law-and-order policies might be on the wane. But by the end of the year the chance of significant change was wrecked.

For several months an extraordinary and volatile debate about criminal justice issues raged, with neoconservative, libertarian, liberal, and radical perspectives competing for political traction.

In April a task force appointed by Chicago mayor Rahm Emanuel confirmed a widely held belief that the city's police "have no regard for the sanctity of life when it comes to people of color." In June the U.S. Supreme Court was deeply split in *Utah v. Strieff*. Justice Clarence Thomas, writing for the majority, said that the court had found no evidence of "systemic or recurrent" police misconduct during police street operations. In her dissent Justice Sonia Sotomayor responded in unusually straightforward language, saying that "many innocent people are subjected to the humiliations of . . . unconstitutional searches," and "unlawful police stops corrode all our civil liberties and threaten all our lives."[49]

This decorous judicial debate was viscerally echoed on the streets and in publications. On July 7 an African American man ambushed and killed five police officers in Dallas; ten days later an African American veteran who had served with the marines in Iraq killed two police officers and one sheriff's deputy in Baton Rouge. In response the National Law Enforcement Officers Memorial Fund reported "a very alarming, shocking increase in the number of officers who are literally being assassinated because of the uniform they wear and the job that they do." The right-wing Manhattan Institute took out a full-page ad in the *New York Times* to promote a new book by Heather MacDonald, *The War on Cops*, which claims "police everywhere are being vilified by activists and organizations claiming to speak for those most vulnerable to violent crime."

In response, on July 21 a coalition of black racial justice organizations held demonstrations in several cities to protest police shootings. By

August the Black Lives Matter movement had spread to other countries, including England, where protests in several cities called attention to police brutality, racial disparities in sentencing policies, treatment of immigrants in detention, and hate crimes. In the United States, although the number of police killed had changed little from previous years, and almost as many police were killed in automobile accidents as by guns, the Right gained the political initiative in reframing the crisis of lawless policing as an assault on law-abiding police officers.[50]

The presidential campaign also was a platform for an argument about crime and justice, and it became nasty and rancorous. Donald Trump successfully mobilized a coalition of old-guard conservatives, evangelical organizations, neonationalists, and government functionaries working as police, guards, and immigration enforcers to fight back against an imagined enemy of terrorists, black anarchists, and violent Mexicans in the same way that Richard Nixon in 1969 had framed the sixties as an assault on traditional American values. In one of many reckless speeches Trump implied to a crowd in Wilmington, North Carolina, that gun owners might need to take matters into their own trigger fingers if Hillary Clinton became president and appointed judges opposed to the Second Amendment.

The same day as Trump's provocation, the Obama administration announced that the Justice Department would begin to keep track of killings by police, and the department's Civil Rights Division issued a blistering indictment of the Baltimore police for a systematic pattern of "unconstitutional stops, searches, and arrests" in African American neighborhoods. Four days later Milwaukee was the scene of a ferocious neighborhood protest, reminiscent of the urban rebellions of the 1960s, after police killed yet another young African American man. In September police killings of black men in Tulsa and Charlotte triggered militant demonstrations.[51]

As protests against police persisted, expressions of solidarity came from unlikely allies. At the beginning of the National Football League season, San Francisco's quarterback, Colin Kaepernick, refused to stand for the national anthem in protest of police killings. "I am not going to stand up to show pride in a flag for a country that oppresses black people and people of color," he announced to the media. "To me, this is bigger than football and it would be selfish on my part to look the other way. There are bodies in the street and people getting paid leave and getting away with murder." Many athletes, professional and amateur, adults and youth, emulated this symbolic gesture, echoing Tommie Smith and John Carlos' black power stance at the 1968 Olympics in Mexico. The sports sociologist Harry Edwards advised the Smithsonian's National Museum of African American History and Culture to immediately acquire Kaepernick's shoes and jersey for exhibition because he had achieved what nobody else had been able to do: "Get the president of the United States, down to the guy shining shoes at the bus station in Atlanta, talking about this." Kaepernick's protest had long-lasting repercussions. "People sometimes forget that love is at the root of our resistance," he said after receiving Amnesty International's Ambassador of Conscience award in April 2018. "As police officers continue to terrorize Black and brown communities, abusing their power, and then hiding behind their blue wall of silence, and laws that allow for them to kill us with virtual impunity, I have realized that our love, that sometimes manifests as Black rage, is a beautiful form of defiance against a system that seeks to suppress our humanity."[52]

On the presidential campaign trail in 2016, Donald Trump's rhetoric moved further right, emphasizing that the police must "be allowed to do their job the way they know how to do it," while Hillary Clinton campaigned with Mothers of the Movement, a group of black women whose children had been killed by police or other violent acts and who were associated with the Black Lives Matter movement. Bernie Sanders called for "fundamental police reform."[53]

Trump and Clinton personified the national debate. "Hillary Clinton isn't afraid to say black lives matter. She isn't afraid to sit at a table with grieving mothers and bear the full force of our anguish," said Lucy McBath, one of the Mothers of the Movement, at the Democratic National Convention. "Stop and frisk worked very well in New York. It brought the crime rate way down," Trump responded at the first presidential debate in September. "You take the gun away from criminals that shouldn't be having it. We have gangs roaming the street. And in many cases, they're illegal immigrants. And they have guns. And they shoot people."[54]

In October the *Washington Post* released a recording of Trump boasting in 2005 about being able to grab women "by the pussy" because "when you're a star, they let you do it." In response thousands of women used social media to share their experiences of sexual abuse after Kelly

Oxford's request to "tweet me your first assaults, they aren't just stats." When professional athletes and the first lady joined the debate, a national conversation about predatory sexual behavior took place. "It's that feeling of terror and violation that too many women have felt when someone has grabbed them, or forced himself on them, and they've said no but he didn't listen," said Michelle Obama in an eloquent, emotional speech that reached a wide audience. "It reminds us of stories we heard from our mothers and grandmothers about how, back in their day, the boss could say and do whatever he pleased to the women in the office, and even though they worked so hard, jumped over every hurdle to prove themselves, it was never enough."[55]

Then, as quickly as the national debates about predatory sexual behavior and crime and injustice had taken center stage, they were sidelined by the sweeping electoral victory for the Right in November 2017. With Donald Trump elected president, Republican domination of Congress and state legislatures, appointment of a hard-line attorney general who as senator had opposed the most modest prison reforms during the Obama presidency, and a decisive shift to the right on the U.S. Supreme Court, the politics of law and order was back in fashion, not as a regression to Nixonland but as a forward-looking shift to a much more explicitly authoritarian use of power. "The problem in our poorest communities," Trump had warned ominously during the campaign, "is not that there are too many police, the problem is that there are not enough police."[56]

9

LIMBO

*On facing the reality of the new
authoritarian disorder, learning from the past,
and thinking boldly about the future.*

So twilight
is
that time
between day and night.
Limbo,
I call it limbo.

—Anna Deavere Smith, *Twilight in Los Angeles*

ZERO TOLERANCE

In August 1966, as I was completing my doctoral degree at Berkeley's School of Criminology, Governor Ronald Reagan announced a plan to create an institute that would teach law enforcement officers "the newest methods in crime prevention and solution." Based in Berkeley, and "with Mr. Hoover's help," Reagan said, "such a school could become a sort of FBI academy of California." J. Edgar Hoover appreciated Reagan's long record of "anti-communist activities" and enthusiastic collaboration with the FBI, but the plan never materialized. Instead Reagan settled for placing his right-hand man, Edwin Meese, on the School of Criminology's Advisory Council. As a prosecutor in the Alameda County District Attorney's Office, Meese had counseled Governor Pat Brown in 1964 to take a tough stand against free speech demonstrators at Berkeley, a decision for which the California Chamber of Commerce recognized him as one of the state's outstanding young men of the year.[1]

In 1969, as Reagan's chief of staff, Meese became the point man for the state's repressive response to student antiwar activism and civil disobedience, including deployment of the "blue meanies"—sheriff's deputies who killed James Rector and blinded Alan Blanchard with buckshot at protests against the University of California's unwillingness to allow almost three acres of urban land to be used as a public park in Berkeley. During the next couple of years Meese played a key part in overseeing the arrest and beating of hundreds of demonstrators, including me. Later, as President Reagan's attorney general (1985–88), Meese would sharpen his reputation as a law-and-order advocate, until he was forced to resign for his complicity and "ethical lapses" in a government contract scandal.

Meese may have lost his cabinet position but not his influence. When he held the Ronald Reagan Chair in Public Policy at the right-wing Heritage Foundation, his views on criminal justice policies helped to shape the punitive turn of the 1980s and caught the attention of Donald Trump, a businessman who by the early 1990s was considering a plunge into national politics. In 2016 President-elect Trump appointed Meese to his presidential transition team, a signal that the reforms initiated during the Obama presidency would be quickly undone.[2]

Since World War II the United States has had two significant moments of national debate about criminal justice issues, both during centrist liberal regimes: in the 1960s a variety of social movements challenged the Johnson administration to go beyond its moderate reform program and put policing under civilian control, and during the last years of the Obama administration widespread repulsion at the injustices of mass incarceration and unchecked police killings triggered fierce debates, and even some new policy proposals, from all sectors of the political spectrum.

The reforms that ensued were modest, selective, and did little to change the basic functioning and governance of criminal justice agencies. Moreover, these breaks with the status quo were short-lived and followed by repressive regimes. The Nixon administration acted on its right-wing rhetoric to expand and further militarize policing, attack civil liberties, and lay the groundwork for the expansion of incarceration in the 1980s. A decade later the Clinton administration gouged large holes in the safety net, propelling millions of families into economic insecurity and the quasi-criminal status of public welfare.

Similarly Obama's efforts to juggle liberal and conservative policy initiatives were quickly erased by a Trump administration eager to roll back Obama's reform agenda and make the United States into "a country of law and order." The election of Donald Trump in November 2016 emboldened the most right-wing tendencies in the criminal justice debate. He made no effort during his campaign to incorporate liberal motifs in his rhetoric or make nuanced concessions to the complexity of policy. Those who wanted to curb police lawlessness and racism were promoting "a war on our police," Trump said. "The attacks on our police, and the terrorism in our cities, threaten our very way of life. Any politician who does not grasp this danger is not fit to lead this country." The Obama administration had been responsible for allowing "border deaths, narco-terrorists, and waves of violent illegal criminals into America," Trump said, as usual with no evidence to back up the claim. In fact an in-depth study by a research team from four universities of 200 metropolitan areas with large immigrant populations reported that the rate of violent crime is lower than it was in the 1980s, and New York's murder rate is the lowest it has been in decades.[3]

The Trump platform in 2016 openly adopted rhetoric and imagery that smacked of classical fascism, a political perspective that had shaped his worldview for several years: an apocalyptic vision of American citizens facing "the possibility of economic and social upheaval" caused by "an economic crash like we've never seen" or a terrorist attack that "would turn Manhattan into Hiroshima II." He promoted a politics of antipolitics that called for draining Washington, D.C., of "career politicians" and a hyperbolic characterization of the United States as "the world's whipping boy," treated like a "punching bag" by China. His call to revive the grandeur of a mythic past emphasized that American borders and patriotism were under attack and that the response required a masculinist revolt against so-called American spinelessness and emasculation. Trump flayed the "established media" while exploiting its fascination with the candidate's flamboyant style, creatively using visual culture and spectacle to evoke "the people" and make his political supporters feel as though they were insiders participating in their own governance.[4]

Prior to and during the campaign Trump regularly characterized the police as beleaguered and "afraid for their jobs, they're afraid of the

mistreatment they get," and terrorists as indulged by the Obama administration's weak policies. "I would leave Guantanamo just the way it is,"
Trump declared, "and I would probably fill it up with more people that
are looking to kill us."[5]

For all that has been said about Trump's mercurial and narcissistic
temperament, his impetuosity and grandstanding, and his tendency to op-
portunistically scavenge a political philosophy from discarded ideolo-
gies, his views about criminal justice, welfare, and race are long standing
and quite consistent.

Donald Trump honed his ideas about crime and criminal justice in the
political and intellectual climate of the 1980s, long before he made law and
order a centerpiece of his 2016 campaign. Following the arrest of five young
men of color, all juveniles, in the brutal rape and beating of a white investment banker jogging in Central Park in 1989, a crime for which they
were falsely arrested and imprisoned for several years before being exon-
erated and compensated, Trump took out a full-page advertisement in four
New York newspapers. "I want to hate these muggers and murderers," he
announced. "They should be forced to suffer and, when they kill, they
should be executed for their crimes." The headline on his ad urged New
York: BRING BACK THE DEATH PENALTY, BRING BACK OUR POLICE. His
endorsement of capital punishment for juveniles put Trump at the fringe
of the far Right.[6]

The Central Park Five were convicted in 1990 and received sentences
ranging from five to fifteen years. The robbing and injury of Trump's
mother in 1991 added personal animus to his political convictions. When
the mugger was arrested, Trump bragged that his brother "contacted the
judge and made a point of being in the courtroom during the trial, so
the family presence would be felt. The Trumps believe in getting even."
The defendant, who was sixteen years old at the time of his arrest, was
tried as an adult and received a three- to nine-year sentence.[7]

More than a decade after the Central Park rape, Matias Reyes, who was
already serving a life sentence for murder and multiple rapes, confessed
to the crime for which the five young men had been convicted, leading
in 2002 to the vacation of their conviction and in 2014 to a $41 million
settlement with the city of a civil suit for malicious prosecution. In an
opinion piece written for the New York *Daily News*, Trump denounced
the settlement, calling it a "disgrace . . . Settling doesn't mean innocence . . .

Speak to the detectives on the case and try listening to the facts. These young men do not exactly have the pasts of angels."[8]

When Trump decided to articulate more fleshed-out policies on police and prisons, he looked to the circle of intellectuals around his "favorite crime expert," James Q. Wilson of broken windows fame. "Wilson's anthology of expert opinions, *Crime*, is must reading," Trump noted in *The America We Deserve*, ghostwritten in 2000. He cribbed the chapter "The Safe Streets We Deserve" from a briefing book coauthored by Edwin Meese and issued by the Heritage Foundation for right-wing political candidates; it railed against indulgent welfare programs, lenient judges, habitual offenders, and police departments weakened by "the substitution of politically correct racial, ethnic, or gender 'diversity' quotas for competence and merit."[9]

Following the lead of Wilson and Meese, Trump advocated a "zero-tolerance policy toward anyone who is getting in the way of the safer America we all deserve . . . Government's number-one job is to ensure domestic tranquility, and that means tranquilizing the criminal element." He welcomed the expansion of imprisonment in the 1980s, wildly pontificating in his 2000 book, despite impressive evidence to the contrary, that "America doesn't use prisons much more than any civilized nation . . . No, the problem isn't that we have too many *people* locked up. It's that we don't have enough *criminals* locked up."[10]

Trump pledged to further gut what was left of public welfare by replacing "the great failed social programs of our country" with a revival of volunteerism as a substitute for government services. His version of noblesse oblige recalled the Victorian charity movement, which put the social good in the hands of wealthy individual benefactors. "We should back public policies that encourage, not discourage, this purest form of public service," he advocated in 2000, "particularly tax reduction, which would leave more money in the hands of the middle class."[11]

In his 2011 book, *Time to Get Tough*, which was geared toward a political campaign—"A great leader can bring America together"—Trump made immigrants, particularly Mexican immigrants, synonymous with a propensity for criminality, again the evidence be damned. Nothing about the argument was subtle. Why, he asked, "have we suddenly become an annex of Mexico's prison system?" He called for a crackdown on undocumented immigrants during the Obama administration's unprecedented crackdown on immigrants, which broke all records for rounding up people whose visas had expired and deporting those with criminal records. "We should not let ourselves become the dumping ground for other countries' undesirables," Trump proclaimed while the Obama administration set up special courts to speed up the process of detaining and criminalizing people who tried to enter the country illegally. Desperate to find a tiny difference with Obama's immigration policies, Trump objected to the "resort-like accommodations" in detention centers, where people await- ing a deportation hearing were offered health and welfare classes, movie nights, and bingo. Such soft, sentimental liberalism was making the United States into a laughingstock, Trump claimed.[12]

STANDING UP FOR LAW ENFORCEMENT

The 2016 elections resulted in an unprecedented victory for the Right at all levels of government. The Trump administration came to power on a law-and-order platform, promising to undo the reforms of the Obama era, go after "illegal immigrant criminals" and "Muslim extremists," and "reclaim our streets and neighborhoods." As President Trump made "Standing Up for Our Law Enforcement Community" one of his six po- litical priorities and issued executive orders encouraging state and local police to "perform the functions of immigration officers" while making "a chargeable criminal offense" grounds for deportation without a judicial hearing and conviction. The administration's association of Mexicans with violent crime and Muslims with terrorism renewed and expanded the racialization of dangerousness.[13]

After his election Trump nominated a strict constructionist to the Supreme Court and a virulent reactionary with a history of racist views for attorney general, and the Senate confirmed both. As a Democrat from Illinois, U.S. representative Luis Gutiérrez, observed, "If you have nos- talgia for the days when blacks kept quiet, gays were in the closet, immi- grants were invisible and women stayed in the kitchen, Senator Jefferson Beauregard Sessions is your man." Sessions had piled up such a record of racist comments and practices as the U.S. attorney for the Southern Dis- trict of Alabama in the 1980s—including characterizing the NAACP and ACLU as "communist-inspired" and unsuccessfully prosecuting civil rights activists (the Marion Three) for voter fraud—that in 1986, despite

Ronald Reagan's endorsement, even the Republican-controlled Senate refused to confirm Sessions' appointment as a federal judge.[14]

As attorney general Sessions announced that he was steering the Justice Department away from efforts begun by his predecessor to rein in lethal violence and racist abuse by urban police through federal oversight and imposition of specific department-wide reforms. Worried that imposing consent decrees might "reduce morale of the police officers," as well as "push back against being out on the street in a proactive way," Sessions wanted to make sure that "the individual misdeeds of bad actors" did not taint departments or undermine public safety. This decision signaled a return to a "bad apple," rather than a systems, approach to police malpractice. To Sessions crimes by the police were of much less concern than "the rising levels of violence against law enforcement" that came as "no surprise," given "divisive rhetoric that treats police officers like the problem" and "the enemy." But it was a surprise to criminologists and record keepers because the number of police killed on the job had dropped in 2017 to its second-lowest total in fifty years. Like his boss, Sessions learned quickly how to package misinformation in the guise of established truths, as in falsely asserting "a rise in vicious gangs" and the largest surge in the murder rate since 1968.[15]

The new Justice Department quickly made clear that its priorities were radically different from the previous administration's. It reversed Obama's decisions to decrease the federal government's use of private prisons, restrict the ability of states to use assets seized during arrests, and limit the transfer of military surplus, such as armored vehicles, to police departments. Sessions indicated that he intended to investigate universities for practicing "reverse discrimination" against white and Asian students, and in a blatant effort to curb free speech, he tried to obtain the IP addresses of about 1.3 million visitors to an anti-Trump website that helped to organize protests on Inauguration Day.[16]

As was the case with Obama's Justice Department, which in 2016 distributed $5.5 billion in grants to local law enforcement agencies, Trump's Justice Department quickly made use of economic incentives to selectively promote its policies. It revoked funding for an innovative community policing project in Los Angeles, a decision that was probably payback for California's unwillingness to cooperate with the crackdown by the Department of Homeland Security (DHS) on undocumented immigrants.

Similarly the Justice Department replaced the Community-Based Violence Prevention Initiative, which focused on street-level outreach programs, with Project Safe Neighborhoods, which funds police efforts to go after gangs. DHS used the same tactic to reward its allies and punish its opponents through its grant-making capacity. It canceled a $400,000 grant, authorized by the Obama administration, to Life After Hate, a group working with former members of white supremacist groups who are open to giving up their racist ideology, in favor of organizations that target Muslim extremism.[17]

Officials speaking on behalf of Immigration and Customs Enforcement (ICE), the largest investigative agency in DHS, welcomed "President Trump's commitment to enforce our immigration laws" and give "clear direction" to ICE to step up deportations. The administrative machinery, thanks to the previous government, was in place and ready to do so. Obama had given the go-ahead to more than three million deportations in the hope that this concession to the Right would prompt Congress to pass comprehensive immigration reform and create a path to citizenship for many undocumented immigrants. When this failed, Julia Preston of *The Marshall Project* notes, Obama worked "to restrain the deportations machine his administration had created." Obama directed ICE to give priority to people accused of serious crimes and those involved in border violations. All that the Trump administration needed to do was shift ICE's priorities to give noncriminal cases the same attention as criminal cases. Trump's orders, as the *New York Times* noted, "expanded prosecutorial priorities so broadly that, as a practical matter, there no longer exist any priorities at all."

In the first quarter of 2017 ICE arrests increased by 37 percent over the previous year. Given their fear of surprise raids and reluctance to trust public officials, the families of undocumented immigrants have been much more cautious about reporting crime, especially sexual assaults and domestic violence, and they tend to avoid public events. There are reports of immigrants getting rounded up while dropping their children off at school. Church attendance has dropped. "People leave their loved ones in the emergency room and run away," the chief executive of a New York hospital reported. In Atlanta, where immigration-related arrests increased by 40 percent in 2017, many immigrants have stopped driving their cars for fear of being stopped for petty infractions.

"If you're in this country illegally," the director of Atlanta's DHS office said, "you should be scared."[18]

The long-term threat to civil liberties and political freedom emanates from changes taking place throughout the carceral state, not only in the nation's leading institutions. While a great deal of attention was being paid to the possibility of impeaching or removing Trump and to his unvarnished bigotry and bombastic rhetoric, his administration was quickly transforming the appellate levels of the federal judiciary, as well as stimulating a significant shift to the right in legislative policies at the state level. Whether a President Trump or President Mike Pence is in the White House, their right-wing policies mean everyday criminal justice policies are irretrievably hardened, posing an enormous challenge to the progressive movement for the next decade.

Pence, who was responsible for turning Trump's dystopian vision into mundane policies, rose to national prominence as a member of Congress (2002–11) and then as governor of Indiana. He helped to build the right-wing, evangelical Christian base of the Republican Party by campaigning for restriction of birth control to married women and for criminalizing abortion. In Congress he made a case for teaching "intelligent design" alongside evolution and became a leader of the far Right caucus. As governor he was an ardent advocate of the Religious Freedom Restoration Act, which would have legalized discrimination against gays and lesbians by businesses. A leading proponent of unregulated capitalism, Pence has close ties to the right-wing Koch brothers, who bankrolled his political career and envisioned him as presidential material. In return Pence helped to bring into the Trump administration sixteen high-ranking officials with ties to the Kochs.[19]

With Trump's endorsement the administration's strategy for the judiciary was to appoint several extremists to lifelong positions as federal appellate judges. The group of mostly conservative white men, recommended by the Federalist Society and Heritage Foundation, included nominees rated "not qualified" by the American Bar Association and who supported "conversion therapy" for gay youth, described transgender children as part of Satan's plan, and compared *Roe v. Wade* to the *Dred Scott* decision. For a position on a court in the Eastern District of North Carolina, which has never had an African American judge, the Trump administration nominated Thomas Alvin Farr, who, as a protégé of the notoriously racist senator Jesse Helms, had been active in efforts to suppress black voting rights—in the words of a federal court, with "almost surgical precision." After another candidate was forced to withdraw his quest for a seat on the U.S. District Court in Alabama when reporters exposed his posts defending the Ku Klux Klan, the Justice Department retained him in a unit that advises the president on judicial appointments. While the publicity generated by these nominations forced at least three candidates to withdraw from consideration, Trump's appointments represented the most effective stacking of the federal judiciary since the Nixon presidency, potentially shaping legal doctrines for a generation: the twelve regional federal appeals courts decide about sixty thousand cases annually, compared with about eighty heard by the Supreme Court.[20]

At the state level, where the Republican Party in 2017 controlled the governorship in thirty-three states, and the governorship and legislatures in twenty-five states, conservative activists moved quickly to pass right-wing policies.[21]

The attack on reproductive rights was as widespread as were efforts to expand the right to own guns. Arizona imposed new and burdensome restrictions on abortion providers. Iowa stripped Planned Parenthood of Medicaid funding, resulting in the closure of one-third of the agency's clinics in the state. Missouri restricted the ability of people on Medicaid to receive insurance payments for birth control and other reproductive health services. Kentucky passed a law banning most abortion procedures after eleven weeks, and Idaho requires abortion providers to report to the state all patients who received abortions and how many abortions they have received in the past. Texas' legislature authorized criminal and civil penalties for late-term abortions and prohibited the donation of human fetal tissue from abortions, although a federal court later enjoined Texas' late-term abortion ban. It also took a federal court to undo Indiana's selective abortion ban on the grounds that it posed an undue burden on women seeking abortions. Ohio banned abortions in cases where the fetus shows signs of Down syndrome, another piece of legislation blocked by a federal judge.[22]

Several states have in mind a challenge to the U.S. Supreme Court's decision in Roe v. Wade that authorizes abortion up to twenty-four weeks when a fetus may be viable outside the womb. Mississippi banned abortion before fifteen weeks. Ohio Republicans have proposed a ban on all abortions with no exceptions, and Iowa passed a bill that bans abortions when a fetal heartbeat is detectable, usually at six weeks. At the national level, the Trump administration proposed withholding federal funds from agencies such as Planned Parenthood that provide or refer patients for abortions.[23]

Meanwhile New Hampshire passed legislation that allows people to carry concealed guns without a permit, and Florida increased the level of proof required of prosecutors in the state's Stand Your Ground law, under which George Zimmerman had been charged and acquitted of the murder of Trayvon Martin. At the national level in 2017 the National Rifle Association lobbied Congress to require all states to recognize concealed carry permits from states in which they are recognized, thus equating gun licenses with drivers' and marriage licenses. Despite national protests in favor of stricter gun regulations in 2018, the NRA continued to gain victories at the state level: Iowa passed a resolution supporting a state constitutional amendment for the right to bear arms, West Virginia restricted employers from banning guns at work, Wyoming and Idaho passed Stand Your Ground laws, Nebraska shielded gun ownership records from public records requests, and Colorado considered a repeal of its large capacity ammunition ban. NRA representatives even mocked survivors of the shooting in Parkland, Florida. "No one would know your names," said a host of the NRA's television station, if a student had not killed seventeen people at Marjory Stoneman Douglas High School.[24]

State governments in 2017 also adopted a range of policies that increase punishments for protest and civil disobedience and whittle away at what is left of undocumented immigrant rights. Texas passed a ban on sanctuary cities that also makes it a crime for police officers to refuse to comply with ICE regulations. Georgia required its Bureau of Investigations to publish a list of all immigrants with criminal records who are released from ICE custody in Georgia. Mississippi passed legislation prohibiting cities or public universities from adopting sanctuary policies that would impede cooperation with federal immigration officials. Tennessee added longer sentences for criminal convictions in cases in which the defendant was illegally in the country at the time of the offense and had been previously deported for a criminal offense. At the national level, in 2018 Trump proposed further restrictions on immigration and asylum policies, and ordered the National Guard to carry out immigration enforcement at the U.S.-Mexico border.[25]

Most of the new state legislation was concentrated in areas of the South and Midwest that were also Trump territory. A coalition of conservative organizations, Right on Crime, has been effective at the state level in co-opting a liberal reform agenda by advocating a reduced prison population as a cost-saving measure, increased financial restitution to victims of crime, and a higher level of proof against corporations charged with crime. The conservative organization also lobbied Congress to enact legislation that would essentially eliminate strict liability in cases involving economic crimes.[26]

It is telling that Right on Crime stays silent on abuses by law enforcement and has no interest in reforming the governance and oversight of policing. A particularly important trend in state-level carceral politics is the wave of "back the badge" bills that increase penalties for assaulting cops, including petty assault enhancements that are likely to be used as tools to punish activists. Encouraged to go after Black Lives Matter groups by the Heritage Foundation and nationally known right-wing ideologues, including Edwin Meese and former New York police chief Bernard Kerik, many states passed "blue lives matter" legislation. These laws designate attacks on police as hate crimes in Kentucky; impose a life sentence without parole for the murder of an officer in Mississippi; establish thirteen as the minimum age for trying juveniles as adults for assaults on police in Georgia; and extend prison sentences for crimes against police in Arkansas, Utah, Nevada, Kansas, North Dakota, and South Dakota. Similarly Oklahoma, in response to the Dakota Access Pipeline protests, has significantly increased penalties for trespass or vandalism against refineries, pipelines, and oil- and gas-processing plants.[27]

These laws provide county and state prosecutors with additional tools to coerce protesters to accept plea deals and to increase the punishment of those who fight charges and are judged guilty. The message of this swath of legislation is clear: don't organize, don't protest, and don't cause trouble.

FISSURES

The shift to the right is real, the floating of authoritarian measures ominous. But we are not yet under the gaze of a panopticon administered by an omniscient centralized system of command and control. We certainly

live in dangerous and messy times, but the carceral state is rife with political and legal fissures and is by no means a closed system.

For all the tough talk during the presidential campaign, Trump's first
executive orders relating to crime and criminal justice were weak on substance. One order made it a governmental priority to go after drug cartels and human traffickers, as if it was not already a priority. It called for
a "comprehensive and decisive approach" without providing any additional funds or resources. A second order advocated measures to stop
violence against the police but did not specify any federal legislation. Its
main value was symbolic, an effort to upset a popular narrative that projects cops as agents, not victims, of out-of-control violence. The third order commanded the attorney general to establish a task force to generate
ideas for reducing serious crime, a tried-and-true delaying device for covering up a lack of imaginative and strategic thinking.[28]

In 2017 the White House could not count on other sectors of government for support or loyalty. Leaks from intelligence agencies made it necessary for Trump to fire his national security adviser, Michael T. Flynn, after
allegations surfaced about his ties to foreign governments. In May the president also fired FBI director James Comey, the former deputy attorney general who once told federal prosecutors that they needed to toughen up and
take on crimes in high places. Trump variously claimed that Comey's mis-
handling of allegations about Hillary Clinton's emails and his inability to
"effectively lead the Bureau" were grounds for his dismissal. A month later,
at a sensational Senate hearing watched by millions, Comey accused the
president of lying about the reasons for his dismissal and of trying to derail
an investigation into collusion between Russian officials and the Trump
campaign during the 2016 elections. In response to the subsequent political
crisis, the Justice Department appointed Robert S. Mueller III, a former FBI
director, as a special counsel to resume Comey's investigation.[29]

The law-and-order president quickly became a person of considerable
interest to the Justice Department, facilitated by Sessions, who recused
himself from Mueller's inquiry. During Trump's first year as president federal grand juries indicted Flynn and three other functionaries associated
with the Trump campaign or administration. Flynn and George Papado-
poulos, a foreign policy adviser, pleaded guilty to lying to the FBI about
their interactions with representatives of the Russian government; former
Trump campaign chairman Paul Manafort was charged with conspiracy

to launder money and other felonies; and Rick Gates, another campaign staffer, was charged with financial crimes. In 2018, as grand juries empaneled by Mueller piled on indictments of a lawyer at a top-tier New York law firm, several Russian operatives, and internet companies, and as a federal judge revoked Manafort's $10 million bail and sent him to jail for alleged witness tampering, loyalists in Trump's inner circle began to bicker and take action to save their own skins and careers. In two different federal courts on the same day in August, a jury found Manafort guilty of financial fraud, and Trump's former lawyer, Michael Cohen, pled guilty to violations of campaign finance laws by arranging payoffs to the two women who claimed they had affairs with the future president.[30]

As Mueller's probe expanded to include possible obstruction of justice and financial crimes, the president, who had once expressed "great respect" for the courage of the FBI and Justice Department, initiated an unprecedented assault on their reputations, deriding the FBI's leadership as disgraceful and the "worst in history." Trump accused the Justice Department of politicizing "the sacred investigative process in favor of the Democrats and against Republicans," thus feeding right-wing conspiracy theories that the "deep state" was plotting his downfall. When a high-level FBI agent resigned in protest, he made a point of announcing that he was joining "the growing chorus of people who believe that the relentless attacks on the bureau undermine not just America's premier law enforcement agency but also the nation's security."[31]

The FBI has a long history of politicization, especially during J. Edgar Hoover's reign, and agents have occasionally left the bureau because of disagreements about policies. But this was the first time that a president has waged such a sustained public attack on the bureau's legitimacy and tried to whip up public opinion against his own attorney general. By March 2018 Trump and Sessions were no longer on speaking terms, with the president publicly berating his appointee as "DISGRACEFUL," and Sessions forced to defend his own "integrity and honor."[32]

With the publication of James Comey's memoir in April 2018, the battle of words between the president and the seventh director of the FBI escalated into trash talk. The president "treats women like they're pieces of meat," Comey said in a television interview. "He is morally unfit to be president." Comey is a "slimeball," tweeted Trump. The president's tendency to demand absolute loyalty from his staff and appointees reminded

Comey of "New York Mafia social clubs" with "the boss as the dominant center of everything." Comey belongs in jail for leaking classified information, retorted Trump. He will go down in history as "the WORST FBI Director in History, by far . . . He is not smart."[33]

On another front the legal battle about the new government's policies on immigration revealed a deep rift with and within the judiciary. In January 2017 Trump signed an executive order that for ninety days banned immigration from seven majority-Muslim countries: Iran, Iraq, Libya, Somalia, Sudan, Syria, and Yemen. It suspended the admission of Syrian refugees indefinitely and of all other refugees for 120 days. The purpose of this order was supposedly to evaluate and strengthen vetting procedures against potential terrorists. It potentially involved revocation of 60,000 to 100,000 visas, depending on estimates by different government officials.

When Bob Ferguson, attorney general for the State of Washington, decided to take on Trump's executive order, he enlisted the support of major corporations, including Expedia and Amazon, as well as Minnesota's attorney general. In February Judge James Robart of the U.S. District Court in Seattle imposed a temporary nationwide halt to the order, raising questions about its constitutional validity. While Trump publicly derided "the opinion of this so-called judge" as ridiculous, he did not send alt-right thugs to close down the courts but rather sent Justice Department lawyers to appeal the decision. A federal appeals panel unanimously rejected Trump's bid to reinstate his ban on travel, writing, "It is beyond question that the federal judiciary retains the authority to adjudicate constitutional challenges to executive action."[34]

A leading neoconservative law professor, who had drafted memos for George W. Bush that articulated a rationale for "enhanced interrogation techniques," registered "grave concerns" about Trump's use of executive power. "A successful president need not have a degree in constitutional law," John Yoo, a law professor at Berkeley, wrote in the *New York Times*. "But he should understand the Constitution's grant of executive power." Trump's nominee for the vacancy on the U.S. Supreme Court is said to have called Trump's attack on the judiciary demoralizing and disheartening.[35]

Even when the U.S. Supreme Court in June 2017 ruled partially in favor of the government and lifted the immigration ban, it restricted the policy to "foreign nationals who lack any bona fide relationship with a person or entity in the United States." The court's decision led to months of administrative and legal squabbling about who was and was not eligible for entry into the United States. By early 2018 the Trump administration had received judicial approval to ban entry to the United States of most individuals from Chad, Iran, Libya, North Korea, and Syria and to increase the level of vetting for applicants from Somalia and Venezuela. But several state governments and civil liberties organizations continued to challenge specific elements of the ban. Moreover, many federal judges intervened to slow down the implementation of executive orders. Beneficiaries included Indonesian Christians in New Jersey, Somalis in Florida, and about 800,000 Dreamers—young people brought without papers into the United States by their parents. The Dreamers had been protected by Obama's Deferred Action for Childhood Arrivals (DACA) program, which Trump rescinded in September 2017. In April 2018, the U.S. Supreme Court in a majority decision that included the concurrence of Trump's appointee held that a law requiring deportation of immigrants convicted of "crimes of violence" was insufficiently specific. "Vague laws," Justice Neil Gorsuch wrote, "invite arbitrary power."[36]

Despite opposition from federal judges at the regional level, at the national level the shift to the right was steady and relentless. The Justice Department made it more difficult for asylum seekers to gain entry into the United States by removing domestic abuse and the threat of gang violence as grounds for asylum. In June 2018 the U.S. Supreme Court in a split decision ruled that the president has wide authority to limit immigration on the basis of national security. In her dissent, Justice Sotomayor compared Trump's ban to the Supreme Court's 1944 decision that upheld the forcible internment of Japanese Americans during World War II. Both cases, she argued, represented capitulation to the government's "discriminatory policy motivated by animosity toward a disfavored group." Activists won a small victory when nationwide protests forced the Trump administration to revoke an order to detain and separate thousands of children from their families when immigration authorities arrest the parents. The chant of "Abolish ICE" was a popular slogan at large rallies held in several cities. But the euphoria was short-lived. Justice Anthony M. Kennedy's announcement of his decision to retire from the U.S. Supreme Court handed President Trump an opportunity to create a stable conservative majority for the first time since before the New Deal. The court's new alignment, observes Harvard Law School professor Noah Feldman, could decisively shift American judicial doctrines and politics further right for a genera-

tion and bolster efforts by state governments to further restrict or eliminate a woman's right to an abortion.[37]

Similar schisms exist within the policing establishment, although they
are not as wide as within the judiciary. Many police chiefs, leading law
enforcement organizations (such as the Fraternal Order of Police and
National District Attorneys Association), and most rank-and-file officers
applauded the Trump agenda. The FOP, encouraged by Trump's commitment to combat the "dangerous anti-police atmosphere," welcomed revocation of Obama's executive order to limit use of military surplus. But
there was dissent, too, with resistance from some police chiefs to Trump's
order to crack down on undocumented immigrants and refugees protected by sanctuary cities. "We are not going to work in conjunction with
Homeland Security on deportation efforts," Los Angeles police chief Charlie Beck said shortly after Trump was elected president. "That is not our
job, nor will I make it our job." When the mayor of Oakland, California,
warned community-based organizations that an immigrant raid was coming, ICE's acting director called it a "reckless decision" and likened Libby
Schaaf to a "gang lookout yelling 'Police!'"[38]

In late July 2017 Trump addressed police in Brentwood, New York, and
essentially encouraged police to rough up suspects. Various police organizations and several police chiefs were quick to object. "It's not what policing is about today," a Los Angeles Police Department commissioner
said. On another occasion, when Trump promoted his political agenda at
the apolitical Boy Scout Jamboree, a former CIA director said that Trump's
speech gave him "the creeps." Also, some officers broke rank with their
law-and-order colleagues by rallying in Brooklyn in August to demonstrate
support for Colin Kaepernick's decision to refuse to stand for the national
anthem. "I'm law enforcement, and he didn't disrespect me," one officer
said in response to claims from the White House that the quarterback's
action was unpatriotic.[39]

A similar, albeit muted, debate continued about the state of prisons and
jails. As the White House and attorney general called for an increase in
the use of incarceration, even advocating imposition of the death penalty in
cases involving "extremely large quantities of drugs," Right on Crime continued to make the case for exempting "nonviolent offenders" from imprisonment and finding ways to achieve public safety with less expensive and
less intrusive policies. Another national organization, Law Enforcement

Leaders to Reduce Crime and Incarceration, composed of nearly two hundred police chiefs and prosecutors—including Manhattan's district attorney, Cyrus R. Vance, Jr.; former Dallas police chief David O. Brown; and former New York police chief William Bratton—issued a report in February 2017 calling for an increase in mental health and drug treatment programs and alternatives to prosecution and incarceration. "For many nonviolent and first-time offenders," their report argued in a not-so-subtle dig at Trump's policies, "prison is not only unnecessary from a public safety standpoint, it also endangers our communities." Contrary to Sessions' emphasis on the police as a military operation and "the thin blue line that stands between law-abiding people and criminals," Law Enforcement Leaders made the case for greater "cooperation between law enforcement and the community."[40]

These tensions within professional organizations show that criminal justice agencies are not fully united behind Trump's law-and-order agenda, that there is not yet a consolidated national policy to increase the power of the police or deport millions without due process. At the same time differences are often tactical rather than a matter of principle, as in figuring out the most effective mix of hard and soft measures of control. Vigorous debate about a reform agenda continues within government, but conservative and libertarian politics dominate it. Overall the policing and guarding fraternity was delighted that the language of reform associated with Obama's Justice Department was scrubbed from the White House website. The killing by police of unarmed black men—as in the case of Stephon Clark in his grandparents' backyard in Sacramento in March 2018—continued unabated, as did intense protests against the police.[41]

RESISTANCE TO CHANGE

American criminal justice institutions have demonstrated a remarkable resiliency and resistance to meaningful reform. The challenges we face are extensive and stretch far beyond the problems of mass imprisonment and unruly police. What people routinely refer to as the criminal justice system is inextricably linked to a much more expansive set of institutions that incorporates a complex network of agencies and operations, public and private, stretching from unregulated transnational homeland security operations and brutalist maximum-security prisons to punitive public welfare regulations and social engineering campaigns carried out in the name of nation building.

The carceral state is resistant to reform because it is not only a mopping-up operation, limited to managing social outcasts and a specific population of lawbreakers at the margins of society. It also plays a critically important role in legitimating and preserving inequality, criminalizing opposition movements, and backing up democratic institutions with fiercely repressive power, as it regularly claims to need during periods of exceptional emergencies. State violence is a routine and regular phenomenon of governance. That social groups defined as politically dangerous or economically expendable are also overrepresented in arrest, conviction, and incarceration statistics is no accident.[42]

A second reason for the carceral state's immunity to structural reform is its deep roots. While some extraordinary changes are recent, such as the now-dominant influence of homeland security in shaping national and local priorities of governance, the emergence of immigration enforcement as a parallel criminal justice operation, the growing inseparability of public and private policing, these newer developments rest on foundational principles of long standing. They include a double system of injustice that specializes in criminalizing the poor and selectively enforcing public order in working-class communities, a model of policing that emphasizes military functions over peacekeeping and public service, and the pervasive fastening of race to crime, which makes color and criminality appear to be natural and normal companions.

Fighting for reforms that alleviate human suffering is important as a matter of principle but also because no one can ever predict when a seemingly isolated and small-scale issue will become something much bigger: a protest against police violence in one city that became Black Lives Matter; a strike by prisoners in solitary confinement in a remote prison in northern California that became a cause célèbre around the world; and yet another school shooting, this time in a high school in Parkland, Florida—the 239th nationwide since 2012, when Adam Lanza killed twenty Sandy Hook elementary schoolchildren and six adults in Newtown, Connecticut—that prompted school walkouts, a White House summit meeting, a campaign to get the National Rifle Association out of political campaigns, and a decision by Walmart and Dick's Sporting Goods, two of the country's leading gun sellers, to end the sale of assault-style weapons in their stores. "We will flex our muscles at the ballot box," promised student activists.[43]

At the same time, most efforts to reform criminal justice institutions have either failed or had a sting in their tail. There are several reasons for this sorry record.

First, most government-led initiatives tend to focus on changing the attitudes and behavior of criminal justice functionaries who have the least power and the least ability to change organizational culture and priorities. The frontline workers (such as beat cops, guards, and social workers), who are the most visible representatives of social control operations, get the most attention from reformers. They are mobilized to confront protesters on the streets, caught on camera shooting suspects on the run, neglecting a prisoner to death, and telling clients to wait patiently at the end of the line. The communities to which they are dispatched see them as agents of control and humiliation rather than public service, which in turn leads to mutually reinforcing hostile relationships, what Debs described as a system designed to "forbid any intimacy with the human touch."[44]

Whenever public outrage erupts and formal investigations look into abuses and atrocities, staffers at the lowest level are usually targeted for punishment or remedial action, such as sensitivity training, wearing body cameras, learning to recognize the signs of implicit bias, and taking multicultural education classes. For example, the lowest-ranking military guards at Abu Ghraib—not their leaders up the chain of command or the architects of diabolical cruelties—were prosecuted for violating prisoners' human rights.[45]

This approach assumes some kind of psychological or educational deficiency in people who choose careers in prisons, policing, and community corrections, as if they are predisposed to authoritarianism, racism, sexism, and callousness. But many go into this kind of work with a commitment to public service and providing help to people in desperate need, or they are simply in search of a job that they hope will be more than mindless repetition. They are not, as the sociologist Stan Cohen points out, "disguised paratroopers of the state," inherently dedicated to malice. Yet most of them end up objectifying and alienating the communities and clients with whom they work, hardened to the suffering they see every day.[46]

"Warm people enter the system wanting desperately to change it," a former prison administrator observed in 1973, "but the problems they find are so enormous and the tasks so insurmountable that these warm people turn cold. In time they can no longer allow themselves to feel, to love, to care. To survive, they must become callous." This kind of disillusionment affects even the most idealistic criminal justice professionals. "I started out with some kind of avenging zeal to protect these people who'd been ensnared in the clutches of the law," a public defender confessed. "And I grew progressively sourer and had progressively less patience with them as I stayed there, and it finally got so that my animosities for them were very thinly disguised."[47]

Changing individual behavior requires taking on organizational culture. Low-level personnel have little control over the policies they are required to enforce. They work in organizations based on a military chain of command and are expected to behave like combatants managing dangerous populations. They worry about job security and holding on to jobs that are more privileged than most working-class jobs. Their day-to-day tasks are increasingly de-skilled and fragmented, making it difficult to appreciate the larger framework in which they operate. Meanwhile their managers up the bureaucracy—police chiefs, wardens, prosecutors, judges, politicians, and policy makers—are inclined by training, ideological preference, and self-preservation to be "advocates of the status quo, of conservative precedent, of hallowed routines."[48]

The second approach to reform focuses on organizational and policy matters but is often cosmetic and sometimes counterproductive or weakened by a failure to coordinate efforts or make connections to related concerns and constituencies. For example, in 2017 state officials in Oklahoma made twenty-seven technical policy recommendations for reducing the prison population by 7 percent during the next ten years and saving the state $1.9 billion. But they did not even mention race or acknowledge that in Oklahoma one out of every fifteen African American men aged eighteen and older is incarcerated and that the black rate of imprisonment is 2,625 per 100,000, whereas the white rate is 580 per 100,000.[49] How is it possible to address mass imprisonment without tackling racial inequality?

Many reform campaigns focus on important issues, such as abolition of the death penalty, voting rights for the formerly incarcerated, alternatives to imprisonment, community-based policing, and doing away with monetary bail, which is inherently discriminatory against poor people. That progressive groups, in one form or another, have been trying without success for about fifty years to correct these injustices should explain why focusing on a single issue is problematic. If the Vera Institute's 1961 proposal to release most defendants on their "own recognizance" still makes good sense from a policy perspective, why have politicians blocked its implementation?

Consider also a flurry of proposals to provide reintegration and reentry services to people who have been in jail or prison. Of course, releasing most prisoners into their communities is preferable to making them do more time, but these programs, typically outsourced to underfunded religious and nonprofit groups, are at best stopgap measures that do not address the needs of hundreds of thousands of men and women who return every year to depleted communities. As the ethnographer Alessandro De Giorgi notes, these former inmates have been disqualified from most reasonably paid jobs, which makes them "socioeconomic pariahs who are essentially unemployable." At worst, reentry services take on functions of surveillance and regulation through electronic monitoring and behavior modification. At the same time parsimonious handouts pit a small sector of welfare beneficiaries against the majority of people in need. Only a massive public welfare program, which the United States has never implemented, could begin to undo the structural problems of institutionalized poverty and inequality that affect millions of people, including those who have been incarcerated.[50]

A third barrier to effective reform is erected not by the government but by disparate social justice movements that too often fail to find common ground. This problem is partly rooted in the absence of a stable, oppositional, national political party that can serve as a repository of historical memory and make sure that intergenerational communication takes place. Struggles for equality in the United States have usually been uneven and precarious, with improvements in rights and quality of life for one group often coming at the expense of others.

Soon after African Americans made unprecedented, albeit brief, political gains during Reconstruction, American Indians were subjected to slaughter, military conquest, and reservations, while their children faced transportation to government-run boarding schools that attempted, in the words of a government official, to impress upon them "the exalting egotism of American civilization." While white women were fighting for and eventually winning the right to suffrage, Puerto Ricans lost full citizenship rights and did not even have the right to vote for their own governor until 1948. After World War II previously despised Jews quickly moved into the middle-class mainstream, while Japanese Americans were still recovering from the economic and psychological shock of their wartime imprisonment.

The approximately 200,000 middle-class Cubans who fled Cuba in 1959 after Fidel Castro's victory, and the South Vietnamese elites who left Saigon at the end of the Vietnam War, found a much more hospitable United States than did the Cambodian and Laotian refugees in the mid-1970s, the mostly Afro-Cuban Marielitos in the early 1980s, or the Haitians throughout the 1980s, all of whom arrived with nothing and found a country paved with hard stone.

In the 1980s, as ACT UP and the Gay Liberation Front, with its slogan of FIGHTING FOR OUR LIVES, forced the Reagan administration to take serious notice of the spread of HIV/AIDS, and as LGBTQ organizations in subsequent decades successfully challenged deeply held bigoted views about monolithic sexuality and opened the door to same-sex marriage, the courts simultaneously struck down affirmative action policies, and African Americans once again became overrepresented in jails and prisons.

We see this tension in efforts to pit the model minority, usually middle-class Asian Americans, against urban African Americans, and "deserving immigrants," usually the sons and daughters of undocumented immigrants who came here as children, against their parents, who are constantly under suspicion. Trump himself has expressed contradictory attitudes about the Dreamers. On the one hand, Trump described the Dreamers as "good for everyone immigrants" who deserve a path to citizenship if they "do a great job." On the other hand, in September 2017 he announced that the Deferred Action for Childhood Arrivals program would be phased out. I am reminded of how Carlos Bulosan summed up his experience as an immigrant in the United States: "So kind and yet so cruel."[51]

SORROW OF THE DISCONNECTED

Not all efforts at structural change are doomed to failure, nor do all reforms inevitably lead to a widening of social control. Many acts of solidarity and unity have risen from what James Baldwin called the "sorrow of the disconnected," including the nineteenth-century labor movement, which linked exploited labor in prisons and factories; the post-Reconstruction civil rights movement, which understood how the convict lease system, chain gang, and lynching were part of a broader effort to suppress basic rights; and the post–World War II civil rights and black liberation movements, which incorporated prisoners and victims of police brutality in struggles for social justice and forged intimate and reciprocal connections between communities and criminal justice institutions. A wage strike by mostly Filipino workers in rural California in 1965 led to the creation a year later of the Chicano-led United Farm Workers and inspired a national boycott of non-union grapes, as well as a mass movement that, according to the labor activist Frank Bardacke, "for a very brief time, made everything seem possible." The recently opened Legacy Museum in Montgomery, built on the site of a former warehouse where enslaved people were held, makes connections between the racial terrorism of the Jim Crow South and mass incarceration today.[52]

Feminist and antiracist organizations in the late 1990s began joint efforts to reconcile deep differences between movements against state violence and those combating interpersonal violence, calling for them to recognize the connections between mass incarceration and violence against women, between "struggles for personal transformation and healing [and] struggles for social justice." Recently black women and queer people of color have played a leadership role in organizing communities against police violence and in expressing utopian visions of new kinds of personal relationships. An intergenerational movement to expose predatory sexual behavior in high places, prompted in 2016 by reports of Trump's misogyny, was renewed with vigor and depth by the far-reaching #MeToo movement in the wake of about the Hollywood producer Harvey Weinstein and USA Gymnastics doctor Larry Nassar. "It's about time," Justice Ruth Bader Ginsburg, eighty-four, said when asked about the struggle. "Every woman of my vintage knows what sexual harassment is, although we didn't have a name for it," she told a Sundance Film Festival audience. "When I see women appearing every place in numbers, I'm less worried about a backlash than I might have been twenty years ago."[53]

In addition to connecting our sorrows, engaging in public debate, and doing everything we can to, as the civil rights leader Fannie Lou Hamer liked to say, "bring this thing out to the light," progressive movements also need to articulate a program of structural reforms that would both make a difference in everyday lives and substantially alter relations of power.[54] To do this does not require starting with a blank slate.

We can learn a great deal from the experiences of post–World War II activists and social movements, although we should not fall into the pit of nostalgia. There is a difference between understanding the ideas and struggles that motivated us then and dogmatically resurrecting the past as though it is a template for action. The world has changed profoundly in the last fifty years, and we face extraordinary new challenges. When I wrote a manifesto for a radical criminology in 1974, I seemed to know where we were going, no doubt a sign of youthful arrogance as well as the heady optimism of the era. Now we live in a long, uncertain interregnum, when the old regime is crumbling and the new one has not yet emerged, when, as Antonio Gramsci put it, a "great variety of morbid symptoms appear."[55]

Eric Hobsbawm's warning in 1994 about the instability of the world is even more relevant now: "The old maps and charts which guided human beings, singly and collectively, through life no longer represent the landscape through which we move . . . We do not know where our journey is taking us, or even ought to take us." Or, as the sociologist Immanuel Wallerstein put it, also in 1994, we are "in the midst of a whirlpool," uncertain where the ideological currents are heading. We have no maps to guide us on land, and we need to wear a life jacket when we get to the water. It does not look promising! Recognizing that we live in a moment of global uncertainty and chaos does not mean, however, that we need to start from ground zero or wander aimlessly into the future.[56]

To reform criminal justice institutions, we can build upon demands of the 1970s: massive decarceration; closing of juvenile prisons; abolition of capital punishment; ending the racial and class double standards applied to arrests, judicial proceedings, and imprisonment; taking seriously the victimization of women; and civilizing the police. Restoration of voting rights to millions of people with felony records and elimination of financial ability as a basis for bail would dramatically address major injustices in the carceral state. As for prisons, the United Nations offers a list of basic human rights for prisoners, known as the Nelson Mandela

Rules: "Respect for prisoners' inherent dignity and value as human beings"; "an absolute prohibition on engaging, actively or passively, in acts that may constitute torture"; a ban on the use of indefinite or prolonged solitary confinement; programs that "minimize any difference between prison life and life at liberty" and provide education and job-training for those in need; and restorative justice policies that encourage nonpunitive solutions to interpersonal crimes.[57]

Other states need to follow the lead of Rick Raemisch, director of Colorado's prison system, who spent twenty hours in solitary confinement and became convinced that making prisoners endure years without "regular social interactions" or "lock[ing] up someone who is severely mentally ill and let[ting] the demons chase him around the cell" is inhumane. The latter practice is routinely carried out against tens of thousands of prisoners around the country. Under Raemisch Colorado's prison system has limited solitary confinement to a maximum of fifteen days and reduced the number of inmates subjected to "administrative segregation" from seven hundred to eighteen.[58]

As long as the United States is not in compliance with United Nations standards, it has no business exporting American models of law enforcement and community corrections around the world. Also, issuing formal apologies and financial compensation to victims of human rights violations in CIA prisons around the world—such as the decision taken by the British government regarding its collusion with the United States in the case of Libyan dissidents tortured at a black site in Thailand—would be a good beginning to a reparative process.[59]

Given the current political climate in the United States, the adoption of these proposals would represent a significant break with the past. But this is not enough. We also need a bolder vision that links critiques of criminal justice operations with larger economic and social injustices, a vision that goes beyond expressions of outrage to construction of an agenda for radical change. A variety of grassroots groups are venturing into and beyond electoral politics, planting the seeds of such a strategy and experimenting with new kinds of organizations built for the long haul.[60]

In the spirit of these efforts I suggest that struggles to address out-of-control policing should include reining in private security operations, which play a significant role in enforcing public order and operate outside any kind of democratic regulation.

Following the example of early-twentieth-century activists who proposed that the governance of prisons be shared with the incarcerated, and of late-twentieth-century activists who proposed a public-service peace force, we should explore how to limit the police to investigations of serious crimes and transfer most of their day-to-day functions to social agencies and new kinds of community-based institutions that could handle interpersonal harms at the local level. As the sociologist Alex Vitale notes, people's security is too important to be left to the police: "We can use the power of communities and government to make our cities safer without relying on police, courts, and prisons."[61]

In addition to continuing campaigns to reduce the unacceptable cost of state prisons, we should tackle regulation of the unaccountable billions of dollars spent on homeland security, international criminal justice programs, and intelligence operations contracted out to private companies.

The campaign to reduce mass incarceration needs to address with equal vigor mass detention and mass deportation of immigrants.

Activists and reformers who argue that making criminal justice institutions more fair and humane requires a focus on local issues need to keep in mind the decisive role historically played by the federal government in whipping up, leading, and funding many wars on crime, including the latest campaign in the name of homeland security.[62]

Moral exhortation to reduce violent crime in what Trump called urban "war zones," and to separate serious from nonserious offenders, would be more compelling and effective if criminal justice agencies were equally vigilant against economic criminals and state officials who peddle practices and policies that, in Debs' words, are responsible for a "stupendous waste of human life." A few thousand corporate and government criminals sentenced to long terms would no doubt generate support for meaningful changes, if the experiences of the California legislator Patrick Nolan, former New York police commissioner Bernard Kerik, and Nixon aide Charles Colson are any indication. All did time for abuse of power and returned to their careers to preach the gospel of penal reform.[63]

Efforts to reintegrate the formerly incarcerated into their communities should be part of a more broadly based welfare rights campaign that recognizes most people's desire to work and be productive and creative; appreciates that taking care of families is real work; does not tie economic entitlements to morality tests or pit women against men, poor whites against communities of color, immigrants against citizens, or the unemployed against the employed in competition for economic resources; and provides the unemployed and people unable to work with the ability to survive with dignity, with access to the same services available to the employed.

As a result of about forty years of law-and-order policies, whenever the subjects of criminal justice, welfare institutions, and deportation orders are imagined publicly, the mostly black and brown images conjured up suggest beings who are broken, damaged, and semihuman, dangerous and unpredictable, better caged than free. The widely held impression is that they are much more of a threat to public safety than weapons dealers, bombers of civilian populations, corrupt military contractors, torturers, tobacco manufacturers, environmental polluters, tax evaders, false advertisers, fraudulent politicians, sexual predators, and modern-day slave traders. It will take an enormous effort of idealism and creativity to undo what has become taken for granted, to respect the incarcerated and criminalized as our sisters and brothers, and to imagine a society in which authoritarianism, coercion, and fear do not play such a major role in governance.

Clearly the Trump victory represented a right-wing politics in ascendancy and an ideology that confirms Paul Gilroy's insight that "the heritage of fascist rule survives inside democracy as well as outside it," but we must be careful not to see fascism everywhere or conflate Trump's right-wing populism with a consolidated authoritarian state. He has more in common with such characters as George Patton, the right-wing U.S. general who was considering a plunge into politics at the time of his death in 1945, than with Hitler, and with Jesse Ventura, the former wrestler and entertainer who in 1993 became governor of Minnesota on the Reform Party ticket, than with Mussolini. It was Ventura who prompted Trump to first aspire to political office. "Nonpoliticians like Ventura are the wave of the future," Trump wrote in 2000.[64]

Persistent inequality, a right-wing government in ascendancy, tensions within ruling and economic elites, and widespread malaise and resistance will again give us many opportunities to express a vision of social justice and organize opposition. And when political openings occur, we need to be ready with a strategy and concrete ideas.

In this chaotic moment dystopian ideas flourish. "Not since Water-

gate," notes Mike Davis, a leading activist intellectual, "has so much uncertainty and potential disorder infected every institution, network, and
power relationship." Although this era is reminiscent of previous defeats
and setbacks, what the historian Leon Litwack describes as the "terrify-
ing sense of personal betrayal and anguish" that accompanies the crash-
ing of great hopes, the past does not precisely reproduce itself and
regression is not inevitable.[65]

We still live in a "world of walls" that the poet Etheridge Knight
evoked so vividly from his prison cell in the late 1960s: "from the walls of
racism...to the walls of fire in Vietnam and Newark, to the gray stone
walls of San Quentin." Making the criminalized human again and ending the tragedy of the punitive state will take new ways of thinking, a
revitalized imagination, and reckoning with a historical legacy that weighs
heavily on the present. Beyond these walls—walls that contain millions
of our brothers and sisters, walls that divide us, walls that constrain our
idealism, walls that partition our ideas, and walls that cut us off from the
past—sweet freedom still faintly calls.[66]

AUTHOR'S NOTE

We shall not cease from exploration
And the end of all our exploring
Will be to arrive where we started
And know the place for the first time.

—T. S. Eliot, "Little Gidding"

Ever tried. Ever failed. No matter. Try Again.
Fail again. Fail better.

—Samuel Beckett, "Worstward Ho"

This is not a book that I expected to write, but here I am, back where I started, and, I hope, failing better than my first explorations more than fifty years ago.

"Our society," I wrote in the awkward and earnest prose of a twenty-year-old undergraduate in 1963, "still hunts the criminal with all its techniques of hostility and oppression dressed in the language and procedure of law." My first views about crime and punishment were shaped during my adolescence in a leftist household in Manchester, England, where I was taught to believe that every problem has a solution and that imprisonment is a relic of the backward past. I was against flogging, criminalization of homosexuality, capital punishment, and "moral righteousness on the Bench." Influenced more by social psychology than Marxism, I was vaguely in favor of "curative treatment tempered with humanity."[1]

As a rebellious teen in the 1950s, I was fortunate to come of age in a moment of massive global change, when activists could choose from an extraordinary array of utopian possibilities—social democracy in postwar Europe and the New Left in the United States, national liberation movements in Africa and Latin America, state communism in the Soviet Union and China, Cuba's bold rebellion, and later Nicaragua's Sandinista experiment in social justice. We had our pick of several visionary blueprints that, we thought, would guide us toward a promised land.

In the early 1960s, through serendipity rather than design, I made my way from medieval Oxford to a graduate program in the School of Criminology in cutting-edge Berkeley, where critical learning and the Free Speech movement shared the same space and where the foundations of the old white boys' club that had forever run elite universities began to shake. I was a beneficiary of an immigration policy (the Johnson-Reed Act of 1924) that, until passage of the 1965 Immigration Act, preferred newcomers from Europe to those from the rest of the world.

That I appeared on paper to be a British gentleman helped my admission to Berkeley. I doubt the program would have been so eager to recruit me if they had known my grandparents were illiterate Jewish immigrants from Eastern Europe and that my parents were former communists. At Berkeley my career benefited from an all-white doctoral program that in effect meant that I did not have to engage in fair competition with all my peers. My classmates included Mimi Silbert, who would go on to build San Francisco's Delancey Street Foundation into a globally recognized nonprofit rehabilitation program, and Tom Murton, who as superintendent of the notorious Cummins State Farm in Arkansas would excavate the prison's buried scandals and later was channeled by Robert Redford in the movie *Brubaker*. The Berkeley program would later include Lee Brown and George Napper, who would become two of the first African American police chiefs of major American cities, and Dick Hongisto, who as a young white cop joined the black-led Officers for Justice in San Francisco before being elected sheriff in 1971 and shaking up the department's hiring practices.

In Berkeley's School of Criminology and Center for the Study of Law and Society, I studied how California's pioneering leadership in postwar corrections, exemplified in the "rehabilitative ideal," not only had failed to transform the essentially punitive nature of incarceration but also had generated new psychologically and medically based instruments of social control.

From 1966 to 1968 I did my postdoctoral work at the University of Chicago, where I received my first in-depth personal lessons in racism and police violence and was jolted into action by the antiracism movement. Witnessing thousands of African Americans paraded in shackles through the jails and courts after the death of Martin Luther King was a transformative moment in my political development as an activist. Helping to raise bail money and coordinate legal representation for the Community Legal Defense Organization was my first organizing project. "Those who are concerned with the conspiratorial aspects of riots," I wrote in a report for the organization, "should also examine to what extent there was a conspiracy between the executive and judicial branches of Chicago government to illegally detain Black defendants and deny them due process."[2]

During my last month in Chicago before returning to Berkeley to teach in the School of Criminology, I experienced the police run riot over demonstrators at the Democratic Party's 1968 national convention. "The police were angry," I observed the day after being beaten as I tried to help a man with a bloody head wound. "Their anger was neither disinterested nor instrumental. It was deep, expressive, and personal. 'Get out of here you cocksuckers,' was their most common cry. It is difficult to objectively describe how the police relished the confrontation."[3]

These two years in Chicago revealed the enormously repressive power of the state and compelled me to reexamine the assumptions of my discipline. Until the 1960s criminology was a closed shop that maintained incestuous ties with governmental departments and criminal justice agencies. Training in this field, with its emphasis on technical measurement and narrow specialization, insulated professionals from the ethical and political consequences of their work. The first academic criminology program in the United States was established on the Berkeley campus in the political science department during World War I by August Vollmer, the City of Berkeley's chief of police and a leading figure in efforts to professionalize policing. Criminology, Vollmer noted in 1916, "is in reality a part or branch of the Police Department, is in direct control of Department, and is intended for the benefit of the men in the service of the Department." Vollmer would go on to make a name for himself in the 1920s as an outsider called in to clean up corruption in the Los Angeles Police Department and as an advocate of a national system of crime statistics when he was head of the International Association of Chiefs of Police. Vollmer's successor at Berkeley, O. W. Wilson, had served as police chief in Fullerton and Wichita before heading up the School of Criminology in 1950. He left in 1960 to become chief of police in Chicago.

Wilson's replacement, Joe Lohman, was a well-connected machine politician and sociologist who had chaired Governor Adlai Stevenson's Illinois Parole Board before being elected sheriff of Cook County and then treasurer of Illinois. Lohman headed the school when I arrived in 1963. He diversified the curriculum by adding social sciences and a research agenda to the school's professional mission, and his political clout brought grants from Washington, D.C. Although he was more liberal than his predecessors, he nevertheless advised university authorities how to crack down on student protests.[4]

Joe Lohman's unexpected death in 1968, the year of worldwide popular revolts, came as new ideas and practices were storming through academia and I was starting my first university job. When I returned to Berkeley from Chicago, I found a School of Criminology in transition from a managerial, patriarchal style of governance to a pluralistic program that housed a radical wing, liberal policy advocates, and old-school police officials and criminalists. It was a lively and exceptional moment in academia: while I joined antiwar activists on the streets in 1969–70, the school gladly took $140,000 (about $878,000 today) from President Nixon's right-wing Justice Department to train police how to control urban disorders.[5]

The school's faculty and researchers included Bernard Diamond, a psychiatrist who testified on behalf of Sirhan Sirhan, Robert Kennedy's assassin; Joel Fort, another psychiatrist, who led a campaign in California in 1972 to decriminalize the use of marijuana; and Caleb Foote, a pioneer in the bail reform movement who had twice done time in a federal prison for draft law violations during World War II, the first time as a pacifist and conscientious objector, then for his public opposition to the internment of Japanese Americans.[6]

My colleagues on the Left were a small but prominent group. Herman Schwendinger and Julia Schwendinger's communist background was evident in their controversial 1970 essay calling for a new paradigm. "Isn't it time to raise serious questions," they asked, "about the assumptions underlying the definition of the field of criminology when a man who steals a paltry sum can be called a criminal while agents of the State can, with impunity, legally reward men who destroy food so that price levels can be maintained while a sizable portion of the population suffers from malnutrition?"[7]

Bob Martinson, a researcher at the school, had been a Freedom Rider in 1961, joining the Congress of Racial Equality's civil disobedience campaign in Mississippi, where he spent thirty-nine days in the Jackson city jail and the infamous state penitentiary at Parchman. "We traveled across half a continent," he wrote in an essay for *The Nation*, "to lend our bodies to the struggle against bigotry." He participated in "a new kind of freedom—tough, critical, unsentimental, knowing—being forged in the jails and prisons of the South."[8]

Another colleague in Criminology, Paul Takagi, who as a Japanese American child had been incarcerated in Manzanar during the war, was an early advocate of reparations for victims of the internment. Takagi's outspoken views about police brutality and support for the 1969 Third World Strike at Berkeley led to his ostracism by the university administration in the mid-1970s after the school was closed down. Despite his tenured status, the university did not relocate him to another department for a year. "They left me slowly twisting in the wind," he recalled years later, "hoping I would go away, and nothing was being done for me. But that's okay, it's nothing new, but it did hurt me. I had been hurt before, and it wasn't as if my life depended on it."[9]

For an extraordinary few years I was in good company that changed my life. I experienced a seamless connection between ideas and practice, a sense of purposeful commitment in the classroom and community, teaching what I believed and believing what I taught, and researching and writing for social justice. We were far too hopeful, as it turned out, but we did not know or care.

In the early 1970s I was part of the first wave of what we called radical criminology, a perspective deeply influenced by Marxism and the New Left. I joined organizations that advocated local governance of police, massive decarceration, making crimes of violence against women a public matter, and holding corporations and government officials responsible for crimes against people. We created the first radical criminology journal—*Crime and Social Justice*, now known as *Social Justice*—and formed a collective to write a manual for antipolice activists. Our writings took on liberal myths about the neutrality of law and benevolence of the state, communicated the subjective experience of oppression, and exposed the raw, mean-spirited underbelly of the American criminal justice system.[10]

For the first time in the twentieth century, criminology ventured beyond its intellectual parochialism, took off its blinders, and welcomed a wide variety of theoretical and interdisciplinary insights. I was exposed to Michel Foucault's "great carceral continuum of disciplinary networks" and the idea that social control is not limited to physical forms of containment. From a civil libertarian perspective, Francis Allen alerted us to "the malevolent use of state power," especially when dressed up in the language of do-gooding. In Erving Goffman's "total institutions," whether penal or medical, patients and prisoners alike were said to experience processes of mortification as "the inmate is made to display a giving up of his will." From British labor historians and cultural theorists we learned how and when certain working-class behaviors became criminalized and why discourses about criminality are a significant component of how power is exercised. Georg Rusche's insights, first developed in Germany in the 1930s and rediscovered in the United States in the late 1960s, helped us to strip away "ideological veils" and reveal the modern prison as a social institution devoted to containing "surplus populations" and to warning the working poor of a fate worse than poverty if they got out of line.[11]

At Berkeley I cotaught an introductory criminology course with Paul Takagi and Barry Krisberg to six hundred students in which we showed a numbing film about the devastating aftermath of the 1945 atomic bombing of Hiroshima and Nagasaki and asked why it wasn't a war crime.[12] I cotaught another class with David Du Bois (stepson of W.E.B. Du Bois); David Du Bois was then editor of the Black Panther Party's newspaper.

In 1972, I helped to organize the first conference for prison activists in California. Our keynote speaker was Afeni Shakur, who along with twenty other members of New York's Black Panther Party had recently been acquitted of various conspiracy charges. "We as a people," was her message, "do not exist except as victims, and to this and much more, we say, No more."[13]

Years later, as a result of information I was able to obtain through the Freedom of Information Act, I would learn that informants in my classes were taking highly selective and sometimes hilarious notes for the FBI and CIA—and recommending my deportation. "Platt has continually and consistently displayed anti-American ideas," an FBI agent reported in

1969–70. "He has expressed anti-police opinions in the past and has led discussions which had an anti-law enforcement tone. He was one of the first individuals to wear extremely long hair . . . He is a dangerous individual."[14]

Berkeley figured prominently in the paranoid imagination of the executive branch. Nixon's national security adviser pronounced himself shell-shocked by the antiwar movement, and Admiral Thomas Moorer, chair of the Joint Chiefs of Staff, claimed in 1970 that a radical "command post" in Berkeley was plotting a military attack on the White House.[15]

Not surprisingly, I was not a criminology professor much longer. Berkeley's chancellor, Albert Bowker, regarded my first book, *The Child Savers* (still in print fifty years later), as "sharply biased" and evocative of "Orthodox Marxism of the 1930s." In a confidential memo to a university committee considering my promotion to a tenured position, he decried my so-called agitating against the police and contribution to the "decline in morale and reduction in size" of the Berkeley Police Department. He added, "I do believe some of his colleagues would be somewhat relieved if he weren't around." A California Superior Court judge backed up the university's decision to fire me, telling readers of the *New Yorker* that freedom of speech "has its price. A worker is free to tell his employer what he thinks of his business judgment; but he should not count on a Christmas bonus."[16]

By the mid-1970s social movements were in retreat and radical ideas had been marginalized. Despite lobbying by academics around the country in defense of academic freedom and sustained protests on the Berkeley campus, including a rally attended by thousands to hear Black Panther Party leader Bobby Seale defend the School of Criminology, in 1976 the university administration and Reagan-led board of regents closed down the oldest such program in the United States on the pretense that its faculty had abandoned its "professional mission." The administration placed the surviving and vetted faculty, with the exception of Paul Takagi, under the ideological guardianship of the law school. Bowker, still Berkeley's chancellor, took a hard line against students who protested the university's decision. "Sometimes," he recalled, "you have to crack a few heads." I was among many people at Berkeley and around the country who lost their jobs, a purge that echoed 1950s McCarthyism. Many activists lost more than their jobs, ending up dead, incarcerated, or in exile.[17]

I was lucky to get another job at a local state university teaching social work, and my research interests shifted to new topics. I joined a Marxist party until, like most leftist organizations in the 1980s, it imploded, leaving in its wake a sense of powerlessness among former cadres. A few years ago I was drawn back to criminology when, after waiting more than half of my lifetime, a national debate about the state of U.S. prisons and police finally erupted, with every political tendency, from right-wing libertarians to recovering liberals and grassroots activists, weighing in on the need for change.

In 2014, by then retired from teaching, I was invited to return as a resident scholar at the Center for the Study of Law and Society in Berkeley, the site of my banishment in the 1970s. It's good to be back where I started and to be among colleagues who are glad to have me around.

RESOURCES

1. STATE OF INJUSTICE

The literature on the current state of American criminal justice institutions is huge. Michelle Alexander's *The New Jim Crow: Mass Incarceration in the Age of Colorblindness* (2010) had a significant impact on the national conversation about race and incarceration. Angela Davis' *Are Prisons Obsolete?* (2003) reflects the insights of a longtime activist. Ta-Nehisi Coates' *Between the World and Me* (2015) is an eloquent statement of moral outrage at the persistence of racial injustice.

Of many academic books on the subject, Marie Gottschalk's *Caught: The Prison State and the Lockdown of American Politics* (2015) and Jonathan Simon's *Mass Incarceration on Trial: A Remarkable Court Decision and the Future of Prisons in America* (2014) are highly recommended, the former for its broad sweep, the latter for providing a glimmer of hope about judicial efforts to reform state prisons. Amy Lerman and Vesla M. Weaver's *Arresting Citizenship: The Democratic Consequences of American Crime Control* (2014) explains how millions of former prisoners have become "custodial citizens" with limited rights, treated as though they have experienced "civil death."

Two lawyers who have worked in the trenches of criminal defense provide thoughtful and moving accounts of their experiences: Bryan Stevenson's *Just Mercy: A Story of Justice and Redemption* (2014) and James Forman, Jr.'s, *Locking Up Our Own: Crime and Punishment in Black America* (2017).

Several important books, not always in agreement, explain how law and order became a bipartisan political issue: Naomi Murakawa's *The First Civil Right: How Liberals Built Prison America* (2014), Elizabeth Hinton's *From the War on Poverty to the War on Crime: The Making of Mass Incarceration in America* (2016), Michael Javen Fortner's *Black Silent Majority: The Rockefeller Drug Laws and the Politics of Punishment* (2015), and Jonathan Simon's *Governing Through Crime: How the War on Crime Transformed American Democracy and Created a Culture of Fear* (2007).

Beth Richie's *Arrested Justice: Black Women, Violence, and America's Prison Nation* (2012) and Alice Goffman's *On the Run: Fugitive Life in an American City* (2014) pay attention to a neglected topic: the victimization of women by the carceral state.

Lorna Rhodes' *Total Confinement: Madness and Reason in the Maximum Security Prison* (2004) is a devastating account of a supermax prison. Keramet Reiter's *23/7: Pelican Bay Prison and the Rise of Long-Term Solitary Confinement* (2016) illuminates the horrors of solitary confinement.

The Sentencing Project (http://www.sentencingproject.org/) and the Prison Policy Initiative (http://www.prisonpolicy.org/) provide indispensable resources, statistics, reports, and analysis in a readable format, with creatively presented tables and charts.

Since 2008 several organizations from a variety of political perspectives have weighed in on how to reform prisons and police. See, for example, Right on Crime (http://rightoncrime.com/), the Brennan Center for Justice (http://www.brennancenter.org/), and *The Marshall Project* (https://www.themarshallproject.org).

Important historical and theoretical work that continues to be widely studied since the 1970s includes Michel Foucault's *Discipline and Punish* (1977), Georg Rusche and Otto Kirchheimer's *Punishment and Social Structure* (1967), and Stuart Hall and colleagues' *Policing the Crisis: Mugging, the State and Law and Order* (1978, 2013). Foucault's lectures are now available in *The Punitive Society: Lectures at the Collège de France, 1972–1973* (2015), thoughtfully edited by Bernard Harcourt. James Q. Wilson's *Thinking About Crime* (1977) shaped conservative government policies for decades and influenced Donald Trump's views about crime, as did George Kelling and Wilson's 1982 essay in *The Atlantic*, "Broken Windows: The Police and Neighborhood Safety."

On the term *carceral* and its various uses, a good place to begin is Foucault's *Discipline and Punish* and Bernard Harcourt's "Course Content" in Foucault's *The Punitive Society*. The original formulation of *social death* is in Orlando Patterson's *Slavery and Social Death: A Comparative Study* (1982). More recent work that develops Patterson's framework includes Joshua Price's *Prison and Social Death* (2015) and Lisa Marie Cacho's *Social Death: Racialized Rightlessness and the Criminalization of the Unprotected* (2012). Elaborating on Patterson's idea, the sociologist Avery Gordon ("Some Thoughts on Haunting and Futurity," 2011) defines social death as "the process by which a person is socially negated or made a human non-person as the terms of their incorporation into a society."

For an eloquent critique from an unlikely source of how the carceral state subjects the poor and communities of color to "civil and literal death," a must-read is Justice Sonia Sotomayor's U.S. Supreme Court dissent in *Utah v. Strieff* (2016). Katherine Beckett and Naomi Murakawa ("Mapping the Shadow Carceral State," 2012) and Marie Gottschalk in *Caught* make a persuasive case for a capacious understanding of criminal justice institutions. I expand their perspective to include private security, intelligence operations, and the global reach of American criminal justice programs.

Susan Sontag's *Regarding the Pain of Others* (2003) and Eva Hoffman's *After Such*

Knowledge: Memory, History, and the Legacy of the Holocaust (2004) help us to consider ethical responsibilities when investigating and reporting on social injustices.

For a literary take on the carceral state, I recommend revisiting Franz Kafka's *In the Penal Colony* (1948). Charles Dickens' account of his visit to a prison in Pennsylvania in 1842, available in *American Notes* (1972), still resonates more than 175 years later.

2. DOUBLE SYSTEM

Du Bois writes eloquently about the double system in his 1903 book, *The Souls of Black Folk.*

For how jails and prisons have become de facto mental hospitals for the poor, see Ram Subramanian et al., *Incarceration's Front Door: The Misuse of Jails in America* (2015); and Jeremy Travis, Bruce Western, and Steve Redburn, eds., *The Growth of Incarceration in the United States: Explaining Causes and Consequences* (2014).

Herman Schwendinger and Julia Schwendinger's important 1970 essay, "Defenders of Order or Guardians of Human Rights?," called for criminology to break out of its constricted worldview and take on crimes against humanity. To understand how corporations and what used to be called white-collar criminals routinely experience impunity, start with Jerome Hall's *Theft, Law and Society* (1952), then move on to Edwin Sutherland's important 1944 essay, "Is 'White Collar Crime' Crime?" and Gregg Barak's more recent *Theft of a Nation* (2012). In his 2014 polemic, "The Financial Crisis," Judge Jed Rakoff asks in his subtitle, "Why have no high-level executives been prosecuted?" Jesse Eisinger's *The Chickenshit Club: Why the Justice Department Fails to Prosecute Executives* (2017) provides some answers.

On the functional equivalency of welfare and imprisonment, see Julilly Kohler-Hausmann, *Getting Tough: Welfare and Imprisonment in 1970s America* (2017); Loïc Wacquant, *Punishing the Poor* (2009); and Joe Soss, Richard C. Fording, and Sanford F. Schram, *Disciplining the Poor: Neoliberal Paternalism and the Persistent Power of Race* (2011).

For a critical history of the American antiwelfare state, see Michael Katz, *In the Shadow of the Poorhouse: A Social History of Welfare in America* (1986). Theda Skocpol's *Protecting Soldiers and Mothers* (1992) is the definitive work on nineteenth-century welfare. Jacob Hacker's *The Divided Welfare State* (2002) is the best account of the United States' two-tiered welfare system. Linda Gordon's *Pitied but Not Entitled: Single Mothers and the History of Welfare* (1994) brings a much-needed radical feminist perspective to the history of public welfare.

A great deal has been written about the punitive turn in welfare policy in the 1990s. For trenchant critiques by leading feminist academics (including Mimi Abramovitz, Eileen Boris, Nancy Fraser, Linda Gordon, Gwendolyn Mink, Frances Fox Piven, and Rickie Solinger), see three special issues of the journal *Social Justice*: "Women and Welfare Reform" (1994), "Disdained Mothers and Despised Others" (1998), and "Welfare and Punishment in the Bush Era" (2001). David Zucchino's *Myth of the Welfare Queen* (1997) illustrates the important role of right-wing ideology in promoting antiwelfare policies. Trump lays out his antiwelfare prejudices in his 2000 book, *The America We Deserve.*

For the grim everyday realities of criminal justice operations, Caleb Foote's 1959 essay, "The Bail System and Equal Justice," can be read as a critique of today's class system of bail. Issa Kohler-Hausmann's essays on misdemeanor courts (2013 and 2014) paint a detailed portrait of injustices in the lower courts. Since the 1960s the Vera Institute of Justice (https://www.vera.org/) has continued against all odds to fight miserable conditions in local jails. For a critique of the legal profession's collaboration with criminal courts, it is worth revisiting Robert Lefcourt's *Law Against the People* (1971); for a contemporary cri de coeur see Judge Rakoff's "Why Innocent People Plead Guilty" (2014). On the original insight that the criminal courts promote administrative cooperation rather than adversarial combat, see Jerome Skolnick's "Social Control in the Adversary System" (1967) and Abraham Blumberg's "The Practice of Law as a Confidence Game" (1967).

3. EXCEPT FOR

Literature on the topic of contemporary incarceration, or mass imprisonment, as it is known, is extensive. A good place to find a summary of the empirical evidence is the National Research Council's 2014 report: Jeremy Travis, Bruce Western, and Steve Redburn's *The Growth of Incarceration in the United States: Explaining Causes and Consequences*. For up-to-date information on national trends, presented with imaginative graphics, check out the invaluable websites of the Sentencing Project (www.sentencingproject.org) and the Prison Policy Initiative (www.prisonpolicy.org). Important regional case studies include Ruth Gilmore's *Golden Gulag: Prisons, Surplus, Crisis, and Opposition in Globalizing California* (2007), Mona Lynch's *Sunbelt Justice: Arizona and the Transformation of American Punishment* (2010), and Robert Perkinson's *Texas Tough: The Rise of America's Prison Empire* (2010).

The New Red Barn, written by a former prison administrator, William Nagel, warned us in 1973 about the racism and inhumanity of mass imprisonment, but nobody in power was listening.

While academics are in wide agreement that racism is a core aspect of imprisonment, why this is the case has several interpretations. Thorsten Sellin was among the first sociologists to seriously examine the legal relationship in *Slavery and the Penal System* (1976). Several contemporary writers, such as Loïc Wacquant and Marie Gottschalk, explain the punitive turn as rooted in neoliberalism, whereas Jordan Camp's *Incarcerating the Crisis: Freedom Struggles and the Rise of the Neoliberal State* (2016) and Dan Berger's *Captive Nation: Black Prison Organizing in the Civil Rights Era* (2014) focus on the state's response to struggles for racial justice. Naomi Murakawa's *The First Civil Right: How Liberals Built Prison America* (2014) digs deeper into the origins of post–World War II racism, and in *The Condemnation of Blackness: Race, Crime, and the Making of Modern Urban America* (2010), Khalil Muhammad excavates the origins of scientific racism and criminality.

Most accounts of the relationship between racism and criminal justice operations address the experiences of African Americans, Latinos, Asian Americans, and Native Americans as separate and unique. Eleanor Conlin Casella's *The Archaeology of*

Institutional Confinement (2007) and Laleh Khalili's *Time in the Shadows: Confinement in Counterinsurgencies* (2013) help us to understand the interrelationship of different kinds of racial experiences in carceral institutions.

For detailed accounts that reveal the mechanics of criminalization and group repression, see Benjamin Madley, *An American Genocide: The United States and the California Indian Catastrophe, 1846–1873* (2016); David Wallace Adams, *Education for Extinction: American Indians and the Boarding School Experience, 1875–1928* (1995); William D. Carrigan and Clive Webb, *Forgotten Dead: Mob Violence Against Mexicans in the United States, 1848–1928* (2013); and Jean Pfaelzer, *Driven Out: Roundups, Resistance, and the Forgotten War Against Chinese Americans* (2007). John Helmer's 1975 book, *Drugs and Minority Oppression,* led the way in explaining how twentieth-century drug wars were often racially motivated.

For the history of Reconstruction and context, see W.E.B. Du Bois' *Black Reconstruction in America: An Essay Toward a History of the Part Which Black Folk Played in the Attempt to Reconstruct Democracy in America, 1860–1880* (1973); and Eric Foner, *Reconstruction: America's Unfinished Revolution, 1863–1877* (1988). Leon Litwack relentlessly documents the horrific aftermath of Reconstruction in *Trouble in Mind: Black Southerners in the Age of Jim Crow* (1998).

Several excellent case studies explore how the defeat of Reconstruction was linked to the criminalization of African American men and women. See, for example, Sarah Haley, *No Mercy Here: Gender, Punishment, and the Making of Jim Crow Modernity* (2016); Mary Ellen Curtin, *Black Prisoners and Their World, Alabama 1865–1900* (2000); Talitha L. LeFlouria, *Chained in Silence: Black Women and Convict Labor in the New South* (2015); David Oshinsky, *"Worse Than Slavery": Parchman Farm and the Ordeal of Jim Crow Justice* (1997); Douglas Blackmon, *Slavery by Another Name: The Re-Enslavement of Black Americans from the Civil War to World War II* (2008); and Alex Lichtenstein's *Twice the Work of Free Labor: The Political Economy of Convict Labor in the New South* (1996). Mary Church Terrell's "Peonage in the United States: The Convict Lease System and the Chain Gangs," written in 1907, is a model of analytical clarity and moral outrage.

Rebecca McLennan's *The Crisis of Imprisonment: Protest, Politics, and the Making of the American Penal State, 1776–1941* (2008) makes a compelling case that the convict lease system was a national, not southern, phenomenon.

4. ON GUARD

As of July 2018, the federal government does not keep reliable statistics on police-initiated killings, nor does it mandate police departments to report all such occurrences. It is necessary, then, to rely on private databases (such as killedbypolice.net) and invaluable journalistic reporting (such as the *Washington Post*'s Fatal Force project, which is regularly updated at https://www.washingtonpost.com/graphics/national/police-shootings-20187/). For an in-depth study of the death of Eric Garner, see Matt Taibbi's *I Can't Breathe: A Killing on Bay Street* (2017).

The analysis of the history of policing draws in part on *The Iron Fist and the*

Velvet Glove: An Analysis of the U.S. Police, first published in 1975, of which I was a coauthor, and in particular on the contributions of Elliott Currie, Sidney Harring, and Gerda Ray. The third edition, published in 1982, is still in print. Alex Vitale's *The End of Policing* (2017) provides a much-needed critical overview of contemporary police militarism.

Throughout the twentieth century, various government commissions, task forces, and academic investigations called for reforms of the police. See, for example, Gunnar Myrdal's *An American Dilemma* (1944), *The Challenge of Crime in a Free Society* (1967) by the President's Commission on Law Enforcement and Administration of Justice (appointed by Lyndon Johnson), and Jerome Skolnick's *The Politics of Protest* (1969). The final report of the President's 2015 Task Force on 21st Century Policing, appointed by Obama, provides a good overview of current dominant ideas about reform before the Trump presidency. Jodi Rios' "Flesh in the Street" (2016) reveals why one too many police killings ignited street protests.

Of several official investigations of police malpractice and racism by the Justice Department's Civil Rights Division during the Obama administration, see especially *Investigation of the Baltimore City Police Department* (2016), and for an uncompromising investigation at the local level, see the (Chicago) Police Accountability Task Force's *Recommendations for Reform: Restoring Trust Between the Chicago Police and the Communities They Serve* (2016).

For the history and professionalization of modern policing, important texts include Jean-Paul Brodeur's *The Policing Web* (2010), Egon Bittner's *The Function of the Police in Modern Society* (1970), and Robert Fogelson's *Big-City Police* (1977). Clifford Shearing and Philip Stenning's *Private Policing* (1987) was one of the first anthologies to draw attention to a neglected topic. Richard Slotkin's important book, *The Fatal Environment: The Myth of the Frontier in the Age of Industrialization, 1800–1890* (1985) makes connections between military operations against Native peoples and policing operations against the labor movement.

On the history of political policing, Robert Goldstein's *Political Repression in America: From 1870 to the Present* (1978) provides an overview from 1870 to the 1970s; Frank Donner's *The Age of Surveillance: The Aims and Methods of America's Intelligence System* (1980) and *Protectors of Privilege: Red Squads and Police Repression in Urban America* (1990) fill in the important details.

On the history of the racial anxieties of the FBI and federal government, see Kenneth O'Reilly's *Racial Matters: The FBI's Secret File on Black America, 1960–1972* (1989); the 1951 petition to the United Nations by the Civil Rights Congress, edited by William Patterson, *We Charge Genocide* (1952); and David Garrow's *The FBI and Martin Luther King, Jr.* (1981). Paul Takagi's 1974 article, "A Garrison State in a 'Democratic' Society," was the first academic critique of police killings.

Edward J. Escobar's *Race, Police, and the Making of a Political Identity: Mexican Americans and the Los Angeles Police Department, 1900–1945* (1999) is an important history of policing Latinos in a major city. Victor Rios' ethnography, *Punished: Policing the Lives of Black and Latino Boys* (2011), provides a sense of what it is like to be targeted by the police. For an incisive, expressive analysis of police racism, nothing tops James Baldwin's 1960 essay in *Esquire*, "Fifth Avenue, Uptown: A Letter from Harlem," reprinted in *Nobody Knows My Name: More Notes of a Native Son* (1961).

5. THE INSECURITY SYNDROME

On the federalization of the carceral state, and how Democrats and Republicans colluded in its development, Elizabeth Hinton's *From the War on Poverty to the War on Crime: The Making of Mass Incarceration in America* (2016) is a must read. My *Politics of Riot Commissions, 1917–1970: A Collection of Official Reports and Critical Essays* (1971) includes excerpts from the reports and critiques of national commissions in the 1960s and 1970s. The *Task Force Report on Science and Technology* (1967) from the President's Commission on Law Enforcement and Administration of Justice is a key document for understanding the rise of policing by corporate security.

The punitive turn in immigration policies has a large, specialized literature. See, for example, Judith Greene, Bethany Carson, and Andrea Black's *Indefensible: A Decade of Mass Incarceration of Migrants Prosecuted for Crossing the Border* (2016), Tanya Maria Golash-Boza's *Deported: Immigrant Policing, Disposable Labor, and Global Capitalism* (2015), and Marjorie Zatz's *Dreams and Nightmares: Immigration Policy, Youth, and Families* (2015). For the Trump administration's views about the dangers of immigration, see the president's executive orders at https://www.whitehouse.gov/briefing-room /statements-and-releases.

For how urban policing became increasingly a military operation and thoroughly racialized, see Stephen Graham's *Cities Under Siege: The New Military Urbanism* (2011) and Didier Fassin's *Enforcing Order: An Ethnography of Urban Policing* (2013). For background on this development, Mike Davis' *City of Quartz: Excavating the Future in Los Angeles* (1990) is indispensable, and for a global context, see Philip Agee's groundbreaking exposé, *Inside the Company: CIA Diary* (1975).

A growing interdisciplinary literature deals with what is variously called securitization, the security-industrial complex, and the security state; it draws attention to the integration of public policing and private security and their transnational operations. See, for example, Marc Schuilenburg's *The Securitization of Society: Crime, Risk, and Social Disorder* (2015) and Laleh Khalili's *Time in the Shadows: Confinement in Counterinsurgencies* (2013). Bernard E. Harcourt's *The Counterrevolution: How Our Government Went to War Against Its Own Citizens* (2018) argues that counterinsurgency warfare is the "new governing paradigm" in the United States. For a vision of dystopia from the Right, see Peter Huber and Mark Mills' chilling "How Technology Will Defeat Terrorism" (2002).

The nonprofit Gun Violence Archive (http://www.gunviolencearchive.org/), created in 2013, is an excellent resource for statistics about deaths and injuries caused by guns in the United States.

On the dangers of the corporatization of American public life, a good place to begin is Dwight D. Eisenhower, "Farewell Address to the American People."

6. THE PERILS OF REFORM

Much has been written about the role of the media in associating African Americans with dangerousness and criminality. Highly recommended is Russell Lord's case study, *Gordon Parks: The Making of an Argument* (2013), which shows how *Life* magazine in 1948 distorted the work of the noted photographer.

The argument that the Progressive reform tradition has a repressive underside was first developed in Gabriel Kolko's *The Triumph of Conservatism: A Reinterpretation of American History* (1967) and James Weinstein's *The Corporate Ideal in the Liberal State, 1900–1918* (1969), and elaborated in several case studies, including Frances Fox Piven and Richard Cloward's *Regulating the Poor: The Functions of Public Welfare* (1977) and my *The Child Savers: The Invention of Delinquency* (1969).

The role of middle-class women in enforcing tough-minded reforms is explored in Sheila Rowbotham's *Hidden from History* (1973) and Linda Gordon's *Women, the State and Welfare* (1990). On how the child-saving movement affected Native American communities, see David Wallace Adams' *Education for Extinction: American Indians and the Boarding School Experience, 1875–1928* (1994), Margaret Jacobs' *White Mother to a Dark Race: Settler Colonialism, Maternalism, and the Removal of Indigenous Children in the American West and Australia, 1880–1940* (2009), and Cathleen Cahill's *Federal Fathers and Mothers: A Social History of the United States Indian Service, 1869–1933* (2011). Peter Nabokov's *Native American Testimony* (1991) gives readers a sense of how Native American youth experienced the boarding schools.

On moral crusades involving patriotism, sexual purity, health, and disability, see Cecilia O'Leary's *To Die For: The Paradox of American Patriotism* (1999), Margot Canaday's *The Straight State: Sexuality and Citizenship in Twentieth-Century America* (2009), Susan Schweik's *The Ugly Laws: Disability in Public* (2009), Kathy Peiss' *Cheap Amusements: Working Women and Leisure in Turn-of-the-Century New York* (1986), Lisa McGirr's *The War on Alcohol: Prohibition and the Rise of the American State* (2016), Regina Kunzel's *Fallen Women, Problem Girls: Unmarried Mothers and the Professionalization of Social Work, 1890–1945* (1993), Nancy Bristow's *Making Men Moral: Social Engineering During the Great War* (1996), and John D'Emilio's *Sexual Politics, Sexual Communities: The Making of a Homosexual Minority in the United States, 1940–1970* (1983).

The growing literature on the history of eugenics includes Stefan Kühl's *The Nazi Connection: Eugenics, American Racism, and German National Socialism* (1994), my *Bloodlines: Recovering Hitler's Nuremberg Laws, From Patton's Trophy to Public Memorial* (2006), Alexandra Minna Stern's *Eugenic Nation: Faults and Frontiers of Better Breeding in Modern America* (2005), Wendy Kline's *Building a Better Race: Gender, Sexuality, and Eugenics from the Turn of the Century to the Baby Boom* (2001), and Nancy Ordover's *American Eugenics: Race, Queer Anatomy, and the Science of Nationalism* (2003).

To get a sense of how eugenics became mainstream in the 1920s, read Paul Popenoe and Roswell Hill Johnson's dispassionately racist textbook, *Applied Eugenics* (1926). On the role of eugenics in carceral policies against Latinos, see Miroslava Chávez-García's

States of Delinquency: Race and Science in the Making of California's Juvenile Justice System (2012) and Natalia Molina's *Fit to Be Citizens? Public Health and Race in Los Angeles, 1879–1939* (2006). Laura Briggs traces the postwar revival of eugenic policies in the United States in *Reproducing Empire: Race, Sex, Science, and U.S. Imperialism in Puerto Rico* (2002). Moving testimony by women subjected to involuntary sterilization appears in *Against Their Will: North Carolina's Sterilization Program and the Campaign for Reparations* (2012) by Kevin Begos and colleagues. For social work's rationale for enthusiastic postwar participation in sterilization programs, read Moya Woodside's *Sterilization in North Carolina: A Sociological and Psychological Study* (1950). Richard Herrnstein and Charles Murray's influential *The Bell Curve: Intelligence and Class Structure in American Life* (1994) spread eugenic assumptions about intelligence throughout policy circles in the 1990s.

On right-wing perspectives on indulgent welfare policies, it is instructive to compare Marvin Olasky's *The Tragedy of American Compassion* (1995) with Donald Trump's critique of the New Deal and War on Poverty in *The America We Deserve* (2000). Both call for dismantling what little remains of the welfare state.

7. RADICAL VISIONS

To get a sense of the literature that shook up public debates about crime and justice in the 1960s and 1970s, start with popular memoirs, such as *The Autobiography of Malcolm X* (1965), Claude Brown's *Manchild in the Promised Land* (1965), Malcolm Braly's *False Starts: A Memoir of San Quentin and Other Prisons* (1976), and Piri Thomas' *Down These Mean Streets* (1981). The letters of the prison activist George Jackson, published in *Soledad Brother* (1970), had a long-lasting impact on radical prison organizing. The journalist Jessica Mitford's *Kind and Usual Punishment: The Prison Business* (1973) channeled the ideas of the movement to a broad audience. Angela Davis' anthology, *If They Come in the Morning: Voices of Resistance* (1971), was one of the few books of that era to include the experiences of women active in the prison movement. Curtis Dawkins' *The Graybar Hotel* (2017) is a more recent and important contribution to fictional accounts of life inside.

Bruce Franklin's anthology, *Prison Writing in 20th Century America* (1998), is the best introduction to the depth and variety of fiction and poetry written by prisoners. David Suvak's *Memoirs of American Prisons* (1979), an annotated bibliography, provides a comprehensive list of hard-to-find materials.

Of many books written by former prisoners about the horrors of prison life and what to do about them, start with Austin Reed's compelling account written in the mid-nineteenth century, *The Life and Adventures of a Haunted Convict*, published in 2016. Eugene V. Debs' *Walls and Bars* (1963), about his experiences in the 1920s, still stands out as a model of analysis and action. From the perspective of a prison warden who tries to do the right thing, Tom Murton's *Accomplices to the Crime* demonstrates what happens when a reformer goes up against political realities. Heather Thompson's *Blood in the Water: The Attica Uprising of 1971 and Its Legacy* (2016) is the definitive account of the revolt and subsequent repression that sent a warning to the prisoners' movement.

8. THE DISTANT PRESENT

The origins of the bipartisan political consensus regarding law-and-order policies are explored in Lisa McGirr's *The War on Alcohol* (2016), Naomi Murakawa's *The First Civil Right* (2014), and Elizabeth Hinton's *From the War on Poverty to the War on Crime* (2016). They make the case that on issues relating to crime control, telling the difference between Republicans and Democrats is difficult.

For a vivid example of how politics can change a candidate's progressive views into the hard-nosed pragmatism of an officeholder, contrast the early Barack Obama in *The Audacity of Hope: Thoughts on Reclaiming the American Dream* (2006) with President Obama's farewell statement in "The President's Role in Advancing Criminal Justice Reform" (2017).

The sociologist Stuart Hall and his colleagues in England help readers understand how ideas and ideology, as well as economics and politics, have played, and continue to play, a critical role in promoting an authoritarian response to the "crime problem." See, in particular, Hall's *The Hard Road to Renewal: Thatcherism and the Crisis of the Left* (1988) and Hall and colleagues' *Policing the Crisis: Mugging, the State and Law and Order* (1978, 2013).

To appreciate the vitality of debates about crime and justice during Obama's second term, compare the wildly divergent ideas of right, liberal, and radical think tanks through the websites of Right on Crime (http://rightoncrime.com/), *The Marshall Project* (https://www.themarshallproject.org), the Brennan Center (http://www.brennancenter.org/), and Black Lives Matter (http://www.joincampaignzero.org/#vision).

For a discussion of the many problems involved in trying to document the staffing and funding of carceral agencies, see the appendix.

9. LIMBO

To trace the development of Donald Trump's ideas about crime, police, and prisons, start with his 2000 book, *The America We Deserve*. He relies here on the work of James Q. Wilson and the Heritage Foundation's briefing book for the 1998 election (*Issues '98* by Stuart Butler and Kim Holmes), in particular a chapter by Edwin Meese and colleagues ("Crime: Turning the Tide in America"). In *Time to Get Tough: Making America #1 Again* (2011), Trump ties immigration from Mexico to the crime problem. The flurry of anticrime executive orders issued by Trump during his first weeks in office is archived at https://www.whitehouse.gov/briefing-room/statements-and-releases. Jane Mayer's essay for the *New Yorker* (2017) provides a useful overview of Vice President Mike Pence's political career and ideology. Attorney General Jeff Sessions summed up his views about policing in a speech to the National Fraternal Order of Police on August 28, 2017.

For efforts by a centrist group of current and former police chiefs and prosecutors to counter Trump's bellicose law-and-order policies, see the work by Law Enforcement Leaders to Reduce Crime and Incarceration (*Fighting Crime and Strengthening Criminal Justice*, 2017).

Paul Gilroy's *Against Race: Imagining Political Culture Beyond the Color Line* (2000) explores the fascist tradition within democracy. To gain understanding of the conservatism of state bureaucracies, it is worth returning to two classic texts: Ralph Miliband's *The State in Capitalist Society* (1969) and Harry Braverman's *Labor and Monopoly Capital: The Degradation of Work in the Twentieth Century* (1974).

For challenges facing progressive movements in the wake of the collapse of left-wing politics around the world, see Eric Hobsbawm's *The Age of Extremes: A History of the World, 1914–1991* (1994) and Immanuel Wallerstein's 1994 essay, "The Agonies of Liberalism: What Hope Progress?" In *The End of Policing* (2017) Alex Vitale argues that we need to think about a world in which police play a minimal role.

In his novel *Giovanni's Room* (1957), James Baldwin evokes the "sorrow of the disconnected." The contradictory aspects of the immigrant experience are movingly captured in Carlos Bulosan's *America Is in the Heart: A Personal History* (1973).

NOTE ON STATISTICAL SOURCES

Despite the American obsession with data collection, information about the size, scope, and cost of criminal justice agencies is often inconsistent and piecemeal, in part because of the time lapse between reporting and publishing, in part because of changes in the ways in which data are collected and sorted. There have been allegations in the past, especially while John Ashcroft was U.S. attorney general (2001–2004), that the U.S. Department of Justice's decisions about data collection were subject to political manipulation. But the main problem is the failure of Congress and the federal government to authorize mandatory reporting and to do the job professionally.[1]

Much of the spending, employment, and operations of the carceral state occur at the state and local levels. The Justice Department's Bureau of Justice Statistics produces national surveys and estimates and publishes annual or biennial data series on prisons, jails, law enforcement, and court processes (www.bjs.gov). The bureau publishes the *Census of State and Local Law Enforcement Agencies* (www.bjs.gov/index.cfm?ty =dcdetail&iid=249) every four years; it is particularly useful for researching the public police.

INCARCERATION

For data about incarceration and changes over time, see the chart that follows as well as Cahalan, *Historical Corrections Statistics in the United*

States, 1850–1984; Guerino, Harrison, and Sabol, *Prisoners in 2010*; Snell, *Correctional Populations in the United States, 1993*; Carson and Anderson, *Prisoners in 2015*.

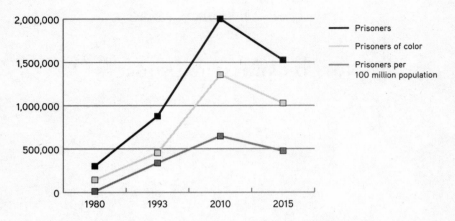

Source: Cahalan, *Historical Corrections Statistics in the United States, 1850–1984*, 64; Guerino, Harrison, and Sabol, *Prisoners in 2010*, 1, 26; Snell, *Correctional Populations in the United States, 1993*, iv; Carson and Anderson, *Prisoners in 2015*, 6.

If you are interested in comparing the number of African American men who are incarcerated and in college, start with the following BJS reports: West and Sabol, *Prisoners in 2007*; Carson and Sabol, *Prisoners in 2011*; and Minton and Golinelli, *Jail Inmates at Midyear 2013—Statistical Tables*. Information about African Americans in college can be found in Bureau of the Census, "Table 1: Population by Sex and Age, for Black Alone and White Alone," in the data series *The Black Population Alone in the United States: 2007*, available at https://www.census.gov/data/tables/2007/demo/race/ppl-ba07.html.

CRIMINAL JUSTICE EMPLOYMENT

Numbers by themselves do not make it possible to compare past and present. To figure out the extent of growth requires taking into account how the rate of employment has changed over time, such as how many police are hired per 100,000 residents of a city, and making a comparison of the rate of population growth and the rate of growth in criminal justice personnel. In both instances the evidence confirms a significant increase in policing and guarding jobs. This chart shows how the rate of criminal justice employment has changed over thirty-seven years.

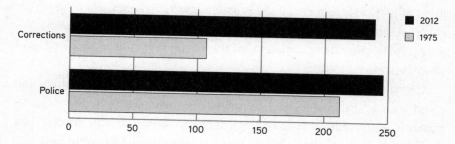

Source: Cahalan, *Historical Corrections Statistics in the United States, 1850–1984*, 64; Guerino, Harrison, and Sabol, *Prisoners in 2010*, 1, 26; Snell, *Correctional Populations in the United States, 1993*, iv; Carson and Anderson, *Prisoners in 2015*, 6.

To estimate changes in the number and rate of public police employment, see the BJS publications Kyckelhahn, *Justice Expenditure and Employment Extracts, 2012*; Lindgren, *Justice Expenditure and Employment Extracts, 1992*; and Reaves, *Number of Full-Time Sworn Law Enforcement Officers*.

To estimate changes in the number and rate of employment in prisons and jails, see the following BJS publications: Cahalan, *Historical Corrections Statistics in the United States, 1850–1984*; BJS, "Prisoners in State and Federal Institutions on December 31, 1979"; Guerino, Harrison, and Sabol, *Prisoners in 2010*; Bureau of Justice Statistics, *Justice Expenditure and Employment in the U.S., 1988* (Washington, D.C.: Bureau of Justice Statistics, 1991), http://www.bjs.gov/content/pub/pdf/jeeus88.pdf; Kyckelhahn, *Justice Expenditure and Employment Extracts, 2012*; and Bureau of the Census, "Population and Housing Estimates," https://www.census.gov/programs-surveys/popest.html.

Additional information about recent employment is available in the 1984 BJS report *Justice Expenditure and Employment in the US, 1971–79*; Office of Personnel Management, *Sizing Up the Executive Branch*; the Bureau of Prisons website (https://www.bop.gov/about/agency/); estimates by the Bureau of Labor Statistics for "correctional treatment specialists"; and the BJS series on state courts.

No centralized source of information exists for private security, the largest criminal justice employment sector, and poor design or sporadic response to surveys compromises all major data sources. The best estimate is an unpublished 2010 report commissioned by the U.S. Department of Justice: Strom et al., *The Private Security Industry*. An even earlier study—Cunningham, Taylor, and Hallcrest Systems, *The Hallcrest Report* (1991)—provides estimates that the Strom report used as the basis of its estimates.

Given that private security employees outnumber public police, and given the central role played by private security firms in the carceral state, this information is critically important. Based on the limited data available, the chart below shows what the rate of policing might look like if public and private police were combined.

Year	Private Police per 100,000	Private + Public Local and State Police per 100,000
1980	251	541
1990	350	630
2010	356	650

Source: Strom et al., *The Private Security Industry*, 34; Reaves, *Law Enforcement Officers*.

To compare carceral and noncarceral workforces, and to find information about employment beyond public agencies, start with the Bureau of Labor Statistics' Employment Projections database, available at www.bls .gov. For calculating specific employment patterns, the BLS "Employment Projections—Occupational Data" series has useful information at http://www.bls.gov/emp/ep_data_occupational_data.htm.

Beyond the BLS data, information can be retrieved from professional organizations and state government reports. For example, the California Budget Project publishes information about the state workforce at www.cbp.org, and data about the size of the legal profession are available from the American Bar Association's "Lawyer Demographics" reports on the field's demographics (such as https://www.americanbar.org

/content/dam/aba/migrated/marketresearch/PublicDocuments/lawyer _demographics_2013.authcheckdam.pdf). For estimates of the number of teachers, use the National Center for Education Statistics, "Fast Facts—2015," http://nces.ed.gov/fastfacts/display.asp?id=372.

Using all these sources, and recognizing the limits of available data, the breakdown of carceral state employees looks like this:

Private security: 1.7 million (2010)

Public policing (including state and local police, and support staff): 1.25 million (2012)

State prisons: 448,000 (2012)

Local jails: 213,300 (2015)

Federal prisons: 39,900 (2015)

U.S. Department of Homeland Security: 250,000 (2017)

U.S. Department of Justice: 112,000 (2013)

U.S. intelligence agencies: 100,000 (2006)

Probation and parole: 90,000 (2012)

Prosecutors: 33,000 (2007)

Judges: 27,570 (state court trial judges, 2011)

Public defenders: 15,000 (2007)

COST

Many claims are made about the cost of criminal justice institutions, but they vary considerably, depending on the subject matter and databases. Moreover, they usually omit programs that in economic terms are far more consequential: homeland security, intelligence agencies, the export of American criminal justice programs, and public projects contracted out to private companies. The economics of the carceral state is an "unknown unknown," to use Rumsfeld's reckoning, but a few examples reveal that budgets for policing and guarding are a fraction of the overall cost.

To research spending on the carceral state, start with the Bureau of the Census' State Government Finances Historical Database, which contains yearly information about criminal justice expenditures that goes back decades. For estimates of the cost of the carceral state, use Barnett et al., *2012*

Census of Governments: Finance—State and Local Government Summary Report, as well as Bureau of the Census, County Area Finance Database (available at http://www2.census.gov/pub/outgoing/govs/special60/).

For historical state budget information, start with census.gov/govs /state/historical_data.html. It is also necessary to draw upon a range of government reports to compile funding information, as these data are often disaggregated. Kyckelhahn, *Justice Expenditure and Employment Extracts 2012* and Lindgren, *Justice Expenditure and Employment Extracts 1992*, help establish public agency expenditures from the municipal to the federal levels. Note that the Lindgren report also includes historical data from before the 1990s.

For information about expenditures on the carceral state before the 1980s, consult the Law Enforcement Assistance Administration, U.S. Department of Justice, *Trends in Expenditure and Employment Data for the Criminal Justice System, 1971–1974* (Washington, D.C: USGPO, 1976), and Center for National Security Studies, *Law and Disorder IV* (Washington, D.C.: Center for National Security Studies, 1976).

Local spending on policing, adjusted for inflation, went from $29.3 billion in 1972 to $33.7 billion in 1982, $70.2 billion in 2002, and $84.1 billion in 2012. But the recent cost of policing needs to also take into account significant investments by the federal government that local criminal justice expenditures usually do not account for. According to a 2014 report issued by the Executive Office of the President, in a five-year period between 2009 and 2014, federal agencies provided nearly $18 billion in "funds and resources" for state and local law enforcement agencies. In 2012 the annual subsidy of $3 billion was in addition to the $84.1 billion spent on the police by all local governments that year.[2]

Kyckelhahn, *State Corrections Expenditures, FY 1982–2010*, provides data on corrections spending. For total state spending, see Bureau of the Census, State Government Finances Historical Database, available at http://www2.census.gov/pub/outgoing/govs/special60/.

OTHER DATABASES

The Federal Bureau of Investigation's *Uniform Crime Report* series (ucr.fbi .gov) contains information about police and arrests, although it mostly focuses on tracking the level of crime rather than carceral state operations (http://www2.census.gov/pub/outgoing/govs/special60/). The *UCR* may also suffer from irregular reporting by state and local agencies. Be aware that arrest data are an inadequate measure of levels of crime, given that most crimes are not reported to the police, and most corporate crime is not criminally prosecuted.

The National Vital Statistics System of the Centers for Disease Control and Prevention (www.cdc.gov/nchs/nvss/) provides yearly mortality data for the United States, including deaths in custody and deaths that result from law enforcement actions. The CDC relies on the reporting agencies to report these deaths accurately, but the NVSS is a useful starting point for researching carceral state violence. For data about deaths and injuries caused by guns, see the Gun Violence Archive (http://www .gunviolencearchive.org/). Killedbypolice.net and the *Washington Post's* Fatal Force project (https://www.washingtonpost.com/graphics/national /police-shootings-2017/) provide up-to-date information on killings by police.

ACKNOWLEDGMENTS

This book has been long in the writing, the result of many conversations and the picking of many brains.

It started as a very civil argument with Jonathan Simon about criminology's radical and liberal traditions that we tried out before a class in the law school at Berkeley in 2012 and in a workshop at the University of Edinburgh's law school in 2014.

I am especially grateful to Jonathan Simon, faculty director, and Rosann Greenspan, executive director, for inviting me to return to the Center for the Study of Law and Society at Berkeley, where I started and nearly ended my academic career more than fifty years ago. Here I have had the opportunity and privilege to learn from Berkeley faculty, students, and visiting scholars and to try out ideas with the Carceral Studies Working Group.

Thank you to Chase Burton, who worked with me for three years as much more than my research assistant, writing dozens of meticulous memos, digging into arcane sources for statistical data, and staying the the long, winding course.

My comrades on the journal *Social Justice* have made the journey since the 1970s much less lonely. Paul Takagi and Hi Schwendinger were there from the beginning. Special thanks to Greg Shank and Stefania De Petris, and to my coauthors of *The Iron Fist and the Velvet Glove*, especially

Elliott Currie, Sid Harring, and Gerda Ray for their historical contributions.

I was fortunate to present work in progress and get feedback on the manuscript for this book as it unfolded. My experience in 2013 with the European Research Council's Corpses of Mass Violence and Genocide project, led by Elisabeth Gessat Anstett and Jean-Marc Dreyfus, taught me about the necessity of interdisciplinary research and a resolutely ethical viewpoint. For hosting my talks I want to thank Dario Melossi at the University of Bologna, and Maartje van der Woude at the University of Leiden in 2015; Lois Presser and Michelle Brown at the University of Tennessee's New Directions in Critical Criminology conference, and Robert Koulish at the University of Maryland's Crimmigration in the Shadow of Sovereignty conference in 2016; and the Dutch Society of Criminology and Dutch Law and Society Association's invitation to speak on "The Responsibility of Intellectuals" in Rotterdam in September 2017.

Many people offered advice, leads, reading lists, and solace: Gregg Barak, Eduardo Bautista, Dan Berger, Michelle Brown, Margaret Cahalan, Jordan Camp, Troy Challenger, Ernest Chavez, Leonidas Cheliotis, David Edgar, Keith Feldman, Bruce Franklin, Alessandro De Giorgi, Craig Gilmore, Ruthie Gilmore, Paul Gilroy, Bob Gould, Sarah Haley, Jeff Halper, Christina Heatherton, Rachel Herzing, Pat Hilden, Steve Hinshaw, Susan Hoffman, Ericka Huggins, Nancy Scheper Hughes, Satsuki Ina, Anil Kalhan, Erin Kerrison, James Kilgore, Johann Koehler, Barry Krisberg, Regina Kunzel, Adam Lankford, Jenna Lloyd, Toussaint Losier, Peter Manning, Marc Mauer, Rebecca McClennan, Meghan McDowell, Armando Lara Millán, Laurindo Dias Minhoto, Michele Phelps, Mark Rabine, Milton Reynolds, Jodi Rios, Victoria Robinson, Ashley Rubin, Judah Schept, Stuart Schrader, Phil Scraton, Micol Seigel, Mimi Silbert, Alex Minna Stern, Pat Sutton, Sara Theiss, Alex Vitale, Geoff Ward, Vron Ware, Steve Wasserman, Sharon Weill, Bob Weiss, Bill Welsh, Rob Werth, and Marjorie Zatz.

If only I had been able to discuss the ideas for this book with Stuart Hall (1932–2014). "You might want to give this some thought," he would have said.

Loving thanks to my godmother, Juanita Rothman, who years ago introduced me to the work of W. G. Sebald. Whenever I got stuck during this project she reminded me that "the problem with writers is that they think too much and don't write enough," and then she'd tell me to "get cracking."

Colleagues and friends who took time off from hectic schedules to read the prospectus and drafts of chapters: I acknowledge your generosity and encouragement. I wanted you to say, "Do not change one word" but am glad that you didn't: Lynn Cooper, Alessandro De Giorgi, Jon Frappier, Jerry Hewitt, Elizabeth Hinton, George Lipsitz, Ed McCaughan, Peter Panuthos, Jeannie Pfaelzer, Steve Platt, Janelle Reinelt, David Stein, Maartje van der Woude, Dick Walker, and Geoff Ward.

My agent, Don Fehr, coaxed me to turn rough ideas into a book proposal. Karen Wolny, my editor at St. Martin's Press, persisted in demanding that I make my ideas accessible to a wide audience and made invaluable suggestions at every stage of the project. I was lucky to have both in my corner. Thanks to Michael Flamini for shepherding the book through its final stages. It took a village at St. Martin's Press to take care of a rigorous editing process and production, and reach out to potential readers: Sarah Becks, Alan Bradshaw, Donna Cherry, Nikolaas Eickelbeck, Gabrielle Gantz, Katherine Haigler, Gwen Hawkes, Polly Kummel, Martin Quinn, Jason Reigal, and Kelly Too.

Extra credit and eternal gratitude go to Cecilia O'Leary, my longtime partner in life and work, and Dennis Sherman, my oldest American friend, who critically read every word, draft after draft after draft, and demanded that I fail better.

Tony Platt
Berkeley, California

PHOTO CREDITS

1. "Carlisle Indian School in 1884." Photograph by John N. Choate. Cumberland County Historical Society, Carlisle, PA.
2. "Student Body of the Carlisle Indian School in 1892." Photograph by John N. Choate. Cumberland County Historical Society, Carlisle, Pa.
3. "Only Healthy Seed," ca. 1930s. Design by Haywood Norfolk. Galton Institute, London.
4. "Tule Lake Stockade," California, 1945. Photographer unknown. Courtesy of Tule Lake Committee.
5. "Central Processing at McAllen Border Patrol Facility, Texas," June 17, 2018. Photograph by U. S. Customs and Border Protection/Getty Images.
6. "Police Officers Removing Sit-Down Strikers from the Yale and Towne Manufacturing Plant, Detroit," 1937. Photographer unknown. U.S. Farm Security Administration/International News Photo, Library of Congress # 20177 62187.
7. "Social Worker Lupe Marshall Confronts Police at the Memorial Day Massacre of 1937," May 30, 1937. Photographer unknown. Roosevelt University Archives. Courtesy of Illinois Labor History Society.
8. "War Relocation Authority Security Roust," 1945. Photograph by Robert H. Ross. Courtesy of John Ross and Tule Lake Committee.
9. "Chicago Police Carry the Body of Fred Hampton," December 4, 1969. Photographer unknown. *Chicago Daily News*/Associated Press.
10. "The Water Cure, Philippines," ca. 1900s. Photographer unknown. National Archives (111-SC-98202).
11. "Tiger Cages, Vietnam," 2010. Photograph by Alan Travers. Courtesy of Alan Travers.

12. "The Hooded Man," ca. 2004. Photograph by Sergeant Ivan Frederick. http://static1.1.sqspcdn.com/static/f/707453/24424599/1393297101010/Tauschinger DempseyFigure9_72dpi.jpg.

13. "Lynndie England with Dog Leash," ca. 2004. Photographer unknown. https://zkm.de/media/bild/2014_aufstand_jean_jaque_lebel_le_labyrinthe.jpg.

14. "Braceros at the Hidalgo Processing Center, Texas," 1956. Photograph by Leonard Nadel. Leonard Nadel Photographs and Scrapbooks, Archives Center, National Museum of American History, Smithsonian Institution.

15. "Mass Arrests, Jackson, Mississippi," 1965. Photograph by Matt Herron.

16. "Huntsville Texas Prison," 1968. Photograph by Danny Lyon, Magnum Photos.

17. "Huntsville Texas Prison," 1968. Photograph by Danny Lyon, Magnum Photos.

18. "Leesburg Stockade, Georgia," 1963. Photograph by Danny Lyon, Magnum Photos.

19. "Food Stamp Line, New York," 1939. Photographer unknown. U. S. Department of Agriculture. National Archives and Records Administration, 20111110-OC-AMW-0051.

20. "Workers Unemployed by the Freeze in California," 2007. Photograph by Michael Raphael. FEMA photograph #29783.

21. "Dellwood, Missouri, Criminal Court," 2015. Photograph by Laurie Skrivan / *St. Louis Post-Dispatch*.

22. "GOP [Republican] National Convention: General Views, Ike," 1964. Photograph by Warren K. Leffler / *U.S. News & World Report*. Library of Congress.

23. "Chief Justice Warren E. Burger Administering the Oath of Office to Richard M. Nixon," 1973. Photograph by Architect of the Capitol. Library of Congress.

24. "1989 Presidential Inauguration, George H. W. Bush, Opening Ceremonies, Capitol, Swearing In," 1989. Photograph by Jeff Tinsley. Smithsonian National Archives.

25. "Chief Justice William Rehnquist Administering the Oath of Office to Bill Clinton on the West Front of the U.S. Capitol, January 20, 1997," 1997. Photograph by Architect of the Capitol. AOC no. 73564.

26. "George W. Bush Delivers His Inaugural Address," 2001. Photograph by Lou Briscese, USAF. Armed Forces Press Service.

27. "Trump Inaugural Address and Crowd," 2017. Photograph by B. Allen. Voice of America.

28. "Trump with Fraternal Order of Police," 2017. Photograph by the White House.

29. "Atlanta, GA," 1963. Photograph by Danny Lyon, Magnum Photos.

30. "Elise Green Confronts Police at Protests in Charlotte After Police Shooting," 2016. Photograph by Sean Rayford, Getty Images.

31. "Not in Service," 2016. Photograph by Adam W. Rhew.

NOTES

COLLECTIONS

E. S. Gosney Papers, California Institute of Technology, Pasadena, California.
J. R. Haynes Papers, John Randolph Haynes Foundation, University of California, Los Angeles, http://www.haynesfoundation.org/about/index.asp.
Arthur Franklin Raper Papers, 1913–1979 (#3966), Manuscripts Department, University Library, University of North Carolina, Chapel Hill.
Register of the Civil Rights Congress, Los Angeles, late 1940s–1950s, Southern California Library for Social Studies and Research, http://www.oac.cdlib.org/findaid/ark:/13030/tf3p3003dn/.

1. STATE OF INJUSTICE

1. Ashley Southall, "Officer Defends His Takedown of Tennis Star," *New York Times,* September 20, 2017; Ashley Southall, "Officer May Lose Vacation Days for Tackling Tennis Star," *New York Times,* September 27, 2017.
2. Pamela Manson, "U.S. Supreme Court Rules for Police in Utah Search Case," *Salt Lake Tribune,* September 23, 2016.
3. Utah v. Strieff, 136 S. Ct. 2056, 2070–71 (2016), Sotomayor, S., dissenting.
4. Snyder, *Arrest in the United States, 1980–2009,* 15; Lerman and Weaver, *Arresting Citizenship,* 8; Peter Wagner and Bernadette Rabuy, "Mass Incarceration: The Whole Pie 2017," press release, March 14, 2017, Prison Policy Initiative, Northampton, MA.
5. Wagner and Watch, "State of Incarceration: The Global Context."
6. Gottschalk, "Long Reach of the Carceral State," 440; Alexander, *New Jim Crow*; Nellis, *Color of Justice*; Walsh, "Criminal Justice System"; Kajstura and Immarigeon, *States of Women's Incarceration*; Carson, *Prisoners in 2014.*

7. US Congress, Senate, Permanent Subcommittee on Investigations, *U.S. Vulnerabilities to Money Laundering*; Dominic Rushe, "HSBC 'Sorry' for Aiding Mexican Drug Lords, Rogue States and Terrorists," *The Guardian*, July 17, 2012; Jill Treanor and Dominic Rushe, "HSBC Pays Record $1.9bn Fine to Settle US Money-Laundering Accusations," *The Guardian*, December 11, 2012; Keefe, "Limited Liability."

8. Bill Chappell, "'You Should Resign': Watch Sen. Elizabeth Warren Grill Wells Fargo CEO John Stumpf," NPR.org, September 20, 2016, http://www.npr.org/sections/thetwo-way/2016/09/20/494738797/you-should-resign-watch-sen-elizabeth-warren-grill-wells-fargo-ceo-john-stumpf; Kevin McCoy, "Wells Fargo Fined $185M for Fake Accounts; 5,300 Were Fired," *USA Today*, September 9, 2016; Emily Flitter and Glenn Thrush, "Regulator to Lay a $1 Billion Fine on Wells Fargo," *New York Times*, April 20, 2018; Dayen, "The Trump Administration."

9. "Trump on Criminal Justice: 'We Have to Get a Lot Tougher,'" *MSNBC.com*, August 20, 2015, http://www.msnbc.com/morning-joe/watch/trump-on-criminal-justice-reform-509292611802.

10. Timothy Williams and Richard A. Oppel, Jr., "Escapes, Riots, Beatings: Behind Bars in Private Prisons," *New York Times*, April 11, 2018; Larry Siems, "CIA Torture: Lawsuit Settled Against Psychologists Who Designed Techniques," *The Guardian*, August 17, 2017, https://www.theguardian.com/us-news/2017/aug/17/cia-torture-lawsuit-settled-against-psychologists-who-designed-techniques; "The Dark Prisoners: Inside the CIA's Torture Programme," *Al Jazeera*, September 5, 2016, http://www.aljazeera.com/indepth/features/2016/03/dark-prisoners-cia-torture-programme-160326051331796.html; Sheri Fink and James Risen, "Suit Gives New Details of Brutal Interrogations," *New York Times*, June 22, 2017.

11. Kafka, "In the Penal Colony," in *Penal Colony*, 191, 202.

12. Lynn Arrington, "Better Design Means Better Management," *Corrections Today* 49, no. 2 (April 1987): 86; Colin Moynihan, "Noise's Use as a Police Weapon Comes Under Scrutiny," *New York Times*, June 2, 2017; Rupert Neate, "Welcome to Jail, Inc.: How Private Companies Make Money off U.S. Prisons," *The Guardian*, June 16, 2016; Rhodes, *Total Confinement*, 41; David Segal, "Prison Vendors See Continued Signs of a Captive Market," *New York Times*, August 29, 2015; Manny Fernandez, "Delays as Death-Penalty States Scramble for Execution Drugs," *New York Times*, October 9, 2015; Associated Press, "Inmate Who Avoided Execution 7 Times Is Put to Death," *New York Times*, May 27, 2017; Adam Nagourney, "Aloha, and Welcome, Unless You're Homeless," *New York Times*, June 4, 2016; Kevin Sack, "Door-Busting Raids Leave Trail of Blood," *New York Times*, March 19, 2017; Huber and Mills, "How Technology Will Defeat Terrorism."

13. McLennan, *Crisis of Imprisonment*, 54–63.

14. Rhodes, *Total Confinement*, 5, 29; Dickens, *American Notes*, 146, 148, 314.

15. Fassin, *Enforcing Order*, xii.

16. Beckett and Murakawa, "Mapping the Shadow Carceral State," 221–24, 239; Gottschalk, *Caught*, chap. 10.

17. J. Rios, "Flesh in the Street"; Debbie Nathan, "What Happened to Sandra Bland?" *The Nation*, May 9–16, 2016, 12–18; Comfort, *Doing Time Together*; Richie, *Arrested*

Justice; A. Goffman, *On the Run*; Travis, Western, and Redburn, *Growth of Incarceration in the United States*, chap. 9; Lucius Couloute, "For Families of Incarcerated Dads, Father's Day Comes at a Premium" (blog), Prison Policy Initiative, June 13, 2017.

18. Taibbi, *I Can't Breathe*; Jessica Glenza, "Activists Want NYPD Officer Charged as Eric Garner Death Is Ruled a Homicide," *The Guardian*, August 2, 2014; George Joseph, "NYPD Officers Accessed Black Lives Matter Activists' Texts, Documents Show," *The Guardian*, April 4, 2017.

19. Brodeur, *Policing Web*, 346; Seigel, "Objects of Police History"; "Policing/Protest," OurStates, https://www.ourstates.org/#ourstates, accessed May 9, 2017.

20. Michael Klare and Nancy Stein, "The U.S. Public Safety Program," *The U.S. Military Apparatus*, NACLA, August 1972.

21. Balagoon et al., *Look for Me in the Whirlwind*, 351.

22. Foucault, *Punitive Society*, 7–9; Eubanks, *Automating Inequality*; Bagaric, Hunter, and Wolf, "Technological Incarceration," 78, 79.

23. Farah Stockman, "After Serving Their Time, Fighting to Get Out the Vote," *New York Times*, May 13, 2018.

24. Kalhan, "Immigration Surveillance"; Stumpf, "Crimmigration Crisis"; Gottschalk, *Caught*, chap. 10; Kalhan, "Rethinking Immigration Detention"; Anil Kalhan, personal communication with author, April 27, 2017; Nicholas Kulish, Caitlin Dickerson, and Ron Nixon, "Agents Discover a New Freedom on Deportations," *New York Times*, February 26, 2017; Maria Sachetti, "Immigration Arrests Soar Under Trump; Sharpest Spike Seen for Noncriminals," *Washington Post*, May 17, 2017.

25. Newman, *Defensible Space*.

26. Balibar, *We, the People of Europe?*, 62.

27. Strom et al., *Private Security Industry*, 34; Kyckelhahn and Martin, *Justice Expenditure and Employment Extracts, 2010*.

28. Foucault, *Discipline and Punish*, 113; Soss, Fording, and Schram, *Disciplining the Poor*; Lara-Millán, "Public Emergency Room Overcrowding"; A. Goffman, *On the Run*; Wacquant, "Deadly Symbiosis," 107–8.

29. Cohen, "Punitive City," 360.

30. Foucault, *Punitive Society*, 7–9; Robert Ross, preface to Wilde, *De Profundis*, 109.

31. Wilde, *De Profundis and Other Writings*, 157.

32. Inouye, *Long Afterlife*, 5, 6, 9.

33. O. Patterson, *Slavery and Social Death*, 46; A. Gordon, "Some Thoughts on Haunting and Futurity," 10.

34. President Barack Obama and Marilynne Robinson, "A Conversation in Iowa," *The New York Review of Books*, November 5, 2015, 4–8; Trump, *Time to Get Tough*, 137.

35. Travis, Western, and Redburn, *Growth of Incarceration in the United States*, 2.

36. Vivian Wang, "Prison Term for Weiner Is Set, but Where Will He Go?" *New York Times*, September 27, 2017. The quote from Anatole France is from his 1894 novel, *The Red Lily*.

37. Angell, "Abortion Battlefield," 10.

38. Alexander, *New Jim Crow*, 8; Travis, Western, and Redburn, *Growth of Incarceration in the United States*, 2; Obama and Robinson, "A Conversation"; Hernández, Muhammad, and Thompson, "Introduction: Constructing the Carceral State," 19; Kelly Lytle Hernández, Khalil Gibran Muhammad, and Heather Ann Thompson, "The Size and Scope of the Carceral State," *Process: A Blog for American History*, June 26, 2015, http://www.processhistory.org/the-size-and-scope-of-the-carceral-state/; Hernández, *City of Inmates*; Harcourt, "From the Asylum to the Prison."
39. P. Levi, *Drowned and the Saved*, 22–51.
40. "The Slow Demise of Capital Punishment," editorial, *New York Times*, December 29, 2013; Carson, *Prisoners in 2014*; Sentencing Project, "U.S. Prison Population Trends 1999–2015."
41. Ferguson, *Inferno*, 249; Stuntz, *Collapse of American Criminal Justice*, 1; Foucault, *Punitive Society*, 12.
42. Stuart Hall and Phil Scraton, "Law, Class and Control," in Fitzgerald, McLennan, and Pawson, *Crime and Society*; Keramet Reiter, "(Un)Settling Solitary Confinement in California's Prisons" (blog), *Social Justice*, September 28, 2015, http://www.socialjusticejournal.org/?p=3214; Ian Lovett, "California Agrees to Overhaul Use of Solitary Confinement," *New York Times*, September 2, 2015; Movement for Black Lives, "A Vision for Black Lives: Policy Demands for Black Power, Freedom & Justice," July 2016, https://policy.m4bl.org/; George Zornick, "The Disrupters: How the Youth Activists of #NeverAgain Are Upending Gun Politics," *The Nation*, April 30/May 7, 2018, 13–15; John Paul Stevens, "Repeal the Second Amendment," *New York Times*, March 28, 2018; Sarah Maslin Nir, "Thousands of Students in Protest of Violence," *New York Times*, April 21, 2018.
43. Scott Graves, "Since 2007–08, Spending Per State Prisoner Has Increased More Than Twice as Fast as Spending Per K-12 Student," California Budget and Policy Center, press release, April 2018.
44. Zimring, *When Police Kill*; Jon Swaine et al., "Young Black Men Killed by US Police at Highest Rate in Year of 1,134 Deaths," *The Guardian*, December 31, 2015; Jon Swaine and Ciara McCarthy, "Killings by US Police Logged at Twice the Previous Rate Under New Federal Program," *The Guardian*, December 15, 2016; John Sullivan, Reis Thebault, Julie Tate, and Jennifer Jenkins, "Number of Fatal Shootings by Police Is Nearly Identical to Last Year," *Washington Post*, July 1, 2017; Jamiles Lartey, "Police Officers in St. Louis Chant After Breaking Up Protests," *The Guardian*, September 18, 2017.
45. Obama, "President's Role," 855.
46. Sellin, *Pioneering in Penology*.
47. Dickens, *American Notes*, 146; Bacon and American Friends Service Committee, *Struggle for Justice*, v.

2. DOUBLE SYSTEM

1. Du Bois, *Souls of Black Folk*, 141–42.
2. Obama, "President's Role," 820; President's Task Force on 21st Century Policing, *Final Report*; Travis, Western, and Redburn, *Growth of Incarceration in the United States*; (Chicago) Police Accountability Task Force, *Recommendations for Reform*.

3. Alan Blinder, "Donald Blankenship Sentenced to a Year in Prison in Mine Safety Case," *New York Times,* April 6, 2016; Eisinger, *Chickenshit Club,* 316–17; Ben Wolfgang, "Controversial Former Coal Titan in Bid to Clear Name, Win Senate Seat in West Virginia," *The Washington Times,* January 1, 2018; Trip Gabriel, "Ex-Coal Baron Jailed Over Mine Blast Loses West Virginia Primary," *New York Times,* May 9, 2018.

4. Barry Paddock and Oren Yaniv, "Lashawn Marten, Suspect in Fatal Hate Attack on Jeffrey Babbitt in Union Square, Says He's Not Racist," New York *Daily News,* September 13, 2013; Rebecca Rosenberg, "Hate Crime Killer Sentenced to 25 Years in Prison," *New York Post,* September 12, 2017; James C. McKinley, Jr., "Man Who Said He Was Angry at Whites Gets 25 Years for Fatal Punch in Union Sq," *New York Times,* September 13, 2017; Michael Croce, personal communication with author, October 6, 2017.

5. Subramanian et al., *Incarceration's Front Door,* 8, 11–12; Travis, Western, and Redburn, *Growth of Incarceration,* 212.

6. Federal Bureau of Investigation, "Expanded Offense Data: Homicides"; Kochanek et al., "Deaths: Final Data for 2014"; Cahalan, "Trends in Incarceration," 39, 41; Centers for Disease Control and Prevention, "Fatal Injury Reports, National and Regional, 1999–2014," http://webappa.cdc.gov/sasweb/ncipc/mortrate10_us.html; Blincoe et al., *Economic and Societal Impact,* 2–5.

7. Wesley Lowery, "Proposal to Congress Would Require Police to Get De-Escalation Training, Create National Use of Force Standard," *Washington Post,* May 12, 2016; Claudia Dreifus, "Perceptions of Race at a Glance: A MacArthur Grant Winner Tries to Unearth Biases to Aid Criminal Justice," *New York Times,* January 5, 2015; Micol Seigel, "The Myth of Racial Profiling," paper presented at New Directions in Critical Criminology conference, University of Tennessee, Knoxville, May 6–7, 2016.

8. Kevin Fagan, "Sweep 'Just the Beginning'," *San Francisco Chronicle,* April 26, 2018.

9. V. Rios, *Punished;* Monahan and Torres, *Schools Under Surveillance;* Obama, "President's Role," 812.

10. N. Algren et al., *Juvenile Jungle;* May, *Homeward Bound;* J. Edgar Hoover, "Mothers . . . Our Only Hope," in N. Walker, *Women's Magazines 1940–1960,* 45–46.

11. Platt, "'Street' Crime"; Langton, *Victimizations Not Reported.*

12. Harcourt, *Against Prediction.*

13. Williams and Gold, "From Delinquent Behavior to Official Delinquency"; Gold and Reimer, "Changing Patterns of Delinquent Behavior"; Lassiter, "Impossible Criminals," 127.

14. Sarri and Hasenfeld, *Brought to Justice?;* Sarri, *Under Lock and Key;* Lassiter, "Impossible Criminals," 138, 140.

15. Ayers, *A Kind and Just Parent,* 29–30.

16. Platt, "Social Insecurity."

17. Susan Archer, Robin Lindsay, and Dave Horn, "F.B.I. Director James Comey Is Fired by Trump," *New York Times,* May 9, 2017; Devlin Barrett and Philip Rucker, "Trump Said He Was Thinking of Russia Controversy When He Decided to Fire Comey," *Washington Post,* May 11, 2017.

18. Eisinger, *Chickenshit Club,* xiv.

19. Comey, *A Higher Loyalty*, xii.

20. Schwendinger and Schwendinger, "Defenders of Order"; Comey, *A Higher Loyalty*, 56–57.

21. J. Hall, *Theft, Law and Society*, 289–332.

22. Sutherland, "Is 'White Collar Crime' Crime?" 135, 136, 139.

23. The President's Commission on Law Enforcement, *Task Force Report: Crime and Its Impact*, 105, 106; Keefe, "Limited Liability," 29.

24. Sam Whiting, "CNN Series Retraces Steps of Patty Hearst's Ordeal," *San Francisco Chronicle*, February 9, 2018.

25. Rakoff, "Financial Crisis"; Eisinger, *Chickenshit Club*, xv–xvi.

26. Barry Meier, "Opioid's Maker Hid Knowledge of Wide Abuse," *New York Times*, May 29, 2018; Barry Meier, "3 Executives Spared Prison in OxyContin Case," *New York Times*, July 21, 2007; Barry Meier and Eric Lipton, "Under Attack, Drug Maker Turned to Giuliani for Help," *New York Times*, December 28, 2007; Keefe, "Empire of Pain."

27. Barak, *Integrating Criminologies*, 65; Robert H. Tillman and Henry N. Pontell, "Corporate Fraud, Criminal Time," op-ed, *New York Times*, June 29, 2016; Barak, *Theft of a Nation*, 3; Keefe, "Limited Liability," 28; Rakoff, "Financial Crisis"; Jean Eaglesham and Anupreeta Das, "Wall Street Crime: 7 Years, 156 Cases and Few Convictions," *Wall Street Journal*, May 27, 2016.

28. Eisinger, *Chickenshit Club*, xviii, 315–16, 320; Rakoff, "Financial Crisis."

29. Rakoff, "Financial Crisis."

30. Kajstura and Immarigeon, "States of Women's Incarceration"; Swavola, Riley, and Subramanian, *Women and Jails*, 7; Glaze and Kaeble, *Correctional Populations in the United States*; Minton and Zeng, *Jail Inmates in 2015*, 5; Sentencing Project, "Incarcerated Women and Girls."

31. Richie, *Arrested Justice*.

32. Berger, *Captive Nation*, 277; A. Goffman, *On the Run*, 47–53, 87–90, 200, 211; Comfort, *Doing Time Together*.

33. Piven and Cloward, *Poor People's Movements*.

34. Stuart Hall et al., *Policing the Crisis* (2013), 298; Kohler-Hausmann, *Getting Tough*; Wacquant, "Deadly Symbiosis"; Wacquant, "From Slavery to Mass Incarceration," 41; Wacquant, *Punishing the Poor*; Pettit, *Invisible Men*; Holloway, *Living in Infamy*; Piven, "Welfare and Work," 74; Shannon et al., "Growth, Scope, and Spatial Distribution."

35. Hacker, *Divided Welfare State*, 6, 9–10.

36. Skocpol, *Protecting Soldiers and Mothers*, 102, 138.

37. Ibid.; Hacker, *Divided Welfare State*, 92; L. Gordon, *Pitied but Not Entitled*, 37–64.

38. Ira Katznelson, "Was the Great Society a Lost Opportunity?" in Fraser and Gerstle, *Rise and Fall*, 199; Bernstein, "The New Deal," in *Towards a New Past*; Jones, *Labor of Love, Labor of Sorrow*; M. Katz, *In the Shadow of the Poorhouse*, 244–45; L. Gordon, *Pitied but Not Entitled*, 198.

39. L. Gordon, *Pitied but Not Entitled*, 192–99; Schwartz, *Civil Works Administration*, 216–17; Abramowitz, *Regulating the Lives of Women*, 283–87; Escobar, *Race, Police*, 84–90.

40. Duster, "Individual Fairness, Group Preferences," 46–47; Karen Brodkin Sacks, "How Did Jews Become White Folks?" in Gregory and Sanjek, *Race*, 92–97; Massey and Denton, *American Apartheid*, 49–51; Bullard and Grigsby, *Residential Apartheid*; Rothstein, *Color of Law*.

41. Sacks, "How Did Jews Become White Folks?" 90–91; Eric Schmitt, "As Military Pay Slips Behind, Poverty Invades the Ranks," *New York Times,* June 12, 1994.

42. Platt, "End Game"; Hinton, *From the War on Poverty*, 134.

43. Hacker, *Divided Welfare State*, 13–15.

44. Woolsey, "Living on Welfare."

45. Zucchino, *Myth of the Welfare Queen*, 64–65.

46. Platt, "State of Welfare," 16; Zucchino, *Myth of the Welfare Queen*, 65.

47. Gwendolyn Mink, "The End of Welfare?" *Social Justice*, January 17, 2017, http://www.socialjusticejournal.org/the-end-of-welfare/; Tina Sacks, "Death by a Thousand Budget Cuts: The Need for a New Fight for Poor People's Rights," *Social Justice*, January 17, 2017, http://www.socialjusticejournal.org/death-by-a-thousand-budget-cuts-the-need-for-a-new-fight-for-poor-peoples-rights/.

48. Mink, "Faith in Government?" 9.

49. Solinger, "Dependency and Choice"; Boris, "When Work Is Slavery"; Office of Family Assistance, "TANF Caseload Data 2012," March 1, 2013, US Department of Health and Human Services, https://www.acf.hhs.gov/archive/ofa/resource/caseload-data-2012; Office of Family Assistance, "TANF Caseload Data 2016," January 12, 2017, US Department of Health and Human Services, https://www.acf.hhs.gov/ofa/resource/tanf-caseload-data-2016; National Data Bank, "Nutrition Assistance Programs Report—February 2016," US Department of Agriculture, May 4, 2016, http://www.fns.usda.gov/sites/default/files/datastatistics/february-performance-report-2016.pdf.

50. Jason DeParle, "Shrinking Welfare Rolls Leave Record High Share of Minorities," *New York Times,* July 27, 1998; Patricia Williams, "The Saints of Servitude," *New York Times,* October 13, 1996.

51. Gustafson, *Cheating Welfare*.

52. Donald J. Trump, "Presidential Executive Order Promoting Free Speech and Religious Liberty," The White House, May 4, 2017 https://www.whitehouse.gov/presidential-actions/presidential-executive-order-promoting-free-speech-religious-liberty/; Robert Pear and Rebecca R. Ruiz, "Trump Relaxes Employers' Duty on Birth Control," *New York Times,* October 7, 2017.

53. Trump, *America We Deserve*, 241–60; Trump, *Time to Get Tough*, 140; "Remarks by President Trump at the Conservative Political Action Conference," The White House, February 24, 2017, https://www.whitehouse.gov/the-press-office/2017/02/24/remarks-president-trump-conservative-political-action-conference; Mink, "End of Welfare?"; Sacks, "Death by a Thousand Budget Cuts."

54. Soss, Fording, and Schram, *Disciplining the Poor*, 6, 44.

55. Stevenson, "A Presumption of Guilt."

56. Rakoff, "Why Innocent People Plead Guilty," 16.

57. Malega and Cohen, *State Court Organization, 2011*, 1–4. For a detailed discussion of the methodology used to determine these numbers, see the appendix.

58. Rakoff, "Why Innocent People Plead Guilty," 16; J. Rios, "Flesh in the Street"; Timothy Williams, "In South Carolina, No Money and No Lawyer Often Mean Jail Time for Minor Crimes," *New York Times,* October 13, 2017; Civil Rights Division, *Investigation of the Baltimore City Police*, 5–6.

59. Kohler-Hausmann, "Managerial Justice and Mass Misdemeanors"; Kohler-Hausmann, "Misdemeanor Justice," 387.

60. Noonan, *Mortality in Local Jails*; Ansell, *Death Gap*, 93–95.

61. Foote, "Bail System and Equal Justice," 46; Katzive, *New Areas for Bail Reform*; Wald and Freed, "Bail Reform Act of 1966"; Bronson and Berzofsky, *Indicators of Mental Health Problems.*

62. Tribe, "An Ounce of Detention," 371; Ervin, "Preventive Detention," 292.

63. Berg, "Bail Reform Act of 1984"; Bail Reform Act of 1984, 18 U.S.C. 3141–3150, 3142; Harwin, "Detaining for Danger"; Karnow, "Setting Bail for Public Safety"; Wiseman, "Discrimination, Coercion," 123.

64. Cohen, *Pretrial Detention and Misconduct*; Benjamin Weiser, "Rich Defendants' Request to Judges: Lock Me Up in a Gilded Cage," *New York Times,* June 1, 2016.

65. White House Council, "Fines, Fees, and Bail," 7; Timothy Williams, "Report Finds Explosive Growth in Number of Women Held in Local Jails," *New York Times,* August 18, 2016; Subramanian et al., *Incarceration's Front Door*; Minton and Zheng, *Jail Inmates in 2015*; Aiken, *Era of Mass Expansion.*

66. Vera Institute of Justice, *New Orleans: Who's in Jail and Why?* First Quarterly Report, January–March 2016, 4–5.

67. Subramanian et al., *Incarceration's Front Door*, 14; Phillips, *Pretrial Detention and Case Outcomes, Part 1: Nonfelony Cases* (New York: New York City Criminal Justice Agency, 2007), 28; Mary Phillips, "Bail, Detention, and Felony Case Outcomes," *CJA Research Brief*, no. 18 (September 2008): 4–5.

68. Gideon v. Wainright, 372 U.S. 335 (1963); O'Hare, *In Prison*, 169; Du Bois, *Autobiography of W. E. B. Du Bois*, 390.

69. Tony Platt and Randi Pollock, "Channeling Lawyers," in Jacob, *Potential for Reform of Criminal Justice*, 242.

70. President's Commission on Law Enforcement, *Task Force Report: The Courts*, 4, 59; Skolnick, "Social Control in the Adversary System"; *In re Gault*, 387 U.S. 1, 28 (1967); Blumberg, "Practice of Law as a Confidence Game"; Platt, *Child Savers*, 160–72; Greenspan, *Transformation of Criminal Due Process*, 135; Robert Lefcourt, "Lawyers for the Poor Can't Win," in *Law Against the People.*

71. American Bar Association, *Gideon's Broken Promise*; Campbell Robertson, "In Louisiana, the Poor Lack Legal Defense," *New York Times,* March 19, 2016; Oliver Laughland, "The Human Toll of America's Public Defender Crisis," *The Guardian*, September 7, 2016; Williams, "In South Carolina."

72. Forman, *Locking Up Our Own*, 6, 193.

73. Rakoff, "Why Innocent People Plead Guilty," 17.

74. Bellow, "Legal Aid in the United States"; Agnew, "What's Wrong," 930; George, "Development of the Legal Services Corporation"; Regnery, *Poverty Agencies*; Cramton, "Crisis in Legal Services for the Poor"; Quigley, "Demise of Law Reform"; Boehm and Flaherty, "Why the Legal Services Corporation," 2, 9–10; Liebman, "Recent Leg-

islation"; Roth, "It Is Lawyers"; Debra Cassens Weiss, "Trump Budget Eliminates Legal Services Corp. Funding," *American Bar Journal*, March 16, 2017, http://www .abajournal.com/news/article/trump_budget_eliminates_funding_for_legal _services_corp/; Katie Benner, "Justice Dept. Closes Down Unit That Offers Legal Aid," *New York Times*, February 2, 2018.

75. Lippman, "New York's Template," 13; Rhode, *Access to Justice*, 3–4.

3. EXCEPT FOR

1. President Barack Obama and Marilynne Robinson, "A Conversation in Iowa," *The New York Review of Books*, November 5, 2015, 6.
2. Alexander, *New Jim Crow*; Travis, Western, and Redburn, *Growth of Incarceration*; Simon, *Mass Incarceration on Trial*, 25–26; Woolredge et al., "Is the Impact of Cumulative Disadvantage"; Wagner and Knopf, *Racial Geography of Mass Incarceration*.
3. State and federal prisons held an estimated 523,000 African American people in 2015, and jails held 243,400 that year. Carson and Anderson, "Prisoners in 2015," 6; Minton and Zheng, "Jail Inmates in 2015," 4; Subramanian et al., *Incarceration's Front Door*; Sakala, "Breaking Down Mass Incarceration"; Carson, *Prisoners in 2014*, 15; Simon, *Mass Incarceration*, 17; Nellis, *Color of Justice*.
4. Walsh, "Criminal Justice System"; Reaves, *Felony Defendants*, 4, 6; Subramanian et al., *Incarceration's Front Door*, 11; Noonan and Ginder, *Mortality in Local Jails and State Prisons*, 3; Pettit, *Invisible Men*, 1; Sentencing Project, "State-by-State Data"; Rovner, *Declines in Youth Commitments and Facilities*, 4–5.
5. Trump, *Time to Get Tough*, 136–37.
6. Trump, *America We Deserve*, 30–31; Morris and Hawkins, *Letter to the President on Crime Control*, 8; Wilson, *Thinking About Crime*, 51.
7. George Orwell, "Politics and the English Language," in *Why I Write*, 120; Jodi Kantor and Megan Twohey, "Harvey Weinstein Paid Off Sexual Harassment Accusers for Decades," *New York Times*, October 5, 2017; Lassiter, "Impossible Criminals"; The Mayor's Commission on Conditions in Harlem, "The Negro in Harlem," in Platt, *Politics of Riot Commissions*, 178.
8. A. Davis, *Meaning of Freedom*, 39.
9. Andrew Kaczynski, "Attorney General Jeff Sessions: Consent Decrees 'Can Reduce Morale of the Police Officers,'" *CNN.com*, April 14, 2017, http://www.cnn.com/2017 /04/14/politics/kfile-sessions-consent-decrees/; Counterterrorism Division, Federal Bureau of Investigation, *Black Identity Extremists Likely Motivated to Target Law Enforcement Officers*, FBI Intelligence Assessment (Washington, DC: FBI, August 3, 2017), 2; Sam Levin, "Black Activist Jailed for His Facebook Posts Speaks Out About Secret FBI Surveillance," *The Guardian*, May 11, 2018.
10. Kevin Liptak, "Obama Administration Ending Program Once Used to Track Mostly Arab and Muslim Men," *CNN.com*, December 22, 2016, http://www.cnn.com/2016 /12/22/politics/obama-nseers-arab-muslim-registry/; Colin Moynihan, "Last of Three Major Suits Accusing N.Y.P.D. of Spying on Muslims Is Settled," *New York Times*, April 6, 2018.

11. Casella, *Archaeology of Institutional Confinement*.

12. Fogelson, *America's Armories*; Cahalan, "Trends in Incarceration in the United States," 40.

13. Phillips, *Indians and Indian Agents*.

14. Sakala, "Breaking Down Mass Incarceration"; James Dehaven, "Report: Native Americans Make Up Disproportionate Share of Rising Montana Prison Population," *The Missoulian*, March 5, 2016.

15. Roosevelt, "Memorial Day Address"; Dumindin, *Philippine-American War, 1899–1902*.

16. McCoy, *Policing America's Empire*, 135, 295; Madley, "From Africa to Auschwitz"; Khalili, *Time in the Shadows*.

17. Pfaelzer, *Driven Out*, 74–75; Cahalan, "Trends in Incarceration," 40; Takagi and Platt, "Behind the Gilded Ghetto," 10; Helmer, *Drugs and Minority Oppression*, 18–33; Okihiro, *Margins and Mainstreams*.

18. Hester, "Deportability and the Carceral State"; Carrigan and Webb, *Forgotten Dead*; Helmer, *Drugs and Minority Oppression*, 54–79; Chávez-García, *States of Delinquency*, 119.

19. Galarza, *Merchants of Labor*, 258.

20. Gottschalk, *Caught*, 220; Golash-Boza, *Deported*, 7.

21. Sakala, "Breaking Down Mass Incarceration"; Subramanian et al., *Incarceration's Front Door*; Gottschalk, *Caught*, 215; Hester, "Deportability and the Carceral State," 147; Nellis, *Color of Justice*; Carson and Anderson, "Prisoners in 2015"; Minton and Zheng, "Jail Inmates in 2015"; Immigration and Customs Enforcement, "ICE ERO: Immigration Arrests Climb Nearly 40%," US Department of Homeland Security, November 2, 2017, https://www.ice.gov/features/100-days?ex_cid=trumpbeat.

22. Didier Bigo, "Globalized (in)Security: The Field and the Ban-Opticon," in Bigo and Tsoukala, *Terror, Insecurity and Liberty*, 10–48.

23. Pettit, *Invisible Men*, 10; Tonry, "Why Are U.S. Incarceration Rates"; Carson, *Prisoners in 2016*; Murakawa, *First Civil Right*, 6; Wacquant, "Deadly Symbiosis," 96.

24. Du Bois, *Black Reconstruction in America*, 10; W. Johnson, *River of Dark Dreams*, 218–19, 243; Beckert, *Empire of Cotton*, 110; Stampp, *Peculiar Institution*, 206–17.

25. Blackmon, *Slavery by Another Name*, 23; Curtin, *Black Prisoners and Their World*, 6; Lichtenstein, *Twice the Work of Free Labor*, 23; Casella, *Archaeology of Institutional Confinement*, 120–21.

26. E. Foner, *Reconstruction*, 595; J. Franklin, *From Slavery to Freedom*, 303; Foucault, *Punitive Society*, 194.

27. E. Foner, *Reconstruction*, xxv.

28. Du Bois, *Black Reconstruction in America*, 670.

29. Blackmon, *Slavery by Another Name*, 56; Frazier, *Negro in the United States*, 159; Du Bois, *Black Reconstruction in America*, 167–74.

30. Terrell, "Peonage in the United States," 306, 307.

31. Balibar, *We, the People of Europe?*, 58–65; Beckert, *Empire of Cotton*, 182; Rusche and Kirchheimer, *Punishment and Social Structure*, 42.

32. Douglas Hay, "Property, Authority and the Criminal Law," in Hay et al., *Albion's Fatal Tree*, 18–19; Chambliss, "A Sociological Analysis"; Adler, "A Historical Analy-

sis"; E. Thompson, *Making of the English Working Class*, 218; Foucault, *Punitive Society*, 33, 52.

33. Beckert, *Empire of Cotton*, 182.

34. Rawls, *Indians of California*, 93; Tony Platt, "Bitter Legacies: A War of Extermination, Grave Looting and Culture Wars in the American West," in Anstett and Dreyfus, *Human Remains and Identification*, 14–33; Madley, *An American Genocide*, 146, 147.

35. Rawls, *Indians of California*, 85–105; Madley, *An American Genocide*, 162; Caughey, *California*, 391; McMurtry, *Oh What a Slaughter*, 56.

36. Fear-Segal, *White Man's Club*, 223; Adams, *Education for Extinction*; Shaunna Oteka McCovey, "Resilience and Responsibility: Surviving the New Genocide," in M. Moore, *Eating Fire, Tasting Blood*, 289; Meriam, *Problem of Indian Administration*, 329, 330, 332.

37. O'Hare, *In Prison*, 156.

38. Oshinsky, *"Worse Than Slavery,"* 21; Casella, *Archaeology of Institutional Confinement*, 34–35; J. Hall, *Theft, Law and Society*, 111–14.

39. McLennan, *Crisis of Imprisonment*, 4–6; Berkman, *Prison Memoirs of an Anarchist*, 272.

40. Franklin, *From Slavery to Freedom*, 303, 343.

41. McLennan, *Crisis of Imprisonment*, 4; Litwack, *Trouble in Mind*, 270; Oshinsky, *"Worse Than Slavery,"* 58, 60, 76; Perkinson, *Texas Tough*, 105; Curtin, *Black Prisoners and Their World*, 3; LeFlouria, *Chained in Silence*; Haley, *No Mercy Here*.

42. Blackmon, *Slavery by Another Name*, 386–96; Lichtenstein, *Twice the Work of Free Labor*, xvii, xix, 16; Haley, *No Mercy Here*, 12; LeFlouria, *Chained in Silence*, 65; Baradaran, *Color of Money*, 282; Oshinsky, *"Worse Than Slavery,"* 60.

43. Curtin, *Black Prisoners and Their World*, 76–77; Oshinsky, *"Worse Than Slavery,"* 48–52; Lichtenstein, *Twice the Work of Free Labor*, 15–16; Sellin, *Slavery and the Penal System*, 176.

44. Haley, "'Like I Was a Man'"; LeFlouria, *Chained in Silence*, 177–78; Steiner and Brown, *North Carolina Chain Gang*, 6.

45. Oshinsky, *"Worse Than Slavery,"* 44, 70; LeFlouria, *Chained in Silence*; Curtin, *Black Prisoners and Their World*; Haley, *No Mercy Here*, 89; Terrell, "Peonage in the United States," 806.

46. McLennan, *Crisis of Imprisonment*, 119–31; Tony Platt and Barbara J. Yaley, "Prisoners of Labor: The Political Economy of Punishment in California, 1850–1940," unpublished manuscript, 1982, in the author's personal files.

47. Lichtenstein, *Twice the Work of Free Labor*, 54; McLennan, *Crisis of Imprisonment*, 122; Oshinsky, *"Worse Than Slavery,"* 45–46.

48. Oshinsky, *"Worse Than Slavery,"* 59–60, 79; Curtin, *Black Prisoners and Their World*, 85; Perkinson, *Texas Tough*, 105.

49. E. Foner, *Reconstruction*, 603.

50. Litwack, *Trouble in Mind*, 284–85, 315; Equal Justice Initiative, *Lynching in America*; Allen, Lewis, and Litwack, *Without Sanctuary*; Oshinsky, *"Worse Than Slavery,"* 209.

51. About twenty percent of Jews died from starvation, disease, and exhaustion during the Holocaust. Laqueur, "Devoted to Terror," 12; Du Bois, *Black Reconstruction*, 700.

52. Wilkerson, *Warmth of Other Suns*, 10; Isabel Wilkerson, "When Will the North Face Its Racism?" op-ed, *New York Times*, January 10, 2015; Grimshaw, *Racial Violence in the United States*, 60; Baldwin, *Nobody Knows My Name*, 68.

53. Arthur Raper, "Race and Class Pressures," June 1, 1940, unpublished document prepared for Myrdal, *An American Dilemma*. Raper's typescript is in the Arthur Franklin Raper Papers.

54. Ward, *Black Child Savers*, 98.

55. Du Bois, *Souls of Black Folk*, 87.

56. Manion, *Liberty's Prisoners*, 137; Muhammad, *Condemnation of Blackness*, 4; Cahalan, "Trends in Incarceration," 40.

57. Muhammad, *Condemnation of Blackness*, 233; Sellin, "Negro Criminal," 52–53; Casella, *Archaeology of Institutional Confinement*, 35; Oshinsky, *"Worse Than Slavery,"* 137.

58. Sellin, "Negro Criminal," 52, 63; Du Bois to Edwin Embree, May 12, 1931, in Aptheker, *Correspondence of W. E. B. Du Bois*, 1:439.

59. Dayan, "With Law at the Edge of Life"; Muhammad, *Condemnation of Blackness*, 8; McGirr, *War on Alcohol*, 18; Helmer, *Drugs and Minority Oppression*, 47.

60. Dan Baum, "Legalize It All: How to Win the War on Drugs," *Harper's*, April 2016, 22.

61. Frazier, *Negro Youth at the Crossways*, 292; California State Board of Prison Directors, *Biennial Reports, 1893–1940* (Sacramento: State Printing Office, 1940); Cahalan, *Historical Corrections Statistics*, 65.

62. President George H. W. Bush mentioned "the laudable desire to sweep away the debris of racism" at a commencement ceremony at the University of Michigan on May 4, 1991. George H. W. Bush, "Remarks at the University of Michigan Commencement Ceremony in Ann Arbor," May 4, 1991, http://www.presidency.ucsb.edu /ws/?pid=19546.

63. Hinton, *From the War on Poverty*, 25–26. On racism as a legacy, see also Obama, "President's Role," 815.

64. Coates, *Between the World and Me*, 99, 132; Gerstle, "Protean Character of American Liberalism"; Wallerstein, *Unthinking Social Science*.

65. Du Bois, *Souls of Black Folk*, xlviii.

66. Gerstle, "Protean Character of American Liberalism"; Murakawa, *First Civil Right*; Gerstle, *American Crucible*.

67. Fannie Lou Hamer, "To Praise Our Bridges," in D. Abbott, *Mississippi Writers*, 2:326.

68. H. Graham, "Origins of Affirmative Action," 50–62.

69. Platt, "End Game"; Platt, *"The Land That Never Has Been Yet,"* 7–23.

70. Alice Walker, "The Civil Rights Movement," 544.

71. National Advisory Commission on Civil Disorders, *Report*, 1, 2, 484–527.

72. Massey and Denton, *American Apartheid*; Jaynes and Williams, *A Common Destiny*; Bloom and Martin, *Black Against Empire*; Skolnick, *Politics of Protest*, 294; Chicago Riot Study Committee, *Report to Hon. Richard J. Daley*, 37; Locke, "Riot Response," 810.

73. Pettit, *Invisible Men*; National Urban League, *Black Families in the 1974–1975 Depression*, 26; Centers for Disease Control, *Population by Age, Groups, Race, and Sex*

for 1960–97 (Washington, DC.: Centers for Disease Control, 1997). https://www.cdc
.gov/nchs/data/statab/pop6097.pdf; Platt, "No Easy Road to Freedom," 15; Platt, *"The
Land That Never Has Been Yet,"* 15; Bureau of the Census, *Statistical Abstract of the
United States*, 48.

74. National Advisory Commission on Civil Disorders, *Report*, 2; Platt, "Living with
    Inequality"; Bush, "Remarks at the University of Michigan."

75. Bloom, *Closing of the American Mind*, 91–93; Herrnstein and Murray, *Bell Curve*,
    551.

76. Platt and Takagi, "Intellectuals for Law and Order"; Wilson, *Thinking About Crime*,
    61, 70, 208; Jackson Toby, "Open-Ended Sentence," op-ed, *New York Times*, Janu-
    ary 15, 1973; Hirschi and Hindelang, "Intelligence and Delinquency," 577; Robin,
    "Justifiable Homicide by Police Officers," 231; Wilbanks, *Myth*, 5; van den Haag,
    Punishing Criminals.

77. Frye et al., "Rise and Fall," 484, 505; Hinton, *From the War on Poverty*, 308.

78. Hinton, *From the War on Poverty*, 142, 168, 170, 177.

79. Bureau of Justice Statistics, "Prisoners in State and Federal Institutions," 4–5.

80. Nagel, *New Red Barn*, 48, 148–50.

4. ON GUARD

1. Terrence McCoy, "Freddie Gray's Life a Study on the Effects of Lead Paint on Poor
   Blacks," *Washington Post*, April 29, 2015; Jean Marbella, "Beginning of Freddie
   Gray's Life as Sad as Its End, Court Case Shows," *The Baltimore Sun*, April 23, 2015;
   Elizabeth Tobin Tyler, "When Are Laws Strictly Enforced? Criminal Justice, Housing Quality, and Public Health," *HealthAffairs Blog*, November 5, 2015, http://
   healthaffairs.org/blog/2015/11/05/when-are-laws-strictly-enforced-criminal-justice
   -housing-quality-and-public-health/.

2. Civil Rights Division, *Investigation of the Baltimore City Police*, 5, 78, 80.

3. Ryan Gabrielson et al., "Deadly Force, in Black and White," Pro Publica, October 10
   2014, https://www.propublica.org/article/deadly-force-in-black-and-white; Julie
   Tate et al., "Fatal Force," *Washington Post*, https://www.washingtonpost.com/graphics
   /national/police-shootings-2017/, last accessed October 26, 2017; "Young Black Men
   Are 21 Times as Likely as Their White Peers to Be Killed by Police," Equal Justice
   Initiative, October 20, 2014, https://eji.org/news/study-shows-young-black-men-21
   -times-more-likely-to-be-killed-by-police; "Audio: Calls from George Zimmerman,
   Neighbor Capture Last Minutes of Martin's Life," *Washington Post*, May 20, 2012,
   http://www.washingtonpost.com/wp-srv/special/nation/last-minutes-trayvon
   -martin-911-calls/index.html.

4. James C. McKinley, Jr., and Al Baker, "A System, with Exceptions, That Favors Po-
   lice in Fatalities," *New York Times*, December 8, 2014; Kimberly Kindy and Kim-
   briell Kelly, "Thousands Dead, Few Prosecuted," *Washington Post*, April 11, 2015;
   Kevin Rector, "Freddie Gray Case: DOJ Won't Charge Baltimore Police Officers,"
   The Baltimore Sun, September 13, 2017; Sarah Wildman, "Jeff Sessions's Chequered
   Past," *The Guardian*, May 5, 2009.

5. Platt, *Politics of Riot Commissions.*

6. President's Task Force, *Final Report*, 5; Office of the Press Secretary, The White House, "Fact Sheet: Task Force on 21st Century Policing," December 18, 2014; Barack Obama, "Remarks by the President After Meeting with Elected Officials, Community and Faith Leaders, and Law Enforcement Officials," The White House, December 1, 2014.

7. Eric L. Adams, "We Must Stop Police Abuse of Black Men," op-ed, *New York Times*, December 5, 2014; Zimring, *When Police Kill*.

8. Richard Luscombe and Haroon Siddique, "George Zimmerman Acquittal Leads to Protests Across US Cities," *The Guardian*, July 15, 2013, http://www.theguardian .com/world/2013/jul/15/trayvon-martin-protests-streets-acquittal; An Act Relating to Self-Defense Immunity; Amending s. 776.032, F.S.; Requiring That the Burden of Proof in a Criminal Prosecution Be on the Party Seeking to Overcome the Immunity . . . SB 128 Legis. Reg. Sess. 2017–2018 (Fl. 2017); "Policing/Protest," OurStates, https://www.ourstates.org/#ourstates, accessed October 26, 2017.

9. Don Walker, "Milwaukee Officer Shoots Man After Struggle at Red Arrow," *Milwaukee Journal Sentinel*, April 30, 2014; Myra Sanchik, "Call for Change: Family of Dontre Hamilton Rallies in Downtown Milwaukee," *Fox 6 Now*, May 2, 2014; Jessica Glenza, "Activists Want NYPD Officer Charged as Eric Garner Death Is Ruled a Homicide," *The Guardian*, August 2, 2014; Steve Bennish and Eric Robinette, "Man Police Shot in Walmart Killed over Fake Gun, Family Says," *Dayton (Ohio) Daily News*, August 6, 2014; Nisha Chittal, "Family of Man Killed by Cops at Wal-Mart Demands Video," *MSNBC.com*, August 13, 2014; Corina Knoll, "Hundreds Rally in L.A. to Protest LAPD Shooting of Unarmed Black Man," *Los Angeles Times*, August 17, 2014; Michael Wilson, "Officer's Errant Shot Kills Unarmed Brooklyn Man," *New York Times*, November 11, 2014; Dennis Slattery, Terrence Cullen, and Corinne Lestch, "Protesters Call for Arrest of Rookie Cop Who Shot Akai Gurley as Victim's Sister Says He Didn't Deserve to Die," New York *Daily News*, November 22, 2014; Alex Johnson, "Protesters March After Phoenix Police Kill Rumain Brisbon," *NBC News.com*, December 5, 2014, http://www.nbcnews.com/news/us -news/protesters-march-after-phoenix-police-kill-unarmed-black-man-n261836; Lauren Gambino, "U.S. Fury as Officer Cleared over Choke Death," *The Guardian*, December 4, 2014; Adam Chandler, "Eric Garner and Michael Brown: Deaths Without Indictments," *The Atlantic*, December 3, 2014; Andrew Siff, Jonathan Dienst, and Jennifer Millman, "Grand Jury Declines to Indict NYPD Officer in Eric Garner Chokehold Death," *NBC New York.com*, December 3, 2014, http://www .nbcnewyork.com/news/local/Grand-Jury-Decision-Eric-Garner-Staten-Island -Chokehold-Death-NYPD-284595921.html.

10. Halpern, "Cop."

11. J. Rios, "Flesh in the Street," 63–78; Monica Davey and Julie Bosman, "Protests Flare After Ferguson Police Officer Is Not Indicted," *New York Times*, November 24, 2014; Yamiche Alcindor, "Mo. Gov. Declares State of Emergency, Curfew in Ferguson," *USA Today*, August 19, 2014, http://www.usatoday.com/story/news/nation/2014/08 /16/ferguson-missouri-michael-brown-rally-protests/14160469/; Lucy Westcott and Taylor Wofford, "Two Shot, 31 Arrested Overnight in Ferguson After National Guard Steps In," *Newsweek*, August 18, 2014, http://www.newsweek.com/sun-goes

-down-ferguson-protesters-march-ninth-night-265506; A. J. Vicens, "'Hands Up, Don't Shoot': Peaceful Protests Across the Country Last Night," *Mother Jones*, August 15, 2014, http://www.motherjones.com/politics/2014/08/peaceful-ferguson-rallies-mike-brown; Davey and Bosman, "Protests Flare."

12. US Department of Justice, "Remarks by Attorney General Eric Holder at 'Making Cities Safe Through Community Policing,' An Event of the U.S. Conference of Mayors, Little Rock, Arkansas," press release, October 8, 2014; Joseph Goldstein, Mosi Secret, and Marjorie Connolly, "'History Simmers' in Missouri Strife, Holder Says," *The International New York Times*, August 22, 2014.

13. J. Rios, "Flesh in the Street," 63–78; Julia Craven, Ryan Reilly, and Mariah Stewart, "The Ferguson Protests Worked," *Huntington Post*, August 5, 2015; "Campaign Zero," www.joincampaignzero.org/#vision; John Eligon, "From Street to Ballot, Emboldened by Protests," *New York Times*, February 7, 2016; Richard Pérez-Peña, "Angered by Cities' Handling of Police Shootings, Voters Oust 2 Prosecutors," *New York Times*, March 17, 2016; Jamiles Lartey, "Obama on Black Lives Matter: They Are 'Much Better Organizers Than I Was,'" *The Guardian*, February 18, 2016.

14. President's Task Force, *Final Report*, 1, 9; Travis, Western, and Redburn, *Growth of Incarceration*, 332, 333.

15. President's Task Force, *Final Report*, 2, 11, 21; Vitale, *End of Policing*, 4–24.

16. Mark Landler, "Obama Offers New Standards on Police Gear," *New York Times*, December 2, 2014; Adam Goldman, "Trump Reverses Restrictions on Military Hardware for Police," *New York Times*, August 28, 2017.

17. Amanda Ripley and Timothy Williams, "Body Cameras Watch Officers with Little Effect, Study Finds," *New York Times*, October 21, 2017; Vitale, *End of Policing*, 23–24.

18. Peter B. Kraska, "The Military-Criminal Justice Blur," in *Militarizing the American Criminal Justice System*, 7; Balko, *Rise of the Warrior Cop*, 207; Vitale, *End of Policing*, 10; Matt Apuzzo, "Officer Friendly, in a Tank? War Gear Flows to Local Police," *New York Times*, June 9, 2014; April Glaser, "If You Go Near the Super Bowl, You Will Be Surveilled Hard," *Wired.com*, January 31, 2016.

19. Jon Schuppe, "What Would Jeff Sessions Mean for the Future of Police Reform as Attorney General?" NBC News, January 10, 2017, http://www.nbcnews.com/news/us-news/what-would-jeff-sessions-mean-future-police-reform-attorney-general-n703886; Jaweed Kaleem, "Under Obama, the Justice Department Aggressively Pursued Police Reforms. Will It Continue Under Trump?" *Los Angeles Times*, January 12, 2017; Donald J. Trump, "Standing Up for Our Law Enforcement Community," January 21, 2017, https://www.whitehouse.gov/law-enforcement-community; Donald J. Trump, "Presidential Executive Order on Preventing Violence Against Federal, State, Tribal, and Local Law Enforcement Officers," The White House, February 9, 2017, https://www.whitehouse.gov/the-press-office/2017/02/09/presidential-executive-order-preventing-violence-against-federal-state; Office of Public Affairs, US Department of Justice, "Attorney General Sessions Delivers Remarks at the 63rd Biennial Conference of the National Fraternal Order of Police, Nashville, Tennessee," press release, August 28, 2017.

20. Office of Public Affairs, "Attorney General Sessions"; Senator Tom Coburn, *Safety at Any Price: Assessing the Impact of Homeland Security Spending in the U.S.*

(Washington, DC: US Department of Homeland Security, 2012), 4, https://www
.hsdl.org/?abstract&did=726637; Jonathan Martin, "Why Do Small Police Departments Need 18-Ton Armor-Plated Assault Vehicles?" *The Seattle Times*, December 8, 2014, http://blogs.seattletimes.com/opinionnw/2014/12/08/militarization-of
-police-in-washington-state/.

21. Wilson, *Varieties of Police Behavior*, 16.
22. Richie, *Arrested Justice*, 29, 43; Platt, "'Street' Crime."
23. Robert B. Reich, "Secession of the Successful," *The New York Times Magazine*, January 20, 1991.
24. Fogelson, *Big-City Police*, 54, 55.
25. Bittner, *Aspects of Police Work*, 136–56; President's Commission on Law Enforcement, *Task Force Report: The Police*, 16; Parker, *Crime Fighter*, 144.
26. Fogelson, *America's Armories*, 34–35; Fogelson, *Big-City Police*, 45–53.
27. Platt et al., *Iron Fist and the Velvet Glove*, 39.
28. Friedman, *Crime and Punishment in American History*, 359–60.
29. Brodeur, *Policing Web*, 73.
30. Ibid., 27.
31. Robert P. Weiss, "Vanishing Boundaries of Control," in Hucklesby and Lister, *Private Sector and Criminal Justice*, 23–63; H. W. Aurand quoted in *Brodeur, Policing
Web*, 74; Goldstein, *Political Repression in Modern America*; Harring, *Policing a
Class Society*; Brodeur, *Policing Web*, 75.
32. J. Hall, *Theft, Law and Society*, 205.
33. Johnston, *Rebirth of Private Policing*, 20, 72; Robert P. Weiss, "From 'Slugging
Detectives' to 'Labor Relations,'" in Shearing and Stenning, *Private Policing*, 115;
Goldstein, *Political Repression in Modern America*, 12.
34. Fogelson, *America's Armories*, 38, 41–42; Goldstein, *Political Repression in Modern America*, 15.
35. Brodeur, *Policing Web*, 72–75; Gary T. Marx, "The Interweaving of Public and Private Police in Undercover Work," in Shearing and Stenning, *Private Policing*, 182;
Friedman, *Crime and Punishment in American History*, 104; Richardson, *New York
Police*, 195, 196–97.
36. Fogelson, *America's Armories*, 40–45.
37. Ibid., 2.
38. Jerry M. Cooper, "Federal Military Intervention in Domestic Disorders," in Kohn,
United States Military Under the Constitution, 136, 137.
39. Platt, *Bloodlines*, 117–18.
40. Fogelson, *American Armories*, 24; Slotkin, *Fatal Environment*.
41. McCoy, *Policing America's Empire*, 294–96; Katie Reilly, "President Trump Praises
Fake Story About Shooting Muslims with Pig's Blood-Soaked Bullets," *Time*, August 17, 2017, http://time.com/4905420/donald-trump-pershing-pigs-blood-muslim
-tweet/; J. Katz, "What General Pershing."
42. McCoy, *Policing America's Empire*, 294–96; Cooper, "Federal Military Intervention,"
136–37; Preston, *Aliens and Dissenters*.
43. O'Leary, *To Die For*, 228–29; Donald J. Trump, "Inaugural Address: 'This Moment
Is Your Moment,'" *New York Times*, January 21, 2017.

44. Fogelson, *Big-City Police*, 246; Donner, *Protectors of Privilege*, 59–60; Arthur Raper, "Race and Class Pressures," June 1, 1940, 48, Arthur Franklin Raper Papers, unpublished document prepared for Myrdal, *An American Dilemma*.

45. Donner, *Protectors of Privilege*, 47–64; W. Patterson, *We Charge Genocide*, 189.

46. D'Emilio and Freedman, *Intimate Matters*, chap. 5; McGirr, *War on Alcohol*; D'Emilio, *Sexual Politics, Sexual Communities*, 40–52; García, *Mexican Americans*, 222–27; Vigil, *Crusade for Justice*; Escobar, *Race, Police*; Cole, "What James Comey Did," 4; Office of the Inspector General, U.S. Department of Justice, *A Review of Various Actions by the Federal Bureau of Investigation and Department of Justice in Advance of the 2016 Elections* (June 2018), vi.

47. Chris Hawley, "NYPD Monitored Muslim Students All over Northeast," Associated Press, February 18, 2012, http://www.ap.org/Content/AP-In-The-News/2012/NYPD -monitored-Muslim-students-all-over-Northeast; Adam Goldman and Matt Apuzzo, "With Cameras, Informants, NYPD Eyed Mosques," Associated Press, February 23, 2012, http://www.ap.org/Content/AP-In-The-News/2012/Newark-mayor-seeks-probe -of-NYPD-Muslim-spying; Adam Goldman and Matt Apuzzo, "Informant: NYPD Paid Me to 'Bait' Muslims," Associated Press, October 23, 2012, http://www.ap.org /Content/AP-In-The-News/2012/Informant-NYPD-paid-me-to-bait-Muslims; Matt Apuzzo and Al Baker, "New York to Appoint Civilian to Monitor Police's Counterterrorism Activity," *New York Times*, January 7, 2016; David E. Sanger and Maggie Haberman, "In Campaign, Walking a Tightrope over the Fight on Terrorism," *New York Times*, March 23, 2016.

48. Stampp, *Peculiar Institution*, 192, 209–11; Genovese, *Roll, Jordan, Roll*, 619.

49. Reichel, "Southern Slave Patrols"; Archibald, *Policing*, 4–5; Webb, *Texas Rangers*, xv.

50. Hoover, *Masters of Deceit*.

51. K. O'Reilly, *"Racial Matters,"* 13–14; Lowenthal, *Federal Bureau of Investigation*, 120; Donner, *Age of Surveillance*, 45.

52. Banton, *Policeman in the Community*, 173.

53. National Commission on Law Observance, *Report on the Causes of Crime*, 1:122, 246, 249.

54. National Commission on Law Observance, *Report on Penal Institutions*, 331; National Commission on Law Observance, *Report on Lawlessness in Law Enforcement*, 56, 36–37, 67, 71.

55. Raper, "Race and Class," 13; Myrdal, *An American Dilemma*, 1:540–41.

56. Raper, "Race and Class," 19, 22, 23, 30–31, 59.

57. President's Committee on Civil Rights, *To Secure These Rights*, 25–26.

58. W. Patterson, *We Charge Genocide*, 8; Hodding Carter III, introduction, and Reinhold Niebuhr, foreword to Carter and Niebuhr, *Mississippi Black Paper*, xxxi; Banton, *Policeman in the Community*, 172; Sentencing Project, "Regarding Racial Disparities," 1–2.

59. Raper, "Race and Class," 32–33, 39, 46–47. Myrdal (*An American Dilemma*, 2:1342) conceded that "in the North, there is much killing of Negroes by the police," but guessed that "it seems to be more a part of the regular warfare against criminals than it is an expression of race prejudice."

60. Raper, "Race and Class," 37–38.

61. W. Patterson, *We Charge Genocide*, xi, 8–9.

62. James Baldwin, "Fifth Avenue, Uptown: A Letter from Harlem," in *Nobody Knows My Name*, 68.

63. *Report of the Special Committee Authorized by Congress to Investigate the St. Louis Riots*, July 15, 1918, in Platt, *Politics of Riot Commissions*, 69; Chicago Commission on Race Relations, *Negro in Chicago*, 599; Mayor's Commission on Conditions in Harlem, *Negro in Harlem* (1935), in Platt, *Politics of Riot Commissions*, 178.

64. Platt, *E. Franklin Frazier Reconsidered*, 202–12; K. O'Reilly, *"Racial Matters,"* 19.

65. Skolnick, *Politics of Protest*, 243; Wright, *12 Million Black Voices*, 103, 123; Frazier, *Negro in the United States*, 646.

66. Civil Rights Congress, "Local Police Brutality: Is the Police Department Above the Law?" ca. 1947, Register of the Civil Rights Congress, Mss 016. The quotation was lightly edited for punctuation to make it easier to read.

67. Donner, *Protectors of Privilege*, 246–49, 252; Commission of Inquiry into the Black Panthers, *Search and Destroy*, 10–11.

68. Bloom and Martin, *Black Against Empire*, 212; Wilkins and Clark, *Search and Destroy*, viii.

69. Platt et al., *Iron Fist and the Velvet Glove*, 110–15; Robert Wall, "Special Agent for the FBI," in Platt and Cooper, *Policing America*, 114, 115.

70. Medsger, *Burglary*, 169, 170, 226; Garrow, *FBI and Martin Luther King, Jr.*, 105, 125–26; Comey, *A Higher Loyalty*, 136.

71. Bloom and Martin, *Black Against Empire*; Hill, *Deacons for Defense*, 2, 9.

72. Tony Platt and Cecilia O'Leary, "Two Interviews with Ericka Huggins," *Social Justice* 40, no. 1–2 (2014): 59; P. Foner, *Black Panther Speaks*, 3; Newton, "A Citizens' Peace Force," 36.

73. Harold A. Nelson, "The Defenders," in Platt and Cooper, *Policing America*, 206, 207.

74. Harlem Youth Opportunities Unlimited, *Youth in the Ghetto*, 336; Baldwin, "Fifth Avenue, Uptown," 66.

75. Balagoon et al., *Look for Me in the Whirlwind*, 349; Peter H. Rossi et al., "Between White and Black: The Faces of American Institutions in the Ghetto," in National Advisory Commission, *Supplemental Studies*, 109.

76. President's Commission on Law Enforcement, *Challenge of Crime in a Free Society*, 99; President's Commission on Law Enforcement, *Task Force Report: The Police*, 180; Skolnick, "Police and the Urban Ghetto," 4.

77. National Advisory Commission on Civil Disorders, *Report*, 5, 93; Angus Campbell and Howard Schuman, "Racial Attitudes," in National Advisory Commission, *Supplemental Studies*, 43; Rossi, "Between White and Black," 74, 107; Bittner, *Functions of the Police in Modern Society*, 104; Jewelle Taylor Gibbs, "New Morbidity," in *Young, Black, and Male in America*, 285.

78. Skolnick, *Politics of Protest*, 243; Bloom and Martin, *Black Against Empire*, 28; Skolnick and Fyfe, *Above the Law*, 3.

79. Takagi, "A Garrison State in a 'Democratic' Society"; Robin, "Justifiable Homicide by Police Officers," 225–23; Lofton et al., "Underreporting of Justifiable Homicides."

80. Matt Apuzzo and Adam Liptak, "At Supreme Court, Eric Holder's Justice Dept. Routinely Backs Officers' Use of Force," *New York Times,* April 21, 2015; Erwin Chemerinsky, "How the Supreme Court Protects Bad Cops," op-ed, *New York Times,* August 26, 2014.

81. James C. McKinley, Jr., and Al Baker, "Grand Jury System, with Exceptions, Favors Police in Fatalities," *New York Times,* December 7, 2014; Kimberly Kindy and Kimbriell Kelly, "Thousands Dead, Few Prosecuted," *Washington Post,* April 11, 2015; Apuzzo and Liptak, "At Supreme Court"; Chemerinsky, "How the Supreme Court Protects"; Skolnick, *Politics of Protest,* 346.

82. Escobar, *Race, Police,* 84–90; Vigil, *Crusade for Justice;* Provine, Varsanyi, and Lewis, *Policing Immigrants;* Donald J. Trump, "Executive Order: Enhancing Public Safety in the Interior of the United States," The White House, January 25, 2017, https://www.whitehouse.gov/the-press-office/2017/01/25/presidential-executive -order-enhancing-public-safety-interior-united.

83. García, *Mexicans in the Midwest,* 155–56; Acuña, *Occupied America,* 256–59.

84. J. Moore, *Homeboys,* 25–26; Escobar, *Race, Police,* 3.

85. M. García, *Mexican Americans,* 220–21; Trump, *America We Deserve,* 98–99.

86. M. García, *Memories of Chicano History,* 114, 185–86, 272–85; Commission on Civil Rights, *Hearings Before the United States Commission,* 50.

87. Coles, *Eskimos, Chicanos, Indians,* 4:324, 325.

88. Senator Fred R. Harris, foreword to Morales, *Ando Sangrando (I Am Bleeding),* vii.

89. Morales, *Ando Sangrando (I Am Bleeding),* 20, 27.

90. J. Moore, *Homeboys,* 25.

91. Bourgois, *In Search of Respect,* 36, 37.

92. Monica Davey and Mitch Smith, "Racism Stains Chicago Police, Report Finds," *New York Times,* April 14, 2016; (Chicago) Police Accountability Task Force, *Recommendations for Reform,* 1, 6, 7; Civil Rights Division and US Attorney's Office, *Investigation of the Chicago Police Department,* 145.

93. Davey and Smith, "Racism Stains Chicago Police"; (Chicago) Police Accountability Task Force, *Recommendations for Reform,* 1, 6, 7; Civil Rights Division, *Investigation of the Baltimore City Police.*

94. Utah v. Strieff, 136 S. Ct. 2056, 2070 (2016), Sotomayor, S., dissenting.

95. Smith, *Twilight Los Angeles, 1992,* 3, 6.

5. THE INSECURITY SYNDROME

1. US Congress, Senate Select Committee on Intelligence, *Report on Torture,* 5–6; Scott Shane, "2 U.S. Architects of Harsh Tactics in 9/11's Wake," *New York Times,* August 11, 2009; "Psychologist Says Designing CIA Interrogations Caused Him 'Torment,'" *CBS News.com,* July 22, 2017, https://www.cbsnews.com/news/cia-harsh -interrogation-methods-bruce-jessen-james-mitchell-war-on-terror/.

2. Randy James, "Sheriff Joe Arpaio," *Time,* October 13, 2009, http://content.time.com /time/nation/article/0,8599,1929920,00.html; "Sheriff Runs Female Chain Gang," *CNN.com,* October 29, 2003, http://www.cnn.com/2003/US/Southwest/10/29/chain

.gang.reut/; Ashley Hayes, "'America's Toughest Sheriff' No Stranger to Controversy," *CNN.com*, December 15, 2011, http://www.cnn.com/2011/12/15/justice/arizona-arpaio-profile/index.html; Valeria Fernandez, "Arizona's 'Concentration Camp': Why Was Tent City Kept Open for 24 Years?" *The Guardian*, August 21, 2017.

3. Office of Public Affairs, US Department of Justice, "Department of Justice Releases Investigative Findings on the Maricopa County Sheriff's Office," press release, December 15, 2011; Fernanda Santos, "Judge Finds Violations of Rights by Sheriff," *New York Times*, May 24, 2013; Carma Hassan and Darran Simon, "Former Arizona Sheriff Joe Arpaio Found Guilty of Criminal Contempt," *CNN.com*, July 31, 2017, http://www.cnn.com/2017/07/31/us/arpaio-found-guilty/index.html.

4. Julie Hirschfeld Davis and Maggie Haberman, "Trump Pardons Joe Arpaio, Who Became Face of Crackdown on Illegal Immigration," *New York Times*, August 25, 2017; Conor Friedersdorf, "The Arpaio Pardon Is a Flagrant Assault on Civil Rights," *The Atlantic*, August 26, 2017, https://www.theatlantic.com/politics/archive/2017/08/a-flagrant-assault-on-latino-civil-rights/538119/.

5. Harcourt, *Counterrevolution*.

6. James Baldwin, "Fifth Avenue, Uptown: A Letter from Harlem," in *Nobody Knows My Name*, 62.

7. Wolfe, "Political Repression"; Platt, *Politics of Riot Commissions*.

8. National Advisory Commission, *Report*, 1, 267–91, 297–98; Federal Bureau of Investigation, *Prevention and Control of Mobs and Riots*, 31, 87; Bernard B. Kerik, "War Is Being Waged on Our Homeland," *Time*, December 22, 2014.

9. Skolnick, *Politics of Protest*, 65, 263, 241–92; Stark, *Police Riots*; "The Chicago Police Riot," *Life* 65, no. 23 (December 6, 1968): 34–43.

10. Mike Klare, "Bringing It Back," in National Action/Research on the Military-Industrial Complex, *Police on the Homefront*, 71–72; Coates, *Some New Approaches*, 14; US Department of the Army, *Operations Report*, 2; Janowitz, *Social Control of Escalated Riots*, 24; National Advisory Commission, *Report*, 1.

11. National Advisory Commission, *Report*, 16; Hinton, *From the War on Poverty*, 56–57, 89–90; Klare, "Bringing It Back," 69.

12. Hinton, *From the War on Poverty*, 13, 65, 69, 311.

13. Seigel, "Objects of Police History," 159; Platt et al., *Iron Fist and the Velvet Glove*, chap. 5; Hinton, *From the War on Poverty*, 113, 145. FBI file #44-0-18680 details the students' reports about me; I acquired a copy in 1985 through the Freedom of Information Act, and it remains in my files.

14. Platt et al., *Iron Fist and the Velvet Glove*; Platt and Cooper, *Policing America*, 73–90.

15. President's Commission on Law Enforcement, *Task Force Report: Science and Technology*; and *Task Force Report: The Police*, 44; Platt et al., *Iron Fist and the Velvet Glove*, 78, 224–28; Vince Pinto, "Weapons for the Homefront," in National Action/Research, *Police on the Homefront*, 74–89.

16. Hinton, *From the War on Poverty*, 147, 168, 290, 314.

17. Ibid., 29, 116–23, 142, 253–54, 303–5.

18. Platt and O'Leary, "Patriot Acts."

19. US Congress, Senate, Select Committee, *Report on Torture*, 3–22; Slahi, *Guantánamo Diary*; Sheri Fink and James Risen, "Suit Gives New Details of Brutal Interrogations," *New York Times*, June 22, 2017.

20. Barton Gellman and Greg Miller, "'Black Budget' Summary Details U.S. Spy Network's Successes, Failures, and Objectives," *Washington Post*, August 29, 2013; Khalili, *Time in the Shadows*; Dan Froomkin, "Cheney's 'Dark Side' Is Showing," op-ed, *Washington Post*, November 7, 2005; Agee, *Inside the Company*, 8; John D. Negroponte, interview by Chris Matthews, September 11, 2006, transcript available at http://www.dni.gov/files/documents/Newsroom/Speeches%20and%20Interviews /20060911_interview.pdf; Dana Priest and William M. Arkin, "A Hidden World, Growing Beyond Control," *Washington Post*, July 19, 2010.

21. Gottschalk, *Caught*, chap. 10; Kalhan, "Rethinking Immigration Detention"; Kalhan, "Immigration Surveillance"; Office of Personnel Management, "Sizing Up the Executive Branch"; Ron Nixon, "Single-Minded at Homeland Security," *New York Times*, July 14, 2017; Bureau of Labor Statistics, "Employment Projections— Occupational Data," 2012, "occupation.xls" spreadsheet, http://www.bls.gov/emp /ep_data_occupational_data.htm.

22. Department of Homeland Security Press Office, "DHS Announces Grant Allocations for Fiscal Year (FY) 2015 Preparedness Grants," press release, July 28, 2015.

23. Stumpf, "Crimmigration Crisis," 383, 386.

24. Mason, *Dollars and Detainees*, 4–5.

25. Kalhan, "Immigration Surveillance," 20; Marjorie Zatz, personal communication with author, September 28, 2015; Marjorie Zatz, *Dreams and Nightmares*; Gottschalk, *Caught*, chap. 10; Kalhan, "Rethinking Immigration Detention"; Julia Preston, "Low-Priority Immigrants, Still Swept Up in U.S. Deportation Net," *New York Times*, June 25, 2016; Erik Eckolm, "U.S. Is Sued over Health Care for Immigrant Minors," *New York Times*, June 25, 2016.

26. Kalhan, "Immigration Surveillance," 28; Greene, Carson, and Black, *Indefensible*; Preston, "Lost in Court"; Kalhan, "Rethinking Immigration Detention," 46.

27. Executive Office of the President, *Review*, 2–5; Barnett et al., "2012 Census of Governments," 8.

28. Executive Office of the President, *Review*, 7–8; Robert O'Harrow, Sari Horwitz, and Steven Rich, "Holder Limits Seized-Asset Sharing Process That Splits Billions with Local, State Police," *Washington Post*, January 16, 2015.

29. Mona Chalabi, "America in Grave Danger from Terrorists? The Numbers Tell a Different Story," *The Guardian*, November 5, 2017, https://www.theguardian.com /news/datablog/2017/nov/05/america-terrorism-risk-global-data-new york?utm_ source=esp&utm_medium=Email&utm_campaign=GU+Today+USA+-+Collec tions+2017&utm_term=251022&subid=6737138&CMP=GT_US_collection; Anti-Defamation League, "White Supremacist Murders More Than Doubled in 2017," press release, January 17, 2018, https://www.adl.org/news/press-releases/adl-report -white-supremacist-murders-more-than-doubled-in-2017.

30. Adam Lankford, "A Comparative Analysis"; Lankford, "Public Mass Shooters and Firearms"; Lankford, "Are America's Public Mass Shooters Unique?"; Max Fisher

and Josh Keller, "Only One Thing Explains Mass Shootings in the United States," *New York Times,* November 8, 2017.

31. All the figures are from Gun Violence Archive, http://www.gunviolencearchive.org/, accessed November 10, 2017.

32. Lankford, "Are America's Public Mass Shooters Unique?"; Nicholas Kristof with Bill Marsh, "How to Reduce Shootings," op-ed, *New York Times,* November 9, 2017; Rick Rojas and Kristin Hussey, "High Stakes for Gun Companies as Court Weighs Newtown Suit," *New York Times,* November 3, 2017.

33. Brodeur, *Policing Web*; Hobbs et al., *Bouncers*; M. Davis, *City of Quartz*; M. Davis, *Urban Control*; Clifford Shearing and Philip Stenning, "Say CHEESE!," in *Private Policing,* 322.

34. Johnston, *Rebirth of Private Policing,* 191; Sklansky, "Private Police and Democracy," 89, 92.

35. Brodeur, *Policing Web,* 30; Seigel, "Objects of Police History," 155; Johnston, *Rebirth of Private Policing,* 100; Timothy Williams and Richard A. Oppel, Jr., "Escapes, Riots, Beatings: Behind Bars in Private Prisons," *New York Times,* April 11, 2018; Gary T. Marx, "The Interweaving of Public and Private Police in Undercover Work," in Shearing and Stenning, *Private Policing,* 181.

36. Dan Rather and Jeffrey Fager, "Court Martial in Iraq: US Army Soldiers Face Court Martials for Actions at Baghdad's Abu Ghraib Prison," *60 Minutes II,* CBS-TV News, April 28, 2004; Hersh, "Torture at Abu Ghraib"; Spencer Ackerman, "Bad Lieutenant: American Police Brutality, Exported from Chicago to Guantánamo," *The Guardian,* February 18, 2015; Alan Rappeport and Maggie Haberman, "For Donald Trump, 'Get 'Em Out' Is the New 'You're Fired,'" *New York Times,* March 13, 2016; William K. Rashbaum, "Kerik Loan Activity Is Brought to Light After Indictment," *New York Times,* November 24, 2007; Sam Dolnick, "Kerik Is Sentenced in Corruption Case," *New York Times,* February 18, 2010.

37. Jeff Halper, *War Against the People,* 251, 252, 262.

38. Johnston, *Rebirth of Private Policing,* 18–19; C. O'Reilly, "Pluralization of High Policing"; Haley Tsukayama, "Will All Cops Soon Wear Body Cameras? Companies Like Taser Are Counting on It," *Washington Post,* August 20, 2014; Wagner and Rabuy, *Following the Money*; Lichtenstein, "Flocatex and the Fiscal Limits"; Gottschalk, *Caught,* 65; A. Davis, "Prison Industrial Complex," in *Are Prisons Obsolete?,* 84–104; A. Davis, *Meaning of Freedom*; Eldridge, "Big Business"; Coates, *Between the World and Me,* 131–32.

39. A. Davis, *Meaning of Freedom,* 70; Office of the Inspector General, *Review of the Federal Bureau of Prisons' Monitoring of Contract Prisons* (Washington, DC: US Department of Justice, August 2016); Sally Q. Yates, deputy attorney general, "Memorandum re Reducing Our Use of Private Prisons," US Department of Justice, August 18, 2016; Kilgore, *Understanding Mass Incarceration,* 170; Matt Zapotosky, "Justice Department Will Again Use Private Prisons," *Washington Post,* February 23, 2017. In 2012, 137,200 prisoners were held in private facilities. The figure for 2014 was 131,300, suggesting that the use of private prisons may have peaked. See Carson, "Prisoners in 2014."

40. Eisenhower, "Farewell Address."

41. Brodeur, *Policing Web*, 32; Strom et al., *Private Security Industry*.

42. Thomas Dresslar, "How Many Law Enforcement Agencies Does It Take to Subdue a Peaceful Protest?" American Civil Liberties Union, November 30, 2016, https://www.aclu.org/blog/speak-freely/how-many-law-enforcement-agencies-does-it-take-subdue-peaceful-protest; Sam Allard, "How Did an Ohio Kennel Get Involved in Dakota Access Pipeline Security?" *The Cleveland Scene*, September 20, 2016; Juan González, "Jeremy Scahill: TigerSwan Security, Linked to Blackwater, Now Coordinates Intel for Dakota Access," *Democracy Now*, November 21, 2016, https://www.democracynow.org/2016/11/21/jeremy_scahill_tigerswan_security_linked_to; Ernest Scheyder and Terray Sylvester, "Morton County Sheriff Defends Tactics Against Pipeline Protesters," Reuters, December 4, 2016, http://www.reuters.com/article/north-dakota-pipeline-idUSL1N1DZ0ET.

43. Whitaker, "Surveillance State," 350, 351; S. Graham, *Cities Under Siege*, xxii; Christie, *Crime Control as Industry*, 126.

44. Huber and Mills, "How Technology"; Kalhan, "Immigration Surveillance"; Brodeur, *Policing Web*, 304, 349–50.

45. Andreas and Nadelmann, *Policing the Globe*, 206, 235–36; Brodeur, *Policing Web*, 258; C. O'Reilly, "Pluralization of High Policing," 688–93.

46. Bigo, "Globalized (in)Security: The Field and the Ban-Opticon," in Bigo and Tsoukala, *Terror, Insecurity and Liberty*, 12, 19.

47. Andreas and Nadelmann, *Policing the Globe*, 3.

48. Charles T. Call, "Institutional Learning Within ICITAP," in Oakley, Dziedzic, and Goldberg, *Policing the New World Disorder*, 317–18. See also Seigel, "Objects of Police History," and Platt et al., *Iron Fist and the Velvet Glove*, 164.

49. Platt et al., *Iron Fist and the Velvet Glove*, 160–62, 165–66.

50. S. Stern, "A Short Account," 39; Saunders, *Who Paid the Piper?*

51. Juan González and Amy Goodman, "Flashback: A Look Back at the Church Committee's Investigation into CIA, FBI Misuse of Power," *Democracy Now.org*, April 24, 2009, http://www.democracynow.org/2009/4/24/flashback_a_look_back_at_the; Stuart Schrader, "When NACLA Helped Shutter the U.S. Office of Public Safety," *NACLA Report on the Americas* 48, no. 2 (2016): 181–87; Seymour Hersh, "Huge C.I.A. Operation Reported in U.S. Against Antiwar Forces, Other Dissidents in Nixon Years," *New York Times*, December 22, 1974.

52. Agee, *Inside the Company*, 598, 599–622.

53. L. Johnson, *A Season of Inquiry*.

54. J. Kenneth McDonald, "Secrecy, Accountability, and the CIA," in Kohn, *United States Military Under the Constitution*, 396; General Accounting Office, *Foreign Aid*, 1, 2.

55. General Accounting Office, *Foreign Aid*, 1, 15.

56. Platt et al., *Iron Fist and the Velvet Glove*, 168; Jack Anderson, "Closer Look at CIA Dope Link," *San Francisco Chronicle*, February 19, 1975; Andreas and Nadelmann, *Policing the Globe*, 129; G. Thompson, "Trafficking in Terror."

57. Platt et al., *Iron Fist and the Velvet Glove*, 169–71; Andreas and Nadelmann, *Policing the Globe*, 132, 170, 193.

58. David H. Bayley, foreword to Buchanan, *A Field Guide*, 9; Crofton Black and Star Raphael, "REVEALED: The Boom and Bust of the CIA's Torture Sites," *The Bureau*

of Investigative Journalism, October 14, 2015, https://www.thebureauinvestigates
.com/stories/2015-10-14/revealed-the-boom-and-bust-of-the-cias-secret-torture
-sites.

59. Andreas and Nadelmann, *Policing the Globe*, 197, 200; General Accounting Office, *Better Management Oversight*; Molotch, *Against Security*, 9.

60. Call, "Institutional Learning Within ICITAP," 320–23; Bayley, *Changing the Guard*; McLeod, "Exporting U.S. Criminal Justice," 126. The Justice Department stone-walled my emails and phone calls seeking information about ICITAP's budget and personnel.

61. US Congress, House, Committee on the Judiciary, *Investigation of Misconduct and Mismanagement*; Bayley, foreword to Buchanan, *A Field Guide*, 9.

62. Office of the Inspector General, *A Review of ICITAP's Screening Procedures for Contractors Sent to Iraq as Correctional Advisors* (Washington, DC: US Department of Justice, February 2005); Lynch, *Sunbelt Justice*, 169; *60 Minutes II*, "Court Martial in Iraq"; Hersh, "Torture at Abu Ghraib."

63. International Criminal Investigative Training Assistance Program, "Fact Sheets and Resources," US Department of Justice, February 13, 2017, https://www.justice.gov/criminal-icitap/fact-sheets-and-resources; Ron Nixon, "Homeland Security Goes Abroad. Not Everyone Is Grateful," *New York Times,* December 26, 2017.

64. Foucault, *Society Must Be Defended*, 103; Klare, "Bringing It Back," 68; Monte Real, "Secret Cameras Record Baltimore's Every Movement from Above," *Bloomberg Businessweek*, August 23, 2016, https://www.bloomberg.com/features/2016-baltimore-secret-surveillance/; S. Graham, *Cities Under Siege*, xv, xvii; Khalili, *Time in the Shadows*.

65. Feldman, "Securocratic Wars of Public Safety," 349; Bigo, "Globalized (in)Security," 17.

66. Huber and Mills, "How Technology."

67. Bromwich, "Working the Dark Side," 16.

68. Hallsworth and Lea, "Reconstructing Leviathan," 141, 146, 153; Feldman, "Securocratic Wars of Public Safety," 331; Schuilenburg, *Securitization of Society*, 290.

69. Hallsworth and Lea, "Reconstructing Leviathan," 151; Laurindo Dias Minhoto, "Rio 2016 Olympics: Security and Segregation in the Marvelous City," *Social Justice*, September 6, 2016, http://www.socialjusticejournal.org/rio-2016-olympics-security-and-segregation-in-the-marvelous-city; Fassin, *Enforcing Order*, xv.

6. THE PERILS OF REFORM

1. Falconer, "The Segregation of Delinquent Women and Girls," 164.

2. Sellin, *Pioneering in Penology*, 57, 63–70; McLennan, *Crisis of Imprisonment*, 54–61; Dickens, *American Notes*, 57, 148, 313.

3. Platt, "In Recovery from Rehab"; Hinton, *From the War on Poverty*.

4. Parks, "Harlem Gang Leader"; Lord, *Gordon Parks*; Maurice Berger, "Gordon Parks's Harlem Argument," *New York Times,* November 11, 2015, https://lens.blogs.nytimes.com/2015/11/11/gordon-parkss-harlem-argument/.

5. Rainwater and Yancey, *Moynihan Report and the Politics of Controversy*; Platt, *E. Franklin Frazier*, 111–13; President's Commission on Law Enforcement, *Challenge of Crime in a Free Society*, 71, 73.

6. Chute, "Juvenile Court in Retrospect," 7; Chute, "Fifty Years of the Juvenile Court," 1.

7. Lathrop, "Development of the Probation System," 348.

8. Platt, *Child Savers*.

9. Brown, *Manchild in the Promised Land*, 134; Malcolm X and Haley, *Autobiography of Malcolm X*, 153, 455.

10. Sarri, *Under Lock and Key*; Vinter, *Time Out*; President's Commission on Law Enforcement, *Juvenile Delinquency and Youth Crime*, 33, 35.

11. Platt, *Child Savers*, 161–63; *In re* Gault, 387 U.S. 1, 27 (1967).

12. Piven and Cloward, *Regulating the Poor*; Hofstadter, *Age of Reform*, 18.

13. President's Commission on Law Enforcement, *Juvenile Delinquency and Youth Crime*, 7–8.

14. Kolko, *Triumph of Conservatism*, 282; Williams, *Contours of American History*; Weinstein, *Corporate Ideal in the Liberal State*; Wiebe, *Businessmen and Reform*; McGirr, *War on Alcohol*, xvii.

15. Eileen Boris, "Reconstructing the 'Family,'" in Frankel and Dye, *Gender, Class, Race, and Reform*; Odem, *Delinquent Daughters*; Stansell, *City of Women*, 54; Platt, *Child Savers*, 68; Ward, *Black Child Savers*; Chávez-García, *States of Delinquency*.

16. Cooley, "'Nature v. Nurture'"; Wines, *State of Prisons*, 132.

17. L. Gordon, *Women, the State and Welfare*; Rowbotham, *Hidden from History*, 55.

18. Brockway, *Fifty Years of Prison Service*, 421.

19. Platt, *Child Savers*, 51–53.

20. Ibid., 69.

21. Braly, *False Starts*, 43.

22. Arnold and Reed, *In the Land of the Grasshopper Song*, xi; Jacobs, *White Mother to a Dark Race*, 24.

23. Nabokov, *Native American Testimony*, 218–24.

24. Adams, *Education for Extinction*; Fear-Segal, *White Man's Club*; Cahill, *Federal Fathers and Mothers*; Nabokov, *Native American Testimony*, 216–17.

25. Canaday, *Straight State*, 59.

26. Schweik, *Ugly Laws*, 1–4, 289.

27. O'Leary, *To Die For*, chaps. 9 and 10; Cecilia O'Leary and Tony Platt, "Pledging Allegiance," in Scraton, *Beyond September 11*, 173–76; Balch, *Methods of Teaching Patriotism*.

28. Balch, *A Patriotic Primer*; O'Leary, *To Die For*, chaps. 9 and 10, 192.

29. Goldstein, *Saving "Old Glory,"* 93–94; O'Leary, *To Die For*, 244.

30. Canaday, *Straight State*, 19–20.

31. Peiss, *Cheap Amusements*, 165, 178; Kunzel, *Fallen Women, Problem Girls*.

32. O'Hare, *In Prison*, 12.

33. Bristow, *Making Men Moral*, 221–29.

34. Brandt, *No Magic Bullet*, 59; Bristow, *Making Men Moral*, 130; Canaday, *Straight State*, 60–61, 64–65.

35. Dietzler, *Detention Houses and Reformatories*, 3, 4, 11, 69, 74.
36. Falconer, "Segregation of Delinquent Women," 161, 165, 166.
37. Bristow, *Making Men Moral*, 119.
38. Brandt, *No Magic Bullet*, 74, 88.
39. McGirr, *War on Alcohol*, xiv, 69, 71.
40. Dwight D. Eisenhower, "Executive Order 10450," April 27, 1953, 18 FR 2489, 3 CFR, 1949–1953 Comp., 936; D'Emilio, *Sexual Politics, Sexual Communities*, 40–52; Gebhard and Johnson, *Kinsey Data*, 591; Duberman, *Cures*, 20.
41. Platt, *Bloodlines*.
42. Ibid., 60–65.
43. Kühl, *Nazi Connection*; Platt, *Bloodlines*, 59, 61.
44. Platt, *Bloodlines*, 59, 61, 125, 135; Popenoe and Johnson, *Applied Eugenics*, 284–85, 319.
45. Popenoe and Johnson, *Applied Eugenics*, 301.
46. Amy LaPan and Tony Platt, "'To Stem the Tide of Degeneracy,'" in Kirk, *Mental Disorders in the Social Environment*, 139–64; Kunzel, *Fallen Women*, 44, 54; Walkowitz, "Making of a Feminine Professional Identity"; Addams, *A New Conscience and an Ancient Evil*, 131.
47. A. Stern, *Eugenic Nation*, 100, 102; Kline, *Building a Better Race*; Ordover, *American Eugenics*.
48. Blue, *Doing Time in the Depression*; Blue, "Strange Career of Leo Stanley"; Nourse, *In Reckless Hands*; Buck v. Bell, 247 U.S. 200, 207 (1927); Skinner v. Oklahoma ex rel. Williamson, 316 U.S. 535, 541 (1942).
49. J. H. Dodge to E. S. Gosney, July 26, 1926, box 16.5, Gosney Papers; Paul Popenoe to John Randolph Haynes, March 14, 1930, box 77, Human Betterment Foundation folder, Haynes Papers; John Randolph Haynes, "Millions of Human Beings," box 84, insanity folder, ca. 1918, Haynes Papers; John Randolph Haynes Foundation, "John Randolph Haynes," http://www.haynesfoundation.org/about/index.asp.
50. Novak et al., *Ethnic Bias*; Chávez-García, *States of Delinquency*, 136; Molina, *Fit to Be Citizens?*, 146–49.
51. Chávez-García, *States of Delinquency*, 63–68, 71–72; Terman, *The Measurement of Intelligence*, 92.
52. Kline, *Building a Better Race*; Ordover, *American Eugenics*.
53. Briggs, *Reproducing Empire*, 102, 143; A. Davis, "Racism, Birth Control, and Reproductive Rights," in *Women, Race, and Class*, 202–21; Ordover, *American Eugenics*, 161–78.
54. Woodside, *Sterilization in North Carolina*, xiv, 163; Ordover, *American Eugenics*, 165; Begos et al., *Against Their Will*, 1.
55. Begos et al., *Against Their Will*, 9.
56. Ibid., 12–13.
57. Ibid., 3, 71–72, 95.
58. L. Gordon, *Moral Property of Women*; Black Panther Intercommunal News Service, "Sterilization: Another Part of the Plan of Black Genocide," *Black Panther*, May 8, 1971, 15; Ordover, *American Eugenics*, 153.
59. A. Stern, "Sterilized in the Name of Public Health"; Corey G. Johnson, "Female Inmates Sterilized in California Prisons Without Approval," *Center for Investigative*

Reporting, July 7, 2013, http://cironline.org/reports/female-inmates-sterilized -california-prisons-without-approval-4917; Alexandra Minna Stern and Tony Platt, "Sterilization Abuse in State Prisons: Time to Break with California's Long Eugenic Patterns," *Huffington Post*, July 23, 2013, http://www.huffingtonpost.com/alex-stern /sterilization-california-prisons_b_3631287.html.

60. Herrnstein and Murray, *Bell Curve*, 532–33, 551.

61. Wilson, "Rediscovery of Character," 3; Steele, "New Sovereignty," 54; Himmelfarb, *On Looking into the Abyss*, 43; Bennett, *Index of Leading Cultural Indicators*, 12; Olasky, *Tragedy of American Compassion*, 1, 9, 16.

62. Roosevelt, "Memorial Day Address"; Donald J. Trump, "The Inaugural Address," January 20, 2017, https://www.whitehouse.gov/inaugural-address; O'Leary, *To Die For*, chap. 12; Trump, *Time to Get Tough*, 107, 110, 113, 114, 137, 149, 150.

63. Trump, *America We Deserve*, 29, 94, 99; Liz Goodwin, "A 1990s Mugging and the Roots of Donald Trump's Hardline Criminal Justice Views," *Yahoo News*, May 25, 2016, https://www.yahoo.com/news/1990s-mugging-roots-donald-trump-000000 780.html; Yamiche Alcindor, "In Trump Tweets, Blacks Perceive a Callous Rival," *New York Times*, January 16, 2017; Donald J. Trump, "Bring Back the Death Penalty," advertisement in four New York newspapers, May 1, 1989; Trump, "Inaugural Address."

64. Robert E. Moffit, Edwin Meese III, and Patrick F. Fagan, "Crime: Turning the Tide in America," in Butler and Holmes, *Issues '98*, 236.

7. RADICAL VISIONS

1. Jack London, "'Pinched,'" in H. Franklin, *Prison Writing in 20th-Century America*, 49; Debs, *Walls and Bars*, 91.

2. Bhabha, *Nation and Narration*, 4; P. Levi, *Drowned and the Saved*, 29.

3. Paul Goodman, introduction to Berkman, *Prison Memoirs of an Anarchist*, iii; Braly, *False Starts*, 47.

4. Debs, *Walls and Bars*, 49; A. Walker, *In Search of Our Mothers' Gardens*, 240.

5. Reed, *Life and Adventures of a Haunted Convict*, xvii, 217–18.

6. Suvak, *Memoirs of American Prisons*; Morris, *Jailhouse Journalism*.

7. H. Franklin, *Prison Literature in America*, xxx; B. Jackson, *Wake Up Dead Man*, 2; H. Franklin, *Prison Writing in 20th-Century America*, 8, 30, 34; Haley, *No Mercy Here*, 213, 215, 216.

8. Goodman introduction, i; H. Franklin, *Prison Writing in 20th-Century America*, 49, 62, 72; O'Hare, *In Prison*.

9. Berkman, *Prison Memoirs of an Anarchist*, 489–90.

10. H. Franklin, *Prison Writing in 20th-Century America*, 10, 89–90, 102–3, 119; Chester Himes, "To What Red Hell?" *Esquire*, October 1934, 100–5.

11. Miriam Allen De Ford, "Shall Convicts Write Books?" *The Nation*, November 5, 1930, 496; H. Franklin, *Prison Writing in 20th-Century America*, 10–11; Braly, *False Starts*, 40; Cannon, *Letters from Prison*; Flynn, "Venus Over Alderson—New Year's, 1956," in *Alderson Story*, 204.

12. Ina, "Haiku."

13. O'Hare, *In Prison*, 93, 182; Malcolm X and Haley, *Autobiography of Malcolm X*, 172, 173, 174.

14. "The Library Report," in Minton, *Inside*, 17–29.

15. O'Hare, *In Prison*, 12, 13; Carter and Niebuhr, *Mississippi Black Paper*, 21.

16. Robert Martinson, "Prison Notes of a Freedom Rider," *The Nation*, January 6, 1962, 4–5.

17. Begos et al., *Against Their Will*, 15, 20, 183–86; Levi and Waldman, *Inside This Place*, 34, 65, 209.

18. Begel, "An Interview with Willie Tate," 72, 76.

19. John Pallas and Bob Barber, "From Riot to Revolution," in Platt and Takagi, *Punishment and Penal Discipline*, 146–54; King, *Letter from Birmingham Jail*, 23; H. Thompson, *Blood in the Water*; Berger, *Captive Nation*.

20. McLennan, *Crisis of Imprisonment*, 140–41.

21. Ibid., 146; Haley, *No Mercy Here*, 205–6, 246.

22. Schechter, *Ida B. Wells-Barnett and American Reform*; Terrell, "Peonage in the United States," 322.

23. Adams, *Education for Extinction*, 224, 229, 231, 232, 233; Brandt, *The Colored Land*, 80.

24. Gluck, *From Parlor to Prison*, 242–43, 247; "'Pickets' Mutiny in Workhouse," *New York Times*, October 5, 1917.

25. O'Hare, *In Prison*, 10, 14, 15, 17, 64–68.

26. Kate Richards O'Hare, "'Nigger' Equality," *The National Rip-Saw*, March 25, 1912; Gluck, *From Parlor to Prison*, 247–48.

27. O'Hare, *In Prison*, 19; H. Franklin, *Prison Writing in 20th-Century America*, 74; "How Did Kate Richards O'Hare's Conviction and Incarceration for Sedition During World War I Change Her Activism?" Women and Social Movements (Archival Collection), Center for the Historical Study of Women and Gender, Binghamton University, Binghampton, NY, http://womhist.alexanderstreet.com/kro/doclist.htm.

28. Debs, *Walls and Bars*, 54, 59, 61, 64, 108, 159, 161, 162–63, 197–208.

29. Flynn, *Alderson Story*, 56, 177, 180, 181, 190, 191.

30. Sobell, *On Doing Time*, 525.

31. Berger, *Captive Nation*, 10.

32. Belfrage, *Freedom Summer*, 141, 148; Deming, *Prison Notes*, 12, 24, 124–27, 180–81.

33. Martinson, "Prison Notes of a Freedom Rider," 4–5.

34. Malcolm X and Haley, *Autobiography of Malcom X*; Brown, *Manchild in the Promised Land*; Jackson, *Soledad Brother*; Thomas, *Down These Mean Streets*; Melville, *Letters from Attica*.

35. Blake, *Joint*; Pell, *Maximum Security*, 8; Thomas, *Seven Long Times*, 218, 232.

36. James Baldwin, "An Open Letter," in A. Davis, *If They Come in the Morning*, 16, 18; Norman Mailer, introduction to J. Abbott, *In the Belly of the Beast*, xviii.

37. Irwin, *Felon*; Bacon and American Friends Service Committee, *Struggle for Justice*; Levy and Miller, *Going to Jail*; Berrigan, *Widen the Prison Gates*.

38. Hayden, *Trial*, 98.

39. Glenn Fowler, "Thomas Murton, Arkansas Penologist, Dies at 62," *New York Times,* October 19, 1990; Murton and Hyams, *Accomplices to the Crime,* 199, 204.

40. Robert Wall, "Special Agent for the FBI," in Platt and Cooper, *Policing America,* 17–18; Agee, *Inside the Company.*

41. Nagel, *New Red Barn;* Alan Blinder and Manny Fernandez, "Life's Last Moment: Bearing Witness to an Execution," *New York Times,* April 24, 2017.

42. H. Franklin, *Prison Writing in 20th-Century America,* 239, 242, 255; Knight, *Black Voices from Prison,* back cover; Gwendolyn Brooks, preface to Etheridge Knight, *Poems from Prison,* 9.

43. Malcolm X and Haley, *Autobiography of Malcolm X,* 158–59; Elma Lewis, foreword to Norfolk Prison Brothers, *Who Took the Weight?,* xiv–xv.

44. Pfaelzer, *Driven Out;* Tony Platt, "The Yokayo vs. the University of California: An Untold Story of Repatriation," *News of Native California* 26, no. 2 (Winter 2012–13): 9–14; Nourse, *In Reckless Hands;* Indians of All Tribes, "Proclamation," in Josephy, *Red Power,* 42–43; Piven and Cloward, *Poor People's Movements.*

45. Gorz, *Strategy for Labor,* 7–8.

46. O'Hare, *In Prison,* 155, 164, 165, 178, 180, 182–83.

47. A. Davis, *Are Prisons Obsolete?;* CR10 Publications Collective, *Abolition Now!*

48. Debs, *Walls and Bars,* 58–59, 200–1, 203, 206–8.

49. King, *Letter from Birmingham Jail,* 2–3, 8; Malcolm X and Haley, *Autobiography of Malcolm X,* 385, 388.

50. John Pallas and Bob Barber, "From Riot to Revolution," in Platt and Takagi, *Punishment and Penal Discipline,* 146–54; *U.S. New and World Report,* "Why Convicts Riot," December 19, 1952, 18–21.

51. Felber, "'Shades of Mississippi'"; Pallas and Barber 147.

52. Red Family, "A Decade of Prison Rebellions in California, 1961–1971," *War Behind Walls,* September 1971, 8–9, zine published by People's Press, San Francisco, in the author's personal files.

53. Brochier, "Prison Talk," 11.

54. Allen, *Borderland of Criminal Justice;* Bacon and American Friends Service Committee, *Struggle for Justice,* chap. 6; E. Goffman, *Asylums,* 44; Speiglman, "Prison Psychiatrists and Drugs," 24; Red Family, "You'll Never Get Out," *War Behind Walls,* 13.

55. John Filmore, "Strike," in Minton, *Inside,* 72; "History of a Convict Report," in Minton, *Inside,* 202–325.

56. "The Folsom Prisoners' Manifesto of Demands," in Pell, *Maximum Security,* 191–201.

57. *Anvil* 1, no. 1 (June 1971); United Prisoners' Union, "Bill of Rights," 1971, in the author's personal files.

58. H. Thompson, *Blood in the Water,* 120–26; Weiss, "Guest Editor's Interview," 90.

59. Lyon, *Conversations with the Dead,* 13; Morris, *Jailhouse Journalism,* 161, 167.

60. Levy and Miller, *Going to Jail,* 239–43; Gilbert, "'These Criminals,'" 74.

61. Platt et al., *Iron Fist and the Velvet Glove,* 185–97; Newton, "A Citizens' Peace Force," 36, 39.

62. Platt, *Child Savers,* 160–63; William Bush, "Child Savers and Three Cycles," in Platt, *Child Savers,* 201–12.

63. H. Thompson, *Blood in the Water*.

64. H. Franklin, *Prison Writing in 20th-Century America*, 14; Camp, *Incarcerating the Crisis*; Berger, *Captive Nation*; Braly, *False Starts*, 333–34.

65. Alexandra Alter, "A Prisoner Wrote a Book. Now the State Wants Him to Write a Check," *New York Times*, February 19, 2018.

66. McLennan, *Crisis of Imprisonment*, 54–56.

67. Campaign Zero, "We Can End Police Violence in America," 2016, https://www .joincampaignzero.org/; Short Corridor Collective, Special Housing Unit, Pelican Bay State Prison, "Agreement to End Hostilities," August 12, 2012, in the author's personal files.

68. MacFarquhar, "Out and Up."

8. THE DISTANT PRESENT

1. Melville, *Letters from Attica*, 172; H. Thompson, *Blood in the Water*; Camp, *Incarcerating the Crisis*; Berger, *Captive Nation*.

2. Gottschalk, "Long Reach of the Carceral State," 440.

3. Gottschalk, *Caught*; Wacquant, "From Slavery to Mass Incarceration," 44.

4. S. Hall, *Hard Road to Renewal*; Perlstein, *Nixonland*, 46; Weaver, "Frontlash."

5. Hinton, *From the War on Poverty*, 8, 310–13; "Transcript of Eisenhower's Speech to the G.O.P. Convention," *New York Times*, July 15, 1964; Ronald Reagan, "We Will All Become Prisoners," op-ed, *New York Times*, October 7, 1971; Ronald Reagan, "A Time for Choosing," October 27, 1964, http://cdn.constitutionreader.com/files /pdf/constitution/ch123.pdf; Rosenfeld, *Subversives*, 322–27.

6. J. Elliot, "'Willie' Horton Nobody Knows," 204.

7. McGirr, *War on Alcohol*, 190; Hinton, *From the War on Poverty*, 8, 310–13.

8. Peter Applebome, "The 1992 Campaign: Death Penalty; Arkansas Execution Raises Questions on Governor's Politics," *New York Times*, January 25, 1992; Sharon LaFraniere, "Governor's Camp Feels His Record on Crime Can Stand the Heat," *Washington Post*, October 5, 1992.

9. Simon, *Governing Through Crime*; Democratic National Convention, *The 2000 Democratic National Platform: Prosperity, Progress, and Peace*, http://www.presi dency.ucsb.edu/ws/index.php?pid=29612; Republican National Convention, *Republican Platform 2000: Renewing America's Purpose Together*, http://www.presidency .ucsb.edu/ws/?pid=25849.

10. Obama, *Audacity of Hope*, 34; "Barack Obama on Crime," On the Issues, http:// www.ontheissues.org/2016/Barack_Obama_Crime.htm (2008). President Obama's widely cited claim is a tad hyperbolic. In 2013, 750,628 African American men were incarcerated and 960,000 were in college. For a discussion of the relevant data on this issue, see the note on statistical sources in the appendix.

11. Loftin et al., "Underreporting of Justifiable Homicides"; Rob Barry, "Hundreds of Police Killings Are Uncounted in Federal Stats," *Wall Street Journal*, March 12, 2014.

12. Donald Rumsfeld, Pentagon press briefing, February 12, 2002; D. Graham, "Rumsfeld's Knowns and Unknowns."

13. Cohen, "Punitive City," 339.

14. Hernández, Muhammad, and Thompson, "Introduction: Constructing the Carceral State," 19.
15. For a discussion of the problems involved in estimating the staffing and funding of carceral agencies, see the note on statistical sources in the appendix.
16. The number of police per 100,000 residents went from 212 in 1975 to 246 in 2012. President's Commission on Law Enforcement, *Task Force Report, The Police*, 1; Kyckelhahn, *Justice Expenditure and Employment Extracts*; Lindgren, *Justice Expenditure and Employment Extracts*; Reaves, *Number of Full-Time*.
17. For a more detailed breakdown of criminal justice employment and how these numbers were calculated, see the appendix.
18. Braly, *False Starts*, 243.
19. Lichtenstein, "Flocatex and the Fiscal Limits," 117; Gilmore, *Golden Gulag*, 7; Lynch, *Sunbelt Justice*, 4; Subramanian et al., *Incarceration's Front Door*.
20. Cahalan, *Historical Corrections Statistics*, 29, 70; Bureau of Justice Statistics, "Prisoners in State and Federal Institutions"; Guerino, Harrison, and Sabol, *Prisoners in 2010*, 1; Lindgren, *Justice Expenditure and Employment in the U.S., 1988*; Kyckelhahn, *Justice Expenditure and Employment Extracts, 2012*. The per capita rate of imprisonment increased from one in 715 nationally in 1979 to one in 200 in 2010. From 1985 to 1991 the number of guards and other staff working in state prisons increased 70 percent.
21. Jayadev and Bowles, "Guard Labor." See appendix for information about how these numbers were calculated.
22. Estimates vary considerably, depending on the time period and subject matter, from Obama's $80 billion for incarceration in 2016 to the Prison Policy Initiative's $265 billion for all criminal justice agencies in 2017. See Perkinson, *Texas Tough*, 1; Wagner and Rabuy, *Following the Money of Mass Incarceration*; Widra, "Tracking the Impact of the Prison System"; Obama, "President's Role."
23. In 1985, large cities (500,000 residents or more) spent 15 percent of their budgets on policing, up from an average of 12 percent in the 1950s. Melissa S. Kearney et al., *Ten Economic Facts About Crime and Incarceration in the United States* (Washington, DC: Hamilton Project, May 2014), www.hamiltonproject.org/assets/legacy/files/downloads_and_links/v8_THP_10CrimeFacts.pdf.
24. Although the percentage of state budgets allocated to prisons has remained relatively stable for several decades, the cost goes up considerably if the calculation includes subsidies and funding provided to the states by the federal government as well as statewide bond measures to raise money for new prisons. Barnett et al., *2012 Census of Governments: Finance*, 8; Executive Office of the President, *Review*, 2–5; Gilmore, *Golden Gulag*.
25. Department of Homeland Security Press Office, "DHS Announces Grant Allocations for Fiscal Year (FY) 2015 Preparedness Grants," press release, July 28, 2015; Hester, "Deportability and the Carceral State," 150; Anil Kalhan, "The Transformation of Immigration Custody and the Limits of 'Crimmigration,'" unpublished paper, April 2017, in the author's personal files.
26. Gottschalk, *Caught*, 237.
27. LEAA funded about eighty thousand crime-control projects at a cost of about $10 billion (about $25 billion in today's dollars). Hinton, *From the War on Poverty*, 178.

28. Ibid., 2; Rosenfeld, *Subversives*; Federal Bureau of Investigation, "Authorized Positions, 1975–2003," http://www.justice.gov/archive/jmd/1975_2002/2002/html/page96 -99.htm; Murakawa, *First Civil Right*, chap. 4.

29. General Accounting Office, *Foreign Aid*, 2; Bayley, foreword to Buchanan, *A Field Guide*, 9.

30. Kohler-Hausmann, *Getting Tough*, 1–2.

31. I draw upon Tarell McCraney's use of the phrase "distant present" from his 2013 play, *Head of Passes*.

32. Lord, *Gordon Parks*; S. Hall, *Hard Road to Renewal*, 42, 55; S. Hall et al., *Policing the Crisis*, xii; Harcourt, *Exposed*.

33. "The Plague of Violent Crime," *Newsweek*, March 23, 1981; "The Curse of Violent Crime," *Time*, March 23, 1981.

34. Platt and Takagi, "Intellectuals for Law and Order"; Platt et al., *Iron Fist and the Velvet Glove*, 9; National Action/Research, *Police on the Homefront*; Carlan, "Criminal Justice Degree and Policing," 608; Frost and Clear, "Doctoral Education in Criminology."

35. Foucault, *Power/Knowledge*, 47; Brochier, "Prison Talk," 13; Banfield, *Unheavenly City*; Wilson, *Thinking About Crime*; Kelling and Wilson, "Broken Windows"; George Lipsitz, "Policing Place and Taxing Time," in Camp and Heatherton, *Policing the Planet*, 124.

36. Friedman, *Crime and Punishment in American History*, 464–65; Jim Webb, "Why We Must Fix Our Prisons," *Parade*, March 29, 2009.

37. Barack Obama, "Remarks by the President in State of Union Address," The White House, Office of the Press Secretary, January 20, 2015, https://www.whitehouse.gov /the-press-office/2015/01/20/remarks-president-state-union-address-january-20 -2015.

38. Richard A. Viguerie, "A Conservative Case for Prison Reform," op-ed, *New York Times*, June 9, 2013.

39. Husna Haq, "Emptier Prisons: Inmate Population Drops for First Time in 40 Years," *The Christian Science Monitor*, July 9, 2010; Bureau of Justice Statistics, "Jail Population Declines by More Than Two Percent in the 12 Months Ending June 30, 2009," press release, June 3, 2010, https://ojp.gov/newsroom/pressreleases/2010/BJS10079 .htm; "Decline in Black Incarceration for Drug Offenses," press release, Sentencing Project, March 17, 2009; Silber, Subramanian, and Spotts, *Justice in Review*; Porter, *Repurposing*; Sentencing Project, "U.S. Prison Population Trends."

40. Marc Mauer, personal communication with author, April 21, 2015; Jeremy W. Peters, "Rand Paul Focuses on Criminal Justice in Talk to Black Students," *New York Times*, March 13, 2015; "Senator Rand Paul on Criminal Justice System," C-SPAN, March 13, 2015, http://www.c-span.org/video/?324817-1/senator-rand-paul-rky-remarks -bowie-state-university. Right on Crime's platform can be found at rightoncrime.com.

41. Michael Barbaro and Alexander Burns, "In Trump's Voice, It's a New Nixon," *New York Times*, July 19, 2016; Jeremy W. Peters, "'Traditional' Marriage, Border Wall and Coal on Tap," *New York Times*, July 19, 2016; Carl Hulse, "Why Senate Couldn't Pass a Crime Bill Many Backed," *New York Times*, September 16, 2016; Mauer, personal communication.

42. President's Task Force, *Final Report*; Travis, Western, and Redburn, *Growth of Incarceration*; Carl Hulse, "Unlikely Cause Unites the Left and the Right: Justice Reform," *New York Times,* February 19, 2015; Newt Gingrich and Van Jones, "Prison System Is Failing America," *CNN.com,* May 22, 2014, http://www.cnn.com/2014/05/21/opinion/gingrich-jones-prison-system-fails-america/index.html. Also see Right on Crime, Bipartisan Summit on Criminal Justice Reform a Triumph of Cooperation, April 9, 2015, http://rightoncrime.com/2015/04/watch-bipartisan-summit-on-criminal-justice-reform/. *The Marshall Project*'s principles can be found at https://themarshallproject.org.

43. Travis, Western, and Redburn (Committee on Causes and Consequences of Higher Rates of Incarceration), *Growth of Incarceration*, 323; President's Task Force, *Final Report*, 9; Lerman and Weaver, *Arresting Citizenship*.

44. James Kilgore, "Jails: Time to Wake Up to Mass Incarceration in Your Neighborhood," *Truth Out,* March 4, 2015, http://www.truth-out.org/news/item/29322-jails-time-to-wake-up-to-mass-incarceration-in-your-neighborhood. The Black Lives Matter agenda can be found at http://www.joincampaignzero.org/#vision.

45. Zepeda-Millán, *Latino Mass Mobilization*; Coates, *Between the World and Me*.

46. Sheryl Gay Stolberg and Eric Eckholm, "Virginia Felons Get Back Votes," *New York Times,* April 23, 2016; Terry McAuliffe, "Governor McAuliffe Statement on the Virginia Supreme Court Decision on the Restoration of Civil Rights," July 22, 2016, https://governor.virginia.gov/newsroom/newsarticle?articleId=16047; Sentencing Project, "Disenfranchisement News: Minnesota and Maryland Advance Probation and Parole Voting Legislation," March 9, 2015, http://www.sentencing-project.org/news/disenfranchisement-news-minnesota-and-maryland-advance-probation-and-parole-voting-legislation/; (Chicago) Police Accountability Task Force, *Recommendations for Reform*; Flint Taylor, "How Activists Won Reparations for the Survivors of Chicago Police Department Torture," *In These Times,* June 26, 2015, http://inthesetimes.com/article/18118/jon-burge-torture-reparations.

47. Richard A. Oppel, Jr., "After a Boy's Death, a Neighborhood's Pain Lives on," *New York Times,* December 9, 2014; Joseph Goldstein, "Judge Rejects New York's Stop-and-Frisk Policy," *New York Times,* August 12, 2013; Charlie Savage, "Justice Department Plans to Streamline How It Tracks Police Killings," *New York Times,* August 10, 2016.

48. Atul Gawande, "Hellhole," *The New Yorker,* March 30, 2009; Colin Dayan, "Barbarous Confinement," op-ed, *New York Times,* July 17, 2011; Jennifer Medina, "Hunger Strike by California Inmates, Already Large, Is Expected to Be Long," *New York Times,* July 10, 2013; Simon, *Mass Incarceration on Trial*.

49. Monica Davey and Mitch Smith, "Racism Stains Chicago Police, A Report Finds," *New York Times,* April 14, 2016; (Chicago) Police Accountability Task Force, *Recommendations for Reform*; Utah v. Strieff, 136 S. Ct. 2056, 2063, 2070–71 (2016).

50. Katie Shepherd and Christine Hauser, "A Day of Protests over Police Shootings Across U.S.," *New York Times,* July 22, 2016; Sewell Chan, "Black Lives Matter Activists Protest Across Britain Against Racial Inequities," *New York Times,* August 6, 2016; Associated Press, "Shooting Deaths of Officers Spike 78%, Report Says," *San*

Francisco Chronicle, July 28, 2016; Niraj Chokshi, "Deaths in the Line of Duty," *New York Times,* July 28, 2016.

51. Nick Corasanti and Maggie Haberman, "Trump Suggests Gun Owners Act Against Clinton," *New York Times,* August 10, 2016; Savage, "Justice Department Plans to Streamline"; Civil Rights Division, "Investigation of the Baltimore City Police"; Kay Nolan and Niraj Chokshi, "Milwaukee Is Shaken by Eruption of Violence," *New York Times,* August 15, 2016; John Eligon, "Violence in Milwaukee Was No Shock to Some," *New York Times,* August 15, 2016.

52. Bryan Flaherty, "From Kaepernick's Sitting to Trump's Fiery Comments: NFL's Anthem Protests Have Spurred Discussion," *Washington Post,* September 24, 2017, https://www.washingtonpost.com/graphics/2017/sports/colin-kaepernick-national -anthem-protests-and-NFL-activism-in-quotes/?utm_term=.4f7780b6e1c9; Elliott Almond, "Harry Edwards Q&A: Kaepernick Belongs in the Smithsonian," *San Jose Mercury News,* December 31, 2016; Colin Kaepernick's acceptance speech for Amnesty International's Ambassador of Conscience Award, Amsterdam, April 21, 2018.

53. "Trump on Criminal Justice: 'We Have to Get a Lot Tougher,'" MSNBC, August 20, 2015, http://www.msnbc.com/morning-joe/watch/trump-on-criminal-justice-reform -509292611802; Dan Balz and Abby Phillip, "Democratic Debate in Milwaukee Spotlights Fundamental Divide," *Washington Post,* February 11, 2016, https://www .washingtonpost.com/politics/2016/02/11/87452fae-d075-11e5-b2bc-988409ee911b _story.html?utm_term=.3ae9b76154aa; Sabrina Siddiqui, "'Mothers of the Movement' Team with Hillary Clinton in Bid for Black Vote," *The Guardian,* October 14, 2016, https://www.theguardian.com/us-news/2016/oct/24/mothers-of-the-movement -hillary-clinton-african-american-vote.

54. Lucy McBath, speech at National Democratic Convention, July 26, 2016, http://time .com/4424704/dnc-mothers-movement-transcript-speech-video/; Aaron Blake, "The First Trump-Clinton Presidential Debate Transcript, Annotated," *Washington Post,* September 26, 2016, https://www.washingtonpost.com/news/the-fix/wp/2016/09 /26/the-first-trump-clinton-presidential-debate-transcript-annotated/?utm_term =.6cba763651bf.

55. David Farenthold, "Trump Recorded Having Extremely Lewd Conversation About Women in 2005," *Washington Post,* October 8, 2016, https://www.washingtonpost .com/politics/trump-recorded-having-extremely-lewd-conversation-about -women-in-2005/2016/10/07/3b9ce776-8cb4-11e6-bf8a-3d26847eeed4_story.html ?postshare=2491475870527101&tid=ss_tw&utm_term=.3e4e0ae05d63; Max Blau, "Not 'Locker Room Talk': Athletes Push Back Against Trump's Remark," CNN, October 10, 2016, http://www.cnn.com/2016/10/10/politics/locker-room-talk-athletes -respond-trnd/; Bonnie Malkin, "Trump's Groping Boasts Inspire Thousands of Women to Share Sexual Assault Stories on Twitter," *The Guardian,* October 9, 2016, https://www.theguardian.com/us-news/2016/oct/09/women-share-sexual-assault -stories-on-twitter-after-donald-trump-comments; Michelle Obama, "Michelle Obama's Speech on Donald Trump's Alleged Treatment of Women," National Public Radio, October 13, 2016, http://www.npr.org/2016/10/13/497846667/transcript -michelle-obamas-speech-on-donald-trumps-alleged-treatment-of-women.

56. Donald Trump, "Full Text: Donald Trump Campaign Speech in Wisconsin," August 17, 2016, http://www.politico.com/story/2016/08/full-text-donald-trumps-speech-on-227095.

9. LIMBO

1. "Reagan Outlines Plan to Fight Crime in State," *Los Angeles Times*, August 21, 1966; Rosenfeld, *Subversives*, 333; Edwards, *To Preserve and Protect*, 10.
2. Edwards, *To Preserve and Protect*, 11–12, 16; Trump, *America We Deserve*, 99; Robert E. Moffit, Edwin Meese III, and Patrick F. Fagan, "Crime," in Butler and Holmes, *Issues '98*; Justin George, "Trump Justice, Year One: The Demolition Derby," *The Marshall Project*, January 17, 2018, https://www.themarshallproject.org/2018/01/17/trump-justice-year-one-the-demolition-derby?utm_medium=email&utm_campaign=newsletter&utm_source=opening-statement&utm_term=newsletter-20180118-932.
3. Donald Trump's speech to the Republican National Convention, July 21, 2016, http://www.politico.com/story/2016/07/full-transcript-donald-trump-nomination-acceptance-speech-at-rnc-225974; Donald Trump, "Full Text: Donald Trump Campaign Speech in Wisconsin," August 17, 2016, http://www.politico.com/story/2016/08/full-text-donald-trumps-speech-on-227095; Trump, *Time to Get Tough*, 143; Anna Flagg, "Immigration and Crime: What Link Is There?" *New York Times*, March 31, 2018; Ashley Southall, "New York Crime Plunges to Level Unseen Since '50s," *New York Times*, December 28, 2017.
4. Trump, *Time to Get Tough*, 2, 3, 7; Trump, *America We Deserve*, 19, 25, 26; Gilroy, *Against Race*, 156.
5. Trump, *Time to Get Tough*, 137; Trump, *America We Deserve*, 110, 242, 260; Team Fix, "Transcript of the New Hampshire GOP Debate, Annotated," *Washington Post*, February 6, 2016, https://www.washingtonpost.com/news/the-fix/wp/2016/02/06/transcript-of-the-feb-6-gop-debate-annotated/; Alexander Bolton, "Trump Calls for More Prisoners in Gitmo," *The Hill*, December 19, 2015, http://thehill.com/blogs/ballot-box/gop-primaries/263809-trump-calls-for-more-prisoners-in-gitmo.
6. Donald J. Trump, "Bring Back the Death Penalty, Bring Back Our Police," advertisement in four New York newspapers, May 1, 1989.
7. Trump, *America We Deserve*, 96; Oliver Laughland, "Donald Trump and the Central Park Five: The Racially Charged Rise of a Demagogue," *The Guardian*, February 17, 2016; "Update; Youth Is Sentenced in Robbery of Mrs. Trump," *New York Times*, June 26, 1992, http://www.nytimes.com/1992/07/26/nyregion/update-youth-is-sentenced-in-robbery-of-mrs-trump.html.
8. Donald Trump, "Central Park Five Settlement Is a 'Disgrace,'" op-ed, *New York Daily News*, June 21, 2014; Amy Davidson, "Donald Trump and the Central Park Five," *The New Yorker*, June 23, 2014.
9. Trump, *America We Deserve*, 94; Moffit, Meese, and Fagan, "Crime."
10. Trump, *America We Deserve*, 94–95, 98, 100, 101.
11. Ibid., 242, 260.
12. Trump, *Time to Get Tough*, 136, 137, 174, 149–51.

13. Donald J. Trump, "Executive Order: Enhancing Public Safety in the Interior of the United States," The White House, January 25, 2017, https://www.whitehouse.gov/the-press-office/2017/01/25/presidential-executive-order-enhancing-public-safety-interior-united; Donald J. Trump, "Executive Order: Border Security and Immigration Enforcement Improvements," The White House, January 25, 2017, https://www.whitehouse.gov/the-press-office/2017/01/25/executive-order-border-security-and-immigration-enforcement-improvements; Trump, *Time to Get Tough*, 137; Trump, *America We Deserve*, 110; Team Fix, "Transcript of the New Hampshire GOP"; Trump, "Standing Up for Our Law Enforcement Community," The White House, January 21, 2017, https://www.whitehouse.gov/law-enforcement-community.

14. Elizabeth Chuck and Alexandra Jaffe, "Trump Taps Alabama Sen. Jeff Sessions for Attorney General Post," NBC News, November 18, 2016, http://www.nbcnews.com/politics/politics-news/trump-taps-alabama-sen-jeff-sessions-be-attorney-general-n685796; Sarah Wildman, "Jeff Sessions's Chequered Past," *The Guardian*, May 5, 2009, https://www.theguardian.com/commentisfree/cifamerica/2009/may/05/jeff-sessions-arlen-specter-judiciary-committee; Associated Press, "Rights Activists Are Acquitted of Voting Fraud," *New York Times*, July 6, 1985; Amber Phillips, "That Time the Senate Denied Jeff Sessions a Federal Judgeship over Accusations of Racism," *Washington Post*, November 18, 2016, https://www.washingtonpost.com/news/the-fix/wp/2016/11/18/that-time-the-senate-denied-jeff-sessions-a-federal-judgeship-over-accusations-of-racism/?utm_term=.5c1228b928c9.

15. Andrew Kaczynski, "Attorney General Jeff Sessions: Consent Decrees 'Can Reduce Morale of the Police Officers,'" CNN, April 14, 2017, http://www.cnn.com/2017/04/14/politics/kfile-sessions-consent-decrees/; Sheryl Gay Stolberg and Eric Lichtblau, "Sweeping Federal Review Could Affect Consent Decrees Nationwide," *New York Times*, April 3, 2017; Ed Krayewski, "There Still Wasn't a War on Cops in 2017," *Reason*, December 28, 2017, http://reason.com/blog/2017/12/28/there-still-wasnt-a-war-on-cops-in-2017; US Department of Justice, "Attorney General Sessions Delivers Remarks at the 63rd Biennial Conference of the National Fraternal Order of Police," press release, August 28, 2017.

16. Matt Zapotosky, "Justice Department Will Again Use Private Prisons," *Washington Post*, February 23, 2017; Ford, "Bipartisan Opposition"; Adam Goldman, "Trump Reverses Restrictions on Military Hardware for Police," *New York Times*, August 28, 2017; Donald J. Trump, "Presidential Executive Order on Restoring State, Tribal, and Local Law Enforcement's Access to Life-Saving Equipment and Resources," The White House, August 28, 2017, https://www.whitehouse.gov/presidential-actions/presidential-executive-order-restoring-state-tribal-local-law-enforcements-access-life-saving-equipment-resources/; Charlie Savage, "Justice Dept. to Take on Affirmative Action," *New York Times*, August 1, 2017; Taylor Hatmaker, "DOJ Backs Down from Request for IP Addresses That Visited Trump Protest Website," *TechCrunch*, August 22, 2017, https://techcrunch.com/2017/08/22/dreamhost-vs-justice-department-excludes-request-ip-addresses/.

17. Law Enforcement Leaders, *Fighting Crime and Strengthening Criminal Justice*; Kate Mather, "L.A. Asked for $3 Million for Community Policing. The DOJ Said No. Some Fear It's a Sign of What's Ahead," *Los Angeles Times*, December 5, 2017, http://

www.latimes.com/local/lanow/la-me-ln-lapd-funding-20171205-story.html?ex
_cid=SigDig; US Department of Justice, *FY 2018 Performance Budget—Office of
Justice Programs*, May, 2017, https://www.justice.gov/file/969001/download; Ron
Nixon, "Single-Minded at Homeland Security," *New York Times,* July 14, 2017.

18. Immigration and Customs Enforcement, "ICE ERO Immigration Arrests Climb
Nearly 40%," 2017, https://www.ice.gov/features/100-days?ex_cid=trumpbeat; Cait-
lin Dickerson, "Immigration Arrests Rise Sharply as Trump Mandate Is Carried
Out," *New York Times,* May 17, 2017; Preston, "Trump: The New Deportation
Threat"; Vivian Yee, "As Arrests Surge, Immigrants Fear Even Driving," *New York
Times,* November 26, 2017.

19. Meyer, "President Pence Delusion."

20. Shira A. Scheindlin, "Trump's Most Troubling Legacy? His Judges," *New York
Times,* November 10, 2017; Charlie Savage, "Courts Reshaped at Fastest Pace in Five
Decades," *New York Times,* November 12, 2017; Charlie Savage, "Poor Vetting Sinks
Nominees for Federal Judge," *New York Times,* December 19, 2017; William Bar-
ber II, "A Terrible Choice for Judge," op-ed, *New York Times,* December 27, 2017;
Stephanie Mencimer, "Trump Judicial Pick Who Blogged Favorably About the KKK
Had to Withdraw. Now He's at the Justice Department," *Mother Jones*, July 2, 2018,
https://www.motherjones.com/politics/2018/07/trump-judicial-pick-who-blogged
-favorably-about-the-kkk-had-to-withdraw-now-hes-at-the-justice-department/#.

21. Alexander Burns and Mitch Smith, "G.O.P.-Led States Race to Cement Their Priorities," *New York Times,* February 12, 2017.

22. Will Stone, "In Arizona, Doctors Criticize Tightening of Late Abortion Rules,"
National Public Radio, May 26, 2017, https://www.npr.org/2017/05/26/530257471
/in-arizona-doctors-criticize-tightening-of-late-abortion-rules; Nicole Lewis,
"Planned Parenthood Closures in Iowa Raise Fears About National Defunding Plan
in Republican Health-Care Bill," *Washington Post,* June 30, 2017, https://www
.washingtonpost.com/national/planned-parenthood-closes-4-clinics-in-iowa
-fears-more-closures-if-the-republican-health-care-bill-passes/2017/06/30
/d43f4dda-5d00-11e7-a9f6-7c3296387341_story.html?utm_term=.73ad5cf3f6b4; An
Act Relating to Limitations on and Prerequisites for an Abortion, Providing for Li-
censee Discipline, Providing Civil Penalties, and Including Effective Date Provi-
sions, Senate File 471, 87th General Assembly 2017-2018 (Ia. 2017); Alison Dreith,
"An Unecessary Assault on Women with Anti-Abortion 'Domestic Gag Rule,'" op-
ed, *Kansas City Star,* May 21, 2018, http://www.kansascity.com/opinion/readers
-opinion/guest-commentary/article211605604.html; An Act Relating to Abortion
and Declaring an Emergency, Senate Bill 5, Session of 2017 (Ky. 2017); Jessica Ravitz,
"New Restrictions on Abortion in Kentucky Face Immediate Challenge," CNN,
April 12, 2018, https://www.cnn.com/2018/04/12/health/kentucky-de-abortion-ban
/index.html; Associated Press, "Idaho to Require Personal Details of Women Getting Abortions," March 22, 2018, https://wtop.com/national/2018/03/idaho-to
-require-personal-details-of-women-getting-abortions/; Joanna Grossman, "Texas
Strikes Out Again," *Justia*, December 5, 2017, https://verdict.justia.com/2017/12/05
/texas-strikes-federal-court-halts-enforcement-yet-another-unconstitutional-anti
-abortion-law; Mairead McCardle, "Court Says Indiana Ban on Selective Abortion

Is Unconstitutional," *National Review*, April 20, 2018, https://www.nationalreview .com/news/indiana-abortion-ban-unconstitutional-appeals-court/; Tony Marco, "New Ohio Law Prevents Abortions in Down Syndrome Cases," *CNN.com*, December 22, 2017, http://www.cnn.com/2017/12/22/health/ohio-governor-signs-down -syndrome-abortion-ban/index.html; Candace Butera, "A Federal Judge Blocks a Ban on Down Syndrome Abortions in Ohio," *Pacific Standard*, March 14, 2018, https://psmag.com/social-justice/a-federal-judge-blocks-a-ban-on-down-syndrome -abortions-in-ohio.

23. The Editorial Board, "An Ohio Bill Would Ban All Abortions. It's Part of a Bigger Plan," *New York Times*, March 25, 2018; Julie Bosman and Mitch Smith, "Iowa Lawmakers Pass Abortion Bill With Roe v. Wade in Sights," *New York Times*, May 2, 2018; Julie Hirschfeld Davis, "New Abortion Limits Challenge Family Planning Programs," *New York Times*, May 19, 2018.

24. Allie Morris, "New Hampshire Eliminates Concealed Carry License Requirement," *Concord Monitor*, February 23, 2017, http://www.concordmonitor.com/sununu -signs-conceal-carry-bill-8252381; Act Relating to Self-Defense Immunity, Senate Bill 128, 2017 Regular Session (Fl. 2017); Nicholas Fandos, "House Votes to Sharply Expand Concealed-Carry Gun Rights," *New York Times*, December 7, 2017; Russell Berman, "A New Republican Strategy to Dramatically Expand Gun Rights," *The Atlantic*, December 5, 2017, https://www.theatlantic.com/politics/archive/2017/12 /republican-house-vote-concealed-carry-gun-background-checks/547454/; Michael Van Sickler, "Did the NRA Really Suffer a Setback with Florida's Gun Control Legislation?" *Tampa Bay Times*, April 20, 2018, http://www.tampabay.com/florida -politics/buzz/2018/04/20/did-the-nra-really-suffer-a-setback-with-floridas-gun -control-legislation/; Cleve Wootson, Jr., "NRA Host Taunts Parkland Teens: 'No One Would Know Your Names If Classmates Were Still Alive,'" *Washington Post*, March 24, 2018; https://www.washingtonpost.com/news/post-nation/wp/2018/03 /24/nra-host-taunts-parkland-teens-no-one-would-know-your-names-if-classmates -were-still-alive/?utm_term=.5128eadf903d.

25. Jenny Jarvie, "Texas' New Ban on 'Sanctuary Cities' Could Put Police in Jail If They Fail to Enforce Immigration Holds," *Los Angeles Times*, May 4, 2017; Georgia Bureau of Investigation: Publicly Post Certain Information to Extent Permitted by Federal Law, House Bill 452, 2017–2018 Regular Session (Ga. 2017); An Act to Prohibit a State Agency, Department, Political Subdivision of This State, County, Municipality, University, College, Community College or Junior College, or Any Agent, Employee, or Officer Thereof from Creating, Planning, Implementing, Assisting, Participating in, or Enabling a Sanctuary City Policy . . . Senate Bill 2710, 2017 Regular Session (Ms. 2017); An Act to Amend Tennessee Code Annotated, Title 40, Relative to Sentencing, House Bill 1041, 2017–2018 Regular Session (Tn. 2017); "Mid-Year Overview of 2017 State Immigration Legislation," Catholic Legal Immigration Network, August 2017, https://cliniclegal.org/resources/mid-year-overview -2017-state-immigration-legislation; Julie Hirschfeld Davis, "Trump's Immigration Tweets Followed by Policy Plans to Match," *New York Times*, April 2, 2018, https:// www.nytimes.com/2018/04/02/us/politics/trump-immigration-mexico-daca .html?mtrref=www.google.com; Julie Hirschfeld Davis, "Trump Plans to Send Na-

tional Guard to the Mexican Border," *New York Times,* April 3, 2018, https://www
.nytimes.com/2018/04/03/us/politics/trump-border-immigration-caravan.html
?mtrref=www.google.com.

26. "Federal Criminal Justice Reform Legislation Has Conservative Values, Focuses on
Public Safety," press release, Right on Crime, October 6, 2017, http://rightoncrime
.com/2017/10/federal-criminal-justice-reform-legislation-has-conservative-values
-focuses-on-public-safety/.

27. An Act Relating to Hate Crimes. House Bill 14, 2017 Regular Session (Ky 2017); An
Act to Create the 'Back the Badge Act' of 2017; To Amend Section 97-3-19, Mississippi Code of 1972, to Include Emergency Medical Technicians, First Responders
and Utility Workers in the Same Capital Murder Category as Police Officers . . .
House Bill 645, 2017 Regular Session (Ms. 2017); Back the Badge Act of 2017.
Senate Bill 160, 2017–2018 Regular Session (Ga. 2017); Creating a Sentencing En-
hancement for Certain Criminal Offenses Targeting a Current or Former Law En-
forcement Officer, First Responder, or His or Her Family, and to Declare an
Emergency. House Bill 2017, 2017 Regular Session (Ak. 2017); Assault on a Peace
Officer Amendments. House Bill 124, 2017 General Session (Ut. 2017); An Act Re-
lating to Crimes; Enhancing the Criminal Penalty for Certain Crimes Committed
Against First Responders; And Providing Other Matters Properly Relating Thereto.
Senate Bill 541, Emergency Request of Senate Majority Leader (Nv. 2017); Requir-
ing Electronic Recording of Certain Felony Custodial Interrogations . . . Increas-
ing Criminal Penalties for Crimes Committed Against a Law Enforcement
Officer . . . Senate Bill 112, 2017–2018 Regular Session (Ks. 2017); Crimes and Punishments; Making Certain Acts of Trespassing and Vandalism Unlawful; Providing
Penalties; Emergency. House Bill 1123, 2017 Regular Session (Ok. 2017).

28. Donald J. Trump, "Presidential Executive Order on Enforcing Federal Law with Respect to Transnational Criminal Organizations and Preventing International
Trafficking," The White House, February 9, 2017, https://www.whitehouse.gov/the
-press-office/2017/02/09/presidential-executive-order-enforcing-federal-law
-respect-transnational; Donald J. Trump, "Presidential Executive Order on Preventing Violence Against Federal, State, Tribal, and Local Law Enforcement Officers,"
The White House, February 9, 2017, https://www.whitehouse.gov/the-press-office
/2017/02/09/presidential-executive-order-preventing-violence-against-federal
-state; Donald J. Trump, "Presidential Executive Order on a Task Force on Crime
Reduction and Public Safety," The White House, February 9, 2017, https://www
.whitehouse.gov/the-press-office/2017/02/09/presidential-executive-order task-force-
crime-reduction-and-public.

29. Charlie Savage and Eric Lichtblau, "Trump Asks Justice Dept. to Investigate Dam-
aging 'Criminal Leaks,'" *New York Times,* February 17, 2017; Susan Archer, Robin
Lindsay, and Dave Horn, "F.B.I. Director James Comey Is Fired by Trump," *New
York Times,* May 9, 2017; Rebecca R. Ruiz and Mark Landler, "Special Counsel Will
Investigate Russia Influence," *New York Times,* May 18, 2017; Michael S. Schmidt,
"Comey Wanted President Kept at a Distance," *New York Times,* May 19, 2017; Matt
Apuzzo and Emmarie Huetteman, "Trump Tried to Sink Inquiry, Comey Says,"
New York Times, June 9, 2017.

30. Zachary Cohen and Madison Park, "The Four People Charged in Mueller's Investigation," CNN, December 4, 2017, https://www.cnn.com/2017/12/04/politics/whos-charged-russia-investigation/index.html; Matt Apuzzo and Sharon LaFraniere, "Indictment Bares Russian Network to Twist 2016 Vote," *New York Times*, February 17, 2018; Sharon LaFraniere and Kenneth P. Vogel, "Guilty Plea by Lawyer Broadens Mueller Inquiry," *New York Times*, February 21, 2018; Emily Cochrane and Alicia Parlapiano, "Charges Adding Up in Inquiry," *New York Times*, February 24, 2018; Kenneth Vogel and Matthew Goldstein, "How Skadden, the Giant Law Firm, Got Entangled in the Mueller Investigation," *New York Times*, February 24, 2018, https://www.nytimes.com/2018/02/24/us/politics/skadden-law-firm-mueller-investigation.html; Sharon LaFraniere, "Manafort Is Jailed Amid Charges He Tried to Influence Witnesses," *New York Times*, June 16, 2018; "Pleading Guilty, Cohen Implicates President" was the *New York Times'* banner headline on August 22, 2018.

31. Michael S. Schmidt and Maggie Haberman, "Trump Ordered Mueller's Firing but Was Refused," *New York Times*, January 26, 2018; Sharon LaFraniere, Katie Benner, and Peter Baker, "Trump's Unparalleled War," *New York Times*, February 4, 2018; Nash Jenkins, "Trump Is Stepping Up His Attacks on His Own FBI and Justice Department," *Time*, February 8, 2018, http://time.com/5130167/donald-trump-tweet-nunes-memo/; Noah Bierman, "Trump Criticizes Sessions and Vents Frustration at Russia Investigation and Leaders of the Justice Department and FBI," *Los Angeles Times*, July 19, 2017; Stephen Collison and Jeremy Diamond, "Trump Again at War with 'Deep State' Justice Department," *CNN.com*, January 2, 2018, https://www.cnn.com/2018/01/02/politics/president-donald-trump-deep-state/index.html; Josh Campbell, "Why I Am Leaving the F.B.I.," op-ed, *New York Times*, February 3, 2018.

32. Peter Baker and Katie Benner, "Trump Tears into Sessions over Russia Investigation," *New York Times*, March 1, 2018.

33. Michael D. Shear and Peter Baker, "Comey, in Interview, Launches All-Out War Against President," *New York Times*, April 16, 2018; Michael D. Shear, "Annotated Excerpts of ABC's Interview With EX-F.B.I. Chief," *New York Times*, April 16, 2018; Comey, *A Higher Loyalty*, 221.

34. Alexander Burns, "How Washington State Banded Together to Halt Trump's Travel Decree," *New York Times*, February 5, 2017; Donald J. Trump, "Executive Order: Protecting the Nation from Terrorist Entry into the United States," January 27, 2017, https://www.whitehouse.gov/the-press-office/2017/01/27/executive-order-protecting-nation-foreign-terrorist-entry-united-states; Nicholas Kulish, Caitlin Dickerson, and Charlie Savage, "Court Temporarily Blocks Trump's Travel Ban, and Airlines Are Told to Allow Passengers," *New York Times*, February 3, 2017; Martin Pengelly and Alan Yuhas, "Donald Trump Attacks 'So-Called Judge' over Decision to Halt Travel Ban," *The Guardian*, February 4, 2017; Adam Liptak, "Judges Refuse to Reinstate Travel Ban," *New York Times*, February 10, 2017.

35. John Yoo, "Executive Power Run Amok," op-ed, *New York Times*, February 6, 2017; Julie Hirschfeld Davis, "Court Pick Says Trump's Censure Is 'Demoralizing,'" *New York Times*, February 9, 2017.

36. Per curiam opinion in *Trump v. International Refugee Assistance Project* and *Trump v. Hawaii*, 582 U.S. ___ (June 26, 2017); Michael D. Shear and Adam Liptak, "Su-

preme Court Takes Up Travel Ban Case, and Allows Parts to Go Ahead," *New York Times*, June 26, 2017; Donald J. Trump, "Executive Order Protecting the Nation from Foreign Terrorist Entry into the United States," The White House, January 27, 2017, https://www.whitehouse.gov/presidential-actions/executive-order-protecting-nation-foreign-terrorist-entry-united-states/; Donald J. Trump, "Executive Order Protecting the Nation from Foreign Terrorist Entry into the United States," The White House, March 6, 2017, https://www.whitehouse.gov/presidential-actions/executive-order-protecting-nation-foreign-terrorist-entry-united-states-2/; Amy Howe, "Justice to Review Travel Ban Challenge," *SCOTUSblog*, January 19, 2018, http://www.scotusblog.com/2018/01/justices-review-travel-ban-challenge/; Liz Robbins, "Judges Nationwide Are Digging in Their Heels and Delaying Deportations," *New York Times*, February 10, 2018; Adam Liptak and Michael D. Shear, "Justices Refuse White House Bid in 'Dreamer' Case," *New York Times*, February 27, 2018; Adam Liptak, "Law on Deportation of Criminals Is Struck Down," *New York Times*, April 18, 2018.

37. Katie Benner and Caitlin Dickerson, "Sessions Shrinks Paths to Asylum," *New York Times*, June 12, 2018; Adam Liptak and Michael D. Shear, "Justices Uphold Travel Ban in 5–4 Decision," *New York Times*, June 27, 2018; Charlie Savage, "Korematsu, Long a Stain on the Supreme Court, Is Finally Tossed Out," *New York Times*, June 27, 2019; Alexandra Yoon-Hendricks and Zoe Greenberg, "Nationwide Protests Call for an End to Migrant Family Separations," *New York Times*, July 1, 2018; Michael D. Shear, "Trump Set to Tilt Court as Kennedy Retires," *New York Times*, June 28, 2018; Alicia Parlapiano and Jugal K. Patel, "With Kennedy's Retirement, the Supreme Court Loses Its Center," *New York Times*, July 1, 2018; Feldman, "Tipping the Scales."

38. Associated Press, "Police Expect Trump to Keep Word, Lift Limits on Surplus Military Gear," *San Francisco Chronicle*, December 12, 2016; Trump, "Standing Up for Our Law Enforcement Community," The White House, January 23, 2017, https://www.whitehouse.gov/law-enforcement-community; Julie Hirschfeld Davis and Julia Preston, "Trump's Deportation Pledge Could Require Raids and Huge Federal Force," *New York Times*, November 15, 2016; Thomas Fuller, "Chief of Immigration Agency Compares Oakland's Mayor to 'Gang Lookout,'" *New York Times*, March 1, 2018.

39. Barbara Demick and Kurits Lee, "Trump Urges Officers and Immigration Officials to Be 'Rough' on 'Animals' Terrorizing U.S. Neighborhoods," *Los Angeles Times*, July 28, 2017; John McLaughlin, "Trump's Boy Scout Speech Should Give Everyone the Creeps," op-ed, *Washington Post*, July 27, 2017; Vivian Wang, "New York Police Officers Rally in Support of Colin Kaepernick," *New York Times*, August 19, 2017.

40. Kevin Breuninger, "Attorney General Jeff Sessions Outlines When to Use Death Penalty on Drug Traffickers," CNBC, March 21, 2018, https://www.cnbc.com/2018/03/21/attorney-general-jeff-sessions-outlines-death-penalty-use-for-drug-crimes.html; "The Conservative Case for Reform," Right on Crime, n.d., http://rightoncrime.com/the-conservative-case-for-reform/; Timothy Williams and Richard A. Oppel, Jr., "Police Chiefs Contend Trump's Law Enforcement Priorities Are Out of Step," *New York Times*, February 13, 2017; "Attorney General Sessions Delivers"; Law Enforcement Leaders, *Fighting Crime*, 9.

41. Jose A. Del Real, "Police Kill Another Unarmed Black Man, and Another City Seethes," *New York Times*, March 29, 2018; Frances Robles and Jose A. Del Real, "8 Bullets Struck Sacramento Man as He Faced Away," *New York Times*, March 31, 2018.
42. Kelley, "Beyond Black Lives Matter."
43. Jugal K. Patel, "The Toll Since Sandy Hook: More Than 400 People Shot, in over 200 School Shootings," *New York Times*, February 16, 2018; Gun Violence Archive. "Gun Violence Archive 2018," http://www.gunviolencearchive.org/ (accessed May 21, 2018); Julie Turkewitz and Vivian Yee, "With Grief and Hope, Florida Students Take Gun Control Fight on the Road," *New York Times*, February 20, 2018; Everytown, "Everytown for Gun Safety: The Movement to End Gun Violence," https://everytown.org/ (accessed May 21, 2018); Julie Creswell and Michael Corkery, "Dick's Sporting Goods and Walmart Tighten Rules on the Guns They Sell," *New York Times*, March 1, 2018; John Paul Stevens, "Repeal the Second Amendment"; Sarah Maslin Nir, "Thousands of Students in Protest of Violence," *New York Times*, April 21, 2018; Darcy Schleifstein, Zachary Dougherty, and Sarah Emily Baum, "We Won't Let the N.R.A. Win," op-ed, *New York Times*, March 14, 2018.
44. Debs, *Walls and Bars*, 203.
45. Noah Bierman, "Few Have Faced Consequences for Abuses at Abu Ghraib Prison in Iraq," *Los Angeles Times*, March 17, 2015.
46. Cohen, "Punitive City," 360.
47. Nagel, *New Red Barn*, 148; Tony Platt and Randi Pollock, "Channeling Lawyers," in Jacob, *Potential for Reform of Criminal Justice*, 253.
48. Braverman, *Labor and Monopoly Capital*, 403–9; Miliband, *State in Capitalist Society*, 122.
49. Oklahoma Justice Reform Task Force, *Final Report*, February 2017, http://s3.amazonaws.com/content.newsok.com/documents/OJRTFFinalReport%20(1).pdf?embeddedLinkType=document; Nellis, *Color of Justice*.
50. Thompkins, "Expanding Prisoner Reentry Industry"; Wacquant, "Prisoner Reentry as Myth and Ceremony"; Miller, "Devolving the Carceral State"; Alessandro De Giorgi, "Crime Is Up? Decarcerate!" *Social Justice*, November 9, 2113, http://www.socialjusticejournal.org/crime-is-up-decarcerate/; Alessandro De Giorgi, "Reentry to Nothing #1—Get a Job, Any Job," *Social Justice*, May 28, 2014, http://www.socialjusticejournal.org/reentry-to-nothing-1-get-a-job-any-job/.
51. Adams, *Education for Extinction*, 23; Murrin et al., *Liberty, Equality, Power*, 707; John Bodnar, "Immigration," in Foner and Garraty, *Reader's Companion to American History*; "Donald Trump on Russia, Advice from Barack Obama, and How He Will Lead," *Time*, December 7, 2016; Maya Rhodan, "Attorney General Jeff Sessions Says DACA Program Will Be Phased Out," *Time*, September 5, 2017, http://time.com/4927227/daca-undocumented-dreamers-jeff-sessions/; Tal Kopan, "Trump Says He's Open to Pathway to Citizenship 'Incentive' on DACA," *CNN.com*, January 25, 2018, https://www.cnn.com/2018/01/24/politics/trump-citizenship/index.html; Carlos Bulosan, *America Is in the Heart*, 147.
52. Baldwin, *Giovanni's Room*, 119; Bardacke, *Trampling Out the Vintage*, 1; The Legacy Museum, Montgomery, Alabama, https://museumandmemorial.eji.org/.

53. Sudbury, "Toward a Holistic Anti-Violence Agenda"; Critical Resistance and Incite!, "Statement"; Jodi Rios, "The Queering of Protest in Ferguson, Mo," unpublished manuscript; Jodi Rios, personal communication with author, March 2017; Derek Hawkins, "'It's About Time': Ruth Bader Ginsburg Praises #MeToo, Recounts Harassment in Sundance Talk," *Washington Post,* January 22, 2018; Bill Hutchinson, "Supreme Court Justice Ginsburg Shares #MeToo," ABC News, January 22, 2018, http://abcnews.go.com/Politics/supreme-court-justice-ginsburg-shares-metoo -experience/story?id=52518887.
54. Fannie Lou Hamer, "To Praise Our Bridges," in Abbot, *Mississippi Writers,* 2:326.
55. Platt, "Prospects for a Radical Criminology"; Bauman, "Times of Interregnum"; Gramsci, *Selections from the Prison Notebooks,* 276.
56. Hobsbawm, *Age of Extremes,* 585; Wallerstein, "Agonies of Liberalism," 17.
57. Stockman, "After Serving Their Time"; Bob Egelko and Annie Ma, "State Closing in on Bail Overhaul," *San Francisco Chronicle,* February 21, 2018; United Nations General Assembly, "United Nations Standard Minimum Rules for the Treatment of Prisoners (the Mandela Rules)," December 17, 2015, https://documents-dds-ny .un.org/doc/UNDOC/GEN/N15/295/06/PDF/N1529506.pdf?OpenElement.
58. Rick Raemisch, "Putting an End to Long-Term Solitary," op-ed, *New York Times,* October 13, 2017.
59. Declan Walsh, "Britain Offers Its Apology to 2 Libyans Held by C.I.A.," *New York Times,* May 11, 2018.
60. Kelley, "Beyond Black Lives Matter"; Berger, Kaba, and Stein, "What Abolitionists Do"; Taylor, *From #Black Lives Matter*; McClain, "Future of BLM."
61. McDowell, "Insurgent Safety"; Vitale, *End of Policing,* 222.
62. James Forman, Jr., "Justice Springs Eternal," op-ed, *The New York Times Sunday Review,* March 26, 2017.
63. Trump, *America We Deserve,* 98; Debs, *Walls and Bars,* 281; Keller, "Prison Revolt."
64. Gilroy, *Against Race,* 152, 153; Tony Platt, "The Strange and Shocking Similarities Between Donald Trump and 'Old Blood and Guts' Patton," *History News Network,* March 11, 2016, http://historynewsnetwork.org/article/162220; Trump, *America We Deserve,* 19.
65. Mike Davis, "The Great God Trump and the White Working Class," *Jacobin,* February 7, 2017, https://www.jacobinmag.com/2017/02/the-great-god-trump-and-the -white-working-class/; Leon Litwack, "Hellhound on My Trail," in Knopke, Norrell, and Rogers, *Opening Doors,* 25.
66. Knight, *Black Voices,* 6.

AUTHOR'S NOTE

1. Platt, "Vicariously We Punish," 13.
2. Tony Platt, "The Administration of Justice in Crisis: Chicago, April 1968," June 1968, unpublished report, in the author's personal files. The findings in this report were incorporated into "Judicial Response in Crisis," in Skolnick, *Politics of Protest.*
3. Tony Platt, "An Account of Police Violence in Chicago, August 28, 1968," August 29, 1968, unpublished report, in the author's personal files.

4. Koehler, "Development and Fracture of a Discipline," 520, 527; McGirr, *War on Alcohol*, 92, 200–1.
5. National Action/Research, *Police on the Homefront*, 31.
6. Jonathan Simon, Sanford Kadish, and Robert Cole, "In Memoriam, Caleb Foote, 1917–2006," senate.universityofcalifornia.edu/_files/inmemoriam/html/calebfoote.html.
7. Schwendinger and Schwendinger, "Defenders of Order," 149.
8. Martinson, "Prison Notes of a Freedom Rider," 4–5.
9. Takagi, "Growing Up a Japanese Boy," 147.
10. Tony Platt, "If We Know, Then We Must Fight," in Oppenheimer, Murrary, and Levine, *Radical Sociologists and the Movement*.
11. Foucault, *Discipline and Punish*, 297; Hay et al., *Albion's Fatal Tree*; S. Hall et al., *Policing the Crisis*; Rusche and Kirchheimer, *Punishment and Social Structure*, 5.
12. Krisberg, "Teaching Radical Criminology."
13. Balagoon et al., *Look for Me in the Whirlwind*, 348.
14. FBI file #44-0-18680, in the author's personal files. I made the FOIA request in 1985.
15. Eckstein, *Bad Moon Rising*, 128.
16. Albert H. Bowker, memorandum to University Budget Committee, May 1, 1972, in the author's personal files; Robert H. Kroninger, "Punishing Speech," letter to the editor, *The New Yorker*, June 3, 2002.
17. Beverly T. Watkins, "Berkeley Finally Drops Its Criminology School," *The Chronicle of Higher Education* (August 9, 1976): 4; Paul Goodman, "Academic Prejudice: The Unfair Silence in Tenure Decisions," op-ed, *The Sacramento Bee*, February 1, 1990; "3,000 Protest Crim School Closing," *The Black Panther*, June 8, 1974, in the author's personal files; Albert H. Bowker, interview by Harriet Nathan, 1991, University History Series, Online Archive of California, http://oac.cdlib.org/ark:/13030/hb1p3001qq/?brand=oac4.

APPENDIX

1. Fox Butterfield, "Some Experts Fear Political Influence on Crime Data Agencies," *New York Times*, September 22, 2002.
2. Barnett, Sheckells, Peterson, and Tydings, *2012 Census of Governments*, 8; Executive Office of the President, *Review*, 2–5.

REFERENCES

Abbott, Dorothy, ed. *Mississippi Writers: Reflections of Childhood and Youth*. Vol. 2. Jackson: University Press of Mississippi, 1986.

Abbott, Jack Henry. *In the Belly of the Beast: Letters from Prison*. Introduction by Norman Mailer. New York: Vintage, 1981.

Abramowitz, Mimi. *Regulating the Lives of Women: Social Welfare Policy from Colonial Times to the Present*. Boston: South End, 1988.

Acuña, Rodolfo. *Occupied America: A History of Chicanos*. 3d ed. New York: Harper & Row, 1988.

Adams, David Wallace. *Education for Extinction: American Indians and the Boarding School Experience, 1875–1928*. Lawrence: University Press of Kansas, 1994.

Addams, Jane. *A New Conscience and an Ancient Evil*. New York: Macmillan, 1913.

Adler, Jeffrey S. "A Historical Analysis of the Law of Vagrancy." *Criminology* 27, no. 2 (1989): 209–29.

Agee, Philip. *Inside the Company: CIA Diary*. New York: Stonehill, 1975.

Agnew, Spiro. "What's Wrong with the Legal Services Program?" *American Bar Association Journal* 58 (1972): 930–32.

Aiken, Joshua. *Era of Mass Expansion: Why State Officials Should Fight Jail Growth*. Northampton, MA: Prison Policy Initiative, May 31, 2017. https://www.prisonpolicy.org/reports/jailsovertime.html.

Alexander, Michelle. *The New Jim Crow: Mass Incarceration in the Age of Colorblindness*. New York: The New Press, 2010.

Allen, Francis A. *The Borderland of Criminal Justice: Essays in Law and Criminology*. Chicago: University of Chicago Press, 1964.

Allen, James, John Lewis, and Leon Litwack. *Without Sanctuary: Lynching Photography in America*. Santa Fe, NM: Twin Palms, 2004.

American Bar Association Standing Committee on Legal Aid and Indigent Defendants.

Gideon's Broken Promise: America's Continuing Quest for Equal Justice. Chicago: American Bar Association, 2004.

Andreas, Peter, and Ethan Nadelmann. *Policing the Globe: Criminalization and Crime Control in International Relations.* Oxford: Oxford University Press, 2006.

Angell, Marcia. "The Abortion Battlefield." *The New York Review of Books,* June 22, 2017, 8–12.

Ansell, David A. *The Death Gap: How Inequality Kills.* Chicago: University of Chicago Press, 2017.

Anstett, Elisabeth, and Jean-Marc Dreyfus, eds. *Human Remains and Identification: Mass Violence, Genocide and the Forensic Turn.* Manchester: Manchester University Press, 2015.

Aptheker, Herbert, ed. *The Correspondence of W. E. B. Du Bois.* Vol. 1, *Selections, 1877–1934.* Amherst: University of Massachusetts Press, 1973.

Archibald, Carol, ed. *Policing: A Text/Reader.* London: Sage, 2012.

Arnold, Mary Ellicott, and Mabel Reed. *In the Land of the Grasshopper Song: Two Women in the Klamath River Indian Country in 1908–1909.* Introduction by Susan Bernardin. Lincoln: University of Nebraska Press, 2011.

Ayers, William. *A Kind and Just Parent: The Children of Juvenile Court.* Boston: Beacon, 1997.

Bacon, Richard G., and American Friends Service Committee. *Struggle for Justice: A Report on Crime and Punishment in America.* New York: Hill & Wang, 1971.

Bagaric, Mirko, Dan Hunter, and Gabrielle Wolf. "Technological Incarceration and the End of the Prison Crisis." *The Journal of Criminal Law & Criminology* 108, 1 (2018): 73–135.

Balagoon, Kuwasi, et al. (The New York 21). *Look for Me in the Whirlwind: The Collective Autobiography of the New York 21.* New York: Vintage, 1971.

Balch, George T. *A Patriotic Primer for the Little Citizen.* Indianapolis: Levey Bros., 1898.

———. *Methods of Teaching Patriotism in the Public Schools.* New York: D. Van Nostrand, 1890.

Baldwin, James. *Giovanni's Room.* London: Michael Joseph, 1957.

———. *Nobody Knows My Name: More Notes of a Native Son.* New York: Dial, 1961.

Balibar, Étienne. *We, the People of Europe? Reflections on Transnational Citizenship.* Princeton, NJ: Princeton University Press, 2004.

Balko, Radley. *Rise of the Warrior Cop: The Militarization of America's Police Forces.* New York: PublicAffairs, 2013.

Banfield, Edward. *The Unheavenly City.* Boston: Little, Brown, 1972.

Banton, Michael. *The Policeman in the Community.* London: Tavistock, 1964.

Baradaran, Mehrsa. *The Color of Money: Black Banks and the Racial Wealth Gap.* Cambridge, MA: Harvard University Press, 2017.

Barak, Gregg. *Integrating Criminologies.* Boston: Allyn and Bacon, 1998.

———. *Theft of a Nation: Wall Street Looting and Federal Regulatory Colluding.* Lanham, MD: Rowman & Littlefield, 2012.

Bardacke, Frank. *Trampling Out the Vintage: Cesar Chavez and the Two Souls of the United Farm Workers.* London: Verso, 2011.

Barnett, Jeffrey, Cindy Sheckells, Scott Peterson, and Elizabeth Tydings. *2012 Census of Governments: Finance—State and Local Government Summary Report.* Washington, DC: Bureau of the Census, 2014. https://www2.census.gov/govs/local/summary_report.pdf.

Bauman, Zygmunt. "Times of Interregnum." *Ethics and Global Politics* 5, no. 1 (2012): 49–56.

Bayley, David H. *Changing the Guard: Developing the Democratic Police Abroad.* Oxford: Oxford University Press, 2005.

Beckert, Sven. *Empire of Cotton: A Global History.* New York: Alfred A. Knopf, 2015.

Beckett, Katherine, and Naomi Murakawa. "Mapping the Shadow Carceral State: Toward an Institutionally Capacious Approach to Punishment." *Theoretical Criminology* 16, no. 2 (2012): 221–44.

Begel, Debby. "An Interview with Willie Tate." *Crime and Social Justice* 6 (Fall–Winter 1976): 69–76.

Begos, Kevin, Danielle Deaver, John Railey, Scott Sexton, and Paul Lombardo, *Against Their Will: North Carolina's Sterilization Program and the Campaign for Reparations.* Apalachicola, FL: Gray Oak Books, 2012.

Belfrage, Sally. *Freedom Summer.* New York: Viking, 1965.

Bellow, Gary. "Legal Aid in the United States." *Clearinghouse Review* 14 (1980–81): 337–44.

Bennett, William J. *The Index of Leading Cultural Indicators: Facts and Figures on the State of American Society.* New York: Simon & Schuster, 1994.

Berg, Kenneth. "The Bail Reform Act of 1984." *Emory Law Journal* 34 (1985): 685–740.

Berger, Dan. *Captive Nation: Black Prison Organizing in the Civil Rights Era.* Chapel Hill: University of North Carolina Press, 2014.

Berger, Dan, Mariame Kaba, and David Stein. "What Abolitionists Do." *Jacobin*, August 24, 2017. https://www.jacobinmag.com/2017/08/prison-abolition-reform-mass-incarceration.

Berkman, Alexander. *Prison Memoirs of an Anarchist.* New York: Schocken, 1970.

Bernstein, Barton J., ed. *Towards a New Past: Dissenting Essays in American History.* New York: Vintage, 1969.

Berrigan, Philip. *Widen the Prison Gates.* New York: Simon & Schuster, 1973.

Bhabha, Homi K., ed. *Nation and Narration.* London: Routledge, 1990.

Bigo, Didier, and Anastassia Tsoukala, eds. *Terror, Insecurity and Liberty: Illiberal Practices of Liberal Regimes After 9/11.* London: Routledge, 2008.

Bittner, Egon. *Aspects of Police Work.* Boston: Northeastern University Press, 1990.

———. *The Functions of the Police in Modern Society.* Rockville, MD: National Institute of Mental Health, 1970.

Blackmon, Douglas A. *Slavery by Another Name: The Re-Enslavement of Black Americans from the Civil War to World War II.* New York: Anchor, 2008.

Blake, James. *The Joint.* New York: Doubleday, 1971.

Blincoe, L. J. Miller, E. Zaloshnja, and B. A. Lawrence. *The Economic and Societal Impact of Motor Vehicle Crashes, 2010.* Washington, DC: National Highway and Traffic Safety Administration, 2015.

Bloom, Allan. *The Closing of the American Mind*. New York: Simon & Schuster, 1987.

Bloom, Joshua, and Waldo E. Martin, Jr. *Black Against Empire: The History and Politics of the Black Panther Party*. Berkeley: University of California Press, 2013.

Blue, Ethan. *Doing Time in the Depression: Everyday Life in Texas and California Prisons*. New York: New York University Press, 2012.

———. "The Strange Career of Leo Stanley: Remaking Manhood and Medicine at San Quentin State Penitentiary, 1913–1951." *Pacific Historical Review* 78, no. 2 (2009): 210–41.

Blumberg, Abraham S. "The Practice of Law as a Confidence Game: Organizational Cooptation of a Profession." *Law and Society Review* 1 (June 1967): 15–39.

Boehm, Kenneth F., and Peter T. Flaherty. "Why the Legal Services Corporation Must Be Abolished." Heritage Foundation Backgrounder #1057 on Legal Issues, 1995.

Boris, Eileen. "When Work Is Slavery." *Social Justice* 25, no. 1 (1998): 28–46.

Bourgois, Philippe. *In Search of Respect: Selling Crack in El Barrio*. Cambridge: Cambridge University Press, 1995.

Braly, Malcolm. *False Starts: A Memoir of San Quentin and Other Prisons*. Boston: Little, Brown, 1976.

———. *On the Yard*. New York: Little, Brown, 1967.

Brandt, Allan M. *No Magic Bullet: A Social History of Venereal Disease in the United States Since 1880*. New York: Oxford University Press, 1987.

Brandt, Rose K., ed. *The Colored Land: A Navajo Indian Book*. New York: Charles Scribner's Sons, 1937.

Braverman, Harry. *Labor and Monopoly Capital: The Degradation of Work in the Twentieth Century*. New York: Monthly Review Press, 1974.

Briggs, Laura. *Reproducing Empire: Race, Sex, Science, and U.S. Imperialism in Puerto Rico*. Berkeley: University of California Press, 2002.

Bristow, Nancy K. *Making Men Moral: Social Engineering During the Great War*. New York: New York University Press, 1996.

Brochier, J. J. "Prison Talk: An Interview with Michel Foucault." *Radical Philosophy* 16 (Spring 1977): 10–15.

Brockway, Zebulon Reed. *Fifty Years of Prison Service*. New York: Charities Publication Committee, 1912.

Brodeur, Jean-Paul. *The Policing Web*. New York: Oxford University Press, 2010.

Bromwich, David. "Working the Dark Side." *London Review of Books*, January 8, 2015, 15–16.

Bronson, Jennifer, and Marcus Berzofsky. *Indicators of Mental Health Problems Reported by Prisoners and Jail Inmates, 2011–2012*. Washington, DC: Bureau of Justice Statistics, US Department of Justice, 2017.

Brown, Claude. *Manchild in the Promised Land*. New York: Macmillan, 1965.

Buchanan, John. *A Field Guide for USAID Democracy and Governance Officers: Assistance to Civilian Law Enforcement in Developing Countries*. Washington, DC: US Agency for International Development, 2011. http://pdf.usaid.gov/pdf_docs/Pnadu808.pdf.

Bullard, Robert D., and J. Eugene Grigsby III. *Residential Apartheid: The American Legacy*. Los Angeles: UCLA Center for Afro-American Studies, 1994.

Bulosan, Carlos. *America Is in the Heart: A Personal History.* Seattle: University of Washington Press, 1973.

Bureau of Justice Statistics. *Justice Expenditure and Employment in the US, 1971–79.* Washington, DC: US Department of Justice, 1984. https://www.bjs.gov/content/pub/pdf/jeeus7179.pdf.

———. "Prisoners in State and Federal Institutions on December 31, 1979." *National Prisoner Statistics Bulletin* SD-NPS-PSF-7A (May 1980). ttps://www.bjs.gov/content/pub/pdf/psfi79.pdf.

Bureau of the Census. *Statistical Abstract of the United States.* Washington, DC: US Department of Commerce, 1994. https://www.census.gov/library/publications/1994/compendia/statab/114ed.html.

Butler, Stuart M., and Kim R. Holmes. *Issues '98: The Candidates Briefing Book.* Washington, DC: Heritage Foundation, 1998.

Cacho, Lisa Marie. *Social Death: Racialized Rightlessness and the Criminalization of the Unprotected.* New York: New York University Press, 2012.

Cahalan, Margaret. *Historical Corrections Statistics in the United States, 1850–1984.* Washington, DC: Bureau of Justice Statistics, US Department of Justice, 1986. https://www.bjs.gov/content/pub/pdf/hcsus5084.pdf.

———. "Trends in Incarceration in the United States Since 1880: A Summary of Reported Rates and the Distribution of Offenses." *Crime & Delinquency* 25, no. 1 (January 1979): 9–41.

Cahill, Cathleen. *Federal Fathers and Mothers: A Social History of the United States Indian Service, 1869–1933.* Chapel Hill: University of North Carolina Press, 2011.

Camp, Jordan. *Incarcerating the Crisis: Freedom Struggles and the Rise of the Neoliberal State.* Berkeley: University of California Press, 2016.

Camp, Jordan T., and Christina Heatherton, eds. *Policing the Planet: Why the Policing Crisis Led to Black Lives Matter.* London: Verso, 2016.

Canaday, Margot. *The Straight State: Sexuality and Citizenship in Twentieth-Century America.* Princeton, NJ: Princeton University Press, 2009.

Cannon, James P. *Letters from Prison.* New York: Pathfinder, 1968.

Carlan, Phillip. "The Criminal Justice Degree and Policing: Conceptual Development or Occupational Primer?" *Policing* 30, no. 4 (2007): 608–19.

Carrigan, William D., and Clive Webb. *Forgotten Dead: Mob Violence Against Mexicans in the United States, 1848–1928.* New York: Oxford University Press, 2013.

Carson, E. Ann. *Prisoners in 2014.* Washington, DC: Bureau of Justice Statistics, 2015. https://www.bjs.gov/content/pub/pdf/p14.pdf.

———. *Prisoners in 2016.* Washington, DC: Bureau of Justice Statistics, 2018. https://www.bjs.gov/content/pub/pdf/p16.pdf.

Carson, E. Ann, and Elizabeth Anderson. *Prisoners in 2015.* Washington, DC: Bureau of Justice Statistics, 2016. https://www.bjs.gov/content/pub/pdf/p15.pdf.

Carson, E. Ann, and William Sabol. *Prisoners in 2011.* Washington, DC: Bureau of Justice Statistics, 2012. https://www.bjs.gov/content/pub/pdf/p07.pdf.

Carter, Hodding, III, and Reinhold Niebuhr, eds. *Mississippi Black Paper.* New York: Random House, 1965.

Casella, Eleanor Conlin. *The Archaeology of Institutional Confinement*. Gainesville: University Press of Florida, 2007.

Caughey, John W. *California*. New York: Prentice-Hall, 1940.

Chambliss, William J. "A Sociological Analysis of the Law of Vagrancy." *Social Problems* 12, no. 1 (Summer 1964): 67–77.

Chávez-García, Miroslava. *States of Delinquency: Race and Science in the Making of California's Juvenile Justice System*. Berkeley: University of California Press, 2012.

Chicago Commission on Race Relations. *The Negro in Chicago: A Study of Race Relations and a Race Riot*. Chicago: University of Chicago Press, 1922.

(Chicago) Police Accountability Task Force. *Recommendations for Reform: Restoring Trust Between the Chicago Police and the Community They Serve*. Chicago: Police Accountability Task Force, 2016. https://chicagopatf.org/wp-content/uploads/2016/04/PATF_Final_Report_4_13_16-1.pdf.

Chicago Riot Study Committee. *Report to Hon. Richard J. Daley*. Chicago: Chicago Riot Study Committee, 1968.

Christie, Nils. *Crime Control as Industry: Towards GULAGS Western Style*. 3d ed. London: Routledge, 2000.

Chute, Charles L. "Fifty Years of the Juvenile Court." *National Probation and Parole Association Yearbook* (1949): 1–20.

———. "The Juvenile Court in Retrospect." *Federal Probation* 13 (September 1949): 3–8.

Civil Rights Division. *Investigation of the Baltimore City Police Department*. Washington, DC: US Department of Justice, 2016. https://www.justice.gov/crt/file/883296/download.

Civil Rights Division and US Attorney's Office for the Northern District of Illinois. *Investigation of the Chicago Police Department*. Washington, DC: US Department of Justice, 2017. https://www.justice.gov/opa/file/925846/download.

Coates, Joseph F. *Some New Approaches to Riot, Mob, and Crowd Control*. Arlington, VA: Institute for Defense Analysis, 1968.

Coates, Ta-Nehisi. *Between the World and Me*. New York: Spiegel & Grau, 2015.

Cohen, Stanley. "The Punitive City: Notes on the Dispersal of Social Control." *Contemporary Crises* 3 (1979): 339–63.

Cohen, Thomas. *Pretrial Detention and Misconduct in Federal District Courts, 1995–2010*. Washington, DC: Bureau of Justice Statistics, 2013. https://www.bjs.gov/content/pub/pdf/pdmfdc9510.pdf.

Cole, David. "What James Comey Did." *New York Review of Books*, December 8, 2016, 4.

Coles, Robert. *Eskimos, Chicanos, Indians: Children of Crisis*. Vol. 4. Boston: Little, Brown, 1977.

Comey, James. *A Higher Loyalty: Truth, Lies, and Leadership*. New York: Flatiron Books, 2018.

Comfort, Megan. *Doing Time Together: Love and Family in the Shadow of the Prison*. Chicago: University of Chicago Press, 2008.

Commission of Inquiry into the Black Panthers and the Police, chaired by Roy Wilkins and Ramsey Clark. *Search and Destroy: A Report by the Commission of Inquiry into the Black Panthers and the Police*. New York: Metropolitan Applied Research Center, 1973.

Commission on Civil Rights. *Hearings Before the United States Commission on Civil Rights. Hearings Held in Los Angeles, California, January 25, 1960, January 26, 1960; San Francisco, California, January 27, 1960, January 28, 1960*. Washington, DC: US-GPO, 1960.

Cooley, Charles H. "'Nature v. Nurture' in the Making of Social Careers." *Proceedings of the National Conference of Charities and Correction* (1896): 399–405.

Cramton, Roger C. "Crisis in Legal Services for the Poor." *Villanova Law Review* 26, no. 3–4 (March 1981): 521–56.

Critical Resistance and Incite! "Statement on Gender Violence and the Prison-Industrial Complex." *Social Justice* 30, no. 3 (2003): 141–50.

Cunningham, William, Todd Taylor, and Hallcrest Systems. *The Hallcrest Report: Private Security and Police in America*. Boston: Butterworth-Heinemann, 1991.

Curtin, Mary Ellen. *Black Prisoners and Their World, Alabama, 1865–1900*. Charlottesville: University Press of Virginia, 2000.

CR10 Publications Collective. *Abolition Now! Ten Years of Strategy and Struggle Against the Prison Industrial Complex*. Oakland: AK Press, 2008.

Davis, Angela Y. *Are Prisons Obsolete?* New York: Seven Stories Press, 2003.

———, ed. *If They Come in the Morning: Voices of Resistance*. New York: Third Press, 1971.

———. *The Meaning of Freedom*. San Francisco: City Lights, 2012.

———. *Women, Race, and Class*. New York: Random House, 1983.

Davis, Mike. *City of Quartz: Excavating the Future in Los Angeles*. London: Verso, 1990.

———. *Urban Control: The Ecology of Fear*. Westfield, NJ: Open Magazine, 1992.

Dawkins, Curtis. *The Graybar Hotel*. New York: Scribner, 2017.

Dayan, Colin. "With Law at the Edge of Life." *The South Atlantic Quarterly* 113, no. 3 (Summer 2014): 629–39.

Dayen, David. "The Trump Administration Is Letting Wells Fargo Get Away with Grand Theft Auto." *The Nation*, April 23, 2018. https://www.thenation.com/article/the-trump-administration-is-letting-wells-fargo-get-away-with-grand-theft-auto/.

Debs, Eugene Victor. *Walls and Bars*. Chicago: Charles H. Kerr, 1963.

D'Emilio, John. *Sexual Politics, Sexual Communities: The Making of a Homosexual Minority in the United States, 1940–1970*. Chicago: University of Chicago Press, 1983.

D'Emilio, John, and Estelle B. Freedman. *Intimate Matters: A History of Sexuality in America*. New York: Harper & Row, 1988.

Deming, Barbara. *Prison Notes*. New York: Grossman, 1966.

Dickens, Charles. *American Notes*. Edited by John S. Whitley and Arnold Goldman. Harmondsworth, UK: Penguin, 1972.

Dietzler, Mary Macey. *Detention Houses and Reformatories as Protective Social Agencies in the Campaign of the United States Government Against Venereal Diseases*. Washington, DC: USGPO, 1922.

Donner, Frank J. *The Age of Surveillance: The Aims and Methods of America's Intelligence System*. New York: Alfred A. Knopf, 1980.

———. *Protectors of Privilege: Red Squads and Police Repression in Urban America*. Berkeley: University of California Press, 1990.

Duberman, Martin. *Cures: A Gay Man's Odyssey*. New York: Penguin, 1992.

Du Bois, W.E.B. *The Autobiography of W. E. B. Du Bois.* New York: International, 1968.

———. *Black Reconstruction in America: An Essay Toward a History of the Part Which Black Folk Played in the Attempt to Reconstruct Democracy in America, 1860–1880.* New York: Atheneum, 1973.

———. *The Souls of Black Folk.* New York: Alfred A. Knopf, 1993.

Dumindin, Arnaldo. *Philippine-American War, 1899–1902.* 2006. http://philippine -americanwar.webs.com/.

Duster, Troy. "Individual Fairness, Group Preferences, and the California Strategy." *Representations* 55 (1996): 41–58.

Eckstein, Arthur M. *Bad Moon Rising: How the Weather Underground Beat the FBI and Lost the Revolution.* New Haven, CT: Yale University Press, 2016.

Edwards, Lee. *To Preserve and Protect.* Washington, DC: Heritage Foundation, 2005.

Eisenhower, Dwight D. "Farewell Address to the American People." January 17, 1961. https://www.eisenhower.archives.gov/all_about_ike/speeches/farewell_address.pdf.

Eisinger, Jesse. *The Chickenshit Club: Why the Justice Department Fails to Prosecute Executives.* New York: Simon & Schuster, 2017.

Eldridge, Taylor Elizabeth. "The Big Business of Prisoner Care Packages." *The Marshall Project*, December 21, 2017. https://www.themarshallproject.org/2017/12/21/the-big -business-of-prisoner-care-packages.

Elliot, Jeffrey M. "The 'Willie' Horton Nobody Knows." *The Nation*, August 23, 1993, 201–16.

Equal Justice Initiative. *Lynching in America: Confronting the Legacy of Racial Terror.* Montgomery, AL: Equal Justice Initiative, 2015.

Ervin, Sam J., Jr. "Preventive Detention—A Step Backward for Criminal Justice." *Harvard Civil Rights–Civil Liberties Law Review* 6, no. 2 (1971): 291–99.

Escobar, Edward J. *Race, Police, and the Making of a Political Identity: Mexican Americans and the Los Angeles Police Department, 1900–1945.* Berkeley: University of California Press, 1999.

Eubanks, Virginia. *Automating Inequality: How High-Tech Tools Profile, Police, and Punish the Poor.* New York: St. Martin's Press, 2018.

Executive Office of the President. *Review: Federal Support for Local Law Enforcement Equipment Acquisition.* Washington, DC: The White House, 2014. http://info.public intelligence.net/WhiteHouse-LawEnforcementMilitarySurplus.pdf.

Falconer, Martha P. "The Segregation of Delinquent Women and Girls as a War Problem." *The Annals of the American Academy of Political and Social Sciences* 79 (September 1918): 160–66.

Farrell, James T., Nelson Algren, Hal Ellson, et al. *Juvenile Jungle: Stories of Juvenile Delinquency.* New York: Berkley, 1957.

Fassin, Didier. *Enforcing Order: An Ethnography of Urban Policing.* Malden, MA: Polity, 2013.

Fear-Segal, Jacqueline. *White Man's Club: Schools, Race, and the Struggle of Indian Acculturation.* Lincoln: University of Nebraska Press, 2007.

Federal Bureau of Investigation. "Expanded Offense Data: Homicides." In *2014 Crime in the United States.* 2014. https://ucr.fbi.gov/crime-in-the-u.s/2014/crime-in-the-u .s.-2014.

———. *Prevention and Control of Mobs and Riots*. Washington, DC: US Department of Justice, 1967.

Felber, Garrett. "'Shades of Mississippi': The Nation of Islam's Prison Organizing, the Carceral State, and the Black Freedom Struggle." *The Journal of American History* 105, no 1 (June 2018): 71–95.

Feldman, Allen. "Securocratic Wars of Public Safety." *Interventions* 6, no. 3 (2004): 330–50.

Feldman, Noah. "Tipping the Scales." *The New York Review of Books*, July 19, 2018, 8–10.

Ferguson, Robert A. *Inferno: An Anatomy of American Punishment*. Cambridge, MA: Harvard University Press, 2014.

Fitzgerald, Mike, Gregor McLennan, and Jennie Pawson, eds. *Crime and Society: Readings in History and Theory*. London: Routledge & Kegan Paul, 1981.

Flynn, Elizabeth Gurley. *The Alderson Story: My Life as a Political Prisoner*. New York: International, 1963.

Fogelson, Robert M. *America's Armories: Architecture, Society, and Public Order*. Cambridge, MA: Harvard University Press, 1989.

———. *Big-City Police*. Cambridge, MA: Harvard University Press, 1977.

Foner, Eric. *Reconstruction: America's Unfinished Revolution, 1863–1877*. New York: Harper & Row, 1988.

Foner, Eric, and John A. Garraty, eds. *The Reader's Companion to American History*. Boston: Houghton Mifflin, 1991.

Foner, Philip S., ed. *The Black Panther Speaks*. Philadelphia: J. B. Lippincott, 1970.

Foote, Caleb. "The Bail System and Equal Justice." *Federal Probation* 23 (1959): 43–48.

Ford, Matt. "The Bipartisan Opposition to Sessions' New Civil Forfeiture Rules." *The Atlantic*, July 19, 2017. https://www.theatlantic.com/politics/archive/2017/07/sessions-forfeiture-justice-department-civil/534168/.

Forman, James, Jr. *Locking Up Our Own: Crime and Punishment in Black America*. New York: Farrar, Strauss & Giroux, 2017.

Foucault, Michel. *Discipline and Punish: The Birth of the Prison*. New York: Pantheon, 1977.

———. *The Punitive Society: Lectures at the College de France, 1972–1973*, ed. Bernard E. Harcourt. New York: Palgrave Macmillan, 2015.

———. *Power/Knowledge: Selected Interviews and Other Writings, 1972-1977*, ed. C. Gordon. New York: Harvester Wheatsheaf, 1980.

———. *Society Must Be Defended: Lectures at the Collège de France, 1975–76*. London: Allen Lane, 2003.

Frankel, Noralee, and Nancy S. Dye, eds. *Gender, Class, Race, and Reform in the Progressive Era*. Lexington: University of Kentucky Press, 1991.

Franklin, H. Bruce. *Prison Literature in America: The Victim as Criminal and Artist*. Westport, CT: Lawrence Hill, 1982.

———, ed. *Prison Writing in 20th-Century America*. New York: Penguin, 1998.

Franklin, John Hope. *From Slavery to Freedom: A History of Negro America*. 3d ed. New York: Alfred A. Knopf, 1967.

Fraser, Steve, and Gary Gerstle, eds. *The Rise and Fall of the New Deal Order, 1930–1980*. Princeton, NJ: Princeton University Press, 1989.

Frazier, E. Franklin. *The Negro in the United States*. New York: Macmillan, 1949.

———. *Negro Youth at the Crossways: Their Personality Development in the Middle States*. New York: Schocken, 1967.

Friedman, Lawrence. *Crime and Punishment in American History*. New York: Basic Books, 1993.

Frost, Natasha A., and Todd R. Clear. "Doctoral Education in Criminology and Criminal Justice." *Journal of Criminal Justice Education* 18, no. 1 (2007): 35–52.

Frye, Jocelyn C., Robert S. Gerber, Robert H. Pees, and Arthur W. Richardson. "The Rise and Fall of the United States Commission on Civil Rights." *Harvard Civil Rights–Civil Liberties Law Review* 22, no. 2 (Spring 1987): 449–506.

Galarza, Ernesto. *Merchants of Labor: The Mexican Bracero Story*. Charlotte, NC: McNally & Loftin, 1964.

García, Juan R. *Mexicans in the Midwest, 1900–1932*. Tucson: University of Arizona Press, 1996.

García, Mario T. *Memories of Chicano History: The Life and Narrative of Bert Corona*. Berkeley: University of California Press, 1994.

———. *Mexican Americans: Leadership, Ideology, and Identity, 1930–1960*. New Haven, CT: Yale University Press, 1989.

Garrow, David J. *The FBI and Martin Luther King, Jr*. New York: Penguin, 1983. First published by W. W. Norton in 1981.

Gebhard, Paul, and Alan Johnson. *The Kinsey Data: Marginal Tabulations of the 1938–1963 Interviews Conducted by the Institute for Sex Research*. Bloomington: Indiana University Press, 1979.

General Accounting Office. *Better Management Oversight and Internal Controls Needed to Ensure Accuracy of Terrorism-Related Statistics*. Washington, DC: General Accounting Office, 2003.

———. *Foreign Aid: Police Training and Assistance*. Report B-247418, 2. Washington, DC: General Accounting Office, 1992.

Genovese, Eugene D. *Roll, Jordan, Roll: The World the Slaves Made*. New York: Pantheon, 1974.

George, Warren E. "Development of the Legal Services Corporation." *Cornell Law Review* 61 (June 1976): 681–730.

Gerstle, Gary. *American Crucible: Race and Nation in the Twentieth Century*. Princeton, NJ: Princeton University Press, 2001.

———. "The Protean Character of American Liberalism." *American Historical Review* 99, no. 4 (1994): 1043–73.

Gibbs, Jewelle Taylor, ed. *Young, Black, and Male in America: An Endangered Species*. New York: Auburn House, 1988.

Gilbert, David. "'These Criminals Have No Respect for Human Life.'" *Social Justice* 18, no. 3 (Fall 1991): 71–83.

Gilmore, Ruth Wilson. *Golden Gulag: Prisons, Surplus, Crisis, and Opposition in Globalizing California*. Berkeley: University of California Press, 2007.

Gilroy, Paul. *Against Race: Imagining Political Culture Beyond the Color Line*. Cambridge, MA: Harvard University Press, 2000.

Glaze, Lauren, and Danielle Kaeble. *Correctional Populations in the United States, 2013.* Washington, DC: Bureau of Justice Statistics, 2014. https://www.bjs.gov/content/pub /pdf/cpus13.pdf.

Gluck, Sherna, ed. *From Parlor to Prison: Five American Suffragists Talk About Their Lives.* New York: Vintage, 1976.

Goffman, Alice. *On the Run: Fugitive Life in an American City.* Chicago: University of Chicago Press, 2014.

Goffman, Erving. *Asylums: Essays on the Social Situation of Mental Patients and Other Inmates.* New York: Anchor, 1961.

Golash-Boza, Tanya Maria. *Deported: Immigrant Policing, Disposable Labor, and Global Capitalism.* New York: New York University Press, 2015.

Gold, Martin, and David Reimer. "Changing Patterns of Delinquent Behavior Among Americans 13 Through 16 Years Old, 1967–1972." *Crime and Delinquency Literature* 7, no. 4 (December 1975): 483–517.

Goldstein, Robert Justin. *Political Repression in Modern America: From 1870 to the Present.* Cambridge, MA: Schenkman, 1978.

———. *Saving "Old Glory": The History of the Flag Desecration Controversy.* Boulder, CO: Westview, 1995.

Gordon, Avery F. "Some Thoughts on Haunting and Futurity." *Borderlands* 10, no. 2 (2011): 1–21.

Gordon, Linda. *The Moral Property of Women: A History of Birth Control Politics in the United States.* Urbana: University of Illinois Press, 2002.

———. *Pitied but Not Entitled: Single Mothers and the History of Welfare.* Cambridge, MA: Harvard University Press, 1994.

———, ed. *Women, the State and Welfare.* Madison: University of Wisconsin Press, 1990.

Gorz, André. *Strategy for Labor: A Radical Proposal.* Boston: Beacon, 1967.

Gottschalk, Marie. *Caught: The Prison State and the Lockdown of American Politics.* Princeton, NJ: Princeton University Press, 2015.

———. "The Long Reach of the Carceral State: The Politics of Crime, Mass Imprisonment, and Penal Reform in the United States." *Law & Social Inquiry* 34, no. 2 (Spring 2009): 439–72.

Graham, David. "Rumsfeld's Knowns and Unknowns: The Intellectual History of a Quip." *The Atlantic,* March 27, 2014. https://www.theatlantic.com/politics/archive /2014/03/rumsfelds-knowns-and-unknowns-the-intellectual-history-of-a-quip /359719/.

Graham, Hugh Davis. "The Origins of Affirmative Action: Civil Rights and the Regulatory State." *The Annals of American Academy of Political and Social Science* 523 (September 1992): 50–62.

Graham, Stephen. *Cities Under Siege: The New Military Urbanism.* London: Verso, 2011.

Gramsci, Antonio. *Selections from the Prison Notebooks.* Edited by Quintin Hoare and Geoffrey Nowell Smith. New York: International, 1971.

Greene, Judith A., Bethany Carson, and Andrea Black. *Indefensible: A Decade of Mass Incarceration of Migrants Prosecuted for Crossing the Border.* Austin, TX: Grassroots Leadership, 2016.

Greenspan, Rosann. *The Transformation of Criminal Due Process in the Administrative State*. New Orleans: Quid Pro, 2014.

Gregory, Steven, and Roger Sanjek, eds. *Race*. New Brunswick, NJ: Rutgers University Press, 1994.

Griffin, John Howard. *Black Like Me*. Boston: Houghton Mifflin, 1961.

Grimshaw, Allen D. *Racial Violence in the United States*. Chicago: Aldine, 1969.

Guerino, Pat, Paige Harrison, and William Sabol. *Prisoners in 2010*. Washington, DC: Bureau of Justice Statistics, 2011. https://www.bjs.gov/content/pub/pdf/p10.pdf.

Gustafson, Kaaryn S. *Cheating Welfare: Public Assistance and the Criminalization of Poverty*. New York: New York University Press, 2011.

Hacker, Jacob S. *The Divided Welfare State*. Cambridge: Cambridge University Press, 2002.

Haley, Sarah. "'Like I Was a Man': Chain Gangs, Gender, and the Domestic Carceral Sphere in Jim Crow Georgia." *Signs* 39, no. 1 (Autumn 2013): 53–77.

———. *No Mercy Here: Gender, Punishment, and the Making of Jim Crow Modernity*. Chapel Hill: University of North Carolina Press, 2016.

Hall, Jerome. *Theft, Law and Society*. 2d ed. Indianapolis: Bobbs-Merrill, 1952.

Hall, Stuart. *The Hard Road to Renewal: Thatcherism and the Crisis of the Left*. London: Verso, 1988.

Hall, Stuart, Chas Critcher, Tony Jefferson, John Clarke, and Brian Roberts. *Policing the Crisis: Mugging, the State and Law and Order*. London: Macmillan, 2013. Originally published by Macmillan in 1978.

Hallsworth, Simon, and John Lea. "Reconstructing Leviathan: Emerging Contours of the Security State." *Theoretical Criminology* 15, no. 2 (2011): 141–57.

Halper, Jeff. *War Against the People: Israel, the Palestinians, and Global Pacification*. London: Pluto, 2015.

Halpern, Jake. "The Cop." *The New Yorker*, August 10 and 17, 2015. https://www.newyorker.com/magazine/2015/08/10/the-cop.

Harcourt, Bernard E. *Against Prediction: Profiling, Policing and Punishing in an Actuarial Age*. Chicago: University of Chicago Press, 2007.

———. *The Counterrevolution: How Our Government Went to War Against Its Own Citizens*. New York: Basic Books, 2018.

———. *Exposed: Desire and Disobedience in the Digital Age*. Cambridge, MA: Harvard University Press, 2015.

———. "From the Asylum to the Prison: Rethinking the Incarceration Revolution." *Texas Law Review* 84 (2006): 1751–86.

Harlem Youth Opportunities Unlimited. *Youth in the Ghetto*. New York: HARYOU, 1964.

Harring, Sidney L. *Policing a Class Society: The Experience of American Cities, 1865–1915*. 2d ed. Chicago: Haymarket, 2017.

Harrington, Michael. *The Other America: Poverty in the United States*. New York: Macmillan, 1962.

Harwin, Michael. "Detaining for Danger Under the Bail Reform Act of 1984." *Arizona Law Review* 35 (1993): 1091–1122.

Hay, Douglas, Peter Linebaugh, John G. Rule, E. P. Thompson, and Cal Winslow. *Albi-*

on's *Fatal Tree: Crime and Society in Eighteenth-Century England.* New York: Pantheon, 1975.

Hayden, Tom. *Trial.* New York: Holt, Rinehart & Winston, 1970.

Helmer, John. *Drugs and Minority Oppression.* New York: Seabury, 1975.

Hernández, Kelly Lytle. *City of Inmates: Conquest, Rebellion, and the Rise of Human Caging in Los Angeles, 1771–1965.* Chapel Hill: University of North Carolina Press, 2017.

Hernández, Kelly Lytle, Khalil Gibran Muhammad, and Heather Ann Thompson. "Introduction: Constructing the Carceral State." *Journal of American History* 102, no. 1 (2015): 18–24.

Herrnstein, Richard J., and Charles Murray. *The Bell Curve: Intelligence and Class Structure in American Life.* New York: Free Press, 1994.

Hersh, Seymour M. "Torture at Abu Ghraib." *The New Yorker,* May 10, 2004. http://www.newyorker.com/magazine/2004/05/10/torture-at-abu-ghraib.

Hester, Torrie. "Deportability and the Carceral State." *Journal of American History* 102, no. 1 (2015): 141–51.

Hill, Lance. *The Deacons for Defense: Armed Resistance and the Civil Rights Movement.* Chapel Hill: University of North Carolina Press, 2004.

Himmelfarb, Gertrude. *On Looking into the Abyss: Untimely Thoughts on Culture and Society.* New York: Vintage, 1995.

Hinton, Elizabeth. *From the War on Poverty to the War on Crime: The Making of Mass Incarceration in America.* Cambridge, MA: Harvard University Press, 2016.

Hirschi, Travis, and Michel Hindelang. "Intelligence and Delinquency: A Revisionist Review." *American Sociological Journal* 42 (1977): 571–87.

Hobbs, Dick, Philip Hadfield, Stuart Lister, and Simon Winslow. *Bouncers: Violence and Governance in the Night-Time Economy.* New York: Oxford University Press, 2003.

Hobsbawm, Eric. *The Age of Extremes: A History of the World, 1914–1991.* New York: Pantheon, 1994.

Hoffman, Eva. *After Such Knowledge: Memory, History, and the Legacy of the Holocaust.* New York: PublicAffairs, 2004.

Hofstadter, Richard. *The Age of Reform.* New York: Vintage, 1955.

Holloway, Pippa. *Living in Infamy: Felon Disenfranchisement and the History of American Citizenship.* New York: Oxford University Press, 2014.

Hoover, J. Edgar. *Masters of Deceit: The Story of Communism and How to Fight It.* New York: Henry Holt, 1958.

Huber, Peter W., and Mark P. Mills. "How Technology Will Defeat Terrorism." *City Journal* (Winter 2002). https://www.city-journal.org/html/how-technology-will-defeat-terrorism-12213.html.

Hucklesby, Anthea, and Stuart Lister. *Private Sector and Criminal Justice.* London: Palgrave Macmillan, 2018.

Ina, Itaru. "Haiku." Translated by Hisako Ifshini and Leza Lowitz. *Modern Haiku* 34, no. 2 (Summer 2003). http://modernhaiku.org/essays/itaruinahaiku.html.

Inouye, Karen M. *The Long Afterlife of Nikkei Wartime Incarceration.* Stanford, CA: Stanford University Press, 2016.

Irwin, John. *The Felon.* Englewood Cliffs, NJ: Prentice-Hall, 1970.

Jackson, George. *Soledad Brother: The Prison Letters of George Jackson*. Introduction by Jean Genet. New York: Bantam, 1970.

Jackson, H. Bruce. *Wake Up Dead Man: Afro-American Worksongs from Texas Prisons*. Cambridge, MA: Harvard University Press, 1972.

Jacob, Herbert, ed. *The Potential for Reform of Criminal Justice*. Beverly Hills, CA: Sage, 1974.

Jacobs, Margaret D. *White Mother to a Dark Race: Settler Colonialism, Maternalism, and the Removal of Indigenous Children in the American West and Australia, 1880–1940*. Lincoln: University of Nebraska Press, 2009.

Janowitz, Morris. *Social Control of Escalated Riots*. Chicago: University of Chicago Center for Policy Study, 1968.

Jayadev, Arjun, and Samuel Bowles, "Guard Labor." *Journal of Development Economics* 79 (2006): 328–48.

Jaynes, Gerald David, and Robin M. Williams, eds. *A Common Destiny: Blacks and American Society*. Washington, DC: National Academy Press, 1989.

Johnson, Loch K. *A Season of Inquiry: Congress and Intelligence*. Chicago: Dorsey, 1988.

Johnson, Walter. *River of Dark Dreams: Slavery and Empire in the Cotton Kingdom*. Cambridge, MA: Harvard University Press, 2013.

Johnston, Les. *The Rebirth of Private Policing*. London: Routledge, 1992.

Jones, Jacqueline. *Labor of Love, Labor of Sorrow: Black Women, Work, and the Family from Slavery to the Present*. New York: Basic Books, 1985.

Josephy, Alvin M., Jr. *Red Power: The American Indians' Fight for Freedom*. Lincoln: University of Nebraska Press, 1999.

Kafka, Franz. *The Penal Colony: Stories and Short Pieces*. New York: Schocken, 1948.

Kajstura, Aleks, and Russ Immarigeon. *States of Women's Incarceration: The Global Context*. Northampton, MA: Prison Policy Initiative, November 18, 2015. https://www.prisonpolicy.org/global/women/.

Kalhan, Anil. "Immigration Surveillance." *Maryland Law Review* 74, no. 1 (2014): 1–86.

———. "Rethinking Immigration Detention." *Columbia Law Review Sidebar* 110 (July 21, 2010): 42–58.

Karnow, Curtis E. "Setting Bail for Public Safety." *Berkeley Journal of Criminal Law* 13, no. 1 (2008): 1–30.

Katz, Jonathan M. "What General Pershing Was Really Doing in the Philippines." *The Atlantic*, August 18, 2017. https://www.theatlantic.com/international/archive/2017/08/pershing-trump-terrorism/537300/.

Katz, Michael. *In the Shadow of the Poorhouse: A Social History of Welfare in America*. New York: Basic Books, 1986.

Katzive, Marion. *New Areas for Bail Reform: A Report on the Manhattan Bail Reevaluation Project*. New York: Vera Institute, 1968.

Keefe, Patrick Radden. "Empire of Pain." *The New Yorker*, October 30, 2017, 34–49.

———. "Limited Liability." *The New Yorker*, July 31, 2017, 28–33.

Keller, Bill. "Prison Revolt." *The New Yorker*, June 29, 2015. http://www.newyorker.com/magazine/2015/06/29/prison-revolt.

Kelley, Robin D. G. "Beyond Black Lives Matter." *Kalfou* 2, no. 2 (Fall 2015): 330–37.

Kelling, George L., and James Q. Wilson. "Broken Windows: The Police and Neighborhood Safety." *The Atlantic*, March 1982. https://www.theatlantic.com/magazine/archive/1982/03/broken-windows/304465/.

Khalili, Laleh. *Time in the Shadows: Confinement in Counterinsurgencies*. Stanford, CA: Stanford University Press, 2013.

Kilgore, James. *Understanding Mass Incarceration: A People's Guide to the Key Civil Rights Struggle of Our Time*. New York: The New Press, 2015.

King, Martin Luther, Jr. *Letter from Birmingham Jail*. San Francisco: Harper, 1994.

Kirk, Stuart, ed. *Mental Disorders in the Social Environment*. New York: Columbia University Press, 2005.

Kline, Wendy. *Building a Better Race: Gender, Sexuality, and Eugenics from the Turn of the Century to the Baby Boom*. Berkeley: University of California Press, 2001.

Knight, Etheridge. *Black Voices from Prison*. New York: Pathfinder, 1970.

———. *Poems from Prison*. Detroit: Broadside Press, 1968.

Knopke, Harry J., Robert J. Norrell, and Ronald W. Rogers, eds. *Opening Doors: Perspectives on Race Relations in Contemporary America*. Tuscaloosa: University of Alabama Press, 1991.

Kochanek, Kenneth D., Sherry Murphy, Jiaquan Xu, and Betzaida Tejada-Vera. "Deaths: Final Data for 2014." *National Vital Statistics Reports* 65, no. 4 (June 2016). https://www.cdc.gov/nchs/data/nvsr/nvsr65/nvsr65_04.pdf.

Koehler, Johann. "Development and Fracture of a Discipline: Legacies of the School of Criminology at Berkeley." *Criminology* 53, no. 4 (November 2015): 513–44.

Kohler-Hausmann, Julilly. *Getting Tough: Welfare and Imprisonment in 1970s America*. Princeton, NJ: Princeton University Press, 2017.

———. "Managerial Justice and Mass Misdemeanors." *Stanford Law Review* 66 (March 2014): 611–93.

———. "Misdemeanor Justice: Control Without Conviction." *American Journal of Sociology* 119, no. 2 (September 2013): 351–93.

Kohn, Richard H., ed. *The United States Military Under the Constitution of the United States, 1789–1989*. New York: New York University Press, 1991.

Kolko, Gabriel. *The Triumph of Conservatism: A Reinterpretation of American History, 1900–1916*. Chicago: Quadrangle, 1967.

Kraska, Peter B., ed. *Militarizing the American Criminal Justice System: The Changing Roles of the Armed Forces and Police*. Boston: Northeastern University Press, 2001.

Krisberg, Barry. "Teaching Radical Criminology." *Crime and Social Justice* 1 (1974): 64–75.

Kühl, Stefan. *The Nazi Connection: Eugenics, American Racism, and German National Socialism*. New York: Oxford University Press, 1994.

Kunzel, Regina G. *Fallen Women, Problem Girls: Unmarried Mothers and the Professionalization of Social Work, 1890–1945*. New Haven, CT: Yale University Press, 1993.

Kyckelhahn, Tracey. *Justice Expenditure and Employment Extracts, 2012*. Washington, DC: Bureau of Justice Statistics, 2015. https://www.bjs.gov/index.cfm?ty=pbdetail&iid=5239.

———. *State Corrections Expenditures, FY 1982–2010*. Washington, DC: Bureau of Justice Statistics, 2012. https://www.bjs.gov/content/pub/pdf/scefy8210.pdf.

Kyckelhahn, Tracey, and Tara Martin. *Justice Expenditure and Employment Extracts, 2010*. Washington, DC: Bureau of Justice Statistics, 2013. https://www.bjs.gov/index.cfm?ty=pbdetail&iid=4679

Langton, Lynn, Marcus Berzofsky, Christopher Krebs, and Hope Smiley-McDonald. *Victimizations Not Reported to the Police, 2006–2010*. Washington, DC: Bureau of Justice Statistics, August 2012.

Lankford, Adam. "A Comparative Analysis of Suicide Terrorists and Rampage, Workplace, and School Shooters in the United States from 1990 to 2010." *Homicide Studies* 17, no. 3 (2012): 255–74.

———. "Are America's Public Mass Shooters Unique? A Comparative Analysis of Offenders in the United States and Other Countries." *International Journal of Comparative and Applied Criminal Justice* 40, no. 2 (2016): 171–83.

———. "Public Mass Shooters and Firearms: A Cross-National Study of 171 Countries." *Violence and Victims* 31, no. 2 (2016): 187–99.

Laqueur, Thomas. "Devoted to Terror." *London Review of Books*, September 24, 2015.

Lara-Millán, Armando. "Public Emergency Room Overcrowding in the Era of Mass Incarceration." *American Sociological Review* 79 (2014): 866–87.

Lassiter, Matthew D. "Impossible Criminals: The Suburban Imperatives of America's War on Drugs." *Journal of American History* 102 (June 2015): 126–40.

Lathrop, Julia. "The Development of the Probation System in a Large City." *Charities* 13 (January 1905): 344–49.

Law Enforcement Leaders to Reduce Crime and Incarceration. *Fighting Crime and Strengthening Criminal Justice: An Agenda for the New Administration*. New York: Brennan Center for Justice, New York University School of Law, 2017. www.lawenforcementleaders.org.

Lefcourt, Robert, ed. *Law Against the People: Essays to Demystify Law, Order and the Courts*. New York: Vintage, 1971.

LeFlouria, Talitha L. *Chained in Silence: Black Women and Convict Labor in the New South*. Chapel Hill: University of North Carolina Press, 2015.

Lerman, Amy E., and Vesla M. Weaver. *Arresting Citizenship: The Democratic Consequences of American Crime Control*. Chicago: University of Chicago Press, 2014.

Levi, Primo. *The Drowned and the Saved*. London: Michael Joseph, 1988.

Levi, Robin, and Ayelet Waldman, eds. *Inside This Place, Not of It*. San Francisco: McSweeney's Books, 2011.

Levy, Howard, and David Miller. *Going to Jail: The Political Prisoner*. New York: Grove, 1976.

Lichtenstein, Alex. "Flocatex and the Fiscal Limits of Mass Incarceration: Towards a New Political Economy of the Postwar Carceral State." *Journal of American History* 102, no. 1 (June 2015): 1–13.

———. *Twice the Work of Free Labor: The Political Economy of Convict Labor in the New South*. London: Verso, 1996.

Liebman, Benjamin. "Recent Legislation: Congress Imposes New Restrictions on Use of Funds by the Legal Services Corporation." *Harvard Law Review* 110 (1997): 1346–51.

Lindgren, Sue. *Justice Expenditure and Employment Extracts, 1992*. Washington, DC: Bureau of Justice Statistics, 1997. https://www.bjs.gov/content/pub/pdf/CJEE92.PDF.

———. *Justice Expenditure and Employment in the U.S., 1998*. Washington, DC: Bureau of Justice Statistics, 1991. http://www.bjs.gov/content/pub/pdf/jeeus88.pdf.

Lippman, Jonathan. "New York's Template to Address the Crisis in Civil Legal Services." *Harvard Law & Policy Review* 7 (2013): 13–30.

Litwack, Leon. *Trouble in Mind: Black Southerners in the Age of Jim Crow*. New York: Alfred A. Knopf, 1998.

Locke, Hubert G. "Riot Response: The Police and the Courts." *Journal of Urban Law* 45 (Spring–Summer 1968): 805–14.

Loftin, Colin, Brian Wiersema, David McDowall, and Adam Dobrin. "Underreporting of Justifiable Homicides Committed by Police Officers in the United States, 1976–1998." *American Journal of Public Health* 93, no. 7 (July 2003): 1117–21.

Lord, Russell. *Gordon Parks: The Making of an Argument*. New Orleans: New Orleans Museum of Art, 2013.

Lowenthal, Max. *The Federal Bureau of Investigation*. New York: Harcourt Brace Jovanovich, 1950.

Lynch, Mona. *Sunbelt Justice: Arizona and the Transformation of American Punishment*. Stanford, CA: Stanford University Press, 2010.

Lyon, Danny. *Conversations with the Dead: Photographs of Prison Life with the Letters and Drawings of Billy McCune #122054*. New York: Holt, Rinehart and Winston, 1971.

MacFarquhar, Larissa. "Out and Up." *The New Yorker*, December 12, 2016, 54–63.

Madley, Benjamin. *An American Genocide: The United States and the California Indian Catastrophe, 1846–1873*. New Haven, CT: Yale University Press, 2016.

———. "From Africa to Auschwitz: How German South West Africa Incubated Ideas and Methods Adopted and Developed by the Nazis in Eastern Europe." *European History Quarterly* 35, no. 3 (2005): 429–64.

Malega, Roy, and Thomas Cohen. *Special Report: State Court Organization, 2011*. Washington, DC: Bureau of Justice Statistics, 2013. http://www.bjs.gov/content/pub/pdf/sco11.pdf.

Manion, Jen. *Liberty's Prisoners: Carceral Culture in Early America*. Philadelphia: University of Pennsylvania Press, 2015.

Martinson, Robert. "Prison Notes of a Freedom Rider." *The Nation*, January 6, 1962, 4–5.

Mason, Cody. *Dollars and Detainees: The Growth of For-Profit Detention*. Washington, DC: Sentencing Project, July 2012.

Massey, Douglas S., and Nancy A. Denton. *American Apartheid: Segregation and the Making of the Underclass*. Cambridge, MA: Harvard University Press, 1993.

May, Elaine Tyler. *Homeward Bound: American Families in the Cold War Era*. New York: Basic Books, 1988.

Mayer, Jane. "The President Pence Delusion." *The New Yorker*, October 23, 2017, 54–69.

McClain, Dani. "The Future of BLM." *The Nation*, October 9, 2017, 13–16.

McCoy, Alfred W. *Policing America's Empire: The United States, the Philippines, and the Rise of the Surveillance State*. Madison: University of Wisconsin Press, 2009.

McDowell, Meghan G. "Insurgent Safety: Theorizing Alternatives to State Protection." *Theoretical Criminology*, 2017. https://doi.org/10.1177/1362480617713984.

McGirr, Lisa. *The War on Alcohol: Prohibition and the Rise of the American State*. New York: W. W. Norton, 2016.

McLennan, Rebecca M. *The Crisis of Imprisonment: Protest, Politics, and the Making of the American Penal State, 1776–1941.* Cambridge: Cambridge University Press, 2008.

McLeod, Allegra. "Exporting U.S. Criminal Justice." *Yale Law Review* 29 (2010): 83–164.

McMurtry, Larry. *Oh What a Slaughter: Massacres in the American West, 1846–1890.* New York: Simon & Schuster, 2005.

Medsger, Betty. *The Burglary: The Discovery of J. Edgar Hoover's Secret FBI.* New York: Vintage, 2014.

Melville, Sam. *Letters from Attica.* New York: William Morrow, 1972.

Meriam, Lewis. *The Problem of Indian Administration: Report of a Survey Made at Request of Honorable Hubert Work, Secretary of the Interior.* Baltimore: Johns Hopkins University Press, 1928.

Miliband, Ralph. *The State in Capitalist Society.* New York: Basic Books, 1969.

Miller, Reuben Jonathan. "Devolving the Carceral State: Race, Prisoner Reentry, and the Micro-Politics of Urban Poverty Management." *Punishment & Society* 16, no. 3 (2014): 305–35.

Mink, Gwendolyn. "Faith in Government?" *Social Justice* 28, no. 1 (2001): 5–10.

Minton, Robert J., ed. *Inside: Prison American Style.* New York: Vintage, 1971.

Minton, Todd, and Daniela Golinelli. *Jail Inmates at Midyear 2013—Statistical Tables.* Washington, DC: Bureau of Justice Statistics, 2014. https://www.bjs.gov/index.cfm?ty=pbdetail&iid=4988.

Minton, Todd D., and Zhen Zeng. *Jail Inmates in 2015.* Washington, DC: Bureau of Justice Statistics, 2016. https://www.bjs.gov/content/pub/pdf/ji15.pdf.

Mitford, Jessica. *Kind and Usual Punishment: The Prison Business.* New York: Alfred A. Knopf, 1973.

Molina, Natalia. *Fit to Be Citizens? Public Health and Race in Los Angeles, 1879–1939.* Berkeley: University of California Press, 2006.

Molotch, Harvey. *Against Security: How We Go Wrong at Airports, Subways, and Other Sites of Ambiguous Danger.* Princeton, NJ: Princeton University Press, 2012.

Monahan, Torin, and Rodolfo D. Torres, eds. *Schools Under Surveillance: Cultures of Control in Public Education.* New Brunswick, NJ: Rutgers University Press, 2010.

Moore, Joan W. *Homeboys: Gangs, Drugs, and Prison in the Barrios of Los Angeles.* Philadelphia: Temple University Press, 1978.

Moore, Marijo, ed. *Eating Fire, Tasting Blood: An Anthology of the American Indian Holocaust.* Philadelphia: Running Press, 2006.

Morales, Armando. *Ando Sangrando (I Am Bleeding): A Study of Mexican American–Police Conflict.* La Puente, CA: Perspectiva, 1972.

Morris, James McGrath. *Jailhouse Journalism: The Fourth Estate Behind Bars.* Jefferson, NC: McFarland, 1998.

Morris, Norval, and Gordon Hawkins. *Letter to the President on Crime Control.* Chicago: University of Chicago Press, 1977.

Muhammad, Khalil Gibran. *The Condemnation of Blackness: Race, Crime, and the Making of Modern Urban America.* Cambridge, MA: Harvard University Press, 2010.

Murakawa, Naomi. *The First Civil Right: How Liberals Built Prison America.* New York: Oxford University Press, 2014.

Murrin, John, Paul E. Johnson, James McPherson, Alice Fahs, and Gary Gerstle. *Liberty, Equality, Power: A History of the American People.* Fort Worth: Harcourt Brace, 1996.

Murton, Tom, and Joe Hyams. *Accomplices to the Crime.* New York: Grove, 1969.

Myrdal, Gunnar. *An American Dilemma: The Negro Problem and Modern Democracy.* 2 vols. New York: Harper & Brothers, 1944.

Nabokov, Peter, ed. *Native American Testimony: A Chronicle of Indian-White Relations from Prophecy to the Present, 1492–1992.* New York: Viking Penguin, 1991.

Nagel, William G. *The New Red Barn: A Critical Look at the Modern American Prison.* Philadelphia: American Foundation, 1973.

National Action/Research on the Military-Industrial Complex (NARMIC). *Police on the Homefront: A Collection of Essays.* Philadelphia: American Friends Service Committee, 1971.

National Advisory Commission on Civil Disorders (the Kerner Commission). *Report.* New York: E. P. Dutton, 1968.

———. *Supplemental Studies.* Washington, DC: USGPO, 1968.

National Commission on Law Observance and Enforcement. *Report on Lawlessness in Law Enforcement.* Washington, DC: USGPO, 1931.

———. *Report on Penal Institutions.* Washington, DC: USGPO, 1931.

———. *Report on the Causes of Crime.* Vol. 1. Washington, DC: USGPO, 1931.

National Urban League. *Black Families in the 1974–1975 Depression.* Washington, DC: National Urban League, 1975.

Nellis, Ashley. *The Color of Justice: Racial and Ethnic Disparity in State Prisons.* Washington, DC: Sentencing Project, 2016. http://www.sentencingproject.org/wp-content/uploads/2016/06/The-Color-of-Justice-Racial-and-Ethnic-Disparity-in-State-Prisons.pdf.

Newman, Oscar. *Defensible Space: Crime Prevention Through Urban Design.* New York: Macmillan, 1973.

Newton, Huey P. "A Citizens' Peace Force." *Crime and Social Justice* 1 (Spring–Summer 1974): 36–39.

Noonan, Margaret E. *Mortality in Local Jails, 2000–2014—Statistical Tables.* Washington, DC: Bureau of Justice Statistics, 2016. https://www.bjs.gov/content/pub/pdf/mlj0014st.pdf.

Noonan, Margaret, and Scott Ginder. *Mortality in Local Jails and State Prisons, 2000–2012—Statistical Tables.* Washington, DC: Bureau of Justice Statistics, 2014. https://www.bjs.gov/content/pub/pdf/mljsp0012st.pdf.

Norfolk Prison Brothers. *Who Took the Weight? Black Voices from Norfolk Prison.* Foreword by Elma Lewis. Boston: Little, Brown, 1972.

Nourse, Victoria F. *In Reckless Hands: Skinner v. Oklahoma and the Near Triumph of American Eugenics.* New York: W. W. Norton, 2008.

Novak, Nicole, Kate O'Connor, Natalie Lira, and Alexandra Minna Stern. *Ethnic Bias in California's Eugenic Sterilization Program, 1920–1945.* Ann Arbor: University of Michigan Population Studies Center, June 2016.

Oakley, Robert B., Michael J. Dziedzic, and Eliot M. Goldberg. *Policing the New World*

Disorder: Peace Operations and Public Security. Washington, DC: National Defense University Press, 1998.

Obama, Barack. *The Audacity of Hope: Thoughts on Reclaiming the American Dream.* New York: Three Rivers, 2006.

———. "The President's Role in Advancing Criminal Justice Reform." *Harvard Law Review* 130 (2017): 811–66.

Odem, Mary. *Delinquent Daughters: Protecting and Policing Adolescent Female Sexuality in the United States, 1885–1920.* Chapel Hill: University of North Carolina Press, 1995.

Office of Personnel Management. *Sizing Up the Executive Branch: Fiscal Year 2013.* Washington, DC: Office of Personnel Management, 2014. https://www.opm.gov/policy-data-oversight/data-analysis-documentation/federal-employment-reports/reports-publications/sizing-up-the-executive-branch.pdf.

O'Hare, Kate Richards. *In Prison.* New York: Alfred A. Knopf, 1923.

Okihiro, Gary Y. *Margins and Mainstreams: Asians in American History and Culture.* Seattle: University of Washington Press, 1994.

Olasky, Marvin. *The Tragedy of American Compassion.* Washington, DC: Regnery, 1995.

O'Leary, Cecilia E. *To Die For: The Paradox of American Patriotism.* Princeton, NJ: Princeton University Press, 1999.

Oppenheimer, Martin, Martin J. Murray, and Rhonda F. Levine, eds. *Radical Sociologists and the Movement: Experiences, Lessons, and Legacies.* Philadelphia: Temple University Press, 1991.

Ordover, Nancy. *American Eugenics: Race, Queer Anatomy, and the Science of Nationalism.* Minneapolis: University of Minnesota Press, 2003.

O'Reilly, Conor. "The Pluralization of High Policing: Convergence and Divergence at the Public-Private Interface." *British Journal of Criminology* 55, no. 4 (January 2015): 688–710.

O'Reilly, Kenneth. *"Racial Matters": The FBI's Secret File on Black America, 1960–1972.* New York: Free Press, 1989.

Orwell, George. *Why I Write.* New York: Penguin, 2005.

Oshinsky, David M. *"Worse Than Slavery": Parchman Farm and the Ordeal of Jim Crow Justice.* New York: Free Press, 1997.

Ottely, Roy, and William J. Wetherby, eds. *The Negro in New York: An Informal Social History.* New York: Oceana, 1967.

Parker, Alfred E. *Crime Fighter: August Vollmer.* New York: Macmillan, 1961.

Parks, Gordon. "Harlem Gang Leader." *Life,* November 1, 1948, 96–106.

Patterson, Orlando. *Slavery and Social Death: A Comparative Study.* Cambridge, MA: Harvard University Press, 1982.

Patterson, William L. *We Charge Genocide: The Historic Petition to the United Nations for Relief from a Crime of the United States Government Against the Negro People.* 3d ed. New York: Civil Rights Congress, 1952.

Peiss, Kathy. *Cheap Amusements: Working Women and Leisure in Turn-of-the-Century New York.* Philadelphia: Temple University Press, 1986.

Pell, Eve, ed. *Maximum Security: Letters from California's Prisons.* New York: E. P. Dutton, 1972.

Perkinson, Robert. *Texas Tough: The Rise of America's Prison Empire*. New York: Metropolitan Books, 2010.

Perlstein, Rick. *Nixonland: The Rise of a President and the Fracturing of America*. New York: Scribner, 2008.

Pettit, Becky. *Invisible Men: Mass Incarceration and the Myth of Black Progress*. New York: Russell Sage Foundation, 2012.

Pfaelzer, Jean. *Driven Out: Roundups, Resistance, and the Forgotten War Against Chinese Americans*. New York: Random House, 2007.

Phillips, George Harwood. *Indians and Indian Agents: The Origins of the Reservation System in California, 1849–1852*. Norman: University of Oklahoma Press, 1997.

Piven, Frances Fox. "Welfare and Work." *Social Justice* 25, no. 1 (1998): 67–81.

Piven, Frances Fox, and Richard Cloward. *Poor People's Movements: Why They Succeed, How They Fail*. New York: Pantheon, 1977.

———. *Regulating the Poor: The Functions of Public Welfare*. New York: Pantheon, 1971.

Platt, Anthony M. (Tony). *Bloodlines: Recovering Hitler's Nuremberg Laws, from Patton's Trophy to Public Memorial*. Boulder, CO: Paradigm, 2006.

———. *The Child Savers: The Invention of Delinquency*. New Brunswick, NJ: Rutgers University Press, 2009.

———. *E. Franklin Frazier Reconsidered*. New Brunswick, NJ: Rutgers University Press, 1991.

———. "End Game: The Rise and Fall of Affirmative Action in Higher Education." *Social Justice* 24, no. 2 (1997): 103–18.

———. "'If We Know, Then We Must Fight': The Origins of Radical Criminology in the United States." In *Radical Sociologists and the Movement: Experiences, Lessons, and Legacies*. Edited by Martin Oppenheimer, Martin J. Murrary, and Rhonda F. Levine. Philadelphia: Temple University Press, 1991.

———. "In Recovery from Rehab." *South Atlantic Quarterly* 113, no. 3 (Summer 2014): 614–20.

———. "'The Land That Never Has Been Yet': U.S. Relations at the Crossroads." *Social Justice* 24, no. 1 (Spring 1997): 7–23.

———. "'Living with Inequality': Race and the Changing Discourse of Victimization in the United States." *Comparative Law Review* 29, no. 4 (1996): 1–30.

———. "No Easy Road to Freedom: Remapping the Struggle for Racial Equality." *Social Justice* 22, no. 3 (Fall 1995): 9–27.

———, ed. *The Politics of Riot Commissions, 1917–1970: A Collection of Official Reports and Critical Essays*. New York: Macmillan, 1971.

———. "Prospects for a Radical Criminology in the United States." *Crime and Social Justice* 1 (1974): 1–10.

———. "Social Insecurity: The Transformation of American Criminal Justice, 1965–2000." *Social Justice* 28, no. 1 (2001): 138–55.

———. "The State of Welfare, United States 2003." *Monthly Review* 55, no. 5 (October 2003): 13–27.

———. "'Street' Crime—A View from the Left." *Crime and Social Justice* 9 (Spring–Summer 1978): 26–34.

———. "Vicariously We Punish." *Isis* 1435 (February 20, 1963): 13.

Platt, Anthony M., and Lynn Cooper, eds. *Policing America*. Englewood Cliffs, NJ: Prentice-Hall, 1974.

Platt, Tony, and Cecilia O'Leary. "Patriot Acts." *Social Justice* 30, no. 1 (2003): 5–21.

Platt, Tony, and Paul Takagi. "Intellectuals for Law and Order: A Critique of the New 'Realists.'" *Crime and Social Justice* 8 (Fall–Winter 1977): 1–16.

———. eds. *Punishment and Penal Discipline*. San Francisco: Crime and Social Justice Associates, 1980.

Platt, Tony, Susie Bernstein, Lynn Cooper, Elliott Currie, Jon Frappier, Sidney Harring, Pat Poyner, Gerda Ray, Joy Scruggs, and Larry Trujillo. *The Iron Fist and the Velvet Glove: An Analysis of the U.S. Police*. 3d ed. San Francisco: Synthesis, 1982. First published in 1975 by the Center for Research on Criminal Justice, Berkeley, CA.

Popenoe, Paul, and Roswell Hill Johnson. *Applied Eugenics*. New York: Macmillan, 1926.

Porter, Nicole D. *Repurposing: New Beginnings for Closed Prisons*. Washington, DC: Sentencing Project, 2016. http://www.sentencingproject.org/publications/repurposing-new-beginnings-closed-prisons/.

President's Commission on Law Enforcement and the Administration of Justice (the Crime Commission). *The Challenge of Crime in a Free Society*. Washington, DC: USGPO, 1967.

———. *Juvenile Delinquency and Youth Crime*. Washington, DC: USGPO, 1967.

———. *Task Force Report: The Courts*. Washington, DC: USGPO, 1967.

———. *Task Force Report: Crime and Its Impact—An Assessment*. Washington, DC: USGPO, 1967.

———. *Task Force Report: The Police*. Washington, DC: USGPO, 1967.

———. *Task Force Report: Science and Technology*. Washington, DC: USGPO, 1967.

President's Committee on Civil Rights. *To Secure These Rights: The Report of the President's Committee on Civil Rights*. Washington, DC: USGPO, 1947.

President's Task Force on 21st Century Policing. *Final Report*. Washington, DC: Department of Justice, Office of Community Oriented Policing Services, May 2015.

Preston, Julia. "Lost in Court." *The Marshall Project*, January 19, 2018. https://www.themarshallproject.org/2018/01/19/lost-in-court.

———. "Trump: The New Deportation Threat." *The New York Review of Books*, May 25, 2017, 8–12.

Preston, William, Jr. *Aliens and Dissenters: Federal Suppression of Radicals, 1903–1933*. Urbana: University of Illinois Press, 1963.

Price, Joshua. *Prison and Social Death*. New Brunswick, NJ: Rutgers University Press, 2015.

Provine, Doris Marie, Monica W. Varsanyi, and Paul G. Lewis. *Policing Immigrants: Local Law Enforcement on the Front Lines*. Chicago: University of Chicago Press, 2016.

Quigley, William P. "Demise of Law Reform and Triumph of Legal Aid." *Saint Louis University Public Law Review* 17 (1998): 256–58.

Rainwater, Lee, and William L. Yancey, eds. *The Moynihan Report and the Politics of Controversy*. Cambridge, MA: MIT Press, 1967.

Rakoff, Jed S. "The Financial Crisis: Why Have No High-Level Executives Been Prosecuted?" *The New York Review of Books*, January 9, 2014. http://www.nybooks.com /articles/2014/01/09/financial-crisis-why-no-executive-prosecutions.

———. "Why Innocent People Plead Guilty." *The New York Review of Books*, November 20, 2014. http://www.nybooks.com/articles/2014/11/20/why-innocent-people -plead-guilty/.

Rawls, James. *Indians of California: The Changing Image*. Norman: University of Oklahoma Press, 1984.

Reaves, Brian. *Felony Defendants in Large Urban Counties, 2009—Statistical Tables*. Washington, DC: Bureau of Justice Statistics, 2013. http://www.bjs.gov/content/pub /pdf/fdluc09.pdf.

———. *Law Enforcement Officers, 1975–1998 (Sworn Personnel)*. Washington, DC: Bureau of Justice Statistics, 2003. https://www.bjs.gov/index.cfm?ty=pbdetail&iid=2049.

Reed, Austin. *The Life and Adventures of a Haunted Convict*. Edited by Caleb Smith. New York: Modern Library, 2016.

Regnery, Alfred S. *The Poverty Agencies: Community Services Administration, Legal Services Corporation*. Washington, DC: Heritage Foundation, 1980.

Reichel, Philip. "Southern Slave Patrols as a Transitional Police Type." *American Journal of Police* 1 (1988): 51–78.

Reiter, Keramet. *23/7: Pelican Bay Prison and the Rise of Long-Term Solitary Confinement*. New Haven, CT: Yale University Press, 2016.

Rhode, Deborah. *Access to Justice*. Oxford: Oxford University Press, 2004.

Rhodes, Lorna A. *Total Confinement: Madness and Reason in the Maximum Security Prison*. Berkeley: University of California Press, 2004.

Richardson, James F. *The New York Police: Colonial Times to 1901*. New York: Oxford University Press, 1970.

Richie, Beth E. *Arrested Justice: Black Women, Violence, and America's Prison Nation*. New York: New York University Press, 2012.

Rios, Jodi. "Flesh in the Street." *Kalfou* 3, no. 1 (Spring 2016): 63–78.

Rios, Victor. *Punished: Policing the Lives of Black and Latino Boys*. New York: New York University Press, 2011.

Robin, Gerald R. "Justifiable Homicide by Police Officers." *The Journal of Criminal Law, Criminology, and Police Science* 54, no. 2 (June 1963): 225–31.

Roosevelt, Theodore. "Memorial Day Address," May 30, 1902. http://www.theodore -roosevelt.com/images/research/txtspeeches/11.txt.

Rosenfeld, Seth. *Subversives: The FBI's War on Student Radicals, and Reagan's Rise to Power*. New York: Farrar, Straus & Giroux, 2012.

Roth, Jessica. "It Is Lawyers We Are Funding: A Constitutional Challenge to the 1996 Restrictions on the Legal Services Corporation." *Harvard Civil Rights–Civil Liberties Law Review* 33 (1998): 107–58.

Rothstein, Richard. *The Color of Law: A Forgotten History of How Our Government Segregated America*. New York: Liveright, 2018.

Rovner, Joshua. *Declines in Youth Commitments and Facilities in the 21st Century*. Washington, DC: Sentencing Project, 2015. http://sentencingproject.org/doc/publications /Youth-Commitments-and-Facilities.pdf.

Rowbotham, Sheila. *Hidden from History*. London: Pluto, 1973.

Rusche, Georg, and Otto Kirchheimer. *Punishment and Social Structure.* New York: New York University Press, 1967.

Sakala, Leah. *Breaking Down Mass Incarceration in the 2010 Census: State-by-State Rates of Race/Ethnicity.* Northampton, MA: Prison Policy Initiative, May 28, 2010. https://www.prisonpolicy.org/reports/rates.html.

Sarri, Rosemary C. *Under Lock and Key: Juveniles in Jails and Detention.* Ann Arbor: University of Michigan, National Assessment of Juvenile Corrections, 1974.

Sarri, Rosemary C., and Yeheskel Hasenfeld, eds. *Brought to Justice?* Ann Arbor: University of Michigan, National Assessment of Juvenile Corrections, 1976.

Saunders, Frances Stonor. *Who Paid the Piper? The CIA and the Cultural Cold War.* London: Granta Books, 1999.

Schechter, Patricia. *Ida B. Wells-Barnett and American Reform, 1880–1930.* Chapel Hill: University of North Carolina Press, 2001.

Schuilenburg, Marc. *The Securitization of Society: Crime, Risk, and Social Disorder.* New York: New York University Press, 2015.

Schwartz, Bonnie Fox. *The Civil Works Administration, 1933–1934: The Business of Emergency Employment in the New Deal.* Princeton, NJ: Princeton University Press, 1984.

Schweik, Susan M. *The Ugly Laws: Disability in Public.* New York: New York University Press, 2009.

Schwendinger, Herman, and Julia Schwendinger. "Defenders of Order or Guardians of Human Rights?" *Issues in Criminology* 5, no. 2 (Summer 1970): 123–58.

Scraton, Phil, ed. *Beyond September 11: An Anthology of Dissent.* London: Pluto, 2002.

Seigel, Micol. "Objects of Police History." *Journal of American History* 102, no. 1 (June 2015): 152–61.

Sellin, Thorsten. "The Negro Criminal: A Statistical Note." *Annals of the American Academy of Political and Social Science* 140 (November 1928): 52–53.

———. *Pioneering in Penology: The Amsterdam Houses of Correction in the Sixteenth and Seventeenth Centuries.* Philadelphia: University of Pennsylvania Press, 1944.

———. *Slavery and the Penal System.* New York: Elsevier, 1976.

Sentencing Project. "State-by-State Data." Criminal Justice Facts. 2016. http://www.sentencingproject.org/the-facts/#map?dataset-option=SIR.

———. "U.S. Prison Population Trends 1999–2015: Modest Reductions with Significant Variations." Fact Sheet: US Prison Population Trends. 2017. http://www.sentencingproject.org/publications/u-s-prison-population-trends-1999-2015-modest-reductions-significant-variation/.

———. "Report of the Sentencing Project to the United Nations Special Rapporteur on Contemporary Forms of Racism, Racial Discrimination, Xenophobia, and Related Intolerance: Regarding Racial Disparities in the United States Criminal Justice System." March 2018. https://www.sentencingproject.org/wp-content/uploads/2018/04/UN-Report-on-Racial-Disparities.pdf.

———. "Incarcerated Women and Girls, 1980–2016." May 2018. http://www.sentencingproject.org/publications/incarcerated-women-and-girls/.

Shannon, Sarah K. S., C. Uggen, J. Schnittker, M. Thompson, S. Wakefield, and M. Massoglia. "The Growth, Scope, and Spatial Distribution of People with Felony Records in the United States, 1948–2010." *Demography* 54 (2017): 1795–1818.

Shearing, Clifford D., and Philip C. Stenning, eds. *Private Policing*. Newbury Park, CA: Sage, 1987.

Silber, Rebecca, Ram Subramanian, and Maia Spotts. *Justice in Review: New Trends in State Sentencing and Corrections 2014–2015*. New York: Vera Institute of Justice, 2016.

Simon, Jonathan. *Governing Through Crime: How the War on Crime Transformed American Democracy and Created a Culture of Fear*. New York: Oxford University Press, 2007.

———. *Mass Incarceration on Trial: A Remarkable Court Decision and the Future of Prisons in America*. New York: The New Press, 2014.

Sklansky, David Alan. "Private Police and Democracy." *American Criminal Law Review* 43 (2006): 89–106.

Skocpol, Theda. *Protecting Soldiers and Mothers*. Cambridge, MA: Harvard University Press, 1992.

Skolnick, Jerome. "The Police and the Urban Ghetto." *Research Contributions of the American Bar Foundation* 3 (1968): 1–29.

———, dir. *The Politics of Protest: Task Force on Violent Aspects of Protest and Confrontation of the National Commission on the Causes and Prevention of Violence*. New York: Simon & Schuster, 1969.

———. "Social Control in the Adversary System." *Journal of Conflict Resolution* 11 (1967): 52–70.

Skolnick, Jerome H., and James J. Fyfe. *Above the Law: Policy and the Excessive Use of Force*. New York: Free Press, 1993.

Slahi, Mohamedou Ould. *Guantánamo Diary*. Edited by Larry Siems. New York: Little, Brown, 2015.

Slotkin, Richard. *The Fatal Environment: The Myth of the Frontier in the Age of Industrialization*. New York: Atheneum, 1985.

Smith, Anna Deavere. *Twilight Los Angeles, 1992*. New York: Anchor, 1994.

Snell, Tracy. *Correctional Populations in the United States, 1993*. Washington, DC: Bureau of Justice Statistics, 1995. https://www.bjs.gov/content/pub/pdf/cpop93bk.pdf.

Snyder, Howard. *Arrest in the United States, 1980–2009*. Washington, DC: Bureau of Justice Statistics, 2011. https://www.bjs.gov/content/pub/pdf/aus8009.pdf.

Sobell, Morton. *On Doing Time*. New York: Charles Scribner's Sons, 1974.

Solinger, Rickie. "Dependency and Choice: The Two Faces of Eve." *Social Justice* 25, no. 1 (1998): 1–27.

Soss, Joe, Richard C. Fording, and Sanford F. Schram. *Disciplining the Poor: Neoliberal Paternalism and the Persistent Power of Race*. Chicago: University of Chicago Press, 2011.

Speiglman, Richard. "Prison Psychiatrists and Drugs: A Case Study." *Crime and Social Justice* 7 (Spring–Summer 1977): 23–39.

Stampp, Kenneth M. *The Peculiar Institution: Slavery in the Ante-Bellum South*. New York: Alfred A. Knopf, 1961.

Stansell, Christine. *City of Women: Sex and Class in New York, 1789–1860*. New York: Alfred A. Knopf, 1986.

Stark, Rodney N. *Police Riots: Collective Violence and Law Enforcement*. Belmont, CA: Wadsworth, 1972.

Steele, Shelby. "The New Sovereignty." *Harper's*, June 1992, 47–54.

Steiner, Jesse F., and Roy M. Brown. *The North Carolina Chain Gang*. Chapel Hill: University of North Carolina Press, 1927.

Stern, Alexandra Minna. *Eugenic Nation: Faults and Frontiers of Better Breeding in Modern America*. Berkeley: University of California Press, 2005.

———. "Sterilized in the Name of Public Health: Race, Immigration, and Reproductive Control in Modern California." *American Journal of Public Health* 95, no. 7 (2005): 1128–38.

Stern, Sol. "A Short Account of International Student Politics and the Cold War with Particular Reference to the NSA, CIA, etc." *Ramparts*, March 1967, 29–39.

Stevenson, Bryan. "A Presumption of Guilt." *New York Review of Books*, July 13, 2107, 8–10.

———. *Just Mercy: A Story of Justice and Redemption*. New York: Spiegel & Grau, 2014.

Strom, Kevin, Marcus Berzofsky, Bonnie Shook-Sa, Kelle Barrick, Crystal Daye, Nicole Horstmann, and Susan Kinsey. *The Private Security Industry: A Review of the Definitions, Available Data Sources, and Paths Moving Forward*. Research Triangle Park, NC: RTI International, 2010. https://www.ncjrs.gov/pdffiles1/bjs/grants/232781.pdf.

Stumpf, Juliet. "The Crimmigration Crisis: Immigrants, Crime, and Sovereign Power." *American University Law Review* 56, no. 2 (2006): 367–419.

Stuntz, William J. *The Collapse of American Criminal Justice*. Cambridge, MA: Harvard University Press, 2011.

Subramanian, Ram, Ruth Delaney, Stephen Roberts, Nancy Fishman, and Peggy McGarry. *Incarceration's Front Door: The Misuse of Jails in America* New York: Vera Institute of Justice, 2015.

Sudbury, Julia. "Toward a Holistic Anti-Violence Agenda: Women of Color as Radical Bridge-Builders." *Social Justice* 30, no. 3 (2003): 134–40.

Sutherland, Edwin H. "Is 'White Collar Crime' Crime?" *American Sociological Review* 10, no. 2 (1944): 132–39.

Suvak, Daniel. *Memoirs of American Prisons: An Annotated Bibliography*. Metuchen, NJ: Scarecrow, 1979.

Swavola, Elizabeth, Kristine Riley, and Ram Subramanian. *Overlooked: Women and Jails in an Era of Reform*. New York: Vera Institute of Justice, 2016.

Taibbi, Matt. *I Can't Breathe: A Killing on Bay Street*. New York: Spiegel & Grau, 2017.

Takagi, Paul. "Growing Up a Japanese Boy in Sacramento County." *Social Justice* 26, no. 2 (1999): 135–49.

———. "A Garrison State in a 'Democratic' Society." *Crime & Social Justice* 1 (Spring–Summer 1974): 27–33

Takagi, Paul, and Tony Platt. "Behind the Gilded Ghetto: An Analysis of Race, Class and Crime in Chinatown." *Crime and Social Justice* 9 (Spring–Summer 1978): 2–25.

Taylor, Keeanga-Yamahtta. *From #Black Lives Matter to Black Liberation*. Chicago: Haymarket, 2016.

Terrell, Mary Church. "Peonage in the United States: The Convict Lease System and the Chain Gangs." *The Nineteenth Century and After* 62 (July–December 1907): 806–22.

Terman, Lewis. *The Measurement of Intelligence*. Boston: Houghton Mifflin, 1916.

Thomas, Piri. *Down These Mean Streets*. New York: Alfred A. Knopf, 1981.

———. *Seven Long Times*. New York: Praeger, 1974.

Thompkins, Douglas E. "The Expanding Prisoner Reentry Industry." *Dialectical Anthropology* 34 (2010): 589–604.

Thompson, E. P. *The Making of the English Working Class.* New York: Vintage, 1966.

Thompson, Ginger. "Trafficking in Terror." *The New Yorker,* December 14, 2015, 60–69.

Thompson, Heather Ann. *Blood in the Water: The Attica Uprising of 1971 and Its Legacy.* New York: Pantheon, 2016.

Tonry, Michael. "Why Are U.S. Incarceration Rates So High?" *Crime and Delinquency* 45, no. 4 (1999): 419–37.

Travis, Jeremy, Bruce Western, and Steve Redburn, eds. *The Growth of Incarceration in the United States: Explaining Causes and Consequences.* Washington, DC: National Academies Press, 2014.

Tribe, Laurence. "An Ounce of Detention: Preventive Justice in the World of John Mitchell." *Virginia Law Review* 56, no. 3 (1970): 371–407.

Trump, Donald J. *The America We Deserve.* Los Angeles: Renaissance Books, 2000.

———. *Time to Get Tough: Making America #1 Again.* Washington, DC: Regnery, 2011.

US Congress. House. Committee on the Judiciary. *Investigation of Misconduct and Mismanagement at ICITAP, OPDAT, and Criminal Division's Office of Administration.* 106th Cong., 2d sess. Washington, DC: USGPO, 2000.

———. Senate. Permanent Subcommittee on Investigations. *U.S. Vulnerabilities to Money Laundering, Drugs, and Terrorist Financing: HSBC Case History.* 107th Cong., 2d sess. Washington, DC: Permanent Subcommittee on Investigations, 2012.

———. Senate. Select Committee on Intelligence. *Report on Torture: Committee Study of the Central Intelligence Agency's Detention and Interrogation Program.* New York: Melville House, 2014.

US Department of the Army. *Operations Report—Lessons Learned, Civil Disturbances, April 1968.* Washington, DC: Office of the Adjutant General, US Army, 1968.

United Nations General Assembly. "United Nations Standard Minimum Rules for the Treatment of Prisoners (the Mandela Rules)," 2015. https://documents-dds-ny.un.org /doc/UNDOC/GEN/N15/295/06/PDF/N1529506.pdf?OpenElement.

Van den Haag, Ernest. *Punishing Criminals.* New York: Basic Books, 1975.

Vigil, Ernesto B. *The Crusade for Justice: Chicano Militancy and the Government's War on Dissent.* Madison: University of Wisconsin Press, 1999.

Vinter, Robert D., ed. *Time Out: A National Study of Juvenile Correctional Programs.* Ann Arbor: National Assessment of Juvenile Corrections, 1976.

Vitale, Alex S. *The End of Policing.* London: Verso, 2017.

Wacquant, Loïc. "Deadly Symbiosis: When Ghetto and Prison Meet and Mesh." *Punishment & Society* 3, no. 1 (2001): 95–133.

———. "From Slavery to Mass Incarceration." *New Left Review* 13 (January–February 2002): 41–60.

———. "Prisoner Reentry as Myth and Ceremony." *Dialectical Anthropology* 34 (2010): 605–20.

———. *Punishing the Poor.* Durham, NC: Duke University Press, 2009.

Wagner, Peter, and Daniel Knopf. *The Racial Geography of Mass Incarceration.* Northampton, MA: Prison Policy Initiative, July 2015. http://www.prisonpolicy.org /racialgeography/report.html.

Wagner, Peter, and Bernadette Rabuy. *Following the Money of Mass Incarceration.* Northampton, MA: Prison Policy Initiative, January 25, 2017. https://www.prison policy.org/reports/money.html.

Wagner, Peter, and Alison Watch. "State of Incarceration: The Global Context." Press release. Prison Policy Initiative. June 16, 2016. https://www.prisonpolicy.org/global /2016.html.

Wald, Patricia, and Daniel Freed. "The Bail Reform Act of 1966: A Practitioner's Primer." *American Bar Association Journal* 52, no. 10 (1966): 940–45.

Walker, Alice. *In Search of Our Mothers' Gardens.* New York: Harcourt Brace Jovanovich, 1983.

———. "The Civil Rights Movement: What Good Was It?" *American Scholar* (Autumn 1967): 554.

Walker, Nancy A., ed. *Women's Magazines 1940–1960: Gender Roles and the Popular Press.* Boston: Bedford/St. Martin's, 1988.

Walkowitz, Daniel J. "The Making of a Feminine Professional Identity: Social Workers in the 1920s." *American Historical Review* 95 (October 1990): 1051–75.

Wallerstein, Immanuel. "The Agonies of Liberalism: What Hope Progress?" *New Left Review* 204 (March–April 1994): 3–17.

———. *Unthinking Social Science: The Limits of Nineteenth Century Paradigms.* Cambridge, MA: Polity, 1991.

Walsh, Alison. "The Criminal Justice System Is Riddled with Racial Disparities." Prison Policy Initiative, August 15, 2016. https://www.prisonpolicy.org/blog/2016/08/15 /cjrace/.

Ward, Geoff K. *The Black Child Savers: Racial Democracy and Juvenile Justice.* Chicago: University of Chicago Press, 2012.

Weaver, Vesla M. "Frontlash: Race and the Development of Punitive Crime Policy." *Studies in American Political Development* 21 (Fall 2007): 230–65.

Webb, Walter Prescott. *The Texas Rangers: A Century of Frontier Defense.* 2d ed. Austin: University of Texas Press, 1980. First published in 1935.

Weinstein, James. *The Corporate Ideal in the Liberal State, 1900–1918.* Boston: Beacon, 1969.

Weiss, Robert. "Guest Editor's Interview with Frank Smith and Akil Al-Jundi." *Social Justice* 18, no. 3 (Fall 1991): 84–91.

West, Heather C., and William Sabol. *Prisoners in 2007.* Washington, DC: Bureau of Justice Statistics, 2009. https://www.bjs.gov/content/pub/pdf/p07.pdf.

Whitaker, Reg. "The Surveillance State." *The Politics of the Right: Socialist Register* 52 (2016): 347–73.

White House Council of Economic Advisers. "Fines, Fees, and Bail: Payments in the Criminal Justice System That Disproportionately Impact the Poor." Issue Brief, December 2015. https://obamawhitehouse.archives.gov/sites/default/files/page/files /1215_cea_fine_fee_bail_issue_brief.pdf.

Widra, Emily. *Tracking the Impact of the Prison System on the Economy.* Northampton, MA: Prison Policy Initiative, December 7, 2017. https://www.prisonpolicy.org/reports /money.html.

Wiebe, Robert H. *Businessmen and Reform: A Study of the Progressive Movement.* Cambridge, MA: Harvard University Press, 1962.

Wilbanks, William. *The Myth of a Racist Criminal Justice System.* Monterey, CA: Brooks/Cole, 1987.

Wilde, Oscar. *De Profundis.* Preface by Robert Ross. London: Methuen, 1912.

———. *De Profundis and Other Writings.* Introduction by Hesketh Pearson. London: Penguin, 1986.

Wilkerson, Isabel. *The Warmth of Other Suns: The Epic Story of America's Great Migration.* New York: Random House, 2010.

Wilkins, Roy, and Ramsey Clark, chairmen. *Search and Destroy: A Report by the Commission of Inquiry into the Black Panthers and the Police.* New York: Metropolitan Applied Research Center, 1973.

Williams, Jay, and Martin Gold. "From Delinquent Behavior to Official Delinquency." *Social Problems* 20, no. 2 (Fall 1972): 209–29.

Williams, William Appleman. *The Contours of American History.* Chicago: Quadrangle, 1966.

Wilson, James Q. "The Rediscovery of Character: Private Virtue and Public Policy." *The Public Interest* 81 (Fall 1985): 3–16.

———. *Thinking About Crime.* New York: Vintage, 1977.

———. *Varieties of Police Behavior.* Cambridge, MA: Harvard University Press, 1968.

Wines, Enoch C. *The State of Prisons and of Child-Saving Institutions in the Civilized World.* Cambridge, MA: Harvard University Press, 1880.

Wiseman, Samuel. "Discrimination, Coercion, and the Bail Reform Act of 1984: The Loss of the Core Constitutional Protections of the Excessive Bail Clause." *Fordham Urban Law Journal* 36 (2009): 121–56.

Wolfe, Alan. "Political Repression and the Liberal Democratic State." *Monthly Review* 23, no. 7 (December 1971): 18–38.

Woodside, Moya. *Sterilization in North Carolina: A Sociological and Psychological Study.* Chapel Hill: University of North Carolina Press, 1950.

Woolredge, John, James Frank, Natalie Goulette, and Lawrence Travis III. "Is the Impact of Cumulative Disadvantage on Sentencing Greater for Black Defendants?" *Criminology and Public Policy* 14, no. 2 (May 2015): 187–223.

Woolsey, Lynn. "Living on Welfare—A Personal View." *Social Justice* 21, no. 1 (Spring 1994): 87–88.

Wright, Richard. *12 Million Black Voices.* New York: Viking, 1941.

X, Malcolm, and Alex Haley. *The Autobiography of Malcolm X.* New York: Grove, 1965.

Zatz, Marjorie. *Dreams and Nightmares: Immigration Policy, Youth, and Families.* Berkeley: University of California Press, 2015.

Zepeda-Millán, Chris. *Latino Mass Mobilization: Immigration, Racialization, and Activism.* Cambridge: Cambridge University Press, 2017.

Zimring, Franklin E. *When Police Kill.* Cambridge, MA: Harvard University Press, 2017.

Zornick, George. "The Disrupters: How the Youth Activists of #NeverAgain Are Upending Gun Politics." *The Nation,* April 30/May 7, 2018, 13–15.

Zucchino, David. *Myth of the Welfare Queen.* New York: Scribner, 1997.

INDEX

Abu Ghraib prison, 14, 127, 133, 143–144, 246
Addams, Jane, 166–167
adversary system, 29, 46–53, 211
affirmative action, 41–42, 78–82, 172, 249
African Americans
and the civil rights movement, 42, 60, 61, 77–80, 109, 120, 122, 151, 153, 177, 181–182, 185, 187, 188, 195, 221, 250, 251
    criminalization of, 12, 60, 61, 67, 155
    deaths of, 28, 58, 72–74, 85–86, 112
    and eugenics, 164–172
    incarceration of, 57–58, 74–76, 82–83
    and juvenile justice, 29–32, 74–75
    and police, 22, 84–91, 105–113, 115–116
    and public welfare, 37–46
    and "punitive turns," 77
    resistance by, 104, 109–110, 181–183, 187–189, 193–199, 223–224
    and segregation, 80–83
Agee, Philip, 127, 141, 191
Agnew, Spiro, 52, 107
Alexander, Michelle, 5, 200, 218
American Bar Association, 46, 51, 235

American Civil Liberties Union (ACLU), 99, 100, 114, 115, 200, 209
American Civil War, 40, 66, 94, 151
    and Reconstruction, 66–67, 73, 77, 78, 248
American Friends Service Committee, 23, 190
American Protective League, 99
Andersonville Prison, 66
anti-communism, 140
armory, 61, 97
Arpaio, Joe, 118–119
Attica, 88, 182, 189, 195, 197–199, 205

"back the badge" bills, 238
backlash, 223–238
bail, 4, 26, 29, 38, 48–50, 60, 134, 247–248, 251
Baldwin, James, 5, 74, 84, 105, 110, 120, 189, 250
Balibar, Étienne, 16, 117
"ban the box" campaign, 221
Berkeley School of Criminology, 124, 188, 227, 258–264
Berkman, Alexander, 70, 177–178, 187

Bigo, Didier, 137
bipartisanship
    and criminal justice reforms,
        215–226
    and law and order, 120–126, 206–209
Black Codes, 61, 65–74
Black Lives Matter, 8, 13, 21, 60, 89, 101,
    122, 200, 224, 225, 238, 245
Black Panther Party for Self-Defense, 14,
    80, 107–110, 122, 171, 188–189, 194,
    199, 262–263
Blake, James, 4
Blankenship, Don, 26
"boomerang effect," 138–146
Brace, Charles Loring, 98
bracero program, 63–64
Bratton, Bill, 134, 244
Brodeur, Jean-Paul, 94–95
"broken windows" policy, 217, 231
Brown, Michael, Jr., 47, 86, 88
Brown v. Board of Education, 77
Bush, George H. W., 81, 208
Bush, George W., 14, 33, 36, 44, 77,
    118–119, 126, 133, 173

California
    and compulsory sterilization, 167–169,
        172
    genocide in, 61–63, 67–69
    prisoners' movement in, 195–197
    incarceration in, 35–36, 63, 72, 76,
        118–119, 151, 157, 195–196
capital punishment, 21, 26, 150, 199, 209,
    230–231, 251, 257
capitalism, 40, 67–68, 155, 235
carceral state
    cost of, 129, 213, 281–282
    defined, 5, 8, 14–18
    employment in, 278–281
    statistics, 209–215, 277–283
Carpenter, Mary, 157
Central Park Five, 230
chain gangs, 71–75, 102, 118, 154, 177,
    183
Cheney, Dick, 127
Chemerinksy, Erwin, 112
Chicago, 31, 41, 108, 115, 153, 159, 222
Chicano movement, 113–115
child-saving movement, 23, 152–158
Chinatown, 19, 63

Chinese
    and drug laws, 63
    ethnic cleansing of, 19
    in prison, 20, 72
    and resistance, 192
Church Committee, 141
Chute, Charles, 153
civilian review boards, 4, 119, 198–199
civility codes, 11, 159
Civil Rights Act of 1964, 78, 79
Civil Rights Congress, 104, 107
civil rights movement, 38, 78, 80, 104, 153
Clark, Stephon, 244
Clinton, Bill, 35, 43, 53, 206, 208–209, 215
Clinton, Hillary, 32, 100, 225, 239
Coates, Ta-Nehisi, 5, 77, 135, 200, 221
Cohen, Michael, 240
Cohen, Stan, 210, 246
Cold War, 126, 138, 143, 163
Comey, James, 32–33, 95, 100, 239–240
Commission on Training Camp
    Activities, 161–162
communists, 19, 64, 98, 99–100, 104, 106,
    107, 122, 140, 163, 173, 179, 185–186,
    227, 232, 258
Congress for Cultural Freedom, 140
convict lease system, 69–73, 182
Cooley, Charles, 156
CoreCivic (Corrections Corporation of
    America), 128–129, 133, 135
counterinsurgency, 13–14, 47, 66, 95, 98,
    123, 139, 146, 151
Crawford, John, III, 87–88
crime
    by corporations, 7–8, 26, 32–37
    and "quality of life" infractions, 47–48
    media images of, 152, 216
    selective enforcement of, 3–5, 6–8,
        25–29, 31, 32–37
    rates of, 229–230
criminal justice functionaries, 60, 191,
    243–246
criminal justice operations
    cost of, 6, 14, 126–127, 129–130, 142,
        212–215, 281–282
    statistics on, 277–281
criminalization, 11–12, 28–29, 38, 57, 60,
    61, 62–63, 66, 68, 155, 159
criminology, 38–39, 93, 124, 137, 187–188,
    216–218, 227, 251, 258–264

dangerousness, 49, 60, 63, 93, 100, 138, 144–146, 211, 216, 232
Dakota Access Pipeline protests, 136, 238
Daniels, Christopher, 60
Davis, Angela, 60, 135, 189
Debs, Eugene, 175, 185–188, 194, 195, 246, 253
Deferred Action for Childhood Arrivals (DACA), 242, 249
Democratic Party, 79, 80, 215, 259
deportation, 128–129
Dickens, Charles, 10, 23, 150
double system of justice, 5, 25–53
Du Bois, W. E. B., 5, 25, 38, 50, 67, 74–77, 106, 171
Dukakis, Michael, 208

Eastern State Penitentiary, 9–10, 150
Economic Opportunity Act of 1964, 52, 120, 151
Eighteenth Amendment, 162–163
Eisenhower, Dwight D., 136, 163
Emanuel, Rahm, 115, 223
embezzlement, 33
Escobar, Edward, 114
eugenics, 20, 23, 164–174
exceptional state, 57, 61, 65, 88, 126, 145–146, 245

fascism, 229, 253–254
Federal Bureau of Investigation (FBI), 32, 95, 100, 109, 121, 124, 126, 133, 240
    and civil rights crackdowns, 12, 106, 107
    and COINTELPRO, 108
    and James Comey, 240–241
    investigation of financial crimes by, 32–34, 37
    under attack by Trump, 240
    under leadership of J. Edgar Hoover, 240
    and Uniform Crime Reports, 30, 75, 282–283
Ferguson, Missouri, 47, 67, 86, 88, 115
financial fraud, 36
Flynn, Elizabeth Gurley, 179, 186
Folsom Manifesto, 197
Fogelson, Robert, 97
Foote, Caleb, 48, 260

Forman, James, Jr., 52
Fosdick, Raymond, 161
Foucault, Michel, 66, 68, 196, 217, 262
France, Anatole, 19
Franklin, John Hope, 70
Frazier, E. Franklin, 59, 106–107
Freedman's Bureau, 40
Freedom Riders, 181, 188

Galarza, Ernesto, 64
García, Juan, 113
Garner, Eric, 13, 25, 86–88
genocide, 62, 104, 192
GI Bill (Servicemen's Readjustment Act of 1944), 41, 79, 120
Gibbs, Jewelle Taylor, 111
Gideon v. Wainright, 50
Giuliani, Rudy, 35, 133
globalization, 63, 119, 134, 141, 146
Goethe, Charles M., 165
Goffman, Alice, 38
Golash-Boza, Tanya Maria, 64
Gray, Freddie, Jr., 84–86, 116, 188
Guantánamo Bay, Cuba, 127
guns, 18, 67, 90, 92, 100, 124, 131–132, 138, 216, 221, 224, 225, 236–237
Gupta, Vanita, 89
Gurley, Akai, 86, 88

Hacker, Jacob, 40
Hall, Jerome, 34, 96
Hall, Stuart, 206–207
Hallsworth, Simon, 146
Hamer, Fannie Lou, 78, 251
Hampton, Fred, 108
Hayes, Rutherford B., 97
Herrnstein, Richard, 81, 172
Hersh, Seymour, 140
Hinton, Elizabeth, 125, 208
Holder, Eric, 38, 88, 112
Hoover, Herbert, 98, 113
Hoover, J. Edgar, 30, 95, 102, 108–109, 111, 119, 122, 163, 191, 227, 240
Horton, William "Willie," 208–209
House Un-American Activities Committee, 106
houses of correction, 23, 67, 68
HSBC, 7, 33
Human Betterment Foundation, 165, 171
Huggins, Ericka, 108

immigration, 12–13, 15, 29, 47, 49, 65, 113,
    115, 126–127, 134–135, 137, 142, 165,
    214
  and Obama administration, 22,
    128–129
  and Trump administration, 224, 232,
    234, 237, 241, 242, 245
Ina, Itaru, 180
incarceration
  of African Americans, 57–58, 74–76,
    82–83
  of Chinese, 63
  of immigrants, 61
  of Japanese, 17, 61, 179–180, 242, 249,
    260, 261
  of Latinos, 63–65
  of Native Americans, 62
  rates of, 6, 20
  and solitary confinement, 6, 10, 19, 21,
    23, 74, 75, 144, 178, 186, 200, 221,
    222, 245, 252
  of women, 6, 12, 23, 27, 32, 37–38, 49,
    58, 70–72, 75, 149, 157, 162, 178–186,
    195–196
Indian boarding schools, 29, 62, 65, 69,
    158, 248
Indian reservations, 19, 62–63, 248
"insecurity syndrome," 16, 117
International Association of Chiefs of
    Police, 30, 82, 134, 259
International Criminal Investigative
    Training and Assistance Program
    (ICITAP), 143–144, 215
International Workers of the World, 99

Jackson, George, 24, 181–182, 195, 222
Jackson, Leonard "Red," 152, 216
Jessen, Bruce, 8, 117–118
Jim Crow, 19, 40, 69–75, 79, 105, 150, 159,
    181, 205, 250
John Birch Society, 107
Johnson, Lyndon, 28, 42, 78, 111, 120–121,
    123, 151, 152, 165, 206, 214
juvenile justice, 29–32, 51, 74–75, 92,
    153–158, 199, 209, 230, 238, 251

Kaepernick, Colin, 224–225, 243
Kafka, Franz, 9, 20
Kennedy, John F., 78
Kerik, Bernard, 35, 133, 238, 253

Kerner, Otto (Kerner Commission),
    79–80, 111, 121, 123
King, Martin Luther, Jr., 80, 109, 182, 187,
    194–195
Knight, Etheridge, 191, 255

Latinos/Latinas
  and eugenics, 169, 172
  incarceration of, 63–65
  and police, 113–116, 118–119
  and welfare, 40–45
"law and order"
  and the Clinton administration, 206,
    208–209, 215
  history of, 12, 97, 103–104, 123, 254
  and the Nixon administration, 206–208
  at state level, 118, 236–238
  and the Trump administration, 58,
    229–230, 232, 239, 243
Law Enforcement Assistance
    Administration (LEAA), 123–125,
    142, 214
Law Enforcement Leaders to Reduce
    Crime and Incarceration, 243–244
legal services, 52–53
Levi, Primo, 21, 176
Litwack, Leon, 73, 255
Locke, John, 68
London, Jack, 175, 178, 201
lynching, 19, 61, 62, 66, 73, 75, 103, 104,
    160, 250

Madoff, Bernie, 35
Manafort, Paul, 240
managerial reform
  and child-saving movement, 152–158
  and disability, 159
  and eugenics, 164–174
  and Indian boarding schools, 157–158
  and moral purity, 159–164
  and nation-building, 94, 173, 244–245
  and patriotism, 159–160
  and Progressive Era, 23, 71, 77, 94,
    154–156, 159, 164, 170
  and sexual repression, 149, 160–164
Manhattan Institute, the, 136, 145, 223
Marten, Lashawn, 26–27
Martin, Trayvon, 86, 87, 237
Marx, Gary, 96
McDonald, Heather, 223

McGirr, Lisa, 155
McLeod, Allegra, 143
Meese, Edwin, 227–228, 231, 238
Melville, Sam, 189, 198, 205
mental illness, 26–27
#MeToo, 250
"military-industrial complex," 136
militias, 61, 66, 94, 96–97, 101, 182
Mitchell, James, 8, 117–118
Molly Maguires, 95
Moore, Joan, 115
"moral zones," 162
Morales, Armando, 115
Moynihan, Daniel Patrick, 152
Mueller, Robert S., III, 239–240
Muhammad, Khalil, 76
Murray, Charles, 81, 172
Murton, Tom, 190–191
Myrdal, Gunnar, 103, 105, 151

National Advisory Commission on Civil
    Disorders (Kerner Commission), 79,
    87, 123
National Association for the
    Advancement of Colored People
    (NAACP), 86, 102
National Commission on Campus Unrest,
    87, 121
National Crime Victimization Surveys, 31
National Guard, 88, 97, 120, 121
National Rifle Association (NRA), 237,
    245
national security, 12, 15, 19, 60, 98–100,
    102, 118, 126–134, 138–146, 173, 211,
    242
National Urban League, 80
Native Americans
    and boarding schools, 157–158
    criminalization of, 32, 62, 68–69, 158
Negroponte, John, 127
neoliberalism, 206–207
New Deal, 40–41, 78, 120, 151
Newton, Huey, 199
New York Police Department, 100
Nixon, Richard, 49, 76, 82, 108, 120–121,
    125, 140, 206–207

Obama, Barack, 8, 18, 22, 25, 29, 57,
    86–87, 89–90, 91, 112, 118, 129, 209
Obama, Michelle, 226

O'Hare, Kate Richards, 161, 178, 180, 184,
    193
Omnibus Crime Control and Safe Streets
    Act of 1978, 123, 124
Operation Wetback, 63
Orwell, George, 20, 59
outsourcing, 43, 95, 119, 132–133, 135–136

Parker, William, 107, 114, 123
Parks, Gordon, 152
patriotism, 152, 159–160
Patterson, Orlando, 17
Pence, Mike, 235
Pendleton, Clarence, 82
Pershing, John, 99
Personal Opportunity and Work
    Responsibility Act of 1996, 43
Philippine-American War, 62, 98–99,
    138
Pinkerton National Detective Agency,
    94–95, 133, 136
Piven, Frances Fox, 39
Platt, Tony, 227, 251, 257–264
police
    in Baltimore, 47–48, 84–85, 116, 144,
        224
    and civil forfeiture, 130
    and counterinsurgency, 99–102,
        106–109
    and failure to control crime, 91–93
    and foreign policy, 98–99, 138–146
    governance of, 93–100
    history of, 91–116
    and John Birch Society, 107
    killings by, 22, 85–88, 221, 283
    and labor movement, 95–98
    in Los Angeles, 99, 107, 112, 123, 243
    militarization of, 93–100
    and Muslims, 61, 100–101, 234
    in New York, 4, 13, 61, 86, 87, 88, 93, 94,
        97, 100, 115, 134, 222, 225, 240
    and private security, 94–97
    reform of, 89–91
    and racism, 100–116
    riots, 110–112
    and slavery, 101
    and stop and frisk, 16, 26, 47, 111, 222,
        225
    transfer of military equipment to, 130,
        233

police (*cont'd*)
    Trump's relationship with, 22, 58–59,
        91, 113, 226, 229–232, 239
police-industrial complex, 124, 132–138
Poor People's Campaign, 39
Popenoe, Paul, 165–166
President's Commission on Law
    Enforcement and the
    Administration of Justice (Crime
    Commission), 28, 34, 93, 111, 121,
    124, 152, 154, 155
prison-industrial complex, 134
prisoners
    in Attica, 182, 189, 197–198, 205
    in California, 21–22, 151, 167, 189,
        195–197, 200
    as labor force, 10, 70–73, 196
    in Oklahoma, 167
    racial composition of, 6, 64–65, 70,
        75–76, 82–83
    in South, 74, 99
Prisons
    as "adjustment centers," 196
    and gerrymandering, 221
    history of, 57–83
    and rates of incarceration, 6, 12, 21, 37,
        57–58, 65
    and rehabilitation, 23, 32, 194, 196, 197,
        206, 258
    as sites of resistance, 191
    and United Nations standards, 104,
        251–252
    as warehouses of surplus labor, 135
private police, 11, 14–16, 47, 83, 91, 92,
    94–97, 99–100, 132–133, 210–213
private prisons, 135
Progressive Era, 76–77, 94, 154–155, 164,
    170
public defender system, 4, 50–52, 57, 213,
    247
Purdue Pharma, 35–36

racism, 6, 31, 40, 57, 60, 69–70, 74–81, 88,
    89, 101, 102, 104, 106, 108, 111, 116,
    119, 121, 126, 151, 154, 181, 187, 221,
    255, 258
Rakoff, Jed, 37, 46, 52
Raper, Arthur, 103–104, 105
Reagan, Ronald, 42–43, 49, 82, 123, 125,
    207–208, 214, 227

"reconcentration camps," 62
Reed, Austin, 177
Reich, Robert, 93
Religious Freedom Restoration Act, 235
Republican Party, 219–220
resistance, *see* African Americans, Black
    Lives Matter, Black Panther Party,
    Chinese, communists, Latinos,
    Japanese Americans, Native
    Americans, prisoners, socialists,
    women
Rhodes, Lorna, 9
Rice, Tamir, 86
Right on Crime, 219, 238, 243
Roosevelt, Franklin Delano, 40
Roosevelt, Theodore, 62, 93, 123
"rough ride," 84, 85, 188

Salas, Rudy, 116
Salazar, Rubén, 114
Sanders, Bernie, 221, 225
Schweik, Susan, 159
Scott, Walter, 87
Seale, Bobby, 189
security
    cultural preoccupations with, 15, 92
    growth of industry, 16, 22
    and public-private partnerships, 94–96,
        126–127, 132–138, 144–146
Sellin, Thorsten, 75
Sentencing Project, the, 104, 200,
    218
September 11, 2001, 19, 36, 61, 119, 126,
    130–131, 136, 142
Sessions, Jeff, 51, 53, 86, 91, 220, 232–233,
    240, 243
sexism, 20, 31, 37–46, 246
Smith, Anna Deavere, 116
social control, 11, 16, 18, 21, 23, 24, 123,
    124, 149–150, 152–153, 175, 213, 215,
    246, 249, 262
"social death," 17
socialists, 19, 50, 164, 175–176, 179,
    183–185, 193–194
Social Security, 41
Sotomayor, Sonia, 5, 8, 14, 116, 223,
    242
sterilization, 23, 164–174, 181, 192
Stern, Alexandra Minna, 169
Stewart, Terry, 144

Stevenson, Bryan, 46
Strieff, Edward, 3–4
structural reform
    policies, 193–199, 251–254
    and radical tradition, 175–201
    resistance to, 199–200, 244–249
    students, 21–22
Supplemental Nutrition Assistance
    Program (SNAP), 44
Sutherland, Edwin, 34

Task Force on 21st Century Policing, 87,
    89, 112, 220
Tate, Willie, 181–182
Temporary Assistance for Needy Families
    (TANF), 43
Terman, Lewis, 161, 165, 169
Terrell, Mary Church, 72, 183
Texas Rangers, 101
Thomas, Clarence, 5, 223
Thompson, E. P., 68
Toby, Jackson, 81
Tompkins Square Park riot, 97
torture, 117–118
Truman, Harry, 104, 126
Trump administration, 8
    convictions of senior members,
        239–240
    and Department of Justice, 53, 60, 86,
        135, 233–234, 242
    and deportation, 15, 22, 65, 113, 129,
        234, 249
    splits within, 32, 239–241
    and federal judiciary, 235–236
Trump, Donald J.
    as an advocate of "law and order," 22,
        90–91, 114, 119, 173, 217, 219,
        229–232, 243, 253
    and populism, 224–225
    and racism, 18, 58–59, 173–174
    and sexism, 46, 225, 237, 250
    and welfare, 45, 53, 231
    as presidential candidate, 99, 225
    as sexual predator, 225

un-Americanism, 124
Uniform Crime Reports (UCR), 30, 75,
    282–283
United Brands, 34
United Nations, 104

United States
    Agency for International Development
        (USAID), 139, 141, 143
    Army, 97
    Border Patrol (U.S. Customs and
        Border Protection), 128, 214
    Central Intelligence Agency, 117, 127,
        139–141, 252
    Commission on Civil Rights, 82
    Department of Defense, 123, 126–127,
        141
    Department of Homeland Security, 15,
        63, 65, 126–132, 130, 142–144, 204,
        233
    Department of Labor, 26
    Drug Enforcement Agency (DEA), 142
    Immigration and Custom Enforcement
        (ICE), 15
    Office of Public Safety (OPS), 13,
        138–139
U.S. Department of Justice, 134, 224
    Bureau of Justice Statistics, 31, 277–282
    and civil rights crackdowns, 102
    and civil rights investigations, 116, 222
    and deportation, 242
    and investigations of police
        departments, 47, 60, 85–86, 233–234
    and white-collar crimes, 35–36
    and the war on terror, 117–118, 125,
        128–129
Utah v. Strieff, 4–5, 116, 223

Vera Institute, 48–49
Vietnam War, 42, 78, 121, 139
Violence Commission (National
    Commission on the Causes and
    Prevention of Violence), 120–121
Vollmer, August, 93

Wagner Act of 1935, 41
Walker, Alice, 79
"war on crime," 21, 28, 77, 81, 83, 93, 120,
    123, 125, 206
"war on drugs," 21, 123, 125
War on Poverty, 42, 52, 78, 120, 206
"war on terror," 126–138
War Relocation Authority, 17
Warren, Elizabeth, 7
welfare, 37–46
Wells Fargo, 7

Wells, Ida B., 182
Weinstein, Harvey, 59
Westley, William, 106
Whitaker, Reg, 136
Wickersham Commission (National
    Commission on Law Observance and
    Law Enforcement), 102–103, 105, 151,
    214
Wilde, Oscar, 17–18
William J. Burns International Detective
    Agency, 94, 102, 133
Williams, Patricia, 45
Wilson, Darren, 47, 86, 88
Wilson, James Q., 81, 91, 172, 217–218,
    231
Wilson, Woodrow, 161
Wines, Enoch, 157
women
    as activists, 6, 12, 23, 27, 32, 37–38, 49,
        58, 70–72, 75, 149, 157, 162, 178–186,
        195–196

incarcerated, 6, 12, 23, 27, 32, 37–38, 49,
        58, 70–72, 75, 149, 157, 162, 178–186,
        195–196
    as victims of carceral state, 20, 38
    and welfare, 37–46
Woods, Arthur, 94
Workingman's Benevolent Association, 95
World War I, 98–99, 100, 149, 159, 161,
    173
World War II, 41, 61, 78, 100, 114, 120, 249
    and sterilization, 170
    and delinquency rates, 29–30
Wright, Richard, 106

X, Malcolm, 24, 154, 180, 185, 188, 192,
    195

"yellow peril," 63

Zimmerman, George, 86, 87, 237
"zoot-suit" riots, 114